Programming language concepts

—*Third edition*

Carlo Ghezzi, Politecnico di Milano
Mehdi Jazayeri, Technische Universität Wien

John Wiley & Sons
New York Chichester Weinheim Brisbane Toronto Singapore

ACQUISITIONS EDITOR	Regina Brooks
MARKETING MANAGER	Jay Kirsch
PRODUCTION SERVICE	Publication Services
COVER PHOTO	The Granger Collection

This book was set in Times Roman by Carlo Ghezzi, Mehdi Jazayeri and Publication Services.

It was printed and bound by Malloy Lithographers. The cover was printed by Phoenix Color Corporation.

Library of Congress Cataloging in Publication Data:
Ghezzi, Carlo.
    Programming language concepts / Carlo Ghezzi, Mehdi Jazayeri. --
3rd ed.
        p.   cm.
    Includes bibliographical references.
    ISBN 0-471-10426-4 (cloth : alk. paper)
    1. Programming languages (Electronic computers)   I. Jazayeri,
Mehdi.   II. Title.
QA76.7.G48   1997
005. 13'3--dc21   97-1905
                                                             CIP

Printed in the United States of America

10 9 8 7 6 5 4 3 2 1

To Anny and Mary

Table of Contents

List of Figures

List of Sidebars

Preface

The purpose of language is simply that it must convey meaning. (Confucius)

That which can be said, can be said clearly. (Wittgenstein, 1963)

Programming languages are at the heart of computer science. They are the tools we use to communicate not only with computers but also with people. The challenge of designing language features that support clear expression, the puzzle of fitting together different features to make a useful language, and the challenge of appropriately using those features for the clear expression of algorithms make up part of the excitement of the study of programming languages.

This is the third edition of *Programming Language Concepts*. We started writing the first edition in 1980 when it appeared to us that the field of programming languages was becoming stable. We were certainly wrong then! Today the field continues to be dynamic and exciting. New concepts and languages continue to excite large communities of computer scientists— theorists, experimentalists, and practitioners alike. Indeed, programming languages represent one of the few areas of computer science where practitioners and theorists find common ground. Emerging technologies and new application needs require continuous evolution and innovation in the field and are sure to keep the flow of ideas and concepts going for a long time.

This book studies fundamental concepts that underlie the features of programming languages. In the first five chapters we study basic concepts: syntax and semantics, and structuring concepts for data, control, and programs. The emphasis in these chapters is on conventional languages. In Chapters 6, 7, and 8 we use the concepts from the earlier chapters to study different programming language paradigms. In particular, we study object-oriented programming, functional programming, and logic and rule-based programming. Chapter 9 concludes the book by looking at the factors that force the evolution of programming languages and some of the current trends in this evolution. Because of its widespread availability, the main language used for our examples is C/C++. Other languages receiving considerable treatment are ML, Ada 95, Java, and Eiffel. We balance the use of examples from different languages to illustrate certain concepts, and we present the major distinguishing features of each language considered.

Use as a text

This book is designed as a textbook for a junior/senior level course at the undergraduate level. We assume that the student has good programming skills in at least one language. Knowledge of another language will be helpful. Because many examples are in C, knowledge of C will be helpful.

The first five chapters are essential. Each of the following chapters presents concepts first and specific language examples next. The instructor may choose to skip specific languages depending on the emphasis of the course.

Earlier editions and the manuscript of the present edition have been used in courses at both the undergraduate and graduate levels. Teaching support material is available by contacting us, preferably through the Web site given below.

There are many exercises at the end of each chapter. Most of the exercises try to get the student to extend the knowledge gained from the text. Many require checking appropriate language reference manuals. We also find that most students learn from doing programming assignments. In each case, the program should be kept small to illustrate a basic concept. Large programs should be left for software engineering studies.

Changes from the second edition

From the earlier editions, we have retained the emphasis on concepts. Although the spirit of the book is the same, we have virtually rewritten everything to be more rigorous, with emphasis on more concrete examples and more detailed explanation of concepts.

Since the first edition, we have used an abstract machine called SIMPLESEM to describe the run-time structure of languages. This approach has been very popular with most instructors. In Chapter 2 of this edition, we have made the description of SIMPLESEM much more concrete. Check the web site for availability of an interpreter for the language.

The chapter from the previous edition on formal semantics has been merged into Chapter 2, which now covers both syntax and semantics.

There is a new chapter on object-oriented programming languages, with significant examples from C++, Eiffel, Java, and Ada 95. Since the last edition, object orientation has become more clearly understood and has been adopted in many languages. In the text, when we refer to Ada, we mean the current standard Ada, which is known as Ada 95.

Chapter 7, on functional programming, has been changed to use ML instead of FP. There is also a presentation of lambda calculus. ML has also been added to the examples in Chapter 5 on modularity.

We have added sidebars in some chapters. Intended for "cultural enrichment," these sidebars contain information that is of historical or general interest but is not strictly necessary in an introductory languages course.

Acknowledgments

Earlier editions of this book have been translated into several languages and used by many teachers and students around the world. The feedback we have received has helped us in preparing the current edition. We are grateful for the feedback.

We would like to acknowledge the help of the following people with the third edition. Andrew Tolmach of Portland State University, Tim Gottleber of North Lake College, and Donald H. Kraft of Louisiana State University were official reviewers. The detailed comments of Andrew Tolmach were especially helpful. Fabiano Cattaneo, Gianpaolo Cugola, Manfred Hauswirth, and Giovanni Vigna read the entire draft and made valuable comments and suggestions. Flavio De Paoli and Marcello Reina read and commented on parts of the draft. Georg Trausmuth helped with the bibliography. Renate Kainz helped with everything. We also would like to thank Roland Mittermeir and Hanna Oktaba who invited us to give courses based on the manuscript at their universities.

The third edition has been almost entirely rewritten. For the first edition, we had comments from: Jean-Pierre Banâtre, Dan Berry, Laurence Chan, Jon Cohen, Richard LeBlanc, Gyula Magó, Dino Mandrioli, David Moffat, and Kuo-Chung Tai. For the second edition, we had comments from Walter Alvey, Bob Collins, Arthur Fleck, Ray Ford, Mariam Jazayeri, Jon Mauney, and Dave Reisenauer.

December 1996, Vienna
Carlo Ghezzi (ghezzi@elet.polimi.it)
Mehdi Jazayeri (jazayeri@tuwien.ac.at)

For up-to-date information about the book, see the web site at:

http://www.infosys.tuwien.ac.at/pl-book

Introduction

The limits of my language are the limits of my world.
(Wittgenstein)

C H A P T E R   1

This book is concerned with programming languages. Programming languages do not, however, exist in a vacuum: they are tools for writing software. A comprehensive study of programming languages must take this context into account. We begin, therefore, with a discussion of the software development process and the role of programming languages in this process. Sections 1.1 through 1.5 provide a perspective from which to view programming languages and their intended uses. From this perspective, we will weigh the merits of many of the language concepts discussed in the rest of the book.

Programming languages have been an active field of computer science for at least four decades. The languages that exist today are rooted in historical developments, either because they evolved from previous versions or because they derived inspiration from their predecessors. Such developments are likely to continue in the future. To foster an appreciation for this fragment of the history of science, we provide an overview of the main achievements in programming languages in Section 1.6.

Finally, Section 1.7 provides an overview of the concepts of programming languages that will be studied throughout this book. This section explains how the various concepts presented in the remaining chapters fit together.

1.1 Software development process

From the inception of an idea for a software system until it is implemented and delivered to a customer, and even after that, the software undergoes gradual development and evolution. The software is said to have a *life cycle* composed of several phases. Each of these phases results in the development of either a part of the system or something associated with the system, such as a fragment of specification, a test plan, or a users manual. In the traditional *waterfall model* of the software life cycle, the development process is a sequential combination of phases, each having well-identified starting and ending points, with clearly identifiable deliverables to the next phase. Each step may identify deficiencies in the previous one, which then must be repeated, to repair the deficiency.

A sample software development process based on the waterfall model may comprise the following phases:

Requirements analysis and specification. The purpose of this phase is to identify and document the exact requirements for the system. These requirements are developed jointly by users and software developers. The success of a system is measured by how well the software mirrors these stated requirements, how well the requirements mirror the users' perceived needs, and how well the users' perceived needs reflect the real needs. The result of this phase is a requirements document stating *what* the system should do, along with users manuals, feasibility and cost studies, performance requirements, and so on. The requirements document does not specify *how* the system is going to meet its requirements.

Software design. Starting with the requirements document, software developers design the software system. The result of this phase is a *design specification document* identifying all of the modules in the system and their interfaces. Separating requirements analysis from design is an instance of a fundamental "what/how" dichotomy that we encounter quite often in computer science. The general principle involves making a clear distinction between *what* the problem is and *how* to solve the problem. In this case, the requirements phase attempts to specify what the problem is. There are usually many ways that the requirements can be met. The purpose of the design phase is to provide a decomposition into modules that will meet the stated requirements. The design method followed in this step can have a great impact on the quality of the resulting application—in particular, on its understandability and modifiability. It can also affect the choice of the programming language to be used in system implementation.

Implementation (coding). Starting with the design specification, software developers implement the system. The design specification, in this case, states a solution strategy; the goal of the implementation step is to choose how, among the many possible ways, the system shall be coded to meet the design specification. Just as the requirements specification is the *what* for the design phase and the design is the *how*, the design specification is the *what* for the implementation phase and the implementation is the *how*. The result of the implementation phase is a fully implemented and documented system.

Verification and validation. This phase assesses the quality of the implemented system, which is then delivered to the user. Note that this phase should not be concentrated at the end of the implementation step, but should occur in conjunction with every phase of software development to check that intermediate deliverables of the process satisfy their objectives. For example, one should check that the design specification document is consistent with the requirements, which, in turn, should match the user's needs. These checks are accomplished by periodically answering the following two questions:

> "Are we building the product right?"
> "Are we building the right product?"

Two specific kinds of assessment performed during implementation are *module testing* and *integration testing*. Module testing is done by each programmer on the module he or she is working on to ensure that it meets its interface specifications. Integration testing is done on a partial aggregation of modules; it is aimed at uncovering intermodule inconsistencies.

Maintenance. Following delivery of the system, changes to the system may become necessary because of detected malfunctions, a desire to add new capabilities or to improve existing ones, or the need to accommodate changes that occurred in the operational environment (e.g., the operating system of the target machine). These changes are referred to as maintenance. The importance of this phase can be seen in the fact that maintenance costs are typically at least as large as those of all the other phases combined.

Programming languages are used only in some phases of the development process. They are obviously used in the implementation phase, when algorithms and data structures are defined and coded for the modules that form the entire application. Moreover, modern high-level languages are also used in the design phase, to describe precisely the decomposition of the entire application into modules, and the relationships among modules, before any detailed implementation takes place. We will next examine the role of the programming language in the software development process by illustrating the relationship between the programming language and other software development tools in Section 1.2 and the relationship between the programming language and design methods in Section 1.3.

1.2 Languages and software development environments

The work in any of the phases of software development may be supported by computer-aided tools. The phase currently supported best is the coding phase, with such tools as text editors, compilers, linkers, and libraries. These tools have evolved gradually as the need for automation has been recognized. Today, one can normally use an interactive editor to create a program and use the file system to store it for future use. When needed, several previously created and (possibly) compiled programs may be linked to produce an executable program. A debugger is commonly used to locate faults in a program and remove them. These computer-aided program development tools have increased programming productivity by reducing the chances of errors and the time to locate the remaining errors.

Yet, as we have seen, software development involves much more than programming. In order to increase the productivity of software development, computer support is needed for all of its phases. A *software development environment* is an integrated set of tools and techniques that aids in the development of software. The environment is used in all phases of software development: requirements, design, implementation, verification and validation, and maintenance.

An idealized scenario for the use of such an environment is the following. A team of application and computer specialists interacting with the environment develops the system requirements. The environment keeps track of the requirements as they are being developed and updated, and checks for incompleteness or inconsistency. It also provides facilities to validate requirements against the customer's expectations, for example, by providing tools to simulate or animate the requirements. The environment helps in keeping the documentation up to date as changes are being made to the requirements. Following the completion of the requirements document, system designers, interacting with the environment, develop an initial system design and gradually refine it; that is, they specify the needed modules and the module interfaces. Test data may also be produced at this stage. The implementers then start to implement the system based on the design. The environment provides support for these phases by automating some development steps, by suggesting reuse of existing design and implementation components taken from a library, and by recording the relationships among all of the artifacts so that one can trace the effect of a change in, say, the requirements document to changes in the design document and in the code. The tools provided by the software development environment to support implementation are the most familiar. They include programming language processors such as editors, compilers, simulators, interpreters, linkers, and debuggers. For this scenario to work, all of the tools must be compatible and integrated with tools used in the other phases. For example, the programming language must be compatible with the design methods supported by the environment at the design stage and with the design notations used to document designs. The editor used to enter programs might be sensitive to the syntax of the language, so that syntax errors can be caught before they are even entered rather than later, at compile time. A facility for test data generation might also be available for programs written in the language.

Again, the above scenario is an ideal one; it is only approximated by existing commercial support tools, known under the umbrella term of CASE (computer-aided software engineering), and the trend is going in the direction of better support and more complete coverage of the software process.

1.3 Languages and software design methods[1]

A design method is a guideline for producing a design. For example, structured design, top-down design, and object-oriented design methods each suggest a different way of approaching the design process and yield different kinds of designs for the same set of requirements. Design methods guide software designers in the decomposition of a system into logical components which, eventually, must be coded in a language. For example, a top-down procedural design method guides software developers in decomposing a system into modules that realize abstract operations that may be activated by other procedural modules. An object-oriented method guides in decomposing a system into classes of objects.

The relationship between software design methods and programming languages is an important one. Some languages provide better support for some design methods than others. Older languages, such as FORTRAN, were not designed to support specific design methods. For example, the absence of suitable high-level control structures (such as while loops and recursive procedures) in early FORTRAN makes it difficult to systematically design algorithms in a top-down fashion. Conversely, Pascal was designed with the explicit goal of supporting top-down program development and structured programming. In both languages, the lack of constructs to define modules other than routines makes it difficult to decompose a software system into abstract data types.

1. If you don't understand some of the concepts and terms used in this section, don't worry. We will cover them all later.

To understand the relationship between a programming language and a design method, it is important to realize that programming languages may enforce a certain programing style, often called a *programming paradigm*. For example, as we will see, Smalltalk and Eiffel are *object-oriented* languages. They enforce the development of programs based on object classes as the unit of modularization. Similarly, FORTRAN and Pascal, as originally defined, are *procedural* languages. They enforce the development of programs based on routines as the unit of modularization. Languages enforcing a specific programming paradigm can be called *paradigm-oriented*. In general, there need not be a one-to-one relationship between paradigms and programming languages. Some languages, in fact, are *paradigm-neutral* and support different paradigms. For example, C++ supports the development of procedural and object-oriented programs. The most prominent programming language paradigms are presented in the sidebar on page 7.

If the design method and the language paradigm are the same, or the language is paradigm-neutral, then the design abstractions can be directly mapped into program components. Otherwise, if the two clash, the programming effort increases. As an example, an object-oriented design method followed by implementation in a procedural language such as FORTRAN increases the programming effort because the program must implement not only the solution to the problem but also the concepts of the paradigm.

Ideally, the design method and the paradigm supported by the language should be the same. If this is the case, there is a continuum between design and implementation. Most modern high-level programming languages, in fact, can even be used as design notations. For example, a language like Ada or Eiffel can be used to document a system's decomposition into modules even at the stage where the implementation details internal to the module are still to be defined.

Language paradigms

Here is a summary of the most prominent programming language paradigms, with emphasis on the program decomposition style that they promote. This discussion provides a roadmap to some of the main concepts that we study extensively in the rest of the book.

- *Procedural programming.* This is the conventional programming style, where programs are decomposed into computation *steps* that perform complex operations. Routines are used as modularization units to define such computation steps.
- *Functional programming.* The functional style of programming is rooted in the theory of mathematical functions. It emphasizes the computation of *values* by the use of *expressions* and *functions.* The functions are the primary building blocks of the program; they may be passed freely as parameters and may be constructed and returned as result parameters of other functions.
- *Abstract data type programming.* Abstract data type programming recognizes abstract data types as the unit of program modularity. CLU was the first language designed to support this paradigm.
- *Module-based programming.* Module-based programming emphasizes modularization units that are groupings of entities such as variables, procedures, functions, or types. A program is composed of a set of such modules. Modules can be used to specify which services are exported to the outside world by the module. In principle, any kind of service can be provided by a module, not just the ability to generate and use abstract data. Modula-2 and Ada support this style of programming.
- *Object-oriented programming.* The object-oriented programming style emphasizes the definition of classes of objects. Instances of classes are created by the program as needed during program execution. This style is based on the definition of hierarchies of classes and run-time selection of units to execute. Smalltalk, Eiffel, and Java are representative languages of this class. C++ and Ada also support the paradigm.
- *Generic programming.* This style emphasizes the definition of generic modules that may be instantiated, either at compile time or run time, to create the entities—data structures, functions, and procedures—needed to form the program. This approach to programming encourages the development of high-level, generic abstractions as units of modularity. The generic programming paradigm does not exist in isolation. It can exist jointly with object-oriented programing, as in Eiffel, or with functional programming, as in ML. It also exists in languages that provide more than one paradigm, such as Ada and C++.
- *Declarative programming.* This style emphasizes the declarative description of a problem, rather than the decomposition of the problem into an algorithmic implementation. Such programs are closer to a specification than a traditional implementation. Logic languages, like PROLOG, and rule-based languages, like OPS5 and CLIPS, are representative of this class of languages.

1.4 Languages and computer architecture

Design methods influence programming languages in the sense of establishing requirements for the language to meet in order to better support software development. Computer architecture has exerted influence from the opposite direction in the sense of restraining language designs to what can be implemented efficiently on current machines. We can say that languages have been constrained by the ideas of von Neumann, because most current computers are similar to the original von Neumann architecture.

The von Neumann architecture, sketched in Figure 1.1, is based on the idea of a memory that contains data and instructions, a CPU, and an I/O unit. The CPU is responsible for taking instructions from memory one at a time. Machine instructions are very low-level. They require the data to be taken out of memory and manipulated via arithmetic or logic operations in the CPU, with the results copied back to some memory cells. Thus, instruction execution results in changes in the *state* of the machine, which is represented roughly by the contents of the memory.

Conventional programming languages can be viewed as abstractions of an underlying von Neumann architecture. An *abstraction* is a model which highlights the relevant aspects of a phenomenon and ignores its irrelevant details. Conventional programming languages retain as their computational model the underlying von Neumann architecture, but abstract away from the details of the individual steps of execution. Such a model consists of a sequential, step-by-step execution of instructions which change the state of a computation by modifying a repository of values. Sequential execution of language instructions reflects the sequential fetch and execution of machine instructions performed by hardware. The variables of conventional programming languages, which can be modified by assignment statements, reflect the behavior of the memory cells of the computer architecture. Conventional languages based on

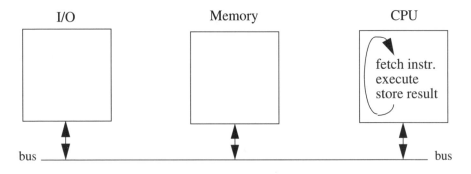

FIGURE 1.1 A von Neumann computer architecture

the von Neumann computational model are often called *imperative languages*. They are also called *state-based languages*, *statement-based languages*, or simply *von Neumann languages*.

Historically, imperative languages have developed through increasingly higher levels of abstraction. In the early times of computing, assembly languages were invented to provide primitive forms of abstraction, such as the ability to name operations and memory locations symbolically. Thus, instead of writing a bit string to denote the increment of the contents of a memory cell by 1, it is possible to write something like

INC DATUM

Many kinds of abstractions were later invented by language designers, such as procedures and functions, data types, exception handlers, classes, and concurrency features. As suggested by Figure 1.2, language developers try to raise the level of programming languages, to make languages easier to use by humans, but still base the concepts of the language on those of the underlying von Neumann architecture.

Some programming languages, namely, *functional* and *logic languages*, have abandoned the von Neumann computational model. Both are based on mathematical foundations rather than on the technology of the underlying hardware: the theory of recursive functions and mathematical logic, respectively. The conceptual foundations of these languages, however, are in conflict with the goal of an efficient implementation. This is not unexpected, since such foundations were not developed for execution on von Neumann

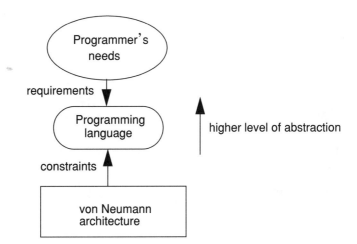

FIGURE 1.2 Requirements and constraints on a language

computers. To improve efficiency, some imperative features have been introduced in most existing unconventional languages.

In analyzing languages, we may view two paradigms: the paradigm that characterizes the computational model, as discussed in this section, and the paradigm that characterizes program organization principles, as discussed in the sidebar on page 7. Imperative, functional, and logic paradigms reflect different underlying computational models of the language. Different program *organization* paradigms can apply—at least in principle—to different computational models. For example, ML provides a functional computational model and supports program organization based on abstract data types. CLOS is a functional language that supports the object-oriented style.

This book considers the prevalent programming languages and the issues that have influenced their design. The primary emphasis of Chapters 2 through 6 is on imperative languages. We cover the important issues in functional programming languages in Chapter 7 and logic languages in Chapter 8.

1.5 Programming language qualities

How can we define the qualities that a programming language should exhibit? In order to understand that, we should keep in mind that a programming language is a tool for the development of software. Thus, ultimately, the quality of the language must be related to the quality of the software.

Software must be reliable. Users should be able to rely on the software; i.e., the likelihood of failures due to faults in the program should be low. As far as possible, the system should be fault-tolerant; i.e., it should continue to provide support to the user even in the presence of infrequent or undesirable events such as hardware or software failures. The reliability requirement has gained importance as software has been called upon to accomplish increasingly complicated and often critical tasks.

Software must be maintainable. As software costs rise and increasingly complex software systems are developed, it is not economically feasible to throw away existing software and develop replacement applications from scratch. Existing software must be modified to meet new requirements. Also, because it is almost impossible to get the real requirements right in the first place, for such complex systems one can only hope to gradually evolve a system into the desired one.

Software must execute efficiently. Efficiency has always been a goal of any software system. This goal affects both the programming language (features that can be implemented efficiently on present-day architectures) and the choice of algorithms to be used. Although the cost of hardware continues to drop even as its performance continues to increase (faster processors and more memory), the need for efficient execution remains because computers are being used in increasingly demanding applications.

These three requirements—reliability, maintainability, and efficiency—can be achieved by adopting suitable methods during software development and appropriate tools in the software development environment, and by certain characteristics of the programming language. We will now discuss language issues that directly support these goals.

1.5.1 Languages and reliability

The reliability goal is promoted by several programming language qualities. A nonexhaustive list is provided below. Most of them, unfortunately, are based on subjective evaluation and are difficult to state in a precise—let alone quantitative—way. In addition, they are not independent concepts: in some cases they are overlapping; in others they may be even conflicting.

Writability. This refers to the possibility of expressing a program in a way that is natural for the problem. The programmer should not be distracted by details and tricks of the language from the more important activity of problem solving. Even though writability is a subjective criterion, we can agree that higher-level languages are more writable than lower-level languages (e.g., assembly or machine language). For example, an assembly language programmer is often forced to consider the addressing mechanisms needed to access certain data, such as the positioning of index registers, and so on. The easier it is to concentrate on the problem-solving activity, the less error-prone is program writing.

Readability. It should be possible to follow the logic of the program and to discover the presence of errors by examining the program. Readability is also a subjective criterion that depends a great deal on matters of taste and style. The provision of specific constructs to define new operations (via routines) and new data types, which keep the definition of such concepts separate from the rest of the program that may use them, enhances readability greatly.

Simplicity. A simple language is easy to master and allows algorithms to be expressed easily, in a way that makes the programmer confident in the correctness of the algorithm. Simplicity can be achieved by minimizing the features of a language, but then this reduces the power of the language. For example, Pascal is simpler but less powerful than C++.

Safety. The language should not provide features that make it possible to write harmful programs. For example, a language that does not provide

goto statements or pointer variables eliminates two well-known sources of danger in a program. Such features may cause subtle errors that are difficult to track during program development, and may manifest themselves unexpectedly in the delivered software. Unfortunately, however, features that decrease the dangers may also reduce power and flexibility.

Robustness. The language supports robustness whenever it provides the ability to deal with undesired events (arithmetic overflows, invalid input, and so on). That is, such events can be trapped and a suitable response can be programmed to respond to their occurrence. In this way, the behavior of the system becomes predictable even in anomalous situations.

1.5.2 Languages and maintainability

Programming languages should allow programs to be easily modifiable. Readability and simplicity are obviously important in this context too. Two main features that languages can provide to support modification are factoring and locality.

Factoring. The language should allow programmers to factor related features into one single unit. As a simple example, if an operation is repeated in several points of the program, it should be possible to factor it in a routine and replace its use by a routine call. In doing so, the program becomes more readable (especially if we give meaningful names to routines) and more easily modifiable (a change to the fragment is localized to the routine's body). As another example, several programming languages allow constants to be given symbolic names. Choosing an appropriate name for a constant promotes readability of the program (e.g., we may use pi instead of 3.14). Moreover, a future need to change the value (e.g., to 3.1415) would necessitate a change only in the definition of the constant, rather than in every use of the constant.

Locality. The effect of a language feature is restricted to a small, local portion of the entire program. Otherwise, if it extends to most of the program, the task of making the change can be exceedingly complex. For example, in abstract data type programming, the change to a data structure defined inside a class is guaranteed not to affect the rest of the program as long as the operations that manipulate the data structure are invoked in the same way.

Factoring and locality are strongly related concepts. In fact, factoring promotes locality in that changes may apply only to the factored portion. Consider, for example, the impact of factoring on changing the number of digits used to represent pi in order to improve accuracy of a geometrical computation.

1.5.3 Languages and efficiency

The need for efficiency has guided language design since the early days of computing. Many languages have had efficiency as a main design goal, either implicitly or explicitly. For example, FORTRAN originally was designed for a specific machine, the IBM 704. The architecture of the IBM 704 was the cause for many restrictions of original FORTRAN, such as the number of array dimensions or the form of expressions used as array indices.

The issue of efficiency, however, has changed considerably. Efficiency is no longer measured only by the execution speed and space. The effort required to produce a program or system initially and the effort required in maintenance can also be viewed as components of the efficiency measure. In other words, in some cases one may be more concerned with productivity of the software development process than with the performance of the resulting products. Moreover, productivity concerns can span several developments rather than just one. That is, one might be interested in developing software components that are *reusable* in future similar applications. Or one might be interested in developing *portable* software (i.e., software that can be moved to different machines) to make it quickly available to different users, even if an ad hoc optimized version for each machine would be faster.

Efficiency is often a combined quality of both the language and its implementation. The language adversely affects efficiency if it disallows certain optimizations to be applied by the compiler. The implementation adversely affects efficiency if it does not take all opportunities into account in order to save space and improve speed. For example, in general, a statement like

```
x = fun (y) + z + fun (y);
```

in C cannot be optimized as

```
x = 2* fun (y) + z;
```

which would presumably be more efficient since it would call the function fun just once. The language feature that allows functions to modify global variables (like z in the example) disallows the optimization.

As another example, the language can affect implementation efficiency by allowing multi-threaded concurrent computations. An implementation adversely affects efficiency if, say, it does not reuse memory space after it is released by the program. Finally, a language that allows visibility to the size of memory words or access to, say, the way floating-point numbers are stored would impede portability and thus increase the effort of moving software to different platforms.

1.6 A brief historical perspective

This section examines the developments in language design briefly by following the evolution of ideas and concepts from a historical perspective.

The software development process originally consisted only of the implementation phase. In the early days of computing, the computer was used mainly in scientific applications. An application was programmed by one person. The problem to be solved (e.g., a differential equation) was well understood. As a result, there was not much need for requirements analysis or design specification or even maintenance. A programming language, therefore, only needed to support one programmer, who was programming what would be by today's standards an extremely simple application. The desire to apply the computer in more and more applications led to its being used in increasingly less understood and more sophisticated environments. This, in turn, led to the need for "teams" of programmers and more disciplined approaches. The requirements and design phases, which up to then essentially were performed in one programmer's head, now required a team, with the results being communicated to other people. Because so much effort and money was being spent on the development of systems, old systems could not simply be thrown away when a new system was needed. Economic considerations forced people to enhance an existing system to meet the newly recognized needs. Also, program maintenance of such "legacy" systems became an important issue.

System reliability is another issue that has gained importance gradually, because of two major factors. One factor is that systems are being developed for users with little or no computer background; these users are not as tolerant of system failures as the system developers. The second factor is that systems are now being applied in critical areas such as chemical or nuclear power plants and patient monitoring, where system failures can be disastrous. In order to ensure reliability, verification and validation became vital.

The perceived shortcomings of programming languages have led to a great number of language design efforts. This book examines these influences on language design and assesses the extent to which the resulting languages meet their goals. Sections 1.6.1 through 1.6.6 describe the historical evolution of programming languages. Table 1 gives a genealogy of selected programming languages discussed in this book. The year associated with each language should be taken as indicative: depending on the availability of the relevant information, it may mean either the year(s) of the language design, of its initial implementation, or of its first available published description. References to relevant published material on the languages listed in Table 1, including standards, can be found in the appendix at the end of the book.

Table 1: Genealogy of selected programming languages

Language	Year	Originator	Predecessor Language	Intended Purpose
FORTRAN	1954–57	J. Backus		Numeric computing
ALGOL 60	1958–60	Committee	FORTRAN	Numeric computing
COBOL	1959–60	Committee		Business data processing
APL	1956–60	K. Iverson		Vector processing
LISP	1956–62	J. McCarthy		Symbolic computing
SNOBOL4	1962–66	R. Griswold		String processing
PL/I	1963–64	Committee	FORTRAN ALGOL 60 COBOL	General purpose
BASIC	1964	J. Kemeny and T. Kurtz	FORTRAN	Educational Interactive
SIMULA 67	1967	O.-J.Dahl	ALGOL 60	Simulation
Algol 68	1963–68	Committee	ALGOL 60	General purpose
Pascal	1971	N. Wirth	ALGOL 60	Educational (gen. purpose)
PROLOG	1972	A. Colmerauer		Artificial intelligence
C	1972	D. Ritchie	Algol 68	Systems programming
Mesa	1974	Committee	SIMULA 67	Systems programming
SETL	1974	J. Schwartz		Very high level lang.
Concurrent Pascal	1975	P. Brinch Hansen	Pascal	Concurrent programming
Scheme	1975	G. Steele and G. Sussman	LISP	Educational (functional programming)
CLU	1974–77	B. Liskov	SIMULA 67	ADT programming

Table 1: Genealogy of selected programming languages

Language	Year	Originator	Predecessor Language	Intended Purpose
Euclid	1977	Committee	Pascal	Verifiable programs
Modula-2	1977	N. Wirth	Pascal	Systems programming
Ada	1979	J. Ichbiah	Pascal SIMULA 67	General purpose Embedded systems
Smalltalk	1971–80	A. Kay	SIMULA 67 LISP	Personal computing
OPS5	1981	Carnegie-Mellon Univ.	LISP	Expert systems
ICON	1983	R. Griswold and M. Griswold	SNOBOL4	String processing
C++	1984	B. Stroutrup	C SIMULA 67	General purpose
CLIPS	1984	NASA	C	C-based expert systems
ML	1984	R. Milner	LISP	Symbolic computing
Oberon-2	1987	N. Wirth et al.	Modula-2	General purpose
Eiffel	1988	B. Meyer	SIMULA 67	General purpose
CLOS	1988	Committee	LISP Smalltalk	OO extension of LISP
Modula-3	1989	Committee (Olivetti and DEC)	Mesa Modula-2	Systems programming
Tcl/Tk	1988	J. K. Ousterhout	OS shell languages	Scripting language
Perl	1990	L. Wall	OS shell languages	Scripting language
Python	1991	G. vanRossum	OS shell languages	Scripting language

Table 1: Genealogy of selected programming languages

Language	Year	Originator	Predecessor Language	Intended Purpose
Java	1995	SUN Micro-systems	C++	Network computing

1.6.1 Early high-level languages

The first attempts towards definition of high-level languages date back to the 1950s. Language design was viewed as a challenging compromise between the users' needs for expressiveness and the machine's limited power. Because hardware was very expensive, execution efficiency concerns were the dominant design constraint.

The most important products of this historical phase were FORTRAN, ALGOL 60, and COBOL. FORTRAN and ALGOL 60 were defined as tools for solving numerical scientific problems, that is, problems involving complex computations on relatively simple data. COBOL was defined as a tool for solving business data-processing problems, that is, problems involving simple computations on large amounts of structured data (e.g., a payroll application).

These languages are among the major achievements in the whole history of computer science, because they proved that the idea of a higher-level language was technically sound and economically viable. Besides that, each of these languages introduced a number of important concepts. For example, FORTRAN introduced modularity via separately developed subprograms and possible sharing of data among modules via a global (COMMON) environment. ALGOL 60 introduced the notion of block structure and recursive procedures. COBOL introduced files and data descriptions, and a very preliminary notion of programming in quasi-natural language.

An even more convincing proof of the validity of these languages is that, apart from ALGOL 60, which did not survive but spawned descendant languages, they are still among the most widely used languages in practice. To be sure, there are other reasons for this long-term success, such as:

- The users' reluctance to move to newer languages, because of the need for compatibility with existing applications or just the fear of change.
- The fact that these languages have been evolving. For example, the present FORTRAN standard (FORTRAN 90) remains compatible with the previous standards (FORTRAN 77 and FORTRAN 66), but modernizes them and overcomes many of their major weaknesses.

1.6.2 Early schisms

As early as in the 1960s there were attempts to define programming languages whose computational models could be based on some well-characterized mathematical principles, rather than on efficiency of implementation.

LISP is one such example. The language definition was based upon the theory of recursive functions and lambda calculus, and gave foundation to a new class of languages called functional (or applicative) languages. Pure LISP is free of the von Neumann concepts of modifiable variables, assignment statements, **goto** statements, and so on. LISP supports only one kind of data structure, the list. LISP programs are themselves written as lists. This uniformity of data and program structure allows LISP interpreters to be specified in LISP in a fairly simple manner.

APL is another language that is rooted in a mathematical style. Its very rich set of operators, especially on arrays, relieves the programmer from using lower-level iterative, element-by-element array manipulations. SNOBOL4 is yet another example of unconventional early languages. It provides string manipulation facilities and pattern matching. It supports a highly declarative programming style.

LISP, APL, and SNOBOL4 are heavy consumers of machine resources (both time and space). All of them require highly dynamic resource management that is difficult to perform efficiently on conventional machines. Yet these languages have become very successful in specialized application areas. Also, they have been adopted by groups of devoted users. For example, LISP is widely used in artificial intelligence. APL is used for rapid prototyping, financial applications, and scientific applications involving heavy usage of matrix operations. SNOBOL4 is used for text manipulations.

An important contribution of LISP and SNOBOL4 was the emphasis on symbolic computation. As we mentioned, in the early days computers were used mainly to solve numerical problems, such as systems of equations. This is why FORTRAN, ALGOL 60, and APL are oriented mostly towards numerical problem solving. At present, however, only a small fraction of application developments are in the area of numeric computation. Major emphasis is on symbolic information processing, such as database applications and text processing. COBOL can be seen as an initial step in this direction, because the language is more oriented towards moving and formatting data than manipulating data through complex numeric computation. In LISP and SNOBOL4 symbolic computation became the central concern of the language.

1.6.3 Consolidation

With the seemingly rapid development of specialized languages in the mid-1960s, a group of researchers at IBM set themselves an ambitious goal: to integrate the most fruitful and original concepts of previous languages into a truly general-purpose, universal programming language. The language was called PL/I. Besides taking concepts from FORTRAN (such as separate modules), ALGOL 60 (block structure and recursive procedures), COBOL (data description facilities), and LISP (dynamic data structures), PL/I introduced less consolidated features, such as exception handling and multitasking facilities.

PL/I was probably too early for its time. It incorporates different features but does not really integrate them in a uniform manner. Also, newer features needed more research and experimentation before being incorporated in the language. As a result, the language is extremely large and complex. So, as time went by, it gradually lost importance.

1.6.4 The next leap forward

Languages designed in the late 1960s introduced interesting concepts that influenced later language designs. We refer primarily to Algol 68, SIMULA 67, and Pascal.

Algol 68 was designed as a successor to ALGOL 60. It is based on the principle of *orthogonality*: language features can be composed in a free, uniform, and noninterfering manner with predictable effects. Algol 68 is a good case study of how different language concepts can interact to provide computational power. Another important concept brought up by the Algol 68 effort is the need for formal language specification. The Algol 68 Report is probably the first complete example of a formal specification for a programming language. The "purity" of Algol 68, the intricacies that can result from an orthogonal combination of language features, and the absence of compromises with such mundane aspects as a user-friendly syntactic notation were responsible for the lack of popularity of Algol 68. The language has been used in universities and research institutions, especially in Europe, but had little industrial application.

SIMULA 67 was also a successor of ALGOL 60, designed to solve discrete simulation problems. In addition to ad hoc constructs for simulation and coroutines that provide a primitive form of parallel execution, the language introduced the concept of class, a modularization mechanism that can group together a set of related routines and data structures. Classes can be organized as hierarchies of increasing specialization. The class concept has influenced most languages designed after SIMULA 67, such as C++, CLU, Smalltalk, Java, and Eiffel.

Pascal has been the most successful among the languages of this period. Although it was conceived primarily as a vehicle for teaching structured programming, there was a rapid expansion of interest in Pascal with the advent of low-cost personal computers. The main appeal of the language is its simplicity and support for disciplined programming. The language has undergone extensive changes and modernization, so that many Pascal dialects now exist. In particular, the language has been extended with modularization and object-oriented features to support development of large programs and reuse of components.

BASIC is another language that was designed in the mid-1960s and has spawned many widely used dialects. The language has a simple algebraic syntax like FORTRAN and limited control and data structures. This simplicity and the ease and efficiency of BASIC implementations have made the language extremely popular. The language itself does not introduce any new linguistic concepts but was among the first available tools to support a highly interactive, interpretive programming style. Recent improvements, such as Visual BASIC, provide high-level facilities for the rapid development of window-based interactive applications.

1.6.5 The experimental 70s

In the 1970s, it became clear that the need to support reliable and maintainable software imposes strong requirements on programming languages. This gave impetus to new research, experimentation, and language evaluations.

Among the most important language concepts investigated in this period were: abstract data types and visibility control to modules, strong typing and static program checking, relationship between language constructs and formal proofs of correctness, generic modules, exception handling, concurrency, and interprocess communication and synchronization. We will discuss most of these concepts in depth in the rest of this book. Some of the influential language experiments were CLU, Mesa, Concurrent Pascal, and Euclid.

Other languages designed in the 1970s that survived their experimental stage and now are used extensively are C and Modula-2. In particular, C became very successful, partly due to the increasing availability of computers running the UNIX operating system, whose development motivated the initial design of the language. C is now among the most widely used languages, because of its power, its efficiency for systems programming, and the availability of efficient implementations on a wide variety of machines. Modula-2 was designed as a successor to Pascal providing specific constructs in support of modular program designs.

On the unconventional side, the family of functional languages continued to flourish, producing several LISP dialects. Among them, Scheme has been adopted widely for instructional purposes in introductory programming courses, as an alternative to conventional languages.

A major contribution to the field of unconventional languages was provided in the early 70s by PROLOG. PROLOG was the starting point of the family of *logic programming languages*. The language had limited success at that time but gained much popularity in the early 80s when the so-called Fifth-Generation Computer Project was launched by the Japanese government, and logic programming was chosen as the basis for the new generation of machines. PROLOG extensions were designed and implemented under the assumption that new generations of parallel machines would be designed to execute logic programs efficiently. Although the revolution predicted by the project did not happen, PROLOG (and other logic languages) found their role in niche software development environments, such as expert systems.

1.6.6 The 80s and object orientation

Developments in functional programming continued in the 80s, producing such languages as Miranda and ML. The important conceptual contribution of ML was to show that programming languages can be made powerful computationally and yet can preserve the ability to prove the absence of certain types of errors without program execution.

New results were also achieved in the family of conventional languages. The desire to unify the programming languages used in embedded computer applications and the need for more reliable and maintainable software led the U.S. Department of Defense (D.O.D) in 1978 to set down the requirements for a programming language to be used as a common language throughout the D.O.D. Because no existing language met the requirements, the D.O.D. sponsored the design of a new language. The result of this process was the Ada programming language, which can be viewed as the synthesis of state-of-the-art concepts of conventional programming languages. Ada has now evolved into the current version, Ada 95, which incorporates several amendments and improvements over the original version, in particular, support for object-oriented programming. In this book, we generally will refer to the language as simply Ada, unless we are specifically discussing features that have been added in the 1995 standard, in which case we will refer to Ada 95.

The origins of object-oriented programming can be traced back to Simula 67. The approach, however, became popular because of the success of Smalltalk in the late 70s and, in particular, of C++. C++ succeeded in implanting object-oriented features into a successful and widely available language like C. This allowed a large population of programmers to incrementally shift from a conventional programming paradigm to one expected to be better. Another attempt to extend C with object-oriented programming facilities was Objective C, which adds Smalltalk-like objects to C. Eiffel is another object-oriented language, aimed at supporting programming with underlying disciplined software engineering principles.

Further advances in the Pascal and Modula-2 tradition are Modula-3 and Oberon-2.

1.6.7 The current stage

For decades, the search for the ideal programming language has been the quest for the Holy Grail of computer science. It is now universally accepted that this approach tries to answer the wrong question. As we mentioned earlier, programmers might be interested in different qualities, and different languages (and different implementations) may indeed provide different answers. So we now realize that the choice of the right language depends on the application. We need to learn how to live with a variety of languages and to be able to move from language to language when needed, as the applications change. Languages evolve and new ones are born as new application requirements emerge.

In the world of information systems applications that was the traditional domain of COBOL, there is an increasing number of application generators. These generators can generate code directly from screen forms that specify the data that should be searched in a database or the reports that must be produced. In certain limited application domains, nonexpert programmers and end users can use such tools to develop nontrivial, practical applications without resorting to a professional programmer. Programming tools of this kind are often called *fourth-generation languages*. Other useful tools for this class of applications are personal *productivity tools* (such as spreadsheets).

Highly interactive applications can be developed rapidly with the aid of *visual languages*, such as Visual BASIC or Visual C++. *Scripting languages*, such as Tcl/Tk, Perl, and Python, which specify activation patterns for existing tool fragments, are an increasingly popular support for rapid application development, which can be useful in developing prototypes.

Specific tools, languages, and environments also exist for developing expert systems, i.e., systems providing problem solving support in specific application domains, based on an explicit representation of knowledge that characterizes the domains. Examples are expert system shells and languages such as OPS5 and the C Language Integrated Production System (CLIPS). CLOS is an object-oriented extension of LISP which can be used for different kinds of artificial intelligence applications, including expert systems.

Finally, C++ seems to be gaining increasing acceptance as a general-purpose programming tool, both because it supports object-oriented programming and because it does not require abandoning more conventional approaches, as more strict approaches would. However, we do not expect the programming language field to reach a stable stage where one language will eventually take over. An important direction for new developments has started already in the area of network-centric computing. Java, a derivative of C++ supporting code mobility on the Internet, can be viewed as the starting point of a new generation of programming languages.

1.7 A bird's-eye view of programming language concepts

This section provides a bird's-eye view of the main concepts of programming languages, which will be the subjects of an in-depth investigation in the remaining chapters. Its purpose is to show how the various concepts that we will present later in the book fit together in a coherent picture. Using a simple C++ program as an example, we look at the kinds of facilities that a programming language must support and the different ways that languages go about providing these facilities.

1.7.1 A simple program

Figure 1.3 shows a part of a C++ program that manipulates a list of phone numbers. As programmers, our inclination on encountering a program is to try to uncover what the program does and how it does it. Our purpose in this book, however, is to learn about the concepts and structure of programming languages. We are interested in the kinds of things one can do with programming languages, rather than the specifics of a given program. What are the inherent capabilities and shortcomings of different programming languages? What makes one language fundamentally different from another, and what makes one language similar to another, despite apparent differences? We will use the simple program in Figure 1.3 to start our exploration of the structure of programming languages. Therefore, in looking at the program, we want to look at not what it does, but what kinds of linguistic facilities were used to write the program.

We have divided the program into three parts, separated by single blank lines. The first part consists of two "#include" statements; the second part consists of three "declaration" statements; and, finally, the third part is the actual code of a function called *main* that supposedly "does the work." We can say that the first part defines the *organization* of the program, in this case in terms of the various files that constitute the program. The second part defines the *environment* in which the program will work by declaring some entities that will be used by the program in this file. These declarations may import entities defined in other files. For example, the line

```
extern phone_list pb;
```

indicates that the variable pb of type phone_list is being used in this program but has been created elsewhere. The third part deals with the actual *computation*. This is the part we most often associate with a program. It contains the program's data and algorithms. Some of the data and processing in this part may use the entities defined in the environment established in the second part. For example, in Figure 1.3 the routines insert and lookup are used in the main program. Another example is the output statement,

```
cout << "Enter 1 to insert, 2 to lookup:" << endl;
```

which uses cout, the standard output device defined in the standard input/output library, iostream.h, which is "included" in the first line of the program.

```
#include <iostream.h>    ⎤
#include "phone.h"        ⎦  part 1: organization

extern phone_list pb;    ⎤
void insert();            ⎬  part 2: environment
number lookup ();        ⎦

main()
{
    int request;
    cout << "Enter 1 to insert, 2 to lookup:" << endl;
    cin >> request;
    if (request == 1)
        insert();
    else if (request == 2)                          part 3: computation
        cout << lookup();
    else
        {cout << "invalid request." << endl;
            exit (1);
        }
}
```

FIGURE 1.3 A phone-list program

Even in this short, simple program, we see that a programming language provides many different kinds of facilities. Let us look more closely at some of the major facilities and the issues involved in designing such language facilities.

1.7.2 Syntax and semantics

Any programming language specifies a set of rules for the *form* of valid programs in that language. For example, in the program of Figure 1.3, we see that many lines are terminated by a semicolon. We see that there are some special characters used, such as { and }. We see that every if is followed by a parenthesized expression. The *syntax* rules of the language state how to form expressions, statements, and programs that *look* right. The semantic rules of the language tell us how to build *meaningful* expressions, statements, and programs. For example, they might tell us that before using the variable request in the if-statement, we must *declare* that variable. They also tell us that the declaration of a variable such as request causes storage to be reserved for the variable. On the other hand, the presence of extern in the declaration of the variable pb indicates that the storage is reserved by some other module and not this one.

Characters are the ultimate syntactic building blocks. Every program is formed by placing characters together in some well-defined order. The syntactic rules for forming programs are rather straightforward. The semantic building blocks and rules, on the other hand, are more intricate. Indeed, most of the deep differences among the various programming languages stem from their different semantic underpinnings.

1.7.3 Semantic elements

In this section, we briefly look at some of the basic semantic concepts in programming languages from the language designer's point of view. We want to see what choices may be available to a language designer and how the designer's decisions affect the programmer.

1.7.3.1 Variables

A variable is the most pervasive concept in traditional programming languages. A variable corresponds to a region of memory which is used to hold *values* that are manipulated by the program. We refer to a variable by its *name*. The syntactic rules specify how variables may be named; for example, they may consist of alphabetic characters. But there are many semantic issues associated with variables. A *declaration* introduces a variable by giving it a name and stating some of its semantic properties. Among the important semantic properties are:

- *Scope*: What part of the program has access to the variable? For example, in the program in Figure 1.3, the scope of the variable request extends to the end of the function called main. That is, the variable may be referred to in any part of the program from the declaration of the variable to the end of the function main. By contrast, the scope of the variable pb is the entire file. That is, if there were other functions besides main, they could also refer to the variable pb. Usually, the location of the variable declaration determines the start of the scope of the variable.

- *Type*: What kinds of values may be stored in the variable, and what operations may be performed on the variable? The variable request is declared to be of type int, and the variable pb is declared of type phone_list. Usually, there are a number of fundamental types defined by the language and there are some facilities for the user to define new types. Languages differ both in terms of the fundamental types and in the facilities for type definition. The fundamental types of traditional languages are dictated by the types that are supported by the hardware. Typically, as in C++, the fundamental types are integer, real, and character. Pascal also has boolean types. There is a large body of work on data types that deals both with the theoretical underpinnings as well as practical implications. We will study many of these issues in detail in Chapter 3.

- *Lifetime*: When is the variable created and when is it discarded? As we said, a variable represents some region of memory which is capable of holding a value. The question is, when is a memory area reserved, or *allocated*, for the variable? Memory may be reserved before the program starts or when the unit in which the declaration occurs is entered, or there could be a statement that explicitly requests the allocation of storage for the variable. Indeed, C++ has all of these kinds of variables: static variables live throughout the execution of the program; automatic variables are allocated when the unit in which they are declared is entered and they are deallocated when the unit terminates; and some variables may be created and destroyed explicitly by the programmer using the operators new and delete.

These issues will be discussed in detail in Chapter 2.

1.7.3.2 Values and references

Having defined some basic issues concerning variables, let us ponder a simple question: what is the *value* associated with a variable? Well, there are at least two answers to this question. Consider an assignment statement of the form:

```
x = y;
```

The *value* referred to by the name y is of a different kind from that referred to by the name x. We have defined a variable as a region of memory. On the right-hand side of this assignment statement we need the contents of that memory, and on the left-hand side we need the address of, or a *reference* to, that region. To enable us to refer to both of these kinds of values, we define two notions: an *l-value* is a value that denotes a memory location and therefore may be used on the left-hand side of an assignment statement; an *r-value* is a value that denotes the contents of a memory location, that is, a value that may be used on the right-hand side of an assignment statement. Referring to the assignment statement above, we need an r-value for y and an l-value for x.

In most languages, the conversions from l-values to r-values are implicit. Some languages, such as C++, also have explicit operators to do the conversions when necessary. For example, the & operator in C++ is the *address-of* operator, which obtains the l-value of its operand. Therefore,

```
x = &y;
```

stores the address of y into x. The & is necessary because the default rule is that on the right-hand side, the r-value is used.

Some contexts require a particular type of value. For example, the left-hand side of an assignment statement requires an l-value. Therefore,

```
3 = y; //error, left-hand side requires l-value
```

is an error because literals in C++ do not have l-values. Instead,

```
y = 3;
```

is legal since the literal 3 is an r-value.

1.7.3.3 Expressions

Expressions are syntactic constructs that allow the programmer to combine values and operations to compute new values. The language specifies syntactic as well as semantic rules for building expressions. Depending on the language, an expression may be constrained to produce a value of only one type or of different types at different times. In the program of Figure 1.3, we see several expressions of different types. For example, request == 1 is an expression of type boolean; "invalid request.\n" is an expression of type array of characters.

In C or C++, for example, an assignment statement produces a value and therefore is also an expression and may be used as a constituent of another expression. Consider

```
a = b = c + d;
```

which assigns (first) to b the value of the expression c+d and then assigns the same value to a. The language Pascal does not allow an assignment statement to be used as part of an expression.

As can be seen from this example, the order in which operations are performed in an expression may influence the value of the expression. Some languages specify the order strictly—for example, right-to-left or based on precedence of operations—and others leave it to the implementer to decide the order. Leaving such issues to the implementation requires the programmer to be more careful because a program that produces the correct result may not necessarily do so when compiled with a different compiler.

The major semantic issue surrounding expressions is the allowable kinds of expressions. Specifically, does the language support expressions that produce only r-values, or can expressions also result in l-values (or even functions)? Chapter 4 will say more about expressions in conventional languages. Chapter 7 will deal with functional languages, which can also be called expression-oriented, since expressions play a central role in such languages.

1.7.4 Program organization

Programs that implement software systems and applications consist of thousands, hundreds of thousands, or even millions of lines of code. These lines together implement a particular system design that consists of many inter-related components, or *modules*. A programming language can provide mechanisms to help the programmer in managing this complexity. To some degree, the structure of the design may be reflected in the structure of the program. As we mentioned, this is straightforward whenever the design method and the programming language paradigm match.

As an example, a program in C++ consists of a number of *files*. By convention, a programmer may implement each design module in one file. Even more, some files may contain modules that are more generally available, referred to as libraries. In the example of Figure 1.3, the program includes a file called iostream.h, which provides the declarations to use the standard input/output library provided by C++. The language does not have any particular facilities for supporting input/output. Instead, a collection of routines make up a library that supports input/output operations. Programs that want to use input/output "include" iostream.h. The other file included by the program is called phone.h. This file is presumably more specific to this application and contains information, such as type definitions, that are shared by different modules of the program.

Being able to break a program into a number of independent parts has many advantages. First, if the parts are independent, they may be implemented and validated by different people. Program debugging and maintenance is also simplified because changes may be isolated to independent modules. Second, it is more practical to store the program in several files rather than one big file. The ability to compile separate parts of the program is important in writing large applications.

In C/C++, the inclusion of files imposes an ordering relationship among the modules of a program. The main program includes some files, which may in turn include other files, and so on. Obviously, the included files must be written before the files that include them. This relationship imposes a hierarchy among the files that constitute the program. There are files that need no other files. These are at the lowest level of the hierarchy—level 0. At the next level are files that only include files from level 0. This file inclusion facility thus supports the direct implementation of hierarchical designs.

Finally, C++ provides support both for procedural and object-oriented programming. The program structure can therefore match a design method based on both decomposition into abstract operations and hierarchies of abstract data types.

Similar considerations hold for Ada. Whereas the correspondence between design modules and program files in C/C++ is rather loose and by convention, in Ada this correspondence is emphasized. Each module has a specification and an implementation. Once the specification of a module is written, other modules that use this module may be written and compiled. This approach reduces the dependence among programmers in that more work may be done in parallel. Ada also supports the concept of a library where module specifications are stored. The language requires that interfaces across independently compiled modules must be checked to ensure that the called and the calling modules agree. On the other hand, the original FORTRAN language also supports independently developed (procedural) modules but does not require type checking across such modules.

The program organization facilities provided by a programming language are dependent on the goals of the language. If the language is intended for writing small programs, for example, for the writing of mathematical algorithms to be run on a calculator, such facilities are not crucial. If, on the other hand, the language is to be used to develop very large programs, these facilities are indispensable. Most modern languages support at least the notion of a module for breaking up a large program into several independent parts. Where the languages differ is in the way the different modules have access to each other's internal entities and in the types of entities that may be imported from other modules. They also differ in the treatment of modules, e.g., whether they can be instantiated and whether they can be compiled separately. These are the specific topics addressed in Chapter 5.

1.7.5 Program data and algorithms

Programming languages provide facilities for implementing algorithms. The algorithms operate on some data to produce some results. This is where programming languages differ the most from each other. The majority of programming languages, including C++, are imperative. As we can see in Figure 1.3, the main program consists of some variable declarations and some statements that operate on these variables. There are also input/output (I/O) statements. The execution of I/O statements modifies the values stored in the memory of the underlying machine; i.e., it modifies the state of the computation.

We will deal with I/O in the next section. For now let us look at the issues relating to data and computation.

1.7.5.1 Data

There are many issues surrounding the idea of data. Look at the simple variable request declared in our example program. It has a type, which in this case is int. It tells us what kinds of values it may hold. Where can such a variable declaration occur in a program? Only at the beginning of a program, or anywhere? When is the variable created? Does it have an initial value? Is it known to other procedures or modules of the program? How can variables be exported to other modules?

Given some elementary data items such as variables, are there mechanisms to combine them? For example, C++ provides arrays and records for building aggregate data structures. What are the kinds of components that a data structure may contain? Can a function be an element of a record? In Pascal the answer is no, and in C++ the answer is yes.

Sophisticated mechanisms for data definition allow the programmer to modularize the data in the program similarly to the way that the algorithms are modularized. For example, in our program in Figure 1.3, we use a file phone.h to store the basic definitions concerning phone data that are used by all other modules. Object-oriented programming languages draw much of their power from the mechanisms they provide to define and refine the definition of complex data items. Chapter 3 is devoted to data types, and Chapter 6 discusses object-oriented programming.

1.7.5.2 Computation

We have already seen expressions as a mechanism for computing values. Expressions are usually made up of elementary values and have a simple structure. *Control structures* are used to structure more complicated computations. For example, mechanisms such as various kinds of loops provide for repeated executions of a sequence of statements. Routine calls allow for the execution of a computation defined elsewhere in the program. Combining expressions, statements, control structures, and routine calls in C++ and other conventional languages allows the programmer to write algorithms using an imperative computation paradigm.

Chapter 4 describes the programming language mechanisms used for structuring computations.

1.7.6 External environment

Programs are seldom self-contained implementations of algorithms. The data they need and the results they expect to compute are normally exchanged with the external environment. In the example of Figure 1.3, the user is asked to type in a request. In other cases, a program might need to access an external database, or a device driver program might need to acquire the value of a particular signal.

How do programs communicate with the external environment? Some languages define specific constructs for input/output. Other languages, such as C/C++, do not provide such facilities. Instead, they rely on libraries external to the language to provide such facilities. For example, iostream.h is the header file that allows the input/output library to become accessible by the program in Figure 1.3 and allows the program to interact with the user. A similar mechanism is used for accessing an external database.

The advantage of language-supported facilities for communication with the external environment is that the programmer has a complete model of the environment and the compiler can do consistency checking. Supporting the facilities in a library makes the language simpler and allows more flexibility. For example, different libraries may be added as new devices, such as graphical ones, become available.

1.8 Bibliographic notes

Software development processes, environments, and methods are covered in software engineering textbooks, such as [Ghezzi91].

For a historical perspective on programming language developments, see [Wexelblat81] and [Bergin96]. These two books are the proceedings of two conferences sponsored by the ACM Special Interest Group on Programming Languages (SIGPLAN) in 1978 and 1993, respectively, on the history of programming languages (HOPL). The Turing lectures by J. Backus, C.A.R. Hoare, and N. Wirth (see [ACM87]) provide stimulating reflections on programming languages and their evolution. In particular, J. Backus takes a strong position in favor of functional languages as opposed to the von Neumann conventional approach.

1.9 Exercises

1. Write a short paper on the costs of programming. Discuss both the costs involved in developing and maintaining programs, and the costs involved in running programs. Discuss the role of the programming language in both.
2. List the main features of your favorite programming language that can help make programs easily maintainable. Also discuss features that hinder maintainability.
3. Write a program that shows why the optimization mentioned in Section 1.5.3 cannot be done in general for C.
4. Provide a succinct characterization of imperative vs. nonconventional (functional and logic) languages.
5. Take one or two languages you have used and discuss the types of expressions you can write in these languages.
6. Take one or two languages you have used and discuss the facilities provided for program organization.
7. Take one or two languages you have used and describe how the language supports interaction with the external environment.

Syntax and semantics

Sentences are not a mixture of words. Sentences are articulated. (Wittgenstein)

C H A P T E R   2

A programming language is a formal notation for describing algorithms for execution by computer. Like all formal notations, a programming language has two major components: syntax and semantics. The syntax is a set of formal rules that specify the composition of programs from letters, digits, and other characters. For example, the syntax rules may specify that each open parenthesis must match a closed parenthesis in arithmetic expressions, and that any two statements must be separated by a semicolon. The semantic rules specify "the meaning" of any syntactically valid program written in the language. Such meaning can be expressed by mapping each language construct into a domain whose semantics is known. For example, one way of describing the semantics of a language is by giving a description of each language construct in English. Such a description, of course, suffers from the informality, ambiguity, and wordiness of natural language, but it can give a reasonably intuitive view of the language. To provide a complete formal description of language semantics, syntactically valid programs are mapped onto mathematical domains. We will provide a preliminary introduction to formal semantics in this chapter, although a full treatment of the subject is out of our scope. Rather, we will focus on a rigorous yet informal description of semantics by specifying the behavior of an abstract processor that executes programs written in the language. This kind of semantic characterization of a language is called *operational semantics*. It could be presented using a rigorous and formal notation. Instead, we will follow a more traditional and informal approach, because it is more easily and intuitively understood by computer programmers and provides a high-level view of the problems found in implementing the language.

This chapter is organized as follows: In Section 2.1 we discuss how the syntax and semantics of a language can be defined. In Section 2.2 we discuss language implementation and introduce the fundamental semantic concept of binding. In Section 2.3 and Section 2.4 we discuss two important concepts of programming languages—variables and routines—and their binding properties. In Section 2.6 we define an abstract semantic processor that can be used to specify operational semantics. In Section 2.7 we discuss how the abstract processor implements the main run-time features of programming languages.

2.1 Language definition

When you read a program, how do you know if it is well formed? How do you know what it means? How does a compiler know how to translate the program? Any programming language must be defined in enough detail to enable these kinds of issues to be resolved. More specifically, a language definition should enable a person or a computer program to determine (1) whether a purported program is in fact valid and (2) if the program is valid, what its meaning or effect is. In general, two aspects of a language—programming or natural language—must be defined: syntax and semantics.

2.1.1 Syntax

Syntax is a set of rules that define the form of a language; they define how sentences may be formed as sequences of basic constituents called *words*. Using these rules we can tell whether a sentence is legal or not. The syntax does not tell us anything about the content (or meaning) of the sentence—the semantic rules tell us that. As an example, C keywords (such as while, do, if, and else), identifiers, numbers, operators, etc. are words of the language. The C syntax tells us how to combine such words to construct well-formed statements and programs.

Words are not elementary. They are constructed out of characters belonging to an *alphabet*. Thus, the syntax of a language is defined by two sets of rules: *lexical rules* and *syntactic rules*. Lexical rules specify the set of characters that constitute the alphabet of the language and the way such characters can be combined to form valid words.

For example, Pascal considers lowercase and uppercase characters to be identical, but C and Ada consider them to be distinct. Thus, according to the lexical rules, "Memory" and "memory" refer to the same variable in Pascal, but to distinct variables in C and Ada. The lexical rules also tell us that <> (or ≠) is a valid operator in Pascal but not in C, where the same operator is represented by !=. Ada differs from both, since "not equal" is represented as /=; the delimiter <> (called "box") stands for an undefined range of an array index.

The distinction between syntactic and lexical rules is somewhat arbitrary. They both contribute to the "external" appearance of the language. Often, we will use the terms "syntax" and "syntactic rules" in a wider sense that includes lexical components as well.

EBNF and syntax diagrams

EBNF is a metalanguage. A metalanguage is a language that is used to describe other languages. We describe EBNF first, and then we show how it can be used to describe the syntax of a simple language (Figure 2.1(a)). The symbols: : =, <, >, |, as well as * and +, when they appear as superscripts, are symbols of the metalanguage: they are *metasymbols*.

A language is described in EBNF through a set of rules. For example, <program> : : = {<statement>*} is a rule. The symbol "∶ ∶=" stands for "is defined as." The symbol "*" stands for "zero or more occurrences of the preceding element." Thus, the rule states that a <program> is defined as an arbitrary sequence of <statement> within brackets "{" and "}". The entities inside the metalanguage brackets "<" and ">" are called *nonterminals*; an entity such as "}" is called a *terminal*. Terminals are what we have previously called words of the language being defined, whereas nonterminals are linguistic entities that are defined by other EBNF rules. The metasymbol "+" denotes one or more occurrences of the previous element (i.e., at least one element must be present, as opposed to "*"). The metasymbol "|" denotes a choice. For example, a <statement> is described in Figure 2.1(a) as either an <assignment>, a <conditional>, or a <loop>.

The lexical rules that provide the EBNF description of identifiers, numbers, and operators are shown in Figure 2.1(b). Here, <operator>, <identifier>, and <number>, which are words of the language being defined, are detailed in terms of elementary symbols of the alphabet.

Figure 2.2 shows the syntax diagrams for the simple programming language whose EBNF syntax rules are shown in Figure 2.1. Nonterminals are represented by boxes and terminals by circles. The nonterminal symbol is defined with a transition diagram having one entry and one exit edge. A string of words is a valid program if it can be generated by traversing the syntax diagram from the entry to the exit edge. In this traversal, if a terminal (circle) is encountered, that word must be in the string being recognized; if a nonterminal (box) is encountered, then that nonterminal must be recognized by traversing the transition diagram for that nonterminal. When a branch in the path is encountered, any one edge may be traversed. Syntax diagrams are similar enough to EBNF to allow you to understand the rules.

How does one define the syntax of a language? Because there are an infinite number of legal and illegal programs in any useful language, we clearly cannot enumerate them all. We need a way to define an infinite set using a finite description. FORTRAN was defined by simply stating some rules in English. ALGOL 60 was defined with a context-free grammar developed by John Backus. This method has become known as BNF or Backus-Naur form (Peter Naur was the editor of the ALGOL 60 report). BNF provides a compact and clear definition for the syntax of programming languages. We illustrate an extended version of BNF (EBNF) in the sidebar on page 35, along with the definition of a simple language. Syntax diagrams provide another way of defining the syntax of programming languages. They are conceptually equivalent to BNF, but their pictorial notation is somewhat more intuitive. Syntax diagrams are also discussed in the sidebar on page 35.

(a) Syntax rules

$<$program$>$: : ={$<$statement$>$* }
$<$statement$>$: : =$<$assignment$>$ | $<$conditional$>$ | $<$loop$>$
$<$assignment$>$: : =$<$identifier$>$ = $<$expr$>$;
$<$conditional$>$: : =**if** $<$expr$>$ { $<$statement$>^+$ } |
      if $<$expr$>$ { $<$statement$>^+$ } **else** { $<$statement$>^+$ }
$<$loop$>$: : =**while** $<$expr$>$ { $<$statement$>^+$ }
$<$expr$>$: : =$<$identifier$>$ | $<$number$>$ | ($<$expr$>$) |
       $<$expr$>$ $<$operator$>$ $<$expr$>$

(b) Lexical rules

$<$operator$>$::= + | - | * | / | = | ≠ | **<** | **>** | ≤ | ≥
$<$identifier$>$::= $<$letter$>$ <ld>*
<ld>::= $<$letter$>$ | <digit>
$<$number$>$::= $<$digit$>^+$
$<$letter$>$::= a | b | c | ... | z
$<$digit$>$::= 0 | 1 | ... | 9

FIGURE 2.1 EBNF definition of a simple programming language

To summarize, the syntactic description of a language has two primary uses:

• It helps the programmer know how to write a syntactically correct program. For example, if one is unsure about the syntax of **if** statements, a look at the EBNF or syntax diagrams can quickly settle any doubts.

• It can be used to determine whether a program is syntactically correct. This is exactly what a compiler does. The compiler writer uses the grammar to write a syntactic analyzer

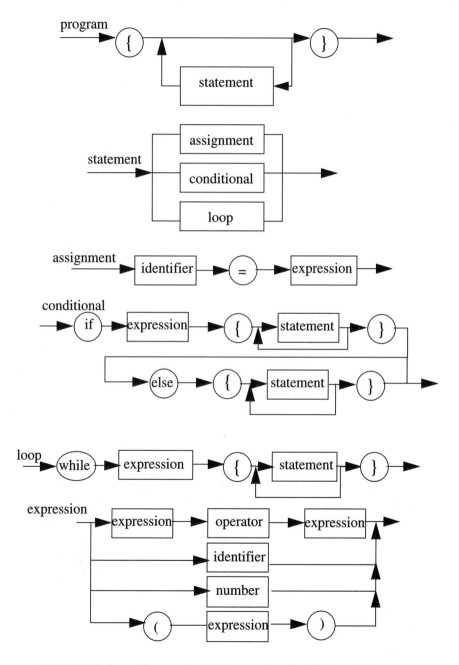

FIGURE 2.2 Syntax diagrams for the language described in Figure 2.1.

(also called parser) that is capable of recognizing all valid programs. This process is now largely automated. In fact, there are programs ("compiler generators") that can use the grammar of the language as input and produce the analyzer as output. LEX and YACC are two well-known UNIX tools that generate lexical and syntax analyzers, respectively, starting from a description of the lexical and syntactic rules of the language. Several versions of these tools exist.

2.1.1.1 Abstract syntax, concrete syntax, and pragmatics

Some language constructs in different programming languages have the same conceptual structure but differ in their appearance at the lexical level. For example, the C fragment

```
while (x != y) {
    ...
};
```

and the Pascal fragment

```
while x <> y do
begin
    ...
end
```

can both be described by simple lexical variants in the EBNF rules of Figure 2.1. They differ from the simple programming language of Figure 2.1 only in the way statements are bracketed (**begin** ... **end** vs. {...}), the "not equal" operator (<> vs. !=), and the fact that the loop expression in C must be enclosed within parentheses. When two constructs differ only at the lexical level, we say that they follow the same *abstract syntax* but differ at the *concrete syntax* level. That is, they have the same abstract structure and differ only in lower-level details.

Although conceptually concrete syntax may be irrelevant, pragmatically it may affect usability of the language and readability of programs. For example, the symbol ≠ is intuitively more readable than !=. As another example, the simple language of Figure 2.1 requires the body of "while" statements and the branches of conditionals to be bracketed by { and }. Other languages, such as C or Pascal, allow brackets to be omitted in the case of single statements. For example, in C one may write:

```
while (x != y)  x = y + 1;
```

Pragmatically, however, this may be error prone. If one more statement needs to be inserted in the loop body, one also needs to add brackets to group the statements constituting the body. Modula-2 addresses this problem at the concrete syntax level, by using the "**end**" keyword to terminate both loop and conditional statements. A similar solution is adopted by Ada. The following are Modula-2 examples:

if x = y **then**	**if** x = y **then**	**while** x = y **do**
...	...	...
end	**else**	**end**
	...	
	end	

In all three fragments, the "..." part can be either a single statement or a sequence of statements separated by semicolons.

2.1.2 Semantics

Syntax defines well-formed programs of a language. Semantics defines the meaning of syntactically correct programs in that language. For example, the semantics of C helps us determine that the declaration

    int vector[10];

causes space for 10 integer elements to be reserved for a variable named vector. The elements of the array may be referenced by an index i, $0 \le i \le 9$. The first element of the vector is vector[0].

As another example, the semantics of C states that the instruction

    if (a > b) max = a; else max = b;

means that the expression a > b must be evaluated and, depending on its value, one of the two given assignment statements is executed. Note that the syntax rules tell us how to form this statement—for example, where to put a ";"—and the semantic rules tell us what the effect of the statement is.

Actually, not all syntactically correct programs have a meaning. Thus, semantics also separates meaningful programs from merely syntactically correct ones. For example, according to the EBNF of the simple language described in Figure 2.1, one could write any expression as a condition of if and while statements. The semantics of the language might require such expressions to deliver a truth value (TRUE or FALSE, not, say, an integer value). In many cases, such rules that further constrain syntactically correct programs can be verified before a program's execution; they are called *static semantics*, as opposed to *dynamic semantics*, which describes the effect of executing the different constructs of the programming language. In such cases, programs can be executed only if they are correct with respect both to syntax and to static semantics. In this section, we concentrate on the latter; i.e., any reference to the term "semantics" implicitly refers to "dynamic semantics."

While syntax diagrams and BNF have become standard tools for syntax description, no such tool has become widely accepted and standard for semantic description. Different formal approaches to semantic definition exist, but none is entirely satisfactory. A brief introduction to formal semantics is provided in Section 2.1.2.1.

In this chapter, and throughout this book, we take an operational approach to describing the semantics of programming languages. In this approach, the behavior of a simple and intuitive abstract processor is used to describe the effects of each language construct. We will describe such a machine in Section 2.6. We will then describe the semantics of programming language constructs in terms of the operations of this machine.

Our machine is abstract. This means that it is not a real machine such as the Apple Macintosh PowerBook Duo 270c or the HP 9000. It is designed to show the run-time requirements of programming languages simply, rather than to execute them efficiently. It can be used as a model for language implementation in the sense that one can derive straightforward, simple implementations by applying the concepts that we discuss here. The resulting implementation, however, probably would be inefficient. To achieve efficiency, any real implementation will have to differ from the model in important ways, for example, in how data structures are arranged and accessed and in the set of machine instructions. The purpose of the model is simply to state the effects of the language, given the structure of the abstract machine. A particular implementation of the language on a given real machine is in no way obligated to implement the structure of the abstract processor used to define the semantics of the language; it is only required to implement the same effects, given the restrictions and structure of the implementation machine.

It is important to separate the semantic issues of the language from the implementation issues (we will come back to this point later). This can be done by keeping in mind which part of the description is a description (or restriction) of the machine and which one is of the language.

2.1.2.1 An introduction to formal semantics

A metalanguage for formal semantics must be based on well-understood mathematical concepts, so that the resulting definition is rigorous and unambiguous. The ability to provide formal semantics makes language definitions independent from the implementation. The description specifies what the language does, without any reference to how this may be achieved by an implementation. Furthermore, it allows an implementation-dependent comparison of different programing language features. Unfortunately, formality does not go hand in hand with readability. Absolute formality can be useful in a reference description, but for most practical uses a rigorous—yet informal—description can suffice.

Here we briefly review two ways of formally specifying semantics: axiomatic semantics and denotational semantics. We do not go deep into the two methods, but rather we provide a preliminary introduction that shows the main differences between them and with respect to the main approach that will be followed in this chapter. The reader who wishes to may skip this section. We base our discussion on the simple language described in Figure 2.1.

Axiomatic semantics views a program as a state machine. Programming language constructs are formalized by describing how their execution causes a state change. A state is described by a first-order logic predicate which defines the property of the values of program variables in that state. Thus the meaning of each construct is defined by a rule that relates the two states before and after the execution of that construct.

A predicate P that is required to hold after execution of a statement S is called a *postcondition* for S. A predicate Q that holds before the execution of S and guarantees that the execution of S terminates and postcondition P holds upon termination is called a *precondition* for S and P. For example, $y = 3$ is one possible precondition for statement

$x = y + 1;$

that leads to postcondition $x > 0$. The predicate $y \geq 0$ is also a precondition for the same statement and the same postcondition. Actually, $y \geq 0$ is the weakest precondition. A predicate W is called the *weakest precondition* for a statement S and a postcondition P if any precondition Q for S and P implies W. Among all possible preconditions for statement S and postcondition P, W is the weakest: it specifies the fewest constraints. It is the necessary and sufficient precondition for a given statement that leads to a certain postcondition. In the example, it is easy to prove that any precondition (e.g., $y = 3$) implies the weakest precondition ($y \geq 0$). This can be stated in first-order logic as

$(y = 3) \supset (y \geq 0)$

Axiomatic semantics specifies each statement of a language in terms of a function asem, called the *predicate transformer,* which yields the weakest precondition W for any statement S and any postcondition P. It also provides composition rules that allow the precondition to be evaluated for a given program and a given postcondition. Let us consider an assignment statement

    x = expr;

and a postcondition P. The weakest precondition is obtained by replacing each occurrence of x in P with the expression expr. We express this weakest precondition with the notation $P_{x \rightarrow expr}$. Thus[1]

    asem(x = expr;, P) = $P_{x \rightarrow expr}$

Simple statements, such as assignment statements, can be combined into more complex actions. For example, let us consider sequences, such as

    S2; S1;

If we know that

    asem(S1;, P) = Q

and

    asem(S2;, Q) = R

then

    asem(S2; S1;, P) = R

The specification of the semantics of selection is straightforward. If B is a boolean expression and L1 and L2 are two statement lists, then let if-stat be the following statement:

    if B **then** L1 **else** L2

If P is the postcondition that must be established by **if**-stat, then the weakest precondition is given by

    asem(**if**-stat, P) = (B ⊃ asem(L1, P)) and (not B ⊃ asem(L2, P))

That is, the function asem yields the semantics of either branch of the selection, depending on the value of the condition. For example, given the following program fragment (x, y, and max are integers)

---

1. This characterization of assignments is correct for simple assignment statements (see Exercise 40).

if $x \geq y$ **then** max = x; **else** max = y;

and the following postcondition Post,

(max = x and $x \geq y$) or (max = y and y > x)

the weakest precondition is easily proven to be true; that is, the statement satisfies the postcondition without any constraints on variables. In fact,

- The weakest precondition for predicate Post and statement max = x is $x \geq y$.
- The weakest precondition for predicate Post and statement max = y is $y \geq x$.
- The weakest precondition for the "if" statement is $(x \geq y \supset x \geq y)$ and $(y > x \supset y \geq x)$, which evaluates to true.

The specification of the semantics of loops is more complex. For simplicity, let us assume that loops always terminate. Let P be the postcondition that must be established by

while B **do** L

where B is a boolean expression and L is a statement list. The problem is that we do not know how many times the body of the loop is executed. Indeed, if we know, for example, that the number of iterations is n, the construct would be equivalent to the sequence of n statements

L; L; ...; L;

In such a case, the semantics of the statement would be straightforward. Since the number of iterations is generally unknown, we relax our requirements. Instead of providing the *weakest* precondition, which gives the exact characterization of semantics, we choose to provide just a precondition, i.e., a sufficient precondition that can be derived for a given statement and a given postcondition. The constraint on the state specified by a (non-weakest) precondition is stronger than that strictly necessary to ensure a certain postcondition to hold after execution of a statement, but nonetheless it provides an approximate specification of what the loop does. Such a precondition Q for a "while" statement and a postcondition P must be such that

- The loop terminates, and
- At loop exit, P holds.

Predicate Q can be written as Q = T and R, where T implies termination of the loop and R implies the truth of P at loop exit. Let us ignore the problem of termination and focus on determining R. This cannot be done mechanically, in general, and requires some ingenuity. A systematic method consists of identifying a predicate I that holds both before and after each loop iteration and such that, when the loop terminates (i.e., when the boolean expression B is false), I implies P. I is called an *invariant* predicate for the loop. Formally, I satisfies the following conditions.

   i) I and B $\supset$ asem(L, I)

   ii) I and not B $\supset$ P

If we are able to identify a predicate I that satisfies both (i) and (ii), then we can take I as the desired precondition R for the loop, because P holds upon termination if R = I holds before executing the loop. In conclusion, the method of loop invariants allows us to approximate the evaluation of the semantics of a "while" statement; the precondition is one possible valid precondition, not necessarily the weakest.

This approximation can be tolerated in practice. In fact, the main use of axiomatic semantics is in proving programs correct, i.e., proving that under certain specified constraints on input data (stated as an input predicate—the precondition for the entire program), the program terminates in a final state satisfying a specified constraint on output data (stated as an output predicate).

Denotational semantics associates each language statement with a function dsem from the state of the program before the execution to the state after execution. The *state* (i.e., the values stored in the memory) is represented by a function mem from the set of variable names ID to values. Each variable name—say, X—is said to denote a value—mem(X). Thus denotational semantics differs from axiomatic semantics in the way states are described (functions vs. predicates). For simplicity, we assume that values can only be of type integer.

Let us start our analysis with arithmetic expressions and assignments. For an expression expr, mem(expr) is defined as error if mem(v) is undefined for some variable v occurring in expr. Otherwise mem(expr) is the result of evaluating expr after replacing each variable v in expr with mem(v).

If x = expr is an assignment statement and mem is the function describing the memory before executing the assignment,

   dsem(x = expr, mem) = error

if mem(v) is undefined for some variable v occurring in expr. Otherwise

   dsem(x = expr, mem) = mem'

where mem'(y) = mem(y) for all y $\neq$ x, mem'(x) = mem(expr).[2]

---

2. This is a simplified formal description that works only for a restricted set of assignment statements (see Exercise 41).

As with axiomatic semantics, denotational semantics is defined compositionally. That is, the state transformation caused by compound statements and, eventually, by the entire program is based on the state transformation caused by each individual statement.

Let us consider a statement list, like

S1; S2;

If

dsem(S1, mem) = mem1

and

dsem(S2, mem1) = mem2

then

dsem(S1; S2;, mem) = mem2

The state error propagates implicitly; i.e., dsem(S, error) = error for any kind of statement S.

Let **if** B **then** L1 **else** L2 be a conditional statement, where B is a boolean expression and L1 and L2 are two statement lists. Its semantics can be defined as follows:

dsem(**if** B **then** L1 **else** L2, mem) = U

where

U = dsem(L1, mem) if mem(B) = true; otherwise

U = dsem(L2, mem)

Finally, let us consider a loop statement like **while** B **do** L. Its semantics can be defined as follows:

dsem(**while** B **do** L, mem)
= mem if mem(B) = false (i.e., if the loop is not entered, there is no change of memory); otherwise
dsem(**while** B **do** L, dsem(L, mem)) if mem(B) = true (i.e., a loop iteration is performed).

By applying the semantic rules provided above to the programs described by the language of Figure 2.1, it is possible to compute the value of function mem for the entire program.

2.2 Language processing

In theory, it is possible to build special-purpose computers to execute directly programs written in any particular language, but this would require a new machine architecture for each programming language. Today's computers directly execute only a very low-level, but general-purpose, language, called the *machine language*. Machine languages are designed on the basis of speed of execution, cost of realization, and flexibility in building new software layers upon them. On the other hand, programming languages often are designed on the basis of the ease and reliability of programming. A basic problem, then, is how a higher-level language eventually can be executed on a computer whose machine language is very different and at a much lower level.

There are generally two extreme alternatives for an implementation: interpretation and translation.

2.2.1 Interpretation

In this solution, the actions implied by the constructs of the language are executed directly (see Figure 2.3(a)). Usually, for each possible action there exists a subprogram—written in machine language—to execute the action. Thus, interpretation of a program is accomplished by calling subprograms in the appropriate sequence.

More precisely, an interpreter is a program that repeatedly executes the following sequence:

1 Get the next statement.
2 Determine the actions to be executed.
3 Perform the actions.

This sequence is quite similar to the pattern of actions carried out by a traditional computer, that is:

1 Fetch the next instruction (i.e., the instruction whose address is specified by the instruction pointer) and advance the instruction pointer (i.e., set the address of the instruction to be fetched next).
2 Decode the fetched instruction.
3 Execute the instruction.

This similarity shows that interpretation can be viewed as a simulation, on a host computer, of a special-purpose machine whose machine language is the higher-level language.

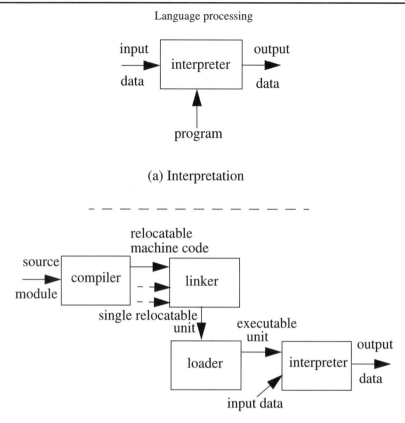

(a) Interpretation

(b) Translation (followed by interpretation)

FIGURE 2.3 Language processing by interpretation (a) and translation (b)

2.2.2 Translation

In this solution, programs written in a high-level language are translated into an equivalent machine-language version before being executed. This translation is often performed in several steps (see Figure 2.3(b)). Program modules might first be separately translated into relocatable machine code; modules of relocatable code are linked together into a single relocatable unit; finally, the entire program is loaded into the computer's memory as executable machine code. The translators used in these steps have specialized names: *compiler*, *linker* (or linkage editor), and *loader*, respectively.

In some cases, the machine on which the translation is performed (the *host machine*) is different from the machine that is to run the translated code (the *target machine*). This kind of translation is called *cross-translation*. Cross-translators offer the only viable solution when the target machine is a special-purpose processor rather than a general-purpose one that can support a translator.

Pure interpretation and pure translation are two ends of a continuous spectrum. In practice, many languages are implemented by a combination of the two techniques. A program may be translated into an intermediate code that is then interpreted. The intermediate code might be simply a formatted representation of the original program, with irrelevant information (e.g., comments and spaces) removed and the components of each statement stored in a fixed format to simplify the subsequent decoding of instructions. In this case, the solution is basically interpretive. Alternatively, the intermediate code might be the (low-level) machine code for a virtual machine that is to be later interpreted by software. This solution, which relies more heavily on translation, can be adopted for generating portable code, that is, code that is executable on different machines. For example, for portability purposes, one of the best-known initial implementations of a Pascal compiler was written in Pascal and generated an intermediate code, called Pcode. The availability of a portable implementation of the language contributed to the rapid diffusion of Pascal in many educational environments. More recently, with the widespread use of the Internet, code portability became a primary concern for network application developers. A number of language efforts have recently been undertaken with the goal of supporting code mobility over a network. The language Java is the best-known and most promising example. The language Java is first translated to an intermediate code, called Java bytecodes, which is interpreted in the client machine.

In a purely interpretive solution, executing a statement may require a fairly complicated decoding process to determine the operations to be executed and their operands. In most cases, this process is identical each time the statement is encountered. Consequently, if the statement appears in a frequently executed part of a program (e.g., in an inner loop), the speed of execution is strongly affected by this decoding process. On the other hand, pure translation generates machine code for each high-level statement. In so doing, the translator decodes each high-level statement only once. Frequently used parts are then decoded many times in their machine-language representation; because this is done efficiently by hardware, pure translation can save processing time over pure interpretation. On the other hand, pure interpretation may save storage. In pure translation, each high-level language statement may expand into tens or hundreds of machine instructions. In a purely interpretive solution, high-level statements are left in the original form and the instructions necessary to execute them are stored in a subprogram of the interpreter. The storage saving is evident if the program is large and uses most of the language's statements. On the other hand, if all of the interpreter's subprograms are kept in main memory during execution, the interpreter may waste space for small programs that use only a few of the language's statements.

Compilers and interpreters differ in the way they can report run-time errors. Typically, with compilation, any reference to the source code is lost in the generated object code. If an error is generated at run time, it may be impossible to relate it to the source language construct being executed. This is why run-time error messages are often obscure and almost meaningless to the programmer. On the opposite side, the interpreter processes source statements and can relate a run-time error to the source statement being executed. For these reasons, some programming environments contain both an interpreter and a compiler for a given programming language. Because of its improved diagnostic facilities, the interpreter is used while the program is being developed. The compiler is then used to generate efficient code, after the program has been validated.

Macro processing is a special kind of translation that may occur as the first step in the translation of a program. A macro is a named source text fragment, called the macro body. Through macro processing, macro names in a text are replaced by the corresponding bodies. In C, one can write macros, which are handled by a preprocessor, which generates source C code through macro expansion. For example, one can use a macro to provide a symbolic name for a constant value, as in the following fragment.

```
#define UPPER_LIMIT 100
...
sum = 0;
for (index = 0; index < UPPER_LIMIT; index++)
{
    sum += a[index];
}
```

2.2.3 The concept of binding

Programs deal with entities, such as variables, routines, and statements. Program entities have certain properties called *attributes*. For example, a variable has a name, a type, a storage area where its value is stored; a routine has a name, formal parameters of a certain type, certain parameter-passing conventions; a statement has associated actions. The values of attributes must be set before they can be used. Setting the value of an attribute is known as *binding*. For each entity, attribute information is contained in a repository called a *descriptor*.

Binding is a central concept in the definition of programming language semantics. Programming languages differ in the number of entities with which they can deal, in the number of attributes to be bound to entities, in the time at which such bindings occur (*binding time*), and in the *stability* of the binding (i.e., whether an established binding is fixed or modifiable).

Some attributes may be bound at language definition time, others at language implementation time, others at program translation time (or compile time), and others at program execution time (or run time). The following is a (nonexhaustive) list of binding examples:

- *Language definition time binding.* In most languages (including FORTRAN, Ada, C, and C++) the type "integer" is bound at language definition time to its well-known mathematical counterpart, i.e., to a set of algebraic operations that produce and manipulate integers.
- *Language implementation time binding.* In most languages (including FORTRAN, Ada, C, and C++) a set of values is bound to the integer type at language implementation time. That is, the language definition states that type "integer" must be supported and the language implementation binds it to a memory representation, which in turn determines the set of values that are contained in the type.
- *Compile-time (or translation-time) binding.* Pascal provides a predefined definition of type "integer" but allows the programmer to redefine it. Thus type "integer" is bound to a representation at language implementation time, but the binding can be modified at translation time.
- *Execution-time (or run-time) binding.* In most programming languages variables are bound to a value at execution time, and the binding can be modified repeatedly during execution.

In the first three examples, the binding is established before run time and cannot be changed thereafter. This kind of binding regime is often called *static*. The term "static" denotes both the binding time (which occurs before the program is executed) and the stability (the binding cannot be changed). Conversely, a binding established at run time is usually modifiable during execution. The fourth example illustrates this case. This kind of binding regime is often called *dynamic*. There are cases, however, where the binding is established at run time and cannot be changed after being established. An example is a language providing (read-only) constant variables that are initialized with an expression to be evaluated at run time.

The concepts of binding, binding time, and stability help clarify many semantic aspects of programming languages. In the next section we will use these concepts to illustrate the notion of a variable.

2.3 Variables

Conventional computers are based on the notion of a main memory consisting of elementary cells, each of which is identified by an *address*. The content of a cell is an encoded representation of a *value*. A value is a mathematical abstraction; its encoded representation in a memory cell can be read and (usually) modified during program execution. Modification implies replacing one encoding with a new encoding. With a few exceptions, programming languages can be viewed as abstractions, at different levels, of the behavior of such conventional computers. In particular, they introduce the notion of variable as an abstraction of the notion of memory cells, the variable name as an abstraction of the address, and the notion of assignment statements as an abstraction of the destructive modification of a cell.

In most of this and the following chapters we will restrict our considerations primarily to these conventional, "assignment-based" programming languages. Alternative languages that support functional and declarative styles of programming will be discussed in Chapters 7 and 8.

Formally, a variable is a 5-tuple <name, scope, type, l-value, r-value>, where

- *name* is a string of characters used by program statements to denote the variable;
- *scope* is the range of program instructions over which the name is known;
- *type* is the variable's type;
- *l-value* is the memory location associated with the variable;
- *r-value* is the encoded value stored in the variable's location.

These attributes are described below, in Section 2.3.1 through Section 2.3.4, along with the different policies that can be adopted for attribute binding. Section 2.3.5 discusses the special case of references and unnamed variables, which diverge from the model we have presented.

2.3.1 Name and scope

A variable's *name* is usually introduced by a special statement, called a *declaration*, and, normally, the variable's *scope* extends from that point until some later closing point, specified by the language. The scope of a variable is the range of program instructions over which the name is known. Program instructions can manipulate a variable through its name within its scope. We also say that a variable is visible under its name within its scope and invisible outside it. Different programming languages adopt different rules for binding a variable name to its scope.

For example, consider the example C program in Figure 2.4. The declaration int x, y; makes variables named x and y visible throughout the program main. The program contains an internal block, which groups a declaration and statements. The declaration int temp; appearing in the block makes a variable named temp visible within the inner block and invisible outside. Thus, it would be an error to use temp as an argument of operation printf.

```
#include <stdio.h>
main()
{
    int x, y;
    scanf("%d %d", &x, &y);
        /* two decimal values are read and stored in the l-values of x and y */
    {
        /* this is a block used to swap x and y*/
        int temp;
        temp = x;
        x = y;
        y = temp;
    }
    printf("%d %d", x, y);
}
```

FIGURE 2.4 A sample C program

In the example, if the inner block declares a new local variable named x, the outer variable named x would no longer be visible in the inner block. The inner declaration masks the outer variable. The outer variable, however, continues to exist even though it is invisible. It becomes visible again when control leaves the inner block.

Variables can be bound to a scope either statically or dynamically. *Static scope binding* (also called *lexical scoping*) defines the scope in terms of the lexical structure of a program; that is, each reference to a variable can be statically bound to a particular (implicit or explicit) variable declaration by examining the program text, without executing it. Static scope binding rules are adopted by most programming languages, such as C, as we saw in the previous example.

Dynamic scope binding defines the scope of a variable's name in terms of program execution. Typically, each variable declaration extends its effect over all the instructions executed thereafter, until a new declaration for a variable with the same name is encountered during execution. APL, LISP (as originally defined), and SNOBOL4 are examples of languages with dynamic scope rules.

As an example, consider the program fragment in Figure 2.5, written in a C-like notation. If the language follows dynamic scoping, an execution of block A followed by block C would cause variable x in the assignment in block C to refer to x declared in block A. Instead, an execution of block B followed by block C would cause variable x in the assignment in block C refer to x declared in block B. Thus, the name x in block C refers either to the x declared in A or the one declared in B, depending on the flow of control followed during execution.

```
{
    /* block A */
    int x;
    ...
}
...
{
    /* block B */
    int x;
    ...
}
...
{
    /* block C */
    ...
    x = ...;
    ...
}
```

FIGURE 2.5 A program fragment in a C-like notation

Dynamic scope rules look quite simple and are rather easy to implement, but they have disadvantages in terms of programming discipline and efficiency of implementation. Programs are hard to read because the identity of the particular declaration to which a given variable is bound depends on the particular point of execution, and so cannot be determined statically.

2.3.2 Type

In this section we provide a preliminary introduction to types. The subject will be examined in more depth in Chapters 3 and 6. We define the type of a variable as a specification of the *set of values* that can be associated with the variable, together with the *operations* that can be legally used to create, access, and modify such values. A variable of a given type is said to be an *instance* of the type.

When the language is defined, certain type names are bound to certain classes of values and sets of operations. For example, type "integer" and its associated operators are bound to their mathematical counterparts. Values and operations are bound to a certain machine representation when the language is implemented. The latter binding may also restrict the set of values that can be represented, based on the storage structure of the target machine.

In some languages, the programmer can define new types by means of type declarations. For example, in Pascal one can write

type vector = **array**[1..10] **of** integer

This declaration establishes a binding—at translation time—between the type name vector and its implementation (i.e., an array of 10 integers, each accessible via an index in the subrange 1..10). As a consequence of this binding, type vector inherits all the operations of the representation data structure (the array); thus, it is possible to read and modify each component of an object of type vector by indexing into the array. Some languages support the implementation of user-defined types (usually called *abstract data types*) by associating the new type with the set of operations that can be used on its instances; the operations are described as a set of routines in the declaration of the new type. The declaration of the new type has the following general form, expressed in Pascal-like syntax:

```
type new_type_name =
{
    data structure representing objects of type new_type_name;
    routines to be invoked for manipulating data objects of type new_type_name;
}
```

To provide a preview of concepts and constructs that will be discussed at length in this text, Figure 2.6 illustrates an example of an abstract data type (a stack of characters) implemented as a C++ class.[3] The class defines the hidden data structure (a pointer s to the first element of the stack, a pointer top to the most recently inserted character, and an integer denoting the maximum size) and five routines to be used for manipulating stack objects. Routines stack_of_char and ~stack_of_char are used to construct and destroy objects of type stack_of_char, respectively. Routine push is used to insert a new element on top of a stack object. Routine pop is used to extract an element from a stack object. Routine length yields the current size of a stack object.

Most languages, including FORTRAN, COBOL, Pascal, C, C++, Modula-2, and Ada, bind variables to their type at compile time, and the binding cannot be changed during execution. This solution is called *static typing*. In these languages, the binding between a variable and its type is specified by a variable declaration. For example, in Pascal one can write:

```
var x, y: integer;
    c: character;
```

By declaring variables to belong to a given type, variables are automatically protected from the application of illegal (or nonsensical) operations.

---

3. A note for the reader who is not familiar with C or C++. The expression *top++ is evaluated as *(top++). The expression top++ increments the value of top and returns the value of top before it is incremented. The expression *--top is evaluated as *(--top). In this case, top is decremented, and the decremented value is used for dereferencing.

```
class stack_of_char{
public:
    stack_of_char(int sz) {
        top = s = new char[size =sz];
    }
    ~stack_of_char() {delete[ ] s;}
    void push(char c) {*top++ = c;}
    char pop() {return *--top;}
    int length() {return top - s;}
private:
    int size;
    char* top;
    char* s;
};
```

FIGURE 2.6 User-defined type in C++

In the example, the compiler can detect the occurrence of illegal assignments, like

```
x := c;
y := not y;
```

because they would violate the above declarations. The ability to perform checks before the program is executed (*static type checking*) contributes to early error detection and enhances program reliability.

In some languages (such as FORTRAN) the first occurrence of a new variable name is also taken as an implicit declaration. The advantage of explicit declarations lies in the clarity of the program and improved reliability, because such things as spelling errors in variable names can be caught at translation time. For example, in FORTRAN the declaration of variable ALPHA followed by an erroneous statement such as ALPA = 7.3, intended to assign a value to it, would not be detected as an error. Rather than being detected as an incorrect occurrence of an undeclared variable ALPA (i.e., as a misspelled ALPHA), the statement would be taken as the implicit declaration of a new variable, ALPA.

Note that the issue of implicit type declarations is not a semantic one. Semantically, FORTRAN and Pascal are equivalent with respect to the typing of variables because they both bind variables to types at translation time. FORTRAN has default rules to determine the particular binding, but the time of binding and its stability are the same in the two languages. The FORTRAN rule that determines the type of a variable is quite simple: it is based on the first letter of the variable's name. The language ML pushes the approach of implicit declaration to its extreme, by not requiring the explicit specification of most types, and yet checking the type of all expressions statically. This is achieved through a *type inference* procedure which determines the type of a variable based on its usage. We will discuss this in Chapter 7.

LISP, APL, SNOBOL4, and Smalltalk are languages that establish a (modifiable) run-time binding between variables and their type. This binding strategy is called *dynamic typing*. Dynamically typed variables are also called *polymorphic variables* (literally, from the ancient Greek, "multiple shape") variables. In such languages, the type of a variable depends on the value that is dynamically associated with it. For example, once an integer value has been assigned to a variable, such a value cannot be treated as if it were, say, a string of characters. That is, once a value is bound to a variable, an implicit binding with a type is also established, and the binding remains in place until a new value is assigned to the variable.

As another example, in LISP, variables are not declared explicitly; their type is determined implicitly by the object they are bound to during execution. The LISP function CAR applied to a list L yields the first element of L, which may be an atom (say, an integer) or a list of, say, strings, if L is a list of lists. If the element returned by CAR is bound to a variable, the type of the variable would be an integer in the former case and a string list in the latter. If such a value is added to an integer value, the operation would be correct in the former case but would be illegal in the latter. Moreover, suppose that the value of the variable is to be printed. The effect of the print operation depends on the type that is dynamically associated with the variable. It prints an integer in the former case and a list of strings in the latter. Such a print routine, which is applicable to arguments of more than one type, is called a *polymorphic,* or *generic, routine.*

In general, dynamic typing prevents programs from being statically type-checked: since the type is not known, it may be impossible to check for type violations before executing the program. In such a case, type violations due to dynamic typing can only be checked at run time, through dynamic type checking. In order to perform dynamic type checking, information about the dynamic type must be kept at run time in suitable object descriptors. For statically typed languages, such descriptors only need to exist at translation time. Perhaps surprisingly, however, there are languages supporting both static type checking and polymorphic variables and routines. This will be discussed at length in Chapters 3, 6, and 7.

Languages can also be *typeless*. Most assembly languages fall under this category. In such a case, variables are untyped, as are the objects to which variables may be bound dynamically. This reflects the behavior of the underlying hardware, where memory cells and registers can contain bit strings that are interpreted as values of any type. For example, the bit string stored in a cell may be added to the bit string stored in a register using integer addition. In such a case, the bit strings are interpreted as integer values.

2.3.3 l-value

The l-value of a variable is the storage area bound to the variable during execution. The *lifetime*, or extent, of a variable is the period of time in which such binding exists. The storage area is used to hold the r-value of the variable. We will use the term *data object* (or simply, object) to denote the pair <l-value, r-value>.

The action that acquires a storage area for a variable—and thus establishes the binding between the variable and its l-value—is called *memory allocation*. The lifetime extends from the point of allocation to the point in which the allocated storage is reclaimed (*memory deallocation*). In some languages, for some kinds of variables, allocation is performed before run time and storage is only reclaimed upon termination (*static allocation*). In other languages, it is performed at run time (*dynamic allocation*), either upon explicit request from the programmer via a creation statement or automatically, when the variable's declaration is encountered, and reclaimed during execution. Section 2.7 presents an extensive analysis of these issues.

In most cases, the lifetime of a program variable is a fraction of the program's execution time. It is also possible, however, to have persistent objects. A persistent object exists in the environment in which a program is executed, and its lifetime has no a priori relation with any given program's execution time. Files are an example of persistent objects. Once they are created, they can be used by different program activations, and different activations of the same program, until they are deleted through a specific command to the operating system. Similarly, persistent objects can be stored in a database and made visible to a programming language through a specific interface.

2.3.4 r-value

The r-value of a variable is the encoded value stored in the location associated with the variable (i.e., its l-value). The encoded representation is interpreted according to the variable's type. For example, a certain sequence of bits stored at a certain location would be interpreted as an integer number if the variable's type is int; it would be interpreted as a string if the type is an array of characters.

l-values and r-values are the main concepts related to program execution. Program instructions access variables through their l-value and possibly modify their r-value. The terms l-value and r-value derive from the conventional form of assignment statements, such as x = y; in C. The variable appearing at the left-hand side of the assignment denotes a location (i.e., the variable's l-value). The variable appearing at the right-hand side of the assignment denotes the contents of a location (i.e., the variable's r-value). Whenever no ambiguity arises, we use the simple term "value" of a variable to denote its r-value.

The binding between a variable and the value held in its storage area is usually dynamic; the binding is established by an assignment operation. An assignment such as b = a; causes a's r-value to be copied into the storage area referred to by b's l-value. That is, b's r-value changes. This, however, is true only for conventional imperative languages, like FORTRAN, C, Pascal, Ada, and C++. Functional and logic programming languages treat variables as their mathematical counterparts: they can be bound to a value by the evaluation process, but once the binding is established it cannot be changed during the variable's lifetime.

Some conventional languages, however, allow the binding between a variable and its value to be frozen once it is established. The resulting entity is, in every respect, a user-defined symbolic constant. For example, in C one can write

    const float pi = 3.1415;

and then use pi in expressions such as

    circumference= 2 * pi * radius;

The variable pi is bound to the value 3.1415 and its value cannot be changed; that is, the translator reports an error if there is an assignment to pi. A similar effect can be achieved in Pascal.

Pascal and C differ in the time of binding between the const variable and its value, although binding stability is the same for both languages. In Pascal the value is provided by an expression that must be evaluated at compile time; i.e., binding time is compile time. The compiler can legally substitute the value of the constant for its symbolic name in the program. In C and Ada the value can be given as an expression involving other variables and constants. Consequently, binding can only be established at run time, when the variable is created.

A subtle question concerning the binding between a variable (that is not a const) and its value is: What is the r-value bound to the variable immediately after it is created? Some languages, for example ML, require a binding to be established when the variable is created. Others support such bindings but do not require them. That is, the declaration of a variable may also specify an initial value for the variable. For example, in C one can write

```
int i = 0, j = 0;
```

Similarly, in Ada one would write

```
i, j: INTEGER := 0;
```

But what if no initialization is provided in the declaration? There are a number of possible approaches that might be followed, but unfortunately most language definitions fail to specify which one they choose. As a result, the problem is solved differently by different implementations of the same language, and thus program behavior depends on the implementation. Moving an apparently correct program to a different platform may produce unforeseen errors or unexpected results.

One obvious and frequently adopted solution to the problem is to ignore it. In this case, the bit string found in the area of storage associated with the variable is considered its initial value. Another solution is to provide a system-defined initialization strategy: for example, integers are initialized to zero, characters to blank, and so on. Yet another solution consists of viewing an uninitialized variable as initialized with a special undefined value, and trapping any read accesses to the variable. This rather clean solution can be enforced in different ways. Its only drawback could be the cost of run-time checks necessary to ensure that a meaningless value is never used in the program.

2.3.5 References and unnamed variables

Some languages allow variables that can be accessed through the r-value of another variable. Such an r-value is called a *reference* (or a *pointer*) to the variable. Variables that are accessed via pointers may even be *unnamed*. The only way to access an unnamed variable is through some other named variable. The unnamed variable might be referenced directly by a named variable. Or it might be referenced by an unnamed variable which, in turn, can be referenced by a named variable. In general, an object can be made accessible via a chain of references (called an *access path*) of arbitrary length, as we will show shortly through examples.

If A = <A_name, A_scope, A_type, A_l-value, A_r-value> is a named variable, the object <A_l-value, A_r-value> is said to be directly accessible through name A_name in A_scope, with an access path of length 0. If B= <--, --, --, B_l-value, B_r-value>, where -- stands for the "don't care" value, is a variable and B_l-value = A_r-value, the object <B_l-value, B_r-value> is said to be accessible through name A_name in A_scope indirectly, with an access path of length 1. Similarly, one can define the concept of an object accessible indirectly through a named variable, with an access path of length i, i>1.

For example, in Pascal we can declare type PI as a pointer to an integer:

```
type PI = ^ integer;
```

We can then allocate an unnamed integer variable and point to it through a variable pxi of type PI:

```
var pxi: PI;
new(pxi);
```

In order to access the unnamed object referenced by pxi, it is necessary to use the *dereferencing* operator ^, which can be applied to a pointer variable to obtain its r-value, which is the l-value of the referenced object. For example, the value of the unnamed variable can be set to zero by writing:

```
pxi^ := 0;
```

The unnamed variable can also be made accessible indirectly through a "pointer to a pointer to an integer," as sketched below:

```
type PPI = ^PI;
var ppxi: PPI;
...
new(ppxi);
ppxi^ := pxi;
```

Here the r-value of variable ppxi is the l-value of an unnamed variable, whose r-value is the l-value of an unnamed object whose r-value is zero. This example is described pictorially in Figure 2.7. The data object whose r-value is zero is accessible indirectly through variable pxi; it is also accessible through variable ppxi, with an access path of length 2.

Pascal allows pointers to point only to unnamed variables. Other languages, such as C, C++, and Ada, allow pointers to refer to named variables. For example, the C fragment

```
int x = 5;
int* px;
px = &x;
```

creates an integer object whose r-value is 5, directly accessible through a variable named x and indirectly accessible (with an access path of length 1) through px, declared as a pointer to an integer. This is achieved by assigning

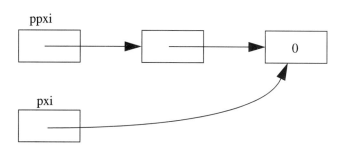

FIGURE 2.7 Access to an unnamed variable

to px the value of the address of x (i.e., &x). Indirect access to x is then made possible by dereferencing px. In C (and C++) the dereferencing operator is denoted by *. For example, the C instruction

    int y = *px;

assigns to y the r-value of the variable pointed at by px (i.e., 5). Two variables are said to *share* an object if each has an access path to the object. A shared object modified via a certain access path makes the modification visible through all possible access paths. Sharing of objects is used to improve efficiency, but it can lead to programs that are hard to read, because the value of a variable can be modified even when its name is not used. In the previous C example, if one writes

    *px = 0;

the contents of the location pointed at by px becomes 0 and, because of sharing, the value of x becomes 0 too.

2.4 Routines

Programming languages allow a program to be composed of a number of units, called *routines*. We use the neutral term "routine" in this chapter to provide a general treatment that enlightens the important principles that are common to most programming languages, without committing to any specific feature offered by an individual language. Routines can be developed in a more or less independent fashion and can sometimes be translated separately and combined after translation. Assembly language subprograms, FORTRAN subroutines, Pascal and Ada procedures and functions, and C functions are well-known examples of routines. In this chapter we will review the main syntactic and semantic features of routines, and in particular the mechanisms that control the flow of execution among routines and the bindings established when a routine is executed. Other, more general kinds of units, such as Ada packages, Modula-2 modules, and C++ classes, will be described in later chapters.

In the programming language world, routines usually come in two forms: procedures and functions. Functions return a value; procedures do not. Some languages, e.g., C and C++, only provide functions, but procedures are easily obtained as functions returning the null type void. Figure 2.8 shows an example of a C function definition.

```
/* sum is a function which computes the sum of the first n positive integers,
1 + 2 + ... + n; parameter n is assumed to be positive */
int sum(int n)
{
    int i, s;
    s = 0;
    for (i = 1; i <= n; ++i)
        s+= i; // Note for non C programmers; this is equivalent to s = s + i
    return s;
}
```

FIGURE 2.8 A C function definition

Like variables, routines have a name, scope, type, l-value, and r-value. A routine name is introduced in a program by a routine *declaration*. Usually the scope of the name extends from the declaration point to some closing construct which is determined either statically or dynamically, depending on the language. For example, in C a function declaration extends the scope of the function till the end of the file in which the declaration occurs.

Routine activation is achieved through a *routine invocation* (or *routine call*), which names the routine and specifies the parameters on which the routine operates. Since a routine is activated by a call, the call statement must be in the routine's scope. Besides having their own scope, routines also define a scope for the declarations that are nested in them. Such *local* declarations are only visible within the routine. Depending on the scope rules of the language, routines can also refer to nonlocal items (e.g., variables) other than those declared locally. Nonlocal items that are visible to every unit in the program are called *global* items.

The *header* of the routine defines the routine's name, its parameter types, and the type of the returned value (if any). In brief, the routine's header defines the *routine type*. In the example of Figure 2.8, the routine's type is:

routine with one int parameter and returning an int

A routine type can be defined precisely by the concept of *signature*. The signature specifies the types of parameters and the return type. A routine fun which behaves like a function, with input parameters of types T1, T2, ..., Tn and returning a value of type R, can be specified by the following signature:

fun: T_1 x T_2 x ...x T_n -> R

A routine call is *type correct* if it conforms to the corresponding routine type. For simplicity, one may assume here that type conformance requires the type of the corresponding formal and actual parameters to be the same. For example, the call

i = sum(10);   /* i is declared as an int */

would be correct with respect to the function definition of Figure 2.8. On the other hand, the call

i = sum(5.3);

would be incorrect.

A routine's l-value is a reference to the memory area which stores the routine *body* (i.e., the routine's executable statements). Activation causes execution of the routine body, which constitutes the r-value that is currently bound to the routine. In the above C example, the r-value is bound to the routine statically, at translation time. A more dynamic binding policy can be achieved by languages which support the concept of variables of type routine, to which a routine value can be assigned. Some languages support the notion of a "pointer to a routine" and provide a way of getting a routine's l-value, which can be assigned (as an r-value) to a pointer. For example, the following C statement declares a pointer ps to a function with an int parameter and returning an int:

int(*ps)(int);

The following assignment

ps = & sum;

makes ps point to the l-value of the previously defined routine sum. A call may then be issued via ps as in the following example:

int i = (*ps)(5); // invokes the r-value of the routine that is currently referred to by ps

The use of pointers to routines allows different routines to be invoked each time a pointer is dereferenced. This provides a way to achieve a dynamic binding policy; this cannot be achieved by directly calling a routine, which is statically bound to its body. Languages that exploit the distinction between a routine l-value and r-value, and allow variables of type routine and pointers to routines to be defined and manipulated, treat routines in much the same way as variables: they are said to treat routines as *first-class objects*.

Some languages (like Pascal, Ada, C, and C++) distinguish between the *declaration* and *definition* of a routine. A routine declaration introduces the routine's header, without specifying the body. The name is visible from the declaration point on, up to the scope end. The definition specifies both the header and the body. The distinction between declaration and definition is exploited to allow routines to call each other in a mutual recursion scheme, as illustrated by the fragment in Figure 2.9.

```
int A(int x, int y); // declaration of a function with two int parameters
                     // returning an int; A is visible from this point on
float B(int z)       //definition of function B; B is visible from this point on
{
    int w, u;
    ...
    w = A(z, u);   //calls A, which is visible at this point
    ...
};
int A(int x, int y) //this is A's definition
{
    float t;
    ...
    t = B(x);      //B is visible here
    ...
}
```

FIGURE 2.9 Routine declaration and definition in C

A routine definition specifies a computational process. At invocation time, an instance of the process is executed for the particular values of the parameters. The representation of a routine during execution is called a *routine instance*. A routine instance is composed of a code segment and an activation record. The *code segment*, whose contents are fixed, contains the instructions of the unit. The contents of the *activation record* (also called *frame)* are changeable. The activation record contains all the information necessary to execute the routine, including, among other things, the data objects associated with the local variables of a particular routine instance. The relative position of a data object in the activation record is called its *offset*. To allow the invoked routine to return control back to its caller, the return pointer is saved as part of the activation record at routine invocation time.

The *referencing environment* of a routine instance U consists of U's local variables, which are bound to objects stored in U's activation record and U's nonlocal variables, which are bound to objects stored in the activation records of other units. The local objects define the *local environment*; the nonlocal objects define the *nonlocal environment*. The modification of a data object bound to a nonlocal variable is called a *side effect*.

If routines can be activated *recursively*, a new unit activation can occur before termination of a previous activation of the same unit. All the instances of the same unit are composed of the same code segment but different activation records. Thus, in the presence of recursion, the binding between an activation record and its code segment is necessarily dynamic. Every time a unit is activated, a binding must be established between an activation record and its code segment to form a new unit instance.

When a routine is activated, parameters may be passed from the caller to the callee. Parameter passing allows for the flow of information among program units. In most cases, only data entities may be passed. In some cases, routines may also be passed. In particular, this feature is offered by languages where routines are first-class objects.

Parameter passing and communication via nonlocal data are two different ways of achieving inter-unit information flow. Unlike communication via global environments, parameters allow for the transfer of different data at each call and provide advantages in terms of readability and modifiability.

It is necessary to distinguish between *formal parameters* (the parameters that appear in the routine's definition) and *actual parameters* (the parameters that appear in the routine's call). Most programming languages use a *positional* method for binding actual to formal parameters in routine calls. If the routine's header is

routine S(F1, F2, ...Fn);

and the routine call is

call S(A1, A2,...An)

the positional method implies that the formal parameter Fi is to be bound to actual parameter Ai, i = 1,2,...n. In some cases the number of actual and formal parameters need not be the same. For example, in C++ formal parameters can be given a default value, which is used in case the corresponding actual parameters are not passed in the call.

For example, given the function header

```
int distance(int a = 0, int b =0);
```

the call distance() is equivalent to distance(0, 0), and the call distance(10) is equivalent to distance(10, 0). To explore this issue further, see Exercise 42.

Besides the positional association method, some languages, including Ada, allow a named parameter association. For example, having defined a procedure with the header

```
procedure Example(A: T1; B: T2 := W; C: T3);
    --parameters A, B, and C are of types T1, T2, and T3, respectively;
    --a default value is specified for parameter B, given by the value of W
```

assuming X, Y, and Z to be of types T1, T2, and T3, respectively, the following calls are legal:

```
Example(X, Y, Z);
    --this is a pure positional association
Example(X, C => Z)
    --X is bound to A positionally, B gets the default value W
    --Z is bound to C in a named association
Example(C => Z, A => X, B => Y);
    --all correspondences are named here
```

We take up the issue of parameter passing in Section 2.7.7, where we give an abstract implementation model and describe the different kinds of parameter passing modes.

2.4.1 Generic routines

Routines factor a code fragment that is executed at different points of the program in a single place and assign it a name. The fragment is then executed through invocation and customized through parameters. Often, however, similar routines must be written several times, because they differ in some detail that cannot be factored through parameters. For example, if a program needs a routine to sort both arrays of integers and arrays of strings, two different routines must be written, one for each parameter type, even if the abstract algorithm chosen for the implementation of the sort operation is the same in both cases.

Generic routines, as offered by some programming languages, provide a solution to this problem. In this section we provide an introductory view of generic routines as they appear in languages like C++ and Ada. More will be said in Chapters 4, 5, 6, and 7. A generic routine can be made parametric with respect to a type. In the previous example, the routine would be generic with respect to the type of the array elements. Type parameters in a generic routine, however, differ from conventional parameters and require a different implementation scheme. A generic routine is a template from which the specific routine is generated through *instantiation*, an operation that binds generic parameters to actual parameters at compile time. Such binding can be obtained via macroprocessing, which generates a new instance (i.e., an actual routine) for each type parameter. Other implementation schemes, however, are also possible.

Figure 2.10 shows an example of a generic swap routine in C++. Generic C++ units are called *templates*. In contrast to Ada, C++ generic routines are not instantiated explicitly. Rather, any use of a generic routine triggers the compiler to instantiate the corresponding executable routine implicitly. For example, given the generic routine in Figure 2.10, the code fragment

```
int i, j;
...
swap(i, j);
```

will instantiate an integer swap routine, and

```
float f, g;
...
swap(f, g);
```

will instantiate a float swap routine.

```
template <class T> void swap(T& a, T& b)
/* the function does not return any value; it is generic with respect to type T;
a and b refer to the same locations as the actual parameters;
swap interchanges the two values*/
{
    T temp = a;
    a = b;
    b = temp;
}
```

FIGURE 2.10   A generic routine in C++

2.5 Aliasing and overloading

As our discussion so far has emphasized, a central issue of programming language semantics has to do with the conventions adopted for naming. In programs, names are used to denote variables and routines. The language uses special operator names, such as + or *, to denote certain predefined operations. So far, we have assumed implicitly that at each point in a program a name denotes exactly one entity, based on the scope rules of the language. Since names are used to identify the corresponding entity, the assumption of unique binding between a name and an entity would make the identification unambiguous. This restriction, however, almost never holds for existing programming languages.

For example, in C one can write the following fragment:

```
int i, j, k;
float a, b, c;
...
i = j + k;
a = b + c;
```

In this example, the operator + in the two instructions of the program denotes two different entities. In the first expression, it denotes integer addition; in the second, it denotes floating-point addition. Although the name of the operator is the same in the two expressions, the binding between the operator and the corresponding operation is different in the two cases, and the exact binding can be established at compile time, since the types of the operands allow for the disambiguation.

We can generalize the previous example by introducing the concept of *overloading*. A name is said to be overloaded if it refers to more than one entity at a given point of a program and yet the specific occurrence of the name provides enough information to allow the binding to be uniquely established. In the previous example, the types of the operands to which + is applied allow for the disambiguation.

As another example, if the second instruction of the previous fragment is changed to

```
a = b + c + b();
```

the two occurrences of name b would (unambiguously) denote, respectively, variable b and routine b with no parameters and returning a float value (assuming that such routine is visible by the assignment instruction). Similarly, in C++, if another routine named b with one int parameter and returning a float value is visible, the instruction

```
a = b() + c + b(i);
```

would unambiguously denote two calls to the two different routines.

Aliasing is the opposite of overloading. Two names are aliases if they denote the same entity at the same program point. This concept is especially relevant in the case of variables. Two aliased variables share the same data object in the same referencing environment. Thus modification of the object under one name would make the effect visible, maybe unexpectedly, under the other.

Although examples of aliasing are quite common, one should use it carefully since this feature may lead to programs that are error-prone and difficult to read. An example of aliasing is shown by the following C fragment:

```
int x = 0;
int *i = &x;
int *j = &x;
```

If a new value is assigned to *i (e.g., *i = 10), the change is also visible by dereferencing j and as a new value of x.

2.6 An abstract semantic processor

In Section 2.1.2 we described several approaches to defining the semantics of programming languages. We said that in this book we will use an operational approach to semantics. To do so, we introduce a simple abstract processor, called SIMPLESEM, and we show how language constructs can be executed by sequences of operations of the abstract processor. In this section, we provide the main features of SIMPLESEM; additional details will be introduced incrementally, as additional language features are introduced.

In its basic form, SIMPLESEM consists of an *instruction pointer* (the reference to the instruction currently being executed), a *memory*, and a *processor*. The memory stores the instructions to be executed and the data to be manipulated. For simplicity, we will assume that these two parts are stored in two separate memory sections: the *code memory* (C) and the *data memory* (D). Both C's and D's addresses start at 0 (zero), and both programs and data are assumed to be stored starting at this address. The instruction pointer (ip) is always used to point to a location in C; it is initialized to 0.

We use the notation D[X] and C[X] to denote the values stored in the Xth cell of D and C, respectively. Thus X is an l-value and D[X] is the corresponding r-value. Modification of the value stored in a cell is performed by the instruction

```
set target, source
```

where the two parameters target and source are, respectively, the address of the cell whose content is to be set, and the expression evaluating the new value. For example, the effect of the instruction

```
set 10, D[20]
```

on the data memory is to copy the value stored at location 20 into location 10.

Input/output in SIMPLESEM is achieved quite simply by using the set instruction and referring to the special registers read and write, which provide for communication of the SIMPLESEM machine with the outside world. For example,

```
set 15, read
```

means that the value read from the input device is to be stored at location 15;

```
set write, D[50]
```

means that the value stored at location 50 is to be transferred to the output device.

We are quite liberal in the way we allow values to be combined in expressions; for example, D[15]+D[33]*D[41] would be an acceptable expression, and

```
set 99, D[15]+D[33]*D[41]
```

would be an acceptable instruction to modify the contents of location 99.

As we mentioned, ip is SIMPLESEM's instruction pointer, which is initialized to zero at each new execution and automatically updated as each instruction is executed. The machine, in fact, operates by executing the following steps repeatedly, until it encounters a special halt instruction:

1 Get the current instruction to be executed (i.e., C[ip]);
2 Increment ip;
3 Execute the current instruction.

Notice, however, that certain programming language instructions might modify the normal sequential control flow, and this must be reflected by SIMPLESEM. In particular, we introduce the following two instructions: jump and jumpt. The former represents an unconditional jump to a certain instruction. For example,

```
jump 47
```

forces the instruction stored at address 47 of C to be the next instruction to be executed; that is, it sets ip to 47. The latter represents a conditional jump, which occurs if an expression evaluates to true. For example, in

```
jumpt 47, D[3] > D[8]
```

the jump occurs only if the value stored in cell 3 is greater than the value stored in cell 8.

SIMPLESEM allows *indirect addressing*. For example,

```
set D[10], D[20]
```

assigns the value stored at location 20 to the cell whose address is the value stored at location 10. Thus, if the value 30 is stored at location 10, the instruction modifies the contents of location 30. Indirection is also possible for jumps. For example,

```
jump D[13]
```

jumps to the instruction stored at location 88 of C, if 88 is the value stored at location 13.

SIMPLESEM, which is sketched in Figure 2.11, is quite simple. It is easy to understand how it works and what the effects of executing its instructions are. In other terms, we can assume that its semantics is intuitively known; it does not require further explanations that refer to other, more basic concepts. The semantics of programming languages can therefore be described by rules that specify how each construct of the language is translated into a sequence of equivalent SIMPLESEM instructions. Since SIMPLESEM instructions are perfectly understood, the semantics of newly defined constructs also becomes known. We will enrich SIMPLESEM gradually as we introduce new programming language concepts.

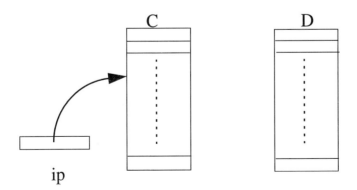

FIGURE 2.11 The SIMPLESEM machine

2.7 Run-time structure

In this section we discuss how the most important concepts related to the execution-time processing of programming languages may be explained using SIMPLESEM. We will proceed gradually, from the most basic concepts to more complex structures that reflect what is provided by modern general-purpose programming languages. We will move through a series of languages that are based on simplified variants of the C programming language. They are named C1 through C5.

Our discussion will show that languages can be classified in several categories, according to their execution-time structure.

Static languages

Exemplified by the early versions of FORTRAN and COBOL, these languages guarantee that the memory requirements for any program can be evaluated before program execution begins. Therefore, all the needed memory can be allocated before program execution. Clearly, these languages cannot allow recursion, because recursion would require an arbitrary number of unit instances, and thus memory requirements could not be determined before execution. (As we will see later, the implementation is not required to perform the memory allocation statically. The semantics of the language, however, gives the implementer the freedom to make that choice.)

Section 2.7.1 and Section 2.7.2 will discuss languages C1, C2, and variant C2', all of which fall under the category of static languages.

Stack-based languages

Historically headed by ALGOL 60 and exemplified by the family of so-called Algol-like languages, this class is more demanding in terms of memory requirements, which cannot be computed at compile time. However, their memory usage is predictable and follows a last-in/first-out (LIFO) discipline. The variables declared in a scope are allocated automatically, as the scope is entered at run time, and deallocated as the scope is exited (such variables are often called *automatic*). Thus the latest allocated activation record is the next one to be deallocated. It is therefore possible to manage SIMPLESEM's D store as a stack to model the execution-time behavior of this class of languages. Notice that an implementation of these languages need not use a stack (although, most likely, it will): deallocation of discarded activation records can be avoided if the store can be viewed as unbounded. In other terms, the stack is part of the semantic model we provide for the language; strictly speaking, it is not part of the semantics of the language.

Section 2.7.3 and Section 2.7.4 discuss the languages C3 and C4, which fall under the category of stack-based languages.

Dynamic languages

These languages have an unpredictable memory usage; i.e, data are allocated dynamically only when they are needed during execution. Such variables are often called *dynamic*. The problem then becomes how to manage memory efficiently. In particular, how can unused memory be recognized and reallocated, if needed? To indicate that D is not handled according to a predefined policy (like a LIFO policy for a stack memory), the term "heap" is used traditionally to refer to the data memory. This class of languages is illustrated by the language C5 in Section 2.7.5.

2.7.1 C1: A language with only simple statements

Let us consider a very simple programming language, called C1, which can be seen as a lexical variant of a subset of C, where we only have simple types and simple statements, and there are no functions. Let us assume that the only data manipulated by the language are those whose memory requirements are known statically, such as integer and floating-point values, fixed-size arrays, and structures. The entire program consists of a main routine (main()), which encloses a set of data declarations and a set of statements that manipulate these data. For simplicity, input/output is performed by invoking the operations get and print to read and write values, respectively.

A C1 program is shown in Figure 2.12, and its straightforward SIMPLESEM representation is shown in Figure 2.13. The D memory shows the activation record of the main program at the start of the program, which contains space for all variables that appear in the program. The C memory shows the SIMPLESEM code.

```
main()
{
    int i, j;
    get(i, j);
    while (i != j)
        if (i > j)
            i -= j;
        else
            j -= i;
    print(i);
}
```

FIGURE 2.12 A C1 program

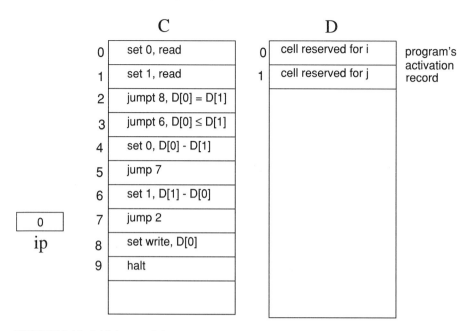

FIGURE 2.13   Initial state of the SIMPLESEM machine for the C1 program in Figure 2.12

2.7.2 C2: Adding simple routines

Let us now add a new feature to C1. The resulting language, C2, allows routines to be defined in a program and allows routines to declare their own local data. A C2 program consists of a sequence of the following items:

- A (possibly empty) set of data declarations (*global data*);
- A (possibly empty) set of routine definitions and/or declarations;
- A *main routine* (main()), which contains its local data declarations and a set of statements, which are automatically activated when the execution starts. The main routine cannot be called by other routines.

Routines may access their local data and any global data that are not redeclared internally. Routines may not be nested, they cannot call themselves recursively, they do not have parameters, and they do not return values (these restrictions will be removed later).

Figure 2.14 shows an example of a C2 program whose main routine gets called initially and causes routines beta and alpha to be called in a sequence.

Under the assumptions we have made so far, the size of each unit's activation record can be determined at translation time, and all activation records can be allocated before execution (*static allocation*). Thus each variable can be bound to a D memory address before execution. Static allocation is a straightforward implementation scheme which does not cause any memory allocation overhead at run time, but can waste memory space. In fact, memory is allocated for a routine even if it is never invoked. Since our purpose is to provide a semantic description, not to discuss an efficient implementation scheme, we assume static allocation. If needed, the run-time model described in Section 2.7.3 could be adapted to provide dynamic memory allocation for the C2 class of languages.

```
int i = 1, j = 2, k = 3;
alpha()
{
    int i = 4, l = 5;
    ...
    i+=k+l;
    ...
};
beta()
{
    int k = 6;
    ...
    i=j+k;
    alpha();
    ...
};
main()
{
    ...
    beta();
    ...
}
```

FIGURE 2.14 A C2 program

Figure 2.15 shows the state of the SIMPLESEM machine after instruction i += k + l of routine alpha has been executed. The first location of each activation record (offset 0) is reserved for the *return pointer*. Starting at offset 1, space is reserved for the local variables. In general, for an instance of unit A, the return pointer will contain the address of the instruction that should be executed after unit A terminates. This does not apply to main, which does not return to a caller. On real computers, however, main is called by the operating system, and after termination main must return control to the operating system. We also maintain an activation record to keep global data at the low address end of store D.

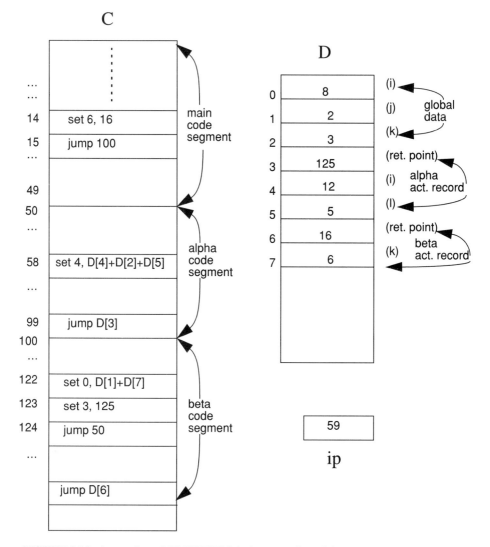

FIGURE 2.15 A snapshot of SIMPLESEM during execution of the program of Figure 2.14

So far, we have implicitly assumed that in C2 the main program and its routines are compiled in one monolithic step. It may be convenient instead to allow the various units to be compiled separately. *Separate compilation* is illustrated by a variant of C2 (called C2') which allows program units to be put into separate files, and each file to be compiled separately in an arbitrary order. The file containing the main program may also contain global data declarations, which may then be imported by other separately compiled units, which consist of single routines. If one of these routines needs to access some globally defined data, it must define them as external. Figure 2.16 shows the same example of Figure 2.14, using separate compilation.

```
file 1                      file 2              file 3

int i = 1, j = 2, k = 3;    extern int k;       extern int i, j;
extern beta();              alpha()             extern alpha();
main()                      {                   beta()
{                              ...              {
    ...                     }                       ...
    beta();                                         alpha();
    ...                                             ...
}                                               }
```

FIGURE 2.16 Program layout for separate compilation

As in the case of C2, a SIMPLESEM implementation can reserve the first location of each activation record (except for main) for the return pointer. Further consecutive locations are then reserved for local variables, which can be bound to their offset within the activation record, as each routine is compiled separately. Since each file is compiled separately, the compiler is unable to bind local variables to their absolute addresses and imported global variables cannot be bound to their offsets in the global activation record. Similarly, routine calls cannot be bound to the starting address of the corresponding code segments.

To resolve such unresolved addresses, a *linker* is used to combine the independently translated modules into a single executable module. The linker assigns the various code segments and activation records to stores C and D and binds any missing information that the compiler was unable to evaluate.

From this discussion we see that C2 and C2' do not differ semantically. Indeed, once a linker collects all separately compiled components, C2' programs and C2 programs cannot be distinguished from each other. Their difference is in terms of the user support they provide for the development of large programs. C2' allows parallel development by several programmers, who might work at the same time on different units.

Separate compilation, as offered by C2', is a simplified version of the facility offered by several existing programming languages, such as FORTRAN and C.

2.7.3 C3: Supporting recursive functions

Let us add two new features to C2: the ability of routines to call themselves (*direct recursion*) or to call one another in a recursive fashion (*indirect recursion*), and the ability of routines to return values, i.e., to behave as functions.

These extensions define a new language, C3, which is illustrated in Figure 2.17 through an example program for computing factorials.

```
int n;
int fact()
{
    int loc;
    if (n > 1) {
        loc = n--;
        return loc * fact();
    }
    else
        return 1;
}
main()
{
    get(n);
    if (n >= 0)
        print(fact());
    else
        print("input error");
}
```

FIGURE 2.17   A C3 example

As we mentioned in Section 2.4, to support mutual recursion between two routines A and B, the program must be written according to the following pattern:

A's declaration (i.e., A's header);
B's definition (i.e., B's header and body);

A's definition;

Let us first analyze the effect of the introduction of recursion. Although each unit's activation record has a known and fixed size, in C3 it is not known how many instances of any unit will be needed during execution. As an example, for the program shown in Figure 2.17, at a given point of execution two activations are generated for the function fact if the value of n is greater than or equal to 2. All different activations have the same code segment, since the code does not change from one activation to another, but they need different activation records for storing the different values of the local environment. As for C2, the compiler can bind each variable to its offset in the corresponding activation record. However, as opposed to C2, in C3 it is not possible to perform the further binding step which transforms it into an absolute address of the D memory until execution time. In fact, an activation record is allocated by the invoking function for each new invocation, and each new allocation establishes a new binding with the corresponding code segment to form a new activation of the invoked function. Consequently, the final binding step which adds the offset of a variable—known statically—to the starting address (called *base address*) of the activation record—known dynamically—can only be performed at execution time. To make this possible, we will use the cell at address zero in D to store the base address of the activation record of the currently executing unit (we call this value CURRENT).

When the current instance of a unit terminates, its activation record is no longer needed. In fact, no other units can access its local environment, and the semantic rule of function invocation requires a new activation record to be freshly allocated for a future invocation. Therefore, after a function completes its current instance, it is possible to free the space occupied by the activation record and make it available to store new activation records in the future. For example, if A calls B which then calls C, the activation records for functions are allocated in the order A, B, C. When C returns to B, C's activation record can be discarded; B's activation record is discarded next, when B returns to A. Because the activation record that is freed is the one that was most recently allocated, activation records can be allocated with a *last-in/first-out* policy on a stack-organized storage.

To make return from an activation possible, the following information needs to be stored in the activation record: the address of the instruction to be executed upon return *(return pointer)* and the base address of the caller's activation record. For language C2, we needed to save only the return pointer because through it the (unique) activation record associated with the caller also becomes known. But since in C3 more than one activation may exist for a given unit, a more general solution becomes necessary. Therefore, we assume that the cell at offset 0 of activation records contains the return pointer, while the cell at offset 1 contains a pointer to the base address of the caller's activation record—this pointer is called the *dynamic link*. The chain of dynamic links originating in the currently active activation record is called the *dynamic chain*. At any time, the dynamic chain represents the dynamic sequence of unit activations.

In order to manage SIMPLESEM's D store as a stack, it is necessary to know, at run time, the address of the first free cell of D, since a new activation record is allocated from that point on. We will use D's cell at address 1 to keep this information (we call this value FREE). Finally, it is necessary to provide memory space for the value returned by the routine, if it behaves as a function.

Since the routine's activation record is deallocated upon return, the returned value must be saved into the caller's activation record. That is, when a functional routine is called, the caller's activation record is extended to provide space for the return value, and the callee writes the returned value into that space (using a negative offset, since the location is in the caller's activation record) before returning.[4]

Figure 2.18 provides an intuitive view of SIMPLESEM's D store. Activation records are allocated one on top of the previous, and the allocated memory grows from the upper part of the store (corresponding to low addresses) downwards.

Since recursion is the main additional feature of C3, we now show how the semantics of routine call and return are specified in terms of SIMPLESEM instructions.

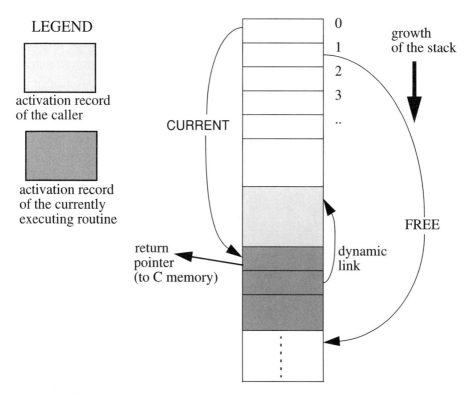

FIGURE 2.18 Structure of the SIMPLESEM D memory implementing a stack

---

4. For further details concerning the management of return values, see Exercise 21.

Routine call

set 1, D[1] + 1	allocate space on the stack for the return value; assume one cell can hold the returned value
set D[1], ip + 4	set the value of the return pointer in the callee's activation record (4 is the number of instructions still needed to implement the routine call)
set D[1] + 1, D[0]	set the dynamic link of the callee's activation record to point to the caller's activation record
set 0, D[1]	set CURRENT, the address of the currently executing activation record
set 1, D[1] + AR	set FREE (AR is size of callee's activation record)
jump start_addr	start_addr is an address of C where the first instruction of the callee's code is stored.

Return from routine

set 1, D[0]	set FREE
set 0, D[D[0] +1]	set CURRENT
jump D[D[1]]	jump to the stored return pointer

We assume that before the execution of a C3 program starts, ip is set to point to the first instruction of main() and the D memory is initialized to contain space for the global data and for the activation record of main(). The activation record contains space just for main's local variables (if any); space for the return pointer and for the dynamic link are not needed, since the main routine does not return to a caller. Its termination simply means that the execution terminates. The values stored in D[0] and D[1] are also assumed to be initialized before execution. D[0] is set to the address of the first location of main's activation record, and D[1] must be set to the address of the first free location following main's activation record.

As an exercise, let us show how the program of Figure 2.17 is executed by the SIMPLESEM machine. The code stored in the C memory is shown in Figure 2.19.

Figure 2.20 provides two snapshots of the D memory: immediately after the first call to fact (case (a)) and at the return point from the third activation of fact when the initially read input value is 3 (case (b)). The reader is urged to try the example on paper, going through all intermediate steps of execution.

Note that the stack-based abstract implementation scheme discussed in this section also can be used for implementing C2. We discussed C2 in terms of static memory allocation, but this was simply an implementation choice. The advantage of a stack-based implementation would be that only the

0 set 2, read	reads the value of n; 2 is the absolute address where global variable n is stored
1 jumpt 10, D[2] < 0	tests the value of n
2 set 1, D[1] + 1	call to fact starts here; but first space for the result is saved
3 set D[1], ip + 4	set return pointer
4 set D[1] + 1, D[0]	set dynamic link
5 set 0, D[1]	set CURRENT
6 set 1, D[1] + 3	set FREE (3 is the size of fact's activation record)
7 jump 12	12 is the starting address of fact's code
8 set write, D[D[1] - 1]	D[1] - 1 is the address where the result of the call to fact is stored
9 jump 11	end of the call
10 set write, "input error"	
11 halt	this is the end of the code of main
12 jumpt 23, D[2] ≤ 1	this is the start of the code of fact; tests the value of n
13 set D[0] + 2, D[2]	assigns n to loc
14 set 2, D[2] - 1	decrements n
15 set 1, D[1] + 1	call to fact starts here; but first space for the result is saved
16 set D[1], ip + 4	set return pointer
17 set D[1] + 1, D[0]	set dynamic link
18 set 0, D[1]	set CURRENT
19 set 1, D[1] + 3	set FREE (3 is the size of fact's activation record)
20 jump 12	12 is the starting address of fact's code
21 set D[0] - 1, D[D[0] + 2] * D[D[1] - 1] store returned value	
22 jump 24	
23 set D[0] - 1, 1	return 1
24 set 1, D[0]	this and the next 2 instructions correspond to the return from the routine
25 set 0, D[D[0] + 1]	
26 jump D[D[1]]	

FIGURE 2.19   SIMPLESEM code for the program in Figure 2.17

minimum amount of data store is allocated at any given time. The disadvantage, of course, is that a more complicated language management scheme is needed.

2.7.4 C4: Supporting block structure

The structuring facilities offered by C3 allow programs to be defined as a sequence of global declarations of data and routines. Routines may call each other in a recursive fashion. In this section we discuss a new extension to our language family, resulting in a new family, C4. The family C4 contains two members: C4' and C4". C4' allows local declarations to appear within any compound statement. C4" supports the ability to nest a routine definition

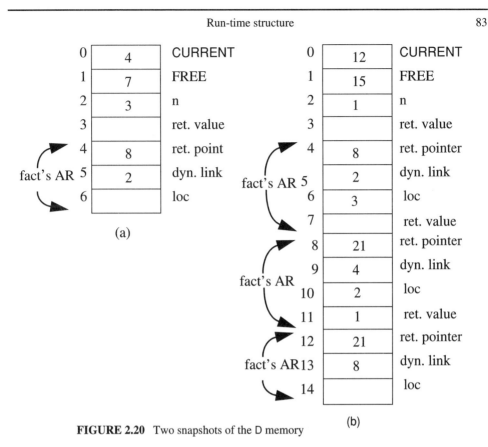

FIGURE 2.20 Two snapshots of the D memory

within another. Conventionally, the new features offered by C4' and C4" are collectively called *block structure*. Block structure is used to control the scope of variables, to define their lifetime, and to divide the program into smaller units. Any two blocks in the program may be either disjoint (i.e., they have no portion in common) or nested (i.e., one block completely encloses the other).

2.7.4.1 Nesting via compound statements

In C4', blocks have the following form of compound statement, which can appear wherever a statement can appear:

{<declaration_list>; <statement_list>}

It is easy to realize that such compound statements follow the aforementioned rule of blocks: they are either disjoint or they are nested. A compound statement defines the scope of its locally declared variables: such variables are visible within the compound statement, including any compound statement nested in it, provided the same name is not redeclared. An inner declaration masks an outer declaration for the same name. Figure 2.21 shows an

```
int f( );
{                                   //block 1
    int x, y, w;                    //1
    while (…)
    {                               //block 2
        int x, z;                   //2
        …
        while (…)
        {                           //block 3
            int y;                  //3
            …
        }                           //end block 3
        if (…)
        {                           //block 4
            int x, w;               //4
            …
        }                           //end block 4
    }                               //end block 2
    if (…)
    {                               //block 5
        int a, b, c, d;             //5
        …
    }                               //end block 5
}                                   //end block 1
```

FIGURE 2.21   An example of nested blocks in C4'

example of a C4' function having nested compound statements. Function f has local declarations for x, y, and w, whose scope extends from //1 to the entire function body, with the following exceptions:

- x is redeclared in //2. From that declaration until the end of the outermost "while" statement the outer x is not visible;
- y is redeclared in //3. From that declaration until the end of the innermost "while" statement, the outer y is not visible;
- w is redeclared in //4. From that declaration until the end of the innermost "if" statement, the outer declaration is not visible.

Similarly, //2 declares variables x and z, whose visibility extends from the declaration until the end of the statement, with one exception. Since x is redeclared in //4, the outer x is masked by the inner x, which extends from the declaration until the end of the "if" statement.

A compound statement also defines the lifetime of locally declared data. Memory space is bound to a variable x when the block in which it is declared is entered during execution. The binding is removed when the block is exited.

To provide an abstract implementation of compound statements for the SIMPLESEM machine, there are two options. One consists of statically including the memory needed by the compound statement in the activation record of the enclosing routine; the other consists of dynamically allocating new memory space corresponding to local data as each compound statement is entered during execution. The former scheme is simpler and more time efficient, while the latter is a more space-efficient implementation. We will discuss the former scheme and leave the latter as an exercise, which can be solved easily after reading Section 2.7.4.2 (see Exercise 27).

Let us refer to the example of Figure 2.21. Note that block 2 and block 5 are disjoint; similarly, block 3 and block 4 are disjoint. Since two disjoint blocks cannot be active at the same time, it is possible to use the same memory cells to store their local values. Thus, the activation record of function f can be defined as shown in Figure 2.22. The figure shows that the same cells may be used to store a and x, b and z, etc.; i.e., the symbol "--" denotes an overlay. The definition of overlays can be done at translation time. With this done, the run-time behavior of C4' is exactly the same as was discussed in the case of C3.

A block structure can be described by a *static nesting tree* (SNT), which shows how blocks are nested in one another. Each node of a SNT describes a

return pointer
dynamic link
x in //1
y in //1
w in //1
x in //2--a in //5
z in //2--b in //5
y in //3--x in //4--c in //5
w in //4--d in //5

FIGURE 2.22 An activation record with overlays

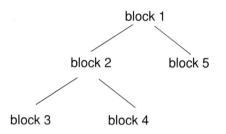

FIGURE 2.23 Static nesting tree for the block structure of Figure 2.21

block; descendants of a node N which represents a certain block denote the blocks that are immediately nested within the block. For example, the program of Figure 2.21 is described by the static nesting tree of Figure 2.23.

2.7.4.2 Nesting via locally declared routines

As we mentioned, block structure may result from the ability to nest compound statements within unnested routines, to nest routine definitions within routines, or both. C and C++ only support the nesting of compound statements within routines. Pascal and Modula-2 allow routine nesting, but do not support nesting of compound statements. Ada allows both.

Let us examine how routine nesting might be incorporated into our language. The resulting language variant will be called C4". As shown in Figure 2.24(a), in C4" a routine may be declared within another routine. Routine f3 can only be called within f2 (e.g., it would not be visible within f1 and main). A call to f3 within f2's body would be a local call (i.e., a call to a locally declared routine). Since f3 is internal to f2, f3 can also be called within f3's body (direct recursion). Such a call would be a call to a nonlocally declared routine, since f3 is declared in the outer routine f2. Similarly, f2 can be called within f1's body (local call) and within both f2's and f3's bodies (nonlocal calls). Moreover, the data declared in //1 are visible from that point until the end of f1 (i.e., //end of block 1), with one exception. If a declaration for the same name appears in internally declared routines (i.e., in //2 or in //3), the internal declarations mask the outer declaration. Also, within a routine, it is possible to access both the local variables and nonlocal variables declared by enclosing outer routines, if they are not masked. In the example, within f3's body, it is possible to access the nonlocal variables x (declared in //2) and u (declared in //1) and the global variable z.

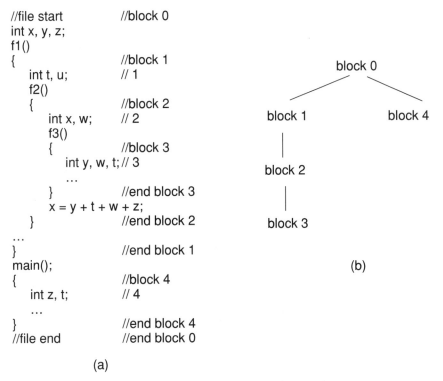

```
//file start              //block 0
int x, y, z;
f1()
{                         //block 1
    int t, u;             // 1
    f2()
    {                     //block 2
        int x, w;         // 2
        f3()
        {                 //block 3
            int y, w, t; // 3
            ...
        }                 //end block 3
        x = y + t + w + z;
    }                     //end block 2
    ...
}                         //end block 1
main();
{                         //block 4
    int z, t;             // 4
    ...
}                         //end block 4
//file end                //end block 0
```

(a)

FIGURE 2.24 A C4" example (a) and its static nesting tree (b)

As shown in Figure 2.24(b), the concept of a static nesting tree can be defined in this case too. Block 0 is introduced to represent the outermost level of the program, which contains the declarations of variables x, y, and z and functions f1() and main().

Let us examine the effect of the following sequence of calls: main calls f1, f1 calls f2, f2 calls f3, and f3 calls f2. Figure 2.25 sketches a portion of the activation record stack corresponding to the example. The description is simplified for readability purposes but shows all the relevant information. For each activation record, we indicate the name of the corresponding routine, the dynamic link, and the names of variables stored in it. Let us suppose that the execution on the SIMPLESEM machine reaches the assignment x = y + t + w + z in f2. The translation process we discussed so far is able to bind variables x and w to their offsets in the topmost activation record (whose initial address is given by D[0], i.e., CURRENT); but what about variables y, t, and z? Surely, they should not be bound according to the most recently established binding for such variable names, since such binding was established by the latest activations of routines f3 (y and t) and main (z).[5] However, the scope rules of C4"

---

5. This would be correct for a language adopting dynamic scoping.

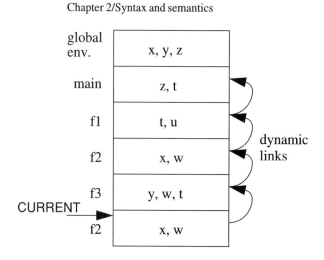

FIGURE 2.25 A sketch of the run-time stack

require variables y and z referenced within f2 to be the ones declared globally, and variable t to be the one declared locally in f1. In other words, the sequence of activation records stored in the stack represents the sequence of unit instances as they are dynamically generated at execution time. But what determine the nonlocal environment are the scope rules of the language, which are based on the static nesting of routine declarations.

On way to make access to nonlocal variables possible is for each activation record to contain a pointer (*static link*) to the activation record of the unit that statically encloses it in the program text. We will use the location of the activation record at offset 2 to store the value of the static link. Figure 2.26 shows the static links for the example of Figure 2.25. The sequence of static links that can be followed from the active activation record is called the *static chain*. Referencing nonlocal variables can be explained intuitively as a search that traverses the static chain. To find the correct binding between a variable and a stack location, the static chain is followed until a binding is found. In our example, the reference to t is bound to a stack location within f1's activation record, whereas references to y and z are bound to a stack location within the global environment—which is as it should be. Notice that in this scheme, the global environment is accessed in the same uniform way as any other nonlocal environment. In such a case, the value of the static link for main's activation record is assumed to be set automatically before execution. In order to use the cell at offset 2 of main's activation record to hold the value of the static link, as we do for any other activation record, the cells at offsets 0 and 1 are kept unused. Alternatively, access to the global environment can be treated as a special case, by using absolute addresses.

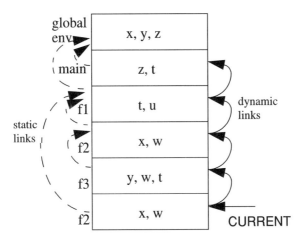

FIGURE 2.26 The run-time stack of Figure 2.25 with static links

In practice, searching along the static chain, which would entail considerable run-time overhead, is never necessary. A more efficient solution is based on the fact that the activation record containing a variable named in a unit U is always a fixed distance from U's activation record along the static chain. If the variable is local, the distance is obviously zero; if it is a variable declared in the immediately enclosing unit, the distance is 1; if it is a variable declared in the next enclosing unit, the distance is 2; and so on. In general, for each reference to a variable, we can evaluate a *distance attribute* between that reference and the corresponding declaration. This distance attribute can be evaluated and bound to the variable at translation time. Consequently, each reference may be statically bound to a pair <distance, offset> within the activation record.

Based on the pair <distance, offset>, it is possible to define the following addressing scheme for SIMPLESEM. If d is the value of the distance, starting from the address of the current activation record (CURRENT, the value stored in D[0]), we traverse d steps along the static chain. The value of the offset is then added to the address so found, and the result is the actual run-time address to the nonlocal data object. We can define this formally in terms of a recursive function fp(d), which can then be easily translated into SIM-PLESEM. Function fp(d), which stands for the frame pointer, defines a pointer to an activation record that is d static links away from the current activation record. It can be defined as:

fp(d) = if d=0 then D[0] else D[fp(d-1)+2]

For example, fp(0) is simply D[0], i.e., the address of the current (topmost) activation record; and fp(1) is D[D[0]+ 2].

Using fp, access to a variable x, with <distance, offset> pair <d, o>, is provided by the following expression:

D[fp(d)+ o]

To take into account the installation of static links in activation records, the semantics of the function call defined in Section 2.7.3 needs to be modified in the case of C4". This can be done in the following way. First, as we did for variables, one can define the concept of distance between a routine call and the corresponding declaration. Thus, if f calls a local routine, then the distance between the call and the declaration is 0. If f contains a call to a function declared in the block enclosing f, the distance is 1. This, for example, would be the case if f calls itself recursively. If f is local to function g, and f contains a call to a function h declared in the block enclosing g, the distance between the call and the declaration is 2, and so on. Therefore, the static link to install for the activation record of the callee, if the callee is declared at distance d, should point to the activation record that is d steps along the static chain originating from the caller's activation record.

In conclusion, the semantics of the routine call can be defined by the following SIMPLESEM code:

Routine call

set 1, D[1] + 1	allocate space on the stack for the return value; assume one cell can hold the returned value
set D[1], ip + 5	set the value of the return pointer in the callee's activation record (5 is the number of instructions still needed to implement the routine call)
set D[1] + 1, D[0]	set dynamic link of callee's activation record to point to the caller's activation record
set D[1] + 2, fp(d)	set the static link of the callee's activation record
set 0, D[1]	set CURRENT, the address of the currently executing activation record
set 1, D[1] + AR	set FREE (AR is size of callee's activation record)
jump start_addr	start_addr is an address of memory C where the first instruction of the callee's code is stored.

2.7.5 C5: Toward more dynamic behaviors

So far we have assumed that the data storage requirements of each unit are known at compile time, so that the required amount of memory can be reserved when the unit is allocated. Furthermore, the mapping of variables to storage within the activation record can be performed at compile time; i.e., each variable is bound to its offset statically. In this section we discuss language features that do not conform to this assumption, and we show how to define the semantics of such features. The corresponding language family is called C5.

2.7.5.1 Activation records whose size becomes known at unit activation

Let us first introduce language C5' by relaxing the assumption that the size of all variables is known at compile time. Such is the case for *dynamic arrays*, that is, arrays whose bounds become known at execution time, when the unit (routine or compound statement) in which the array is declared is activated.

For example, in the Ada programming language, it is possible to define the type

```
type VECTOR is array(INTEGER range <>);
        --defines arrays with unconstrained index
```

and declare the following variables:

```
A: VECTOR(1.. N);
B: VECTOR(1.. M);
        --N and M must be bound to some integer value when these
        --two declarations are processed at execution time
```

The abstract implementation that defines the semantics for this case is rather straightforward. At translation time, storage can be reserved in the activation record for the descriptors of the dynamic arrays. The descriptor includes one cell in which we store a pointer to the storage area for the dynamic array and one cell for each of the lower and upper bounds of each array dimension. As the number of dimensions of the array is known at translation time, the size of the descriptor is known statically. All accesses to a dynamic array are translated as indirect references through the pointer in the descriptor, whose offset is determined statically.

At run time, the activation record is allocated in several stages.

1 Storage is allocated for data whose size is known statically and for descriptors of dynamic arrays.
2 When the declaration of a dynamic array is encountered, the dimension entries in the descriptors are entered, the actual size of the array is evaluated, and the activation record is extended (that is, FREE is increased) to include space for the variable. (This expansion is possible because, being the active unit, the activation record is on top of the stack.)
3 The pointer in the descriptor is set to point to the area just allocated.

Step 1 corresponds to activation record allocation that we have seen already. Steps 2 and 3 are implemented by code that has to be generated for each dynamic array declaration. Without such variables, variable declarations were processed completely at compile time. With dynamic variables, the declaration needs to be processed (or *elaborated*) at run time also. This processing may be done at unit entry time if the size of the dynamic variable is known.

In the previous example, let us suppose that the descriptor allocated when variable A is declared is at offset m. The cell at offset m will point at run time to the starting address of A; the cells at offsets m+1 and m+2 will contain the lower and upper bounds, respectively, of A's index. The run-time actions corresponding to entry into the unit where A's declaration appears will update the value of D[1] (i.e., FREE) to allocate space for A, based on the known value of N, and will set the values of the descriptor at offsets m, m+1, and m+2.

Any access to elements of A are translated to indirect references. Assuming each integer occupies one location of D and supposing that I is a local variable stored at offset s, instruction A[I] = 0 would be translated into SIM-PLESEM as:

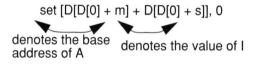

set [D[D[0] + m] + D[D[0] + s]], 0

denotes the base
address of A

denotes the value of I

2.7.5.2 Fully dynamic data allocation

In C1 through C4 all variables are automatic. They are allocated automatically as the scope in which they are declared is entered at run time and they are deallocated as it is exited. Now let us consider another language variation, called C5", in which data can be allocated explicitly, through an executable allocation instruction. In most existing languages, this is achieved by defining pointers to data and by providing statements that allocate such data in a fully dynamic fashion.

For example, in C++ we can define the following type for nodes of a binary tree:

```
struct node {
    int info;
    node* left;
    node* right:
};
```

The following instruction,

```
node* n = new node;
```

which may appear in some code fragment, explicitly allocates a structure with the three fields info, left, and right, and makes it accessible via the pointer n.

According to this allocation scheme, data are allocated explicitly as they are needed. We cannot allocate such data on a stack, as we do for automatically allocated data. For example, suppose that a function append_left is called to generate a new node and make it accessible through the field left of the node pointed at by n. Also, suppose that n is visible by append_left as a nonlocal variable. If the node allocated by append_left were allocated on the stack, it would be lost when append_left returns. The semantics of these dynamically allocated data, instead, is that their lifetime does not depend on the unit in which their allocation statement appears, but lasts as long as they are accessible, i.e., are referred to by some existing pointer variables.

An abstract implementation of this concept using SIMPLESEM is very simple, and consists of allocating dynamic data in D starting from the high-address end. This area of D is also called the *heap*. New data are allocated in the heap as the allocation instructions are executed. We can assume that the size of the SIMPLESEM D store is sufficient to hold all data that are dynamically allocated via the new instruction. Figure 2.27 gives an overall view of how memory D is organized to support both a stack and a heap. We will return to the practical issue of actually implementing dynamic allocation in a memory-efficient way in Chapter 3. From a semantic viewpoint, this simple implementation scheme is sufficient.

2.7.6 The structure of dynamic languages

The term "dynamic languages" implies many things. In general, it refers to those languages that adopt dynamic rather than static rules. For example,

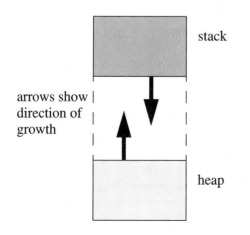

FIGURE 2.27 Organization of the D memory to accommodate a heap

APL, SNOBOL4, and several LISP variants use dynamic typing and dynamic scope rules. In principle, of course, a language designer can make these choices independently of one another. For example, one can have dynamic type rules but static scope rules. In practice, however, dynamic properties are often adopted together.[6]

In this section, we will examine how the adoption of dynamic rules changes the semantics of the language in terms of run-time requirements. In general, a dynamic property implies that the corresponding bindings are carried out at run time and cannot be done at translation time. We will examine dynamic typing and dynamic scoping.

2.7.6.1 Dynamic typing

In a language that uses *dynamic typing*, the type of a variable and therefore the methods of access and the allowable operations cannot be determined at translation time. In Section 2.7.5, we saw that we need to keep a run-time descriptor for dynamic array variables, because their size is unknown at translation time. In that case, the descriptor has to contain the information that cannot be computed at translation time, namely, the starting address and the array bounds. It was possible to keep the descriptor in the activation record because the size of the descriptor was fixed and known at translation time. In the case of dynamically typed variables, we also need to maintain the type of the variable in the descriptor. If the type of a variable may change at run time, then the size and contents of its descriptor may also change. For example, if a variable changes from a two-dimensional array to a three-dimensional array, then the descriptor needs to grow to contain the values of the bounds for the new dimension. This is in contrast to the descriptors of dynamic arrays whose contents were fixed at unit activation time. Every access to a dynamic variable must be preceded by a run-time check on the type of the variable, followed by appropriate address computation, depending on the current type of the variable.

What is maintained for each variable in the activation record for a unit? Since not only the variable's size may change during program execution, but also the size of its descriptor, descriptors must be kept in the heap. For each variable, we maintain a pointer in the activation record that points to the variable's descriptor in the heap, which, in turn, may contain a pointer to the object itself in the heap.

---

6. We already mentioned that there are dynamically typed languages (like ML and Eiffel) that support static type checking.

2.7.6.2 Dynamic scoping

To discuss the effect of dynamic scope rules, let us consider the example program of Figure 2.28. The program is written using a C-like syntax, but it will be interpreted according to an APL-like semantics, i.e., according to dynamic scope rules.

```
sub2() {
    declare x;
    ...
    ... x ...;
    ... y ...;
    ...
}
sub1() {
    declare y;
    ...
    ...x ...;
    ... z ...;
    sub2();
    ...
}
main() {
    declare x, y, z;
    z = 0;
    x = 5;
    y = 7;
    sub1;
    sub2;
    ...
}
```

FIGURE 2.28 An example program in a dynamically scoped language

A program consists of a number of routines and a main program. Each routine declares its local variables (y in the case of sub1; x in the case of sub2; x, y, z in the case of main). Any access to a variable that is not locally declared is implicitly assumed to be an access to a nonlocal variable. A variable declaration does not specify the variable's type: it simply introduces a new name. Routine names are considered as global identifiers.

Since scope rules are dynamic, the scope of a name is dependent on the run-time call chain (i.e., on the dynamic chain), rather than the static structure of the program. In the example shown in Figure 2.28, consider the point when the call to sub1 is issued in main. The nonlocal references to x and z within the activation of sub1 are bound to the global x and z defined by main. When function sub2 is activated from sub1, the nonlocal reference to y is bound to the most recent definition of y, that is, to the data object associated to y in sub1's activation record. Return from routines sub2 and then sub1 causes deallocation of the corresponding activation records and then execution of the call to sub2 from main. In this new activation, the nonlocal reference to y from sub2, which was previously bound to y in sub1, is now bound to the global y defined in main.

An abstract implementation mechanism to reference nonlocal data can be quite simple. Activation records can be allocated on a stack and joined together by dynamic links, as we saw in the case of conventional languages. Each entry of the activation record explicitly records the name of the variable and contains a pointer to a heap area, where the value can be stored. Allocation on a heap is necessary because the amount of storage required by each variable can vary dynamically. For each variable—say, V—the stack is searched by following the dynamic chain. The first association found for V in an activation record is the proper one. Figure 2.29 illustrates the stack for the program of Figure 2.28 when sub2 is called by sub1, which is, in turn, called by main.

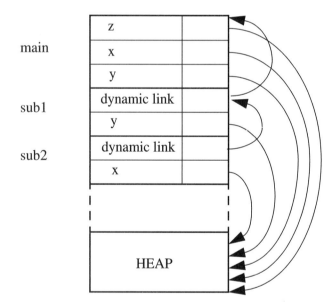

FIGURE 2.29   A view of the run-time memory for the program of Figure 2.28

Although simple, this accessing mechanism is inefficient. Another approach is to maintain a table of currently active nonlocal references. Instead of searching along the dynamic chain, a single lookup in this table is sufficient. We will not discuss this solution any further, but the reader should note that this technique speeds up referencing nonlocal variables at the expense of more elaborate actions to be executed at routine entry and exit. These additional actions are necessary to update the table of active nonlocal references.

2.7.7 Parameter passing

So far we have assumed that routines do not have parameters: we have assumed only that they can return a result value (see Section 2.7.3). We will now remove this limitation by discussing how parameter passing may be implemented on SIMPLESEM. We first address the issue of data parameters, and then we will analyze routine parameters.

2.7.7.1 Data parameters

There are different conventions for passing data parameters to routines. The adopted convention is either predefined by the language or can be chosen by the programmer from several options. In either case, it is important to know which convention is adopted because the choice affects the meaning of programs. The same program may in fact produce different results under different data parameter passing conventions. Three conventions for data parameters are discussed below: call by reference, call by copy, and call by name. Each of them is first introduced informally, and then defined precisely in terms of SIMPLESEM actions.

Call by reference (or by sharing)

The calling unit passes to the called unit the address of the actual parameter (which is in the calling unit's referencing environment). A reference to the corresponding formal parameter in the called unit is treated as a reference to the location whose address is so passed. The effect of call by reference is intuitively described in Figure 2.30. If the formal parameter is assigned a value, the corresponding actual parameter changes value. Thus, a variable that is transmitted as an actual parameter is shared, that is, it is directly modifiable

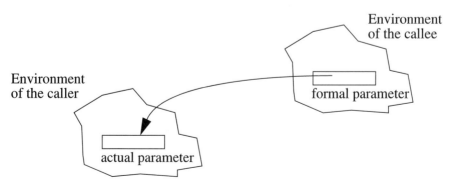

FIGURE 2.30 A view of call by reference

by the subprogram. If an actual parameter is anything other than a variable, for example, an expression or a constant, the subprogram receives the address within the calling unit's activation record of a temporary location that contains the value of the actual parameter. Some languages treat this situation as an error.

Suppose that call by reference is being added to C4. In order to define a SIMPLESEM implementation that specifies semantics precisely, we need to extend the actions described in Section 2.7.3. The callee's activation record must contain one cell for each parameter. At procedure call, the caller must initialize the contents of the cell to contain the address of the corresponding actual parameter. If the parameter cell is at offset off and the actual parameter, which is bound to the pair <d, o>, is not itself a by-reference parameter, the following action must be added for each parameter:

    set D[0] + off, fp(d) + o

If the actual parameter itself is a by-reference parameter, the SIM-PLESEM action should be:

    set D[0] + off, D[fp(d) + o]

When the routine body is executed, parameter access is performed via indirect addressing. Thus, if x is a formal parameter and off is its offset, the instruction

    x = 0;

is translated as

    set D[D[0] + off], 0

Call by copy

In call by copy—unlike in call by reference—formal parameters do not share storage with actual parameters; rather, they act as local variables. Thus, call by copy protects the calling unit from intentional or inadvertent modifications of actual parameters. It is possible further to classify call by copy into three modes, according to the way local variables corresponding to formal parameters are initialized and the way their values ultimately affect the actual parameters. These three modes are call by value, by result, and by value-result.

In *call by value*, the calling unit evaluates the actual parameters and uses these values to initialize the corresponding formal parameters, which act as local variables in the called unit. Call by value does not allow any flow of information back to the caller, since assignments to formal parameters (if permitted) do not affect the calling unit.

In *call by result*, local variables corresponding to formal parameters are not set at subprogram call, but their value, at termination, is copied back into the corresponding actual parameter's location within the environment of the caller. Call by result does not permit any flow of information from the caller to the callee.

In *call by value-result*, local variables denoting formal parameters are both initialized at subprogram call (as in call by value) and delivered upon termination (as in call by result). Information thus flows from the caller to the callee (at the point of call) and from the callee to the caller (at the return point).

A description of the semantics of call by value in terms of a SIMPLESEM implementation is straightforward. The callee's activation record must contain space for by-value parameters, as ordinary local data. The difference here is that the call must provide for initialization of such data. We leave this and the other two cases of call by copy as exercises for the reader.

One might wonder whether call by reference and call by value-result are equivalent. It can be shown that call by reference may produce a different result from call by value-result in the following cases:

1 Two formal parameters become aliases (i.e., the two different names denote the same object).
2 A formal parameter and a nonlocal variable which is visible both by the caller and by the callee become aliases.

We will provide two examples to motivate these statements. The first case may happen if, say, a[i] and a[j] are two integer actual parameters corresponding to the formal parameters x and y, and i happens to be equal to j at the point of call. In such a case, the effect of call by reference is that x and y would be aliased, since they would refer to the same array element. If the routine contains the statements

```
x = 0;
y ++;
```

the result of the call is that the array element of index i (and j) is set to 1. In the case of call by value-result, let a[i] be 10 at the point of call. The call would initialize x and y to 10. Then x becomes 0 and y becomes 11, due to the above assignment statements. Finally, upon return, first 0 is copied back into a[i] and then 11 is copied back into the same cell, if copies are performed in this order. As a result, the array element is set to 11.

As an example of the second case, suppose that a routine is called with one integer actual parameter a which corresponds to the formal parameter x. Let a be visible by the routine as a nonlocal variable. Suppose that the routine contains the following statements:

```
a = 1;
x = x + a;
```

In the case of call by reference, the effect of the call is that a is set to 2. In the case of call by value-result, if a's value is 10 at the call point, the value becomes 11 upon return.

Call by name

The semantics of call by name parameters is defined in terms of textual substitution of every occurrence of a formal parameter in the called routine's body by the corresponding actual parameter. This implies that, as in call by reference, a formal parameter, rather than being a local variable of the subprogram, denotes a location in the environment of the caller. Unlike with call by reference, however, the formal parameter is not bound to a location at the point of call; it is bound to a (possibly different) location each time it is used within the subprogram. Consequently, each assignment to a formal parameter can refer to a different location.

The apparent simplicity of the call-by-name substitution rule can lead to unsuspected complications. For example, the routine in Figure 2.31, which is intended to interchange the values of a and b (a and b are by-name parameters) most likely produces an unexpected result when invoked by the call

```
swap(i, a[i])
```

```
swap(int a, b) {
    int temp;
    temp = a;
    a = b;
    b = temp;
};
```

FIGURE 2.31 A sample routine to illustrate call-by-name parameters

The replacement rule specifies that the statements to be executed are

```
temp = i;
i = a[i];
a[i] = temp;
```

If i = 3 and a[3] = 4 before the call, i = 4 and a[4] = 3 after the call (a[3] is unaffected)!

Another trap is that the actual parameter that is (conceptually) substituted into the text of the called unit belongs to the referencing environment of the caller, not to that of the callee. For example, suppose that procedure swap also counts the number of times it is called and it is embedded in the following fragment.

```
int c;   //global variable
...
swap(int a, b) {
    int temp;
    temp = a; a = b;
    b = temp; c ++;
}
y() {
    int c, d;
    swap(c, d);
};
```

When swap is called by y, the replacement rule specifies that the statements to be executed are

```
temp = c;
c = d;
d = temp;
c ++;
```

However, the location bound to the name c in the last statement belongs to the global activation record, whereas the location bound to the previous occurrences of c belong to y's activation record. This shows that plain macro processing does not provide a correct implementation of call by name if there is a conflict between names of nonlocals in the routine's body and names of locals at the point of call. This example also shows the possible difficulty encountered by the programmer in foreseeing the run-time binding of actual and formal parameters.

Call by name, therefore, can easily lead to programs that are hard to read. It is also surprisingly hard to implement. The basic implementation technique consists of replacing each reference to a formal parameter with a call to a routine (traditionally called *thunk*) that evaluates a reference to the actual parameter in the appropriate environment. One such thunk is created for each actual parameter. Every reference to an actual parameter calls the associated thunk to compute the value of the formal parameter. The overhead of run-time calls to thunks makes call by name costly. Due to these difficulties, call by name is mostly of theoretical and historical interest, and has been abandoned by mainstream programming languages.

Call by reference is the standard parameter passing mode of FORTRAN. Call by name is standard in ALGOL 60, but, optionally, the programmer can specify call by value. SIMULA 67 provides call by value, call by reference, and call by name. C++, Pascal, and Modula-2 allow the programmer to pass parameters either by value (default case) or by reference. For example, the C++ routine declaration

```
void swap(int, int);
```

declares swap as a routine with two by-value parameters, whereas the declaration

```
void swap(int&, int&);
```

declares swap as a routine with two by-reference parameters.

C adopts call by value but allows call by reference to be implemented quite easily via pointers. Ada defines parameter passing based on the intended use, as either **in** (for input parameters), **out** (for output parameters), or **in out** (for input/output parameters), rather than in terms of the implementation mechanism (by reference or by copy). If the mode is not explicitly specified, **in** is assumed by default. More on parameter passing will be discussed in Chapter 4.

2.7.7.2 Routine parameters

Languages supporting variables of type routine are said to treat routines as first-class objects. In particular, they allow routines to be passed as parameters. Such parameters are called *routine* or *procedural parameters*. This facility is useful in some practical situations. For example, a routine S that evaluates an analytic property of a function (e.g., derivative at a given point) can be written without knowledge of the function and can be used for different functions, if the function is described by a routine parameter passed to S. As another example, if the language does not provide explicit features for exception handling (see Chapter 4), one can transmit the exception handler as a routine parameter to the unit that may raise an exception behavior.

Routine parameters behave differently in statically and dynamically scoped languages. Here we concentrate on statically scoped languages. Hints on how to handle dynamically scoped languages are given in the sidebar on page 106.

Consider the program in Figure 2.32. In this program, b is called by main (line 21) with actual parameter a; inside b, the formal parameter x is called (line 15), which in this case corresponds to a. When a is called, it should exc-cute normally just as if it had been called directly; that is, there should be no observable differences in the behavior of a routine called directly or through a formal parameter. In particular, the invocation of a must be able to access the nonlocal environment of a, in this case the global variables u and v. (Note that these variables are not visible in b because they are masked by b's local variables with the same names.) Our current abstract implementation scheme does not work in this case. As we saw in Section 2.7.4, the call to a routine is translated to several instructions. In particular, it is necessary to reserve space for the activation record of the callee and to set up its static link. In the case of "call x" in b, this is impossible at translation time because we do not know what routine x is, let alone its enclosing unit. This information, in general, will only be known at run time. We can handle this situation by passing the size of the activation record and the needed static link at the point of call.

```
1   int u, v;
2   a()
3   {
4       int y;
5       ...
6   };
7   b(routine x)
8   {
9       int u, v, y;
10      c()
11      {...
12          y = ...;
13          ...
14      };
15      x();
16      b(c);
17      ...
18  }
19  main()
20  {
21      b(a);
22  };
```

FIGURE 2.32 An example of routine parameters

In general, how do we know this static link to pass? From the scope rules, we know that in order for a unit U (in this case, main) to pass routine a to routine b, U must either:

a) Have procedure a within its scope, that is, a must be nonlocally visible or local (immediately nested); or

b) a must be a formal parameter to U, that is, some actual procedure was passed to U as a routine parameter.[7]

The two cases can be handled in the following way:

Case (a): The static link to be passed is fp(d), a pointer to the activation record that is d steps along the static chain originated in the calling unit, where d is the distance between the call point where the routine parameter is passed and its declaration (recall Section 2.7.4).

Case (b): The static link to be passed is the one that was passed to the caller.

We leave the task of formulating these rules in terms of SIMPLESEM as an exercise for the reader.

What about calling a routine parameter? The only difference from calling a routine directly is that both the size of the callee's activation record and its static link are simply copied from the parameter area.

The program in Figure 2.32 shows another subtle point: when routine parameters are used in a program, nonlocal variables visible at a given point are not necessarily those of the latest allocated activation record of the unit where such variables are locally declared. For example, after the recursive call to b when c is passed (line 16), the call to x in b (line 15) will invoke c recursively. Then the assignment to y in c (line 12) will not modify the y in the latest activation record for b but in the one allocated prior to the latest one. Figure 2.33 sketches the structure of the run-time stack at this stage. The reader is invited to go through a stepwise construction of the run-time stack as an exercise.

Let us review the impact of routine parameters. First, we had to extend the basic procedure call mechanism to deal with the additional semantic complexity. Procedure calls now have to deal with different cases of objects. Both the procedure call's semantic description and its implementation have increased in complexity. Contrast this with, say, adding a new arithmetic operator to a language that requires hardly any changes to our semantic

---

7. Case (b) cannot occur in the case where U is main, since main cannot be called by other routines.

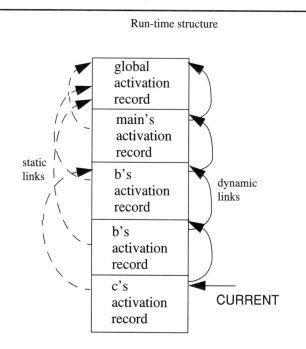

FIGURE 2.33 A sketch of the run-time stack for the program of Figure 2.32

description at all. We can say that the ability to pass procedures as parameters adds to the semantic power (and complexity) of a language. On the other hand, it makes the language more uniform in the way the different language constructs are handled: routines are first-class objects and can be treated uniformly as any other objects of the language.

Routine parameters in dynamically scoped languages

Routines passed as parameters sometimes cause a peculiar problem in languages with dynamic scope rules, such as early versions of LISP. If we consider the program in Figure 2.32 under dynamic scope rules, when routine a is called through x, references to u and v in a will be bound to the u and v in b and not to those in main. This is difficult to use and confusing since when the routine a was written, it was quite reasonable to expect access to u and v in main, but because b happens to contain variables with the same names, they mask out the variables that were probably intended to be used.

Simply stated, the problem is that the nonlocal environment, and therefore the behavior of the routine, is dependent on the dynamic sequence of calls that were made before the routine was activated. Consider several programmers working on different parts of the same program. A seemingly innocuous decision, what to name a variable, can change the behavior of the program entirely.

The problem, however, was discovered very early in the development of LISP, and a new feature was added to the language to allow a routine to be passed along with its naming environment. If a routine is preceded by the keyword FUNCTION, the routine is passed along with its nonlocal environment at the point of call. When such a procedure is invoked, the environment information passed with the parameter is used to set up the current nonlocal environment. A different—and more radical— solution to the problem would be to change the language semantics and adopt static scope rules for the entire language, as most modern LISPs do.

2.8 Bibliographic notes

In this chapter we have studied programming language semantics in an informal but systematic way, by describing the behavior of an abstract language processor. Formal approaches to the definition of semantics are also possible, as we briefly discussed. [Tennent81] and [Winskel93] provide a view of the theoretical foundations of programming languages and their semantics. Our view here is oriented towards language implementation, to allow the reader to understand how machines can support the various language constructs and what the costs of program execution are. We have emphasized the important concepts of binding, binding time, and binding stability. [Johnston71] presents the contour model, an interesting operational model that describes the concepts of binding without referring to the stack-based abstract machine.

The reader who is interested in the details of language implementation should refer to compiler textbooks, such as [Aho86] and [Fischer91]. The SIMPLESEM machine used here is a simplified version of the virtual machines that are used as targets for code generation by compilers which produce portable code. It is similar to the Java Virtual Machine (JVM), whose machine language (JVM bytecodes) is generated by a Java compiler [Lindholm96]. This solution allows JVM bytecodes to be executable on any machine that provides an interpreter.

2.9 Exercises

1. Provide syntax diagrams for the lexical rules of the language described in Figure 2.1.
2. In the example of Figure 2.1 a semicolon is used to terminate each statement in a sequence. That is, a sequence is written as {stat1; stat2; ...; statn;}. Modify the syntax so that the semicolon would be used as a separator between consecutive statements, that is: {stat1; stat2; ...; statn}. Comment on the pragmatic differences between these two choices.
3. Modify both the EBNF and the syntax diagrams of Figure 2.2 to represent Modula-2 if and while statements.
4. Briefly describe scope binding for Pascal variables. Does the language adopt static or dynamic binding?
5. In Section 2.2 we said, "Perhaps surprisingly, there are languages supporting both static type checking and polymorphic variables and routines." Why should one expect, in general, static type checking to be impossible for polymorphic variables and routines?
6. Following the definition of static binding given in Section 2.3, specify the time and stability of the binding between a C (or C++) const variable and its value. How about constants in Pascal?
7. Can the l-value of a variable be accessed only when its name is visible (i.e., within scope)? Why or why not?
8. What is the solution adopted by C, Ada, Modula-2, Java, and Eiffel to the problem of uninitialized variables?
9. In general, it is not possible to check statically that the r-value of an uninitialized variable will not be used during program execution. Why?
10. Does Pascal allow a named variable and a pointer to share the same data object? Why or why not?
11. C and C++ distinguish between declaration and definition for variables. Study this language feature and write a short explanation of why this can be useful.
12. C++ also allows functions to accept more parameters than those specified in the function definition. Why and how is this possible? Write a program to check this feature.
13. What is the difference between macros and routines? Explain the difference in terms of the concept of binding.
14. Describe if and how routines may be passed as parameters in C/C++.
15. Describe the two ways (named vs. positional) provided by Ada to associate actual and formal parameters.
16. Discuss the EQUIVALENCE statement of FORTRAN in the light of aliasing.
17. A routine is called history sensitive if it can produce different results when activated twice with the same values as parameters and visible nonlocal variables. Explain why a language with static memory allocation allows writing history-sensitive routines.
18. Define an algorithm to perform the linkage step for C2'.
19. Write the sequence of SIMPLESEM instructions corresponding to a functional routine call and return to take into account return values. For simplicity, you may assume that return values may be stored in a single SIMPLESEM cell.

20. Write a simple C3 program with two mutually recursive routines, describe their SIMPLESEM implementation, and show snapshots of the D memory.

21. In Section 2.7.3 we assumed function routines to return their output value in a location within the caller's activation record. A number of details were left out of our discussion. For example, we implicitly assumed the cells allocated to hold the result to be released when the caller routine returns. This, however, implies a waste of memory space if a large number of calls are performed. Also, we did not provide a systematic way of generating SIMPLESEM code for the evaluation of expressions that contain multiple function calls, as in

    a = f(x) + b + g(y, z);

Provide solutions to these problems.

22. For the following C3 program fragment, describe each stage in the life of the run-time stack until routine beta is called (recursively), by alpha. In particular, show the dynamic and static links before each routine call.

```
int i = 1, j = 2, k = 3;
beta();
alpha() {
    int i = 4, l = 5;
    ...
    i+=k+l;
    beta();
    ...
};
beta() {
    int k = 6;
    ...
    i=j+k;
    alpha();
    ...
};
main() {
    ...
    beta();
    ...
}
```

23. Based on the treatment of recursive functions, discuss dynamic allocation in the case of C2 and show how the scheme works for the example of Section 2.7.2.

24. In our treatment of C4' using SIMPLESEM, we said, "In order to provide an abstract implementation of compound statements for the SIMPLESEM machine, there are two options. The former consists of statically defining an activation record for a routine with nested compound statements; the latter consists of dynamically allocating new memory space corresponding to local data as each compound statement is entered during execution. The former scheme is simpler and more time efficient, while the latter can lead to a more space-efficient actual implementation." Write a detailed justification for this statement.

25. Consider the following extension to C3. A variable local to a routine may be declared to be **own**. An **own** variable is allocated storage the first time that its enclosing routine is activated, and its storage remains allocated until program termination. Normal scope rules apply, so that the variable is known only within the unit in which it is declared. In essence, the effect of the **own** declaration is to extend the lifetime of the variable to cover the entire program execution. Outline an implementation model for **own** variables. For simplicity, you may assume that **own** variables can only have simple (unstructured) types.

26. Referring to the previous exercise, assume that **own** variables are not automatically initialized to certain default values. Show that this limits their usefulness greatly. (Hint: Show, as an example, how an **own** variable can be used to keep track of the number of times a routine has been called.)

27. Discuss a SIMPLESEM implementation that uses dynamic allocation for C4' nested blocks.

28. Explain why the static and dynamic links have the same value for blocks.

29. Translate the function fp (Section 2.7.4) into SIMPLESEM code.

30. An implementation technique for referencing the nonlocal environment in C4", which differs from the use of static links as presented in Section 2.7.4.2, is based on the use of a *display*. The display is an array of variable length that contains, at any point during program execution, pointers to the activation records of the routines that form the referencing environment—that is, exactly those pointers that would be in the static chain. Let an identifier be bound to the (distance, offset) pair <d, o>. The display is set up such that display[d] yields the address of the activation record which contains the identifier at offset o.

    – Show pictorially the equivalent of Figure 2.26 when displays are used instead of static links. Assume that, like CURRENT and FREE, the display is kept in the initial portion of the data memory.

    – Show the SIMPLESEM actions that are needed to update the display when a routine is called and when a routine returns. Pay special attention to routine parameters.

    – Displays and static chains are two implementation alternatives for the same semantic concept. Discuss the relative advantages and disadvantages of each solution.

31. Check a language of your choice (e.g., Pascal or C++) to see if it allows expressions to be passed by reference. Specify in what cases (if any) this is allowed and provide a concise justification of the behavior. In cases where it does not (if any), write (and run) simple programs which demonstrate the reason.

32. Provide a full description of a SIMPLESEM implementation of call by value.

33. Provide a full description of a SIMPLESEM implementation of call by result. Note that the semantics can be different if the address of the actual result parameter is evaluated at the point of call or at the return point. Why? Show an example where the effect would be different.

34. Can a constant be passed as a by-reference parameter? Check this in a language of your choice.

35. Provide a full SIMPLESEM implementation for call by value-result. Can the abstract implementation for call by reference be used as a semantic description of call by value-result?

36. Consider the example program shown below. Discuss call by reference and call by value-result for swap(a[i], a[j]). What happens if i = j?

```
swap(int x, int y) {
    x = x + y;
    y = x - y;
    x = x - y;
}
```

37. Write a short paper on C macros, comparing them with routines. What are the binding policies adopted by the language? Compare parameter handling for macros with the general parameter passing mechanisms described in this chapter.

38. Discuss how call by reference can be accomplished in C++.

39. Study parameter passing mechanisms in Ada and write a short paper discussing them and comparing them with respect to conventional parameter passing modes.

40. Explain why the axiomatic definition of semantics of assignment statements, given in terms of function asem, is inaccurate in the presence of side effects in the evaluation of the right-hand-side expression and aliasing for the left-hand-side variable.

41. Explain why the denotational definition of semantics of assignment statements, given in terms of function **dsem**, is inaccurate in the presence of side effects in the evaluation of the right-hand-side expression and aliasing for the left-hand-side variable.

42. We observed that in C++ formal parameters can be given a default value, which is used in case the corresponding actual parameters are not passed in the call. For example, given the following function header: int distance(int a = 0, int b =0); the call distance(); is equivalent to distance(0, 0); and the call distance(10); is equivalent to distance(10, 0);. Explain how this language feature interacts with overloading and how this interaction is solved by C++.

Structuring the data

CHAPTER 3

Computer programs can be viewed as functions that are applied to values of certain input domains to produce results in some other domains. In conventional programming languages, this function is evaluated through a sequence of steps that produce intermediate data that are stored in program variables. Languages support the definition of such functions by providing features to describe data, the flow of computation, and the overall program organization. This chapter is on mechanisms for structuring and organizing data; Chapter 4 is on mechanisms for structuring and organizing computations; Chapter 5 is on the mechanisms that languages provide for combining the data and computation structures into a program.

Programming languages organize data through the concept of *type*. Types are used as a way to classify data according to different categories. They are more, however, than pure sets of data. Data belonging to a type also share certain semantic behaviors. A type is thus more properly defined as a set of values and a set of operations that can be used to manipulate them. For example, the type BOOLEAN of languages such as Ada and Pascal consists of the values TRUE and FALSE; Boolean algebra defines operators NOT, AND, and OR for BOOLEANs. BOOLEAN values may be created, for example, as a result of the application of relational operators ($<, \leq, >, \geq, =, \neq$) among INTEGER expressions.

Programming languages usually provide a fixed, built-in set of data types, as well as mechanisms for structuring more complex data types from these built-in ones. Built-in types are discussed in Section 3.1. Constructors that

111

allow more complex data types to be structured starting from built-in types are discussed in Section 3.2. Section 3.4 is about type systems, which are the principles that underlie the organization of a collection of types. The type system adopted by a language affects the programming style enforced by the language. It may also have a profound influence on the reliability of programs, since it may help prevent erroneous uses of data. Moreover, understanding the type system of a language helps us understand subtle and complicated semantic issues. Section 3.5 reviews the type system of existing programming languages. Finally, Section 3.6 is about implementation models.

3.1 Built-in types and primitive types

Any programming language is equipped with a finite set of *built-in* (or *pre-defined*) *types*, which normally reflect the behavior of the underlying hardware. At the hardware level, values belong to the untyped domain of bit strings, which constitutes the underlying universal domain of computer data. Data belonging to this universal domain are then interpreted differently by hardware instructions, according to different types. At the *hardware level*, a type may thus be considered as a view under which data belonging to the universal type may be manipulated. As an example, a hypothetical microcomputer might interpret the bit string "01001010" as integer "74" (coded in two's complement representation) when it is the argument of the machine instruction ADD (which does integer addition). However, it would interpret it as a bit string when it is the argument of the machine instruction CPL (which does bitwise complement). It would interpret it as ASCII character "J" when it is the argument of the instruction PCH (which prints an ASCII character).

The built-in types of a programming language reflect the different views provided by typical hardware. Examples of built-in types are:

- Booleans, i.e., truth values TRUE and FALSE, along with the set of operations defined by Boolean algebra;
- Characters, e.g., the set of ASCII characters;
- Integers, e.g., the set of 16-bit values in the range <–32768, 32767>; and
- Reals, e.g., floating point numbers with given size and precision.

Let us analyze what makes built-in types a useful concept. This discussion will help us identify the properties that types in general (i.e., not only the built-in ones) should satisfy. Built-in types can be viewed as a mechanism for *classifying* the data manipulated by a program. Moreover, they are a way of *protecting* the data against forbidden, or nonsensical, maybe unintended, manipulations of the data. Designating a type for a data item, in fact, indicates which operations may be legally applied to that data. In more detail, the following are possible advantages of introducing built-in types in a programming language:

1 *Hiding of the underlying representation.* This is an advantage provided by the abstractions of higher-level languages over lower-level (machine-level) languages. The programmer does not have access to the underlying bit string that represents a value of a certain type. The programmer may change this bit string only by applying operations, but the change is visible as a new value of the built-in type—not as a new bit string. Invisibility of the underlying representation has the following benefits:

Programming style. The abstraction provided by the language increases program readability by protecting the representation of objects from undisciplined manipulation. This contrasts with the underlying conventional hardware, which does not enforce protection, but usually allows any view to be applied to any bit string. For example, a location containing an integer may be added to one containing a character, or even to a location containing an instruction.

Modifiability. The implementation of abstractions may be changed without affecting the programs that make use of the abstractions. Consequently, portability of programs is also improved; that is, programs can be moved to machines that use different internal data representations. One must be careful, however, regarding the precision of data representation which might change for different implementations. For example, the range of representable integer values is different for 16- and 32-bit machines.

Programming languages provide features to read and write values of built-in types, as well as for formatting the output. Such features may be provided either by language instructions or through predefined routines. Machines perform input/output by interacting with peripheral devices in a complicated and machine-dependent way. High-level languages hide these complications and the physical resources involved in machine input/output (registers, channels, and so on).

2 *Correct use of variables can be checked at translation time.* If the type of each variable is known to the compiler, illegal operations on a variable may be detected when the program is translated. Although type checking does not prevent all possible errors, it improves the reliability of programs. For example, in Pascal or Ada, type checking cannot ensure that J will never be zero in some expression I/J, but it can ensure that it will never be a character.

3 *Resolution of overloaded operators can be done at translation time.* For readability purposes, operators are often overloaded. For example, + is used for both integer and real addition, and * is used for both integer and real multiplication. In each program context, however, it should be clear which specific hardware operation is to be invoked, since integer and real arithmetic are implemented by different machine instructions. If the type of each variable is known to the compiler, the binding between an overloaded operator and its corresponding machine operation can be established at translation time. This makes the implementation more efficient than in dynamically typed languages, for which it is necessary to keep track of types in run-time descriptors.

4 *Accuracy control.* In some cases, the programmer can associate an explicit specification of the accuracy of the representation with a type. For example, FORTRAN allows the user to choose between single- and double-precision floating-point numbers. In C, integers can be short int, int, or long int. Each C compiler is free to choose the appropriate size for its underlying hardware, under the restriction that short int and int are at least 16 bits long, long int is at least 32 bits long, and the number of bits of short int is no more than the number of bits of int, which is no more than the number of bits of long int. In addition, it is possible to specify whether an integer is signed or unsigned. Similarly, C provides both float (for single-precision floating-point numbers) and double (for double-precision floating-point numbers). Accuracy specification allows the programmer to direct the compiler to allocate the exact amount of storage that is needed to represent the data with the desired precision.

Some types can be called *primitive* (or *elementary*). That is, they are not built from other types. Their values are atomic and cannot be decomposed into simpler constituents. In most cases, built-in types coincide with primitive types, but there are exceptions. For example, in Ada both Character and String are predefined. Characters are primitive, but strings are not: data of type String have constituents of type Character. In fact, String is predefined as:

type String **is array** (Positive **range** <>) **of** Character;

It is also possible to declare new types that are elementary. An example is given by enumeration types in Pascal, C, or Ada. For example, in Pascal one may write:

type color = (white, yellow, red, green, blue, black);

The same would be written in Ada as

type color **is** (white, yellow, red, green, blue, black);

Similarly, in C one would write:

enum color {white, yellow, red, green, blue, black};

In the three cases, new constants are introduced for a new type. The constants are ordered; i.e., white < yellow < ... < black. In Pascal and Ada, the built-in successor and predecessor functions can be applied to enumerations. For example, succ(yellow) in Pascal evaluates to red. Similarly, color'pred(red) in Ada evaluates to yellow.

3.2 Data aggregates and type constructors

Programming languages allow the programmer to specify *aggregations* of elementary data objects and, recursively, aggregations of aggregates. They do so by providing a number of *constructors*. Such constructed objects are called *compound objects*. A well-known example is the array constructor, which constructs aggregates of homogeneous-type elements. An aggregate object has a unique name. In some cases, manipulation can be done on a single elementary component at a time, each component being accessible by a suitable selection operation. In many languages, it is also possible to manipulate (e.g., assign and compare) entire aggregates.

Older programming languages, such as FORTRAN and COBOL, provided only a limited number of constructors. For example, FORTRAN only provided the array constructor; COBOL only provided the record constructor. In addition, through constructors, they simply provided a way to define a new *single* aggregate object, not a type. Later languages, such as Pascal, allowed new compound types to be defined by specifying them as aggregates of simpler types. Having defined such a type, any number of instances of the newly defined aggregate can be defined. According to such languages, constructors can be used to define both aggregate objects and new aggregate (*compound*) types.

Because this chapter focuses on data types, we review constructors that generate compound data. One should not, however, ignore that routines can also be seen as constructors that allow elementary instructions to be combined to form new operations. In addition, the distinction between data and routines vanishes in the case of programming languages that treat routines as first-class objects, which can be assigned, be passed as parameters, be fields of data structures, and so on.

Type constructors are discussed and exemplified in Section 3.2.1 through Section 3.2.6. Section 3.2.7 discusses how structured data values can be denoted in some languages by using data constructors. In the discussion, we will first describe the constructors abstractly in terms of a mathematical model, and then we will show how different programming languages provide concrete constructs to represent the abstract model.

3.2.1 Cartesian product

The Cartesian product of n sets $A_1, A_2, \ldots, A_n$, denoted $A_1 \times A_2 \times \ldots \times A_n$, is a set whose elements are ordered n-tuples $(a_1, a_2, \ldots, a_n)$, where each a_k belongs to A_k. For example, regular polygons might be described by an integer—the

number of edges—and a real—the length of each edge. A polygon would thus
be an element in the Cartesian product integer x real.

Programming languages view elements of a Cartesian product as composed of a number of symbolically named *fields*. In the example, a polygon
could be declared as composed of an integer field (no_of_edges) holding the
number of edges and a real field (edge_size) holding the length of each edge.

Examples of Cartesian product constructors in programming languages
are *structures* in C, C++, Algol 68, and PL/I; and *records* in COBOL, Pascal,
and Ada. COBOL was the first language to introduce Cartesian products,
which proved to be very useful in data processing applications. For example,
in a payroll transaction, employees are described by a tuple of attributes (such
as name, address, social security number, salary), some of which, in turn, may
be described by a tuple of attributes (e.g., an address is composed of street
name, number, city, state, and zip code). Such an aggregation can be
described by a record.

As an example of a Cartesian product constructor, consider the following
C declaration, which defines a new type reg_polygon and an object a_pol:

```
typedef struct {
    int no_of_edges;
    float edge_size;
} reg_polygon;
reg_polygon a_pol = {3, 3.45};
```

The regular polygon a_pol is initialized as an equilateral triangle whose edge
is 3.45. The notation {3, 3.45} is used to implicitly define a constant value (also
called a *compound value*) of type reg_polygon (the polygon with 3 edges of
length 3.45).

The fields of an element of a Cartesian product are selected by specifying
their names in an appropriate syntactic notation. In the C example, one may
write

```
a_pol.no_of_edges = 4;
```

to make a_pol quadrilateral. This syntactic notation for selection, which is
common in programming languages, is called the *dot notation*.

In our discussion of elementary types, we saw that one of the advantages
of data types is that they hide the representation of the data objects from the
use of those objects. Instead of manipulating the representation, users apply
only available operations to the objects. As we can see with the structured
type here, however, the representation of aggregate types constructed with
type constructors is not hidden at all. In fact, rather than specialized opera-

tions for the type, the new type only has the generic access operations associated with it for manipulating the representation. For example, we used the representation of the triangle above to convert it to a square, even though this is not generally a sensible operation on triangles. Later, we will see other language constructs that support not only the definition of the representation of a new type (which the aggregate constructors support) but also the allowable associated operations.

3.2.2 Finite mapping

A mathematical function is a rule for associating (or *mapping*) values from one set, called the *domain* of the function, to values in another set, called the *range* of the function. We may describe a function f, which maps from the set of integers to the set of reals, as f: integer → real. A *finite mapping* is a function from a finite set of values of a domain type DT onto values of a range type RT. Such a function may be defined in programming languages using routine definitions. The routine definition encapsulates the rules for associating values of type RT to values of type DT. Such a definition is called *intensional*, because it specifies a rule (the intension) rather than specifying each individual association. In addition, programming languages provide the *array* constructor to define finite mappings as data aggregates. The array aggregate associates (maps) every index of the array to the value stored in the element that has that index. The index range, therefore, is the *domain* of the mapping, and the values stored in the array are the *range* of the mapping. Such a definition is called *extensional*, since all the values of the function are explicitly enumerated.

For example, the C declaration

```
char digits[10];
```

defines a mapping from integers in the domain 0 to 9 to the set of characters, although it does not state which character corresponds to each element of the domain. The following statements,

```
for (i = 0; i < 10; ++i)
    digits[i] = ' ';
```

define one such correspondence by initializing the array to all blank characters. This example also shows that an object in the range of the function is selected by *indexing*, that is, by providing the appropriate value in the domain as an index of the array. Thus the C notation digits[i] can be viewed as the application of the mapping to the argument i. Indexing with a value that is not in the domain yields an error. Some languages specify that such an error is to be trapped. However, such a trap may, in general, occur only at run time.

C arrays provide only simple types of mappings, by restricting the domain type to be an integer subrange whose lower bound is zero. Other programming languages, such as Pascal, require the domain type to be an ordered discrete type. For example, in Pascal, the declaration

var x: **array**[2..5] **of** integer;

defines x to be an array whose domain type is the subrange 2 to 5.

As another example of Pascal, having defined a type computer_manufacturer by enumeration,

type computer_manufacturer = (ibm, dec, hp, sun, apple, toshiba)

one may use the array type constructor to define the following new type to represent data about each computer manufacturer,

type c_m_data = **array**[computer_manufacturer] **of** integer

and then the following data objects:

var c_m_profits, c_m_employees: c_m_data;

For example, c_m_employees[hp] would give the number of employees of computer manufacturer hp. If only the data regarding profits are needed, one could simply define an array data aggregate instead of defining a new type, of which many instances can be generated:

var c_m_profits: **array**[computer_manufacturer] **of** integers;

Languages that allow variables to be initialized when they are declared may also provide a way to initialize array objects. This means that the language must provide a mechanism for constructing constant values of a compound type (see Section 3.2.7). For example, arrays in C may be initialized through a compound value, as shown by the following example:

char digits[5] = {'a', 'b', 'c', 'd', 'e'};

where {'a', 'b', 'c', 'd', 'e'} is a compound value of type "array of 5 characters."

Similarly, in Ada one might write

X: **array** (INTEGER **range** 2.6) **of** INTEGER := (0, 2, 0, 5, -33);

to define an array whose index is in the subrange 2 to 6, where X(2) = 0, X(3) = 2, X(4) = 0, X(5) = 5, X(6) = -33.

It is interesting that Ada uses parentheses "(" and ")" instead of brackets "[" and "]" to index arrays. This makes indexing an array syntactically identical to calling a function. As a consequence, the fact that a mapping is defined extensionally or intensionally does not affect the way the mapping is used, but depends only on how the mapping is defined; that is, it hides the implementation of the mapping abstraction from the user.

Notice that an array element can, in turn, be an array. This allows multidimensional arrays to be defined. For example, the C declaration

```
int x[10][20];
```

declares an integer rectangular array of 10 rows and 20 columns.

In some languages, such as APL, Algol 68, and Ada, indexing can be used to select more than one element of the range. For example, in Ada, X(3..5) selects a subarray of the previously declared array. This operation is called *slicing*, that is, it selects a slice of the array. Slicing is not supported in C.

In a dynamically typed language like SNOBOL4, the array construct does not require that the elements of the domain or range sets be all of the same type. For example, one element might be an integer, another a real, and yet a third a string. In other words, the domain and the range sets can be viewed as the union of all SNOBOL4 types. For example, the following statements create a TABLE T and assign values to some of its elements:

```
T = TABLE()
T<'RED'> = 'WAR'
T<6> = 25
T<4.6> = 'PEACE'
```

In contrast to standard arrays, the TABLE construct in SNOBOL4 does not require the domain type to be an ordered subrange of a discrete type. This construct thus provides the ability to associate any two values together and retrieve values based on their associations, such as T<'RED'>, which yields 'WAR', or T<6>, which yields 25. Such an operation is called *associative retrieval,* and the aggregate is said to be an *associative data structure.*

The domain of a finite mapping is often defined as a finite subset of a (theoretically) infinite set. For example, an array whose index (i.e., its domain set) is in the range 0 to 9 defines a finite mapping whose domain is a finite subset of integers. The strategy for binding the domain of a finite mapping to a specific finite subset of a given type varies according to the language.

Basically, there are three possible choices:

1 *Compile-time binding*. The subset is fixed when the program is written and it is frozen at translation time. This rule was adopted by FORTRAN, C, and Pascal.
2 *Object creation-time binding*. The subset is fixed at run time, when an instance of the variable is created. In Section 2.6.5.1 we called finite mappings of this kind *dynamic arrays*. ALGOL 60 and Ada provide this.
3 *Object manipulation-time binding*. This is the most flexible and the most costly choice in terms of run-time execution. For these so-called *flexible arrays*, the size of the subset can vary at any time during the object's lifetime. This is typical of dynamic languages, such as SNOBOL4 and APL. Of compiled languages, only Algol 68 and CLU offer such features. The C++ standard library contains *vectors*, which are flexible C++ arrays. Since the memory space required for such data may change during execution, allocation must use the heap memory.

3.2.3 Union and discriminated union

Cartesian products defined in Section 3.2.1 allow an aggregate to be constructed through the *conjunction* of its fields. For example, we saw the example of a polygon, which was represented as an integer (the number of edges) *and* a real (the edge size). In this section we explore the *union* constructor, which allows an object (or a type) to be specified by a *disjunction* of fields.

For example, suppose we wish to define the type of a memory address for a machine providing both absolute and relative addressing. If an address is relative, it must be added to the value of some index register in order to access the corresponding memory cell. Using C, we can declare

```
union address {  /* mutually exclusive fields */
    short int offset;
    long unsigned int absolute;
};
```

The declaration is very similar to the case of a Cartesian product. The difference is that here fields are mutually exclusive. That is, any particular data object of type address has either a field offset or a field absolute, but not both.

Values of type address must be treated differently if they denote offsets or absolute addresses. Given a variable of type address, however, there is no automatic way of knowing what kind of value is currently associated with the variable (i.e., whether it is an absolute or a relative address). The burden of remembering which of the fields of the union is current rests on the programmer. A possible solution is to consider an address to be an element of the following type

```
typedef struct {
    address location;
    descriptor kind;
} safe_address;
```

where descriptor is defined as an enumeration:

```
enum descriptor {abs, rel};
```

A safe address is defined as composed of two fields: one holds an address, and the other holds a descriptor. The descriptor field is used to keep track of the kind of the current address. Such a field must be updated for each assignment to the corresponding location field.

The safe_address implementation corresponds to the abstract concept of a *discriminated union*. Discriminated unions differ from unions in that elements of a discriminated union are tagged to indicate which set the value was chosen from. Given an element e belonging to the discriminated union of two sets S and T, a function tag applied to e gives either 'S' or 'T'. Element e can therefore be manipulated according to the value returned by tag.

Type checking must be performed at run time for elements of both unions and discriminated unions. Even with discriminated unions, it is possible for a program to manipulate an element as a member of type T even though it is in fact a member of type S or vice versa. Discriminated unions, however, are potentially safer since they allow the programmer to explicitly take the tag field into consideration before applying an operation to an element. Of course, they cannot prevent the programmer from breaching safety by assigning the tag field a value that is inconsistent with the other fields.

Some languages come close to supporting the notion of discriminated union properly. For example, Pascal offers *variant records* to represent discriminated unions. The following Pascal declarations define a safe address:

```
type natural = 0..maxint;
    address_type = (absolute, offset);
    safe_address =
        record
            case kind: address_type of
                absolute: (abs_addr: natural);
                offset: (off_addr: integer)
        end
```

The type natural (defined as a subrange of nonnegative integers) is used to represent absolute addresses. The type address_type is the enumeration of the possible values of the tag. The field kind of the variant record is called the *tag field.* According to the value of the tag field kind, either field abs_addr or field off_addr can be accessed. Access to field off_addr when the value of the tag field is absolute would result in a run-time error; similarly, access to field abs_addr when the value of the tag field is offset would result in a run-time error.

Although Pascal allows the concept of discriminated union to be more naturally represented than C, it does not make the implementation safer. In Pascal, the tag and the variant parts may be accessed in the same way as ordinary fields. After the tag field of a safe address representing an offset is changed to absolute, it is possible to access field abs_addr. In principle, this should result in a run-time error, because the field should be considered as uninitialized. In practice, however, most Pascal implementations do not perform such a check, in order to improve run-time efficiency. Moreover, the conventional implementation of variant records consists of overlapping all variants over the same storage area. Therefore, by changing the tag field, the machine interprets the string of bits stored in this area under the different views provided by the types of each variant. This is an insecure—although in some cases useful—use of variant records. Viewing the same storage area under different types may be useful in modeling certain practical applications. For example, a program unit that reads from an input device might view a sequence of bytes according to the type of data that is required. In general, however, this is an unsafe programming practice, and should be avoided.

Other languages, such as Ada and ML, provide secure variant records. In such languages, it is not possible to set the tag and the variant part independently of each other.

3.2.4 Powerset

It is often useful to define variables whose value can be a set of elements of a given type T. The type of such variables is powerset(T), the set of all subsets of elements of type T. Type T is called the *base type*. For example, we might be interested in representing a set of compiler options. Suppose that the following set O of options is available

- LIST_S, to produce a listing of the source program;
- LIST_O, to produce a listing of the object program;
- OPTIMIZE, to optimize the object code;
- SAVE_S, to save the source program in a file;
- SAVE_O, to save the object program in a file;
- EXEC, to execute the object code.

A command to the processor can be any subset of O, such as

```
{LIST_S, LIST_O}
{LIST_S, EXEC}
{OPTIMIZE, SAVE_O, EXEC}
```

That is, the type of a command is powerset(O).

Variables of type powerset(T) represent sets. The operations permitted on such variables are set operations, such as union and intersection.

Although sets (and powersets) are common and basic mathematical concepts, only a few languages—notably, Pascal and Modula-2—provide them through built-in constructors and operations. Also, the set-based language SETL makes sets the very basic data-structuring mechanism. For most other languages, set data structures are provided through libraries. For example, the C++ standard library provides many data structures, including sets.

3.2.5 Sequence

A sequence consists of an arbitrary number of occurrences of elements of a certain component type CT. The important property of the sequencing constructor is that the number of occurrences of the component is unspecified; therefore, sequences may be used to represent objects of arbitrary size. Sequential files are an example of a sequence aggregate.

It is rather uncommon for programming languages to provide a constructor for files. In most cases, this is achieved by invoking operating system primitives which access the file system. It is therefore difficult to imagine a common abstract characterization of such a constructor. Perhaps the best example is the file constructor of Pascal, which models the conventional data processing concept of a sequential file. Elements of the file can be accessed sequentially. Modifications to the sequence can be accomplished by appending a new value at the end of an existing file. Files are provided in Ada through standard libraries, which support both sequential and direct files.

Arrays and recursive lists (defined next) may be used to represent sequences, if they can be stored in main memory. If the size of the sequence does not change dynamically, arrays provide the best solution. If the size needs to change while the program is executing, flexible arrays or lists must be used. The C++ standard library provides a number of sequence implementations, including vector and list. Languages such as LISP and PROLOG provide lists as primitives of the language.

3.2.6 Recursion

Recursion is a structuring mechanism for defining aggregates whose size can grow arbitrarily and whose structure can have arbitrary complexity. A recursive data type T is defined as a structure that can contain components of type T. For example, a binary tree can be defined as either empty or as a triple composed of an atomic element, a (left) binary tree, and a (right) binary tree. Formally, if we assume that nil denotes the empty (or null) tree, int_bin_tree (the set of all binary trees of integers) may be described using the union and Cartesian product of sets:

int_bin_tree = {nil} $\cup$ (integer $\times$ int_bin_tree $\times$ int_bin_tree)

As another example, a list of integers may be described recursively as

int_list = {nil} $\cup$ (integer $\times$ int_list)

where nil here denotes the empty list.

Conventional programming languages support the implementation of recursive data types via pointers. Each component of the recursive type is represented by a location containing a pointer to the data object, rather than the data object itself. Thus, in the int_list example, the implementation would be a structure, where one field contains an integer and the other field points to a structure of the same type, and so on. The list itself would be identified by another location containing a pointer to the first element of the list.

The C/C++ and Ada fragments in Figure 3.1 define the type of an integer list and a variable that can point to the head of a specific integer list instance.

Similar implementations of recursive types can be provided in Pascal and Modula-2.

.

(C/C++)	(Ada)
typedef struct {	**type** INT_LIST_NODE;
int val;	**type** INT_LIST_REF **is access** INT_LIST_NODE;
int_list* next;	**type** INT_LIST_NODE is
} int_list;	**record**
int_list* head;	VAL: INTEGER;
	NEXT: INT_LIST_REF;
	end;
	HEAD: INT_LIST_REF;

FIGURE 3.1 Declarations of list elements in C/C++ and Ada

Functional languages, as we will see in Chapter 7, provide a more abstract way of defining and manipulating recursive types, which masks the underlying pointer-based implementation. For example, in ML a list can be denoted as either the empty list nil or as x::xs, the list composed of the head element x and the tail list xs. In order to find an element in a list, we can write the following self-explanatory high-level function:

```
fun find(el, nil) = false
|   find(el, x::xs) =
        if el=x then true
        else find(el, xs);
```

3.2.6.1 Insecurities of pointers

Pointers are a powerful but low-level programming mechanism that can be used to build complex data structures. In particular, they allow recursive data structures to be defined. Like any low-level mechanism, however, they often allow obscure and insecure programs to be written. Just as unrestricted **goto** statements broaden the context from which any labeled instruction can be executed, unrestricted pointers broaden the context from which a data object may be accessed. Let us review a number of cases of insecurities that may arise and possible ways of controlling them.

1 Some languages, such as Pascal or Ada, require pointers to be typed. For example, a Pascal variable p declared of type ^integer is restricted to point to objects of type integer. This allows the compiler to type-check the correct use of pointers and objects pointed to by pointers. On the other hand, other languages, such as PL/I, treat pointers as untyped data objects; i.e., they allow a pointer to address any memory location, no matter what the contents of that location are. In such a case, dynamic type checking should be performed to avoid manipulation of the object via nonsensical operations.

2 C requires pointers to be typed but, unlike Pascal, it also allows arithmetic operations to be applied to pointers. For example, having declared int* p (p is a pointer to objects of type int), one can write p = p + i;, where i is an int variable. This would make p refer to the memory location that is i integer objects beyond the one p is currently pointing to. It is up to the programmer to guarantee that the object pointed by p is an integer. For example, consider the following C fragment:

```
int x = 10;
float y = 3.7;
int* p = &x; /* &x denotes the address of x; thus p now points to x */
p ++;      /* p points to the next location, which contains a float value */
*p += x; /* increment y, interpreted as an int, by 10 */
printf("%f", y); /* reinterprets the modified r-value of y as a float */
```

Although potentially unsafe, pointer arithmetic can be useful in practice. In fact, C pointers and arrays are closely related. The name of an array can also be used as a pointer to its first element, and any operation that can be achieved by array subscripting can also be done with pointers.

Accessing arrays via pointers is in general faster than using the more readable array notation, unless the compiler generates optimized code. Pointers are therefore preferable when efficiency is crucial, thus trading readability for performance. As an example of using a pointer to access an array, consider the following fragment:

```
int n, vect[10];              /* declares an integer vector */
int* p = vect;                /* p points to the first element of vect */
for (n = 0; n < 10; n++)      /* initializes array elements to zero */
*p++= 0;
```

Incrementing a pointer may be done efficiently by a single machine instruction. Thus access to an array element may be faster than using the standard code generated to access an array element indexed by an expression.

3 The r-value of a pointer is an address, i.e., an l-value of an object. If such an object is not allocated, we say that the pointer is *dangling*. A dangling pointer is a serious insecurity, because it refers to a location that is no longer allocated for holding a value of interest. Dangling pointers may arise in languages, such as C, that allow the address of any variable to be obtained (via the & operator) and assigned to a pointer. In the fragment shown in Figure 3.2, since px is a global variable and x is deallocated when the function trouble returns, px is left dangling since the object it points to no longer exists. In order to avoid this problem, languages such as Algol 68 require that in an assignment the scope of the object being pointed to be at least as large as that of the pointer itself. This restriction, however, can only be checked at run time. For example, consider a routine with two formal parameters: x, an integer, and px, a pointer to integers. Whether the assignment px = &x in the routine is legal depends on the actual parameters and obviously is unknown at compile time. As usual, checking the error at run time incurs runtime costs; not checking the error leaves dangling pointers uncaught.

More on this subject will be said for Ada in Section 3.5.3.

4 To avoid the above insecurities, some languages (such as Pascal and Modula-2) further restrict the use of pointers. Pointers are typed; they cannot be manipulated through arith-

```
int* px;
void trouble()
{
    int x;          /* allocates x */
    ...
    px = &x;        /* assigns address of x to global px */
    ...
    return;         /* deallocates x */
}
main( )
{
    ...
    trouble();      /* after the call px is dangling */
    ...
}
```

FIGURE 3.2 An example of dangling pointers in C

metic operators; there is no way to get the address of a named variable. Yet other sources of insecurity may arise in such languages because of *storage deallocation*. Since the amount of heap storage allocated by an executing program can grow large, these languages provide mechanisms for releasing heap storage as it becomes unreferenced, to allow such storage to be reused for new heap variables. Some languages rely on *automatic storage reclamation* to make unused heap storage available as later allocation requests are issued (see Section 3.6.2.7). Other languages provide a standard operator to explicitly deallocate heap storage. For example, Pascal provides a standard routine dispose; C++ provides delete. The operator must be explicitly used by the programmer as necessary. Unfortunately, however, the programmer can request deallocation of a heap variable while objects still are pointing to it, which creates dangling pointers. This error is difficult to check, and most implementations do not provide such checking.

5 Languages that allow pointers to be components of a union may cause further insecurities. For example, if we declare a variable bad of the following type trouble, bad can be assigned an integer value, which is then interpreted as a pointer to access some unpredictable location:

```
union trouble {
    int int_var;
    int* int_ref;
}
```

In the case of C, this is the same as the result of pointer arithmetic. But in a language that does not support pointer arithmetic, union types may cause pointer insecurities. For example, the same undesirable effect may occur in Pascal using variant records.

To resolve the problems associated with pointers, the Java language has eliminated the notion of explicit pointer completely.

3.2.7 Compound values

Besides supporting the ability to define structured variables, some languages also allow constant values of such *compound* (or *composite*) objects to be denoted. For example, in C++ one can write:

```
char hello[] = {'h', 'e', 'l', 'l', 'o', '\0'};
typedef struct {
    float x, y;
} complex;
complex a = {0.0, 1.1};
```

This fragment initializes array hello to the array value {'h', 'e', 'l', 'l', 'o', '\0'}, i.e., the string "hello" ('\0' is the null character, which by convention denotes the end of the string). Structure a is initialized to the structure value {0.0, 1.1}.

Ada provides a rich and elaborate set of facilities to denote constant values of compound objects. For example, the following expressions denote objects of the type INT_LIST_NODE defined in Section 3.2.6.

(VAL => 5, NEXT => **new** INT_LIST_NODE(0, **null**))
   --field NEXT of the object points to a child node
   --the child node is defined positionally; i.e., 0 is the value of field VAL and null
   --is the value of field NEXT

(10, **null**)
   --this node value is described positionally

Array objects also can be denoted in Ada. For example, a variable Y of the following type,

   type BOOL_MATRIX **is array** (0..N, 0..M) **of** BOOLEAN;

can be initialized in the following way:

Y := (1..N - 1 => (0..M => TRUE), **others** => FALSE);
   --all rows except for the first and the last are initialized to TRUE
   --the first and the last are initialized to FALSE

This is an equivalent way of initializing the array:

Y := (0 | M => (0.. N => FALSE), **others** => TRUE);
   --row 0 and M are initialized to FALSE; others are initialized to TRUE

The ability of compound objects to be denoted directly is a syntactic short-hand that frees the programmer from having to construct such values at run time. Moreover, it promotes the sound programming practice of initializing every variable as it is declared.

3.3 User-defined types and abstract data types

Modern programming languages provide some built-in types and many ways of defining new types from them. The simplest way, mentioned in Section 3.1, consists of defining new elementary types by enumerating their values. The constructors reviewed in the previous sections go one step further, since they allow complex data structures to be composed of the built-in types of the language. Modern languages also allow aggregates built through composition of built-in types to be named as new types. Having given a type name to an aggregate data structure, one can declare as many variables of that type as necessary by simple declarations.

For example, after the C declaration that introduces a new type name complex

```
typedef struct {
    float real_part, imaginary_part;
} complex;
```

any number of instance variables may be defined to hold complex values:

```
complex a, b, c, ...;
```

By providing appropriate type names, program readability can be improved. In addition, by factoring the definition of similar data structures in a type declaration, program modifiability is improved. A change that needs to be applied to the data structures is applied to the type, not to all variable declarations. Factorization also reduces the chance of typographical errors and improves consistency.

The ability to assign a type name for a user-defined data structure is only a first step in the direction of supporting data abstraction. As we mentioned in Section 3.1, the two main benefits of introducing types in a language are classification and protection. Types allow the (otherwise unstructured) world of data to be organized as a collection of distinct categories. Types also allow data to be protected from undesirable manipulations by specifying exactly which operations are legal for objects of a given type and by hiding the concrete representation. Of these two properties, only the former is achieved by defining a user-defined data structure as a type. To provide protection, a new type must be defined in terms of a hidden structure and a set of allowable operations. More precisely, we need a construct to define abstract data types. An *abstract data type* is a new type for which we can define the operations to be used for manipulating instances, while the data structure that implements the type is hidden to the users. Next we briefly review the constructs provided by C++ and Eiffel to define abstract data types. Further elaboration of the concepts presented here will be discussed in Chapters 5 and 6. The way abstract data types can be defined in ML is presented in Chapter 7.

3.3.1 Abstract data types in C++

Abstract data types can be defined in C++ through the class construct. A class encloses the definition of a new type and explicitly provides the operations that can be invoked for correct use of instances of the type. As an example, Figure 3.3 shows a class defining the type of the geometrical concept of point.

A class can be viewed as an extension of structures (or records), where fields can be both data and routines. The difference is that only some fields (declared *public*) are accessible from outside the class. Nonpublic fields are hidden to the users of the class. Nonpublic fields can be declared *private*

```
class point {
public:
    point(int a, int b) { x = a; y = b; }      // initializes the coordinates of a new point
    void x_move(int a) { x += a; }             // moves the point horizontally
    void y_move(int b){ y += b; }              // moves the point vertically
    void reset() { x = 0; y = 0; }             // moves the point to the origin
private:
    int x, y;
};
```

FIGURE 3.3 A C++ class defining point

explicitly. A field that is not declared public or private is assumed to be private by default. In the example, the class construct encapsulates both the definition of the data structure defined to represent points (the two integer numbers x and y) and of the operations provided to manipulate points. The operations are described by routines, called *member functions* in the C++ terminology. The data structure that defines a geometrical point (two integer coordinates) is not directly accessible by users of the class. Rather, points can only be manipulated by the operations defined as public routines, as shown by the following fragment:

```
point p1(1, 3);              // instantiates p1 and initializes its value
point p2(55, 0);             // instantiates p2 and initializes its value
point* p3 = new point(0, 0); // p3 points to the origin
p1.x_move(3);                // moves p1 horizontally
p2.y_move(99);               // moves p2 vertically
p1.reset();                  // positions p1 at the origin
```

The fragment shows how operations are invoked on points by means of the dot notation, that is, by writing "object_name.public_routine_name." The only exceptions are the invocations of constructors and destructors. We discuss constructors below; destructors will be discussed in a later example.

3.3.1.1 Constructors

A newly created object—whether it is an instance of a built-in type or a user-defined type—has an initial state. As we have seen, languages often provide mechanisms to initialize a variable when it is created. A *constructor* is used to do the initialization for a user-defined type.

A constructor operation has the same name as the new type being defined (in the example, point). A constructor is invoked automatically when an object of the class is allocated. In the case of points p1 and p2, this is done when the scope in which they are declared is entered. In the case of the dynamically allocated point referenced by p3, this is done when the new instruction is executed. Invocation of the constructor allocates the data structure defined by the class and initializes its value according to the constructor's code.

In general, there may be two kinds of constructors. A *normal constructor* takes as parameters values of components of the object and constructs (initializes) the object from those components. For example, the point constructor in Figure 3.3 takes two integers as parameters. We could also define another constructor, point(), that takes no arguments and initializes the x and y fields to a predefined value, say, zero.

A *copy constructor* is a different kind of constructor. It allows us to build a new object from an existing object without knowing the components that constitute the object. A copy constructor takes as parameter an object of the same type and constructs a copy of that object. In the example, a point copy constructor is able to build a point out of an existing point. The header of the copy constructor for point objects would be

```
point(point&)
```

where point& is a reference to point. That is, the input parameter, a point object, is passed by reference. The copy constructor for point could be implemented simply in this way:

```
point(point& p) {
    x = p.x;
    y = p.y;
}
```

A special use of the copy constructor is in parameter passing. When a parameter is passed by value to a procedure, copy construction is used to build the formal parameter from the argument. Copy construction is somewhat similar to assignment, with the difference that on assignment both objects already exist before the assignment, whereas on copy construction, a new object must be created first and then a value assigned to it.

If a class definition does not provide normal constructors and copy constructors, default definitions are provided by the compiler. The default constructor copies the values of all the members into the constructed object.

3.3.1.2 Genericity

It is also possible to define *generic abstract data types*, i.e., data types that are parametric with respect to the type of their components. The construct provided to support this feature is the *template*. As an example, the C++ template in Figure 3.4 implements an abstract data type stack, which is parametric with

```
template<class T> class Stack{
public:
    Stack(int sz)        {top = s = new T[size = sz];}
    ~Stack()             {delete[ ] s;}   //destructor
    void push(T el)      {*top++ = el;}
    T pop()              {return *--top;}
    int length()         {return top - s;}
private:
    int size;
    T* top;
    T* s;
};

void foo() {
    Stack<int> int_st(30);
    Stack<item> item_st(100);

    ...
    int_st.push(9);

    ...
}
```

FIGURE 3.4 A C++ generic abstract data type and its instantiation

respect to the type of elements that it can store and manage. Figure 3.4 also describes a fragment that defines data objects of instantiated generic types.

3.3.1.3 Destructors

The template also shows an example of a destructor. A *destructor* is recognized by having the name of the class, prefixed by ~ (which stands for "the complement of the constructor"). The purpose of a destructor is to perform a cleanup after the last use of an object. In the example, the cleanup deallocates the array used to store the stack. It is called automatically for automatic objects (i.e., objects allocated in the run-time stack) upon exit from the scope in which the objects are declared. For dynamic objects created using the new operator, deallocation is performed by the delete operator, which must be called explicitly to free the memory when an object becomes inaccessible. The delete operator calls the destructor for the object pointed to. The delete operation, as we already mentioned, may generate dangling references if the object being released is still referenced.

If no destructor is explicitly specified for a class, the language provides for an implicit destruction operation that depends on the types of the encapsulated data. In general, there may be several constructors but only one destructor defined for a class.

3.3.2 Abstract data types in Eiffel

Eiffel provides a class construct to implement abstract data types. Figure 3.5 describes the abstract data type POINT in Eiffel.

In another class, we may declare references to objects of type POINT:

p1, p2: POINT;

Objects can be created and bound to such references using constructors, which are specified in the creation clause of the class. The created objects may then be manipulated according to the type's operations, as shown by the following sample statements (a constructor call is always preceded by !!):

```
!!p1.make_point(4, 7);
!!p2.make_point(55, 0);
p1.move_x(3);
```

```
class POINT export
    x_move, y_move, reset
creation
    make_point
feature
    x, y: INTEGER;
    x_move(a: INTEGER) is
            -- moves the point horizontally
    do
        x := x + a
    end; --x_move
    y_move(b: INTEGER) is
            -- moves the point vertically
    do
        y := y + b
    end; --y_move
    reset is
            -- moves the point to the origin
    do
        x := 0;
        y := 0
    end; -- reset
    make_point(a, b: INTEGER) is
            -- sets the initial coordinates of the point
    do
        x := a;
        y := b
    end -- make_point
end; -- POINT
```

FIGURE 3.5 An Eiffel class defining point

```
p2.move_y(99);
p1.reset();
```

C++ instances of an abstract data type can be either stack objects or heap objects. That is, they can either be associated with automatic variables or be dynamically allocated and referred to by pointers. In the example in Section 3.3.1, the objects associated with variables p1 and p2 are (automatically) allocated on the stack; the objects to which p3 points are dynamically allocated on the heap. In Eiffel, as originally defined, all objects (except for basic values such as integers) are implicitly allocated on the heap and made accessible via pointers. In the example, p1 and p2 are references to POINTs, which are allocated and initialized by the invocation of the creation operation. Later, Eiffel introduced the possibility of declaring a class as expanded, meaning that the possible run-time value is not a reference to the object, but the object itself. By declaring POINT as expanded, p1 and p2 would hold a POINT object as a value, and the creation instruction would become unnecessary. Expanded classes, however, are rarely used in Eiffel. For simplicity, we will ignore this feature in our treatment of the language in this book.

The Eiffel make_point is analogous to the C++ constructor but must be called explicitly to create the object. The C++ concept of copy construction—creating a new object from an existing like object—is not object-specific in Eiffel. Rather, the language provides a function named clone that can be called with an object of any type to create a new object that is a copy of that object.

The Eiffel language supports a set of principles that may guide programmers in the disciplined and methodical development of programs. It is possible to associate a class with an *invariant property*, i.e., a predicate that characterizes all possible correct instances of the type. For example, consider a variant NON_AXIAL_INT_POINT of class POINT that describes the set of points with integer coordinates that do not lie on the axes x or y. The x- and y-coordinates of the elements of class NON_AXIAL_INT_POINT cannot be zero. We can write the invariant property for such a class as:

$$x * y \mathrel{/=} 0$$

where /= is the inequality operator. To ensure that the invariant is satisfied, the exported routines of the class must satisfy suitable constraints. These constraints are stated in Eiffel by defining two predicates for each routine: a *precondition* and a *postcondition*. These two predicates characterize the states in which the routine can start its execution and the states in which the routine should end its execution. A class is said to be consistent if it satisfies the following conditions:

1 For every creation routine, if its precondition holds prior to execution, the invariant holds upon termination.

2 For every exported routine, if the precondition and the invariant hold prior to execution, the postcondition and the invariant hold upon termination.

If these two rules are satisfied, by simple induction one can prove that the invariant will always be true for all reachable object states.

The class NON_AXIAL_INT_POINT is presented in Figure 3.6. The reader should be able to verify manually that conditions 1 and 2 for class consistency hold.

```
class NON_AXIAL_POINT export
    x_move, y_move
creation
    make_point
feature
    x, y: INTEGER;
    x_move(a: INTEGER) is
            -- moves the point horizontally
    require
      x + a /= 0
    do
        x := x + a
    ensure
        x /= 0
    end; --x_move
    y_move(b: INTEGER) is
            -- moves the point vertically
    require
        y + b /= 0
    do
        y := y + b
    ensure
        y /= 0
    end; --y_move
    make_point(a, b: INTEGER) is
            -- sets the initial coordinates of the point
    require
        a * b /= 0
    do
        x := a;
        y := b
    end -- make_point
invariant
    x * y /= 0
end; -- NON_AXIAL_POINT
```

FIGURE 3.6 An Eiffel class defining a point that may not lie on the axes x or y

An Eiffel implementation is not required to provide functionalities to check that all classes are consistent. It does not even force programmers to provide preconditions, postconditions, and invariants: assertions are optional, although their use is a good way to document the code and its design. If assertions are present, an Eiffel implementation can check them at run time. This is an effective way of debugging Eiffel programs. As we will see in Chapter 4, assertions also support systematic ways of error handling.

3.3.2.1 Generic abstract data types

Eiffel supports the implementation of generic abstract data types, via *generic classes*. As an example, Figure 3.7 shows an implementation of the generic abstract data type stack. The definition of preconditions, postconditions, and invariants are left to the reader as an exercise.

```
class STACK[T] export
    push, pop, length
creation
    make_stack
feature
    store: ARRAY[T];
    length: INTEGER;

    make_stack(n: INTEGER) is
        do store.make(1, n);
                --this operation allocates an array with bounds 1, n
            length := 0
        end; --make_stack

    push(x: T) is
        do length := length + 1;
            put(x, length)
                --element x is stored at index length of the array
        end; --push

    pop: T is
        do Result := store@(length);
            -- the element in the array whose index is length is copied in the
            -- language predefined object Result, which always contains the
            -- value returned by the function
            length := length - 1
        end --pop
end --class STACK
```

FIGURE 3.7 An Eiffel abstract data type definition

3.4 Type systems

Data types are fundamental semantic components of programming languages that try to capture the nature of the data manipulated by the programs.

Moreover, programming languages differ in the way types are defined and behave, and typing issues are often quite subtle. Having discussed type concepts informally in different languages, we now review the foundations for a theory of types. We define a *type system* as the set of rules used by a language to structure and organize its collection of types. Understanding the type system adopted by a language is perhaps the major step in understanding the language's semantics. In this section, we introduce a number of concepts that help in understanding and analyzing type systems.

Our treatment in this section is rather abstract and does not refer to any specific programming language features. The only assumption we make is that a type is defined as a set of values and a set of operations that can be applied to such values. As usual, since values in our context are stored somewhere in the memory of a computer, we use the term *object* (or *data object*) to denote both the storage and the stored value. The operations defined for a type are the only ways of manipulating its instance objects: they protect data objects from illegal uses. Any attempt to manipulate objects with illegal operations is a *type error*. A program is said to be *type safe* (or *type secure*) if it is guaranteed to have no type errors, that is, it is guaranteed that its operations always apply to operands of the correct type.

3.4.1 Static versus dynamic program checking

Before focusing our discussion on type errors, we first discuss more generally the kinds of errors that may occur in a program, the different times at which such errors can be checked, and the effect of checking times on the quality of the resulting programs.

Errors can be classified in two categories: language errors and application errors. *Language errors* are syntactic and semantic errors in the use of the programming language. *Application errors* are deviations of the program behavior with respect to the program's specifications. The programming language should facilitate the detection of both kinds of errors. Ideally, it should help prevent them from being introduced in the first place. In general, programs that are readable and well structured are less error prone and easier to check. Here we concentrate on language errors and we use the term "error" to refer to "language error." A discussion of application errors is out of the scope of this book; software design methods address application errors.

Error checking can be accomplished in different ways that can be classified in two broad categories: static and dynamic. *Dynamic checking* requires the program to be executed on sample input data; *static checking* does not. In general, if a check can be performed statically, it is preferable to do so instead of delaying the check to run time for two main reasons. First, potential errors are detected at run time only if one can provide input data that cause the error to be revealed. For example, a type error might exist in a portion of the program that is not executed by the given input data. Second, dynamic checking slows down program execution.

Static checking is often called *compile-time* (or translation-time) *checking*. Actually, the term "compile-time checking" may not be an accurate synonym of "static checking" since programs may be subject to separate compilation and some static checks might occur at link time. For example, the possible mismatch between a routine called by one module and defined in another might be checked at link time. For simplicity, we will continue to use the terms "static checking" and "compile-time (or translation-time) checking" interchangeably.

Static checking, though preferable to dynamic checking, does not uncover all language errors. Some errors only manifest themselves at run time. For example, if div is the operator for integer division, the compiler might check that both operands are integer. However, the program would be erroneous if the value of the divisor is zero. This possibility, in general, cannot be checked by the compiler.

3.4.2 Strong typing and type checking

The type system of a language was defined as the set of rules to be followed to define and manipulate program data. Such rules constrain the set of legal programs that can be written in a language. The goal of a type system is to prevent the writing of type-unsafe programs as much as possible. A type system is said to be *strong* if it guarantees type safety, i.e., if programs written by following the restrictions of the type system are guaranteed not to generate type errors. A language with a strong type system is said to be a *strongly typed language*. If a language is strongly typed, the compiler can guarantee the absence of type errors from programs. A type system is said to be *weak* if it is not strong. Similarly, a *weakly typed language* is a language that is not strongly typed.

In Chapter 2 we introduced the concept of a statically typed language. Such languages are said to obey a *static type system*. Precisely, such a type system requires that the type of every program expression be known at compile time. An example of a static type system can be achieved by requiring that

1 Only built-in types can be used.
2 All variables are declared with an associated type.

3 All operations are specified by stating the types of the required operands and the type of the result.

A statically typed language is a strongly typed language, but there are strongly typed languages that are not statically typed. For example, we will show in Chapters 6 and 7 examples of languages where the binding between a variable and its type cannot be established at compile time, and yet the rules of the type system guarantee type safety; i.e., they guarantee that correctly compiled programs will execute without generating type errors.

In general, there are different ways for a language to achieve a strong type system. Since all of them guarantee type safety, how should a language designer choose a type system when defining a new programming language? There are two conflicting requirements to be accommodated in such a design decision: the size of the set of legal programs and the efficiency of the type-checking procedure performed by the compiler. Since a type system restricts the set of programs that can be written, the rules of the type system might allow only very simple programs. In principle, a type system that restricts the set of legal programs to the empty set is a strong type system. It also supports trivial checking. But it is obviously useless. The previous example of static typing allows for a simple checking procedure, but it is overly restrictive. Dynamic typing, as we will demonstrate in Chapters 6 and 7, is a powerful programming facility that can be combined with strong typing. In such a case, however, a more complex type-checking procedure is required.

3.4.3 Type compatibility

A strict type system might require that if an operation expects an operand of a type T, it may be invoked legally only with a parameter of type T. Languages, however, often allow more flexibility by defining conditions under which an operand of another type, say Q, is also acceptable without violating type safety. In such a case, we say that the language defines whether, in the context of a given operation, type Q is *compatible* with type T. Type compatibility is also sometimes called *conformance* or *equivalence*. When compatibility is defined precisely by the type system, a type-checking procedure can verify that all operations are always invoked correctly, i.e., the types of the operands are compatible with the types expected by the operations. Thus a language defining a notion of type compatibility can still have a strong type system.

To examine the effect of different type compatibility rules, consider the sample program fragment written in a hypothetical programming language given in Figure 3.8.

```
type s1 is struct {
    int y;
    int w;
};
type s2 is struct {
    int y;
    int w;
};
type s3 is struct {
    int y;
};
s3 func(s1 z)
{
...
};
...
s1 a, x;
s2 b;
s3 c;
int d;
...
a = b;          --(1)
x = a;          --(2)
c = func(b);    --(3)
d = func(a);    --(4)
```

FIGURE 3.8 A sample program

The strict conformance rule where a type name is compatible only with itself is called *name compatibility*. Under name compatibility, in the above example, instruction (2) is type correct, since a and x have the same type name. Instruction (1) contains a type error because a and b have different types. Similarly, instructions (3) and (4) contain type errors. In (3) the function is called with an argument of incompatible type; in (4) the value returned by the function is assigned to a variable of an incompatible type.

Structural compatibility is another possible conformance rule that languages may adopt. Type T1 is structurally compatible with type T2 if they have the same structure. This can be defined recursively as follows:

Two types T1 and T2 are structurally compatible if

- T1 is name compatible with T2; or
- T1 and T2 are defined by applying the same type constructor to structurally compatible corresponding type components.

According to structural equivalence, instructions (1), (2), and (3) are type correct. Instruction (4) contains a type error, since type s3 is not compatible with int. Note that the definition we gave does not clearly state what happens with the field names of Cartesian products (i.e., whether they are ignored in the check or are required to coincide, and whether structurally compatible fields are required to occur in the same order). For simplicity, we assume that they are required to coincide and to occur in the same order. In such a case, if we renamed the fields of s2 as y1 and w1, or permuted their occurrence, s2 would no longer be compatible with s1.

Name compatibility is easier to implement than structural compatibility, which requires a recursive traversal of a data structure. Name compatibility is also much stronger than structural compatibility. Actually, structural compatibility goes to the extreme where type names are totally ignored in the check. Structural compatibility makes the classification of data objects implied by types exceedingly coarse.

For example, having defined the following two types,

```
type complex is struct {
    float a;
    float b;
};
type point is struct {
    float a;
    float b;
};
```

the programmer can instantiate variables to represent, say, points on a plane and values of electricity voltage. The type system allows them to be used interchangeably, although most likely the programmer has chosen two different type names in order to keep the different sets of objects separate. In conclusion, name compatibility is often preferable. It prevents two types from being considered compatible just because their representations happen to be identical.

Often programming languages do not take much care in defining the adopted notion of type compatibility. This issue is left to be defined by the implementation. An unfortunate consequence is that different implementations may adopt different notions, and thus a program accepted by one compiler might be rejected by another. This unfortunate case happened, for example, when Pascal was originally defined, although later ISO Pascal defined type compatibility rigorously, mainly based on name compatibility. C adopts structural compatibility for all types except structures, for which name compatibility is required.

Ada adopts name compatibility. In addition, since the language supports the concept of a subtype (see also Section 3.4.5), objects belonging to different subtypes of the same type are compatible. In Ada, when a variable is defined by means of a constructor, as in

IA: **array** (INTEGER **range** 1..100) **of** INTEGER;

a brand new anonymous type is implicitly introduced, followed by a variable declaration:

type ANONYMOUS_1 **is array** (INTEGER **range** 1..100) **of** INTEGER;
IA: ANONYMOUS_1;

Thus, if two variables IA and IB are declared,

IA: **array** (INTEGER **range** 1..100) **of** INTEGER;
IB: **array** (INTEGER **range** 1..100) **of** INTEGER;

the two variables are considered to have incompatible types, since their anonymous type names would be different.

3.4.4 Type conversions

Suppose that an operation at some point of a program expects an object of type T_1. But suppose that the operation is applied to an object of type T_2. If T_1 and T_2 are compatible according to the type system, the application of the operation would be type correct. If they are not, one might wish to apply a type conversion from T_2 to T_1 in order to make the operation possible.

More precisely, let an operation be defined by a function fun expecting a parameter of type T_1 and evaluating a result of type R_1:

fun: $T_1 \rightarrow R_1$

Let x_2 be a variable of type T_2 and y_2 a variable of type R_2. Suppose that T_1 and T_2 (R_1 and R_2) are not compatible. How can fun be applied to x_2 and the result of the routine be assigned to y_2? This would require two conversion functions to be available, t_{21} and r_{12}, transforming, respectively, objects of type T_2 into objects of type T_1 and objects of type R_1 into objects of type R_2:

t_{21}: $T_2 \rightarrow T_1$
r_{12}: $R_1 \rightarrow R_2$

Thus, the intended action can be performed by first applying t_{21} to x_2, evaluating fun with this argument, applying r_{12} to the result of the function, and finally assigning the result to y_2. That is,

i) $y_2 = r_{12}(fun(t_{21}(x_2)))$

In some languages, any allowed conversions are applied automatically by the compiler. Following the Algol 68 terminology, we will call such automatic conversions *coercions*. In the example, if coercions are available, the programmer might simply write

ii) $y_2 = fun(x_2)$

and the compiler would automatically convert ii) into i).

In general, the kind of coercion that may occur at a given point (if any) depends on the context. For example, in C, if we write

x = x + z;

where z is float and x is int, x is coerced to float to evaluate the arithmetic operator + (which stands for real addition), and the result is coerced to int for the assignment. That is, the arithmetic coercion is from int to float, but the assignment coercion is from float to int.

C provides a simple coercion system. In addition, explicit conversions can be applied in C using the *cast* construct. For example, a cast can be used to override an undesirable coercion that would otherwise be applied in a given context. In the above assignment, one can force a conversion of z to int by writing

x = x +(int) z;

Such an explicit conversion in C is semantically defined by assuming that the expression to be converted is implicitly assigned to an unnamed variable of the type specified in the cast, using the coercion rules of the language.

Ada does not provide any coercions. Whenever a conversion is allowed by the language, it must be invoked explicitly. For example, if X is declared as a FLOAT variable and I is an INTEGER, assigning X to I can be accomplished by the instruction

I := INTEGER(X);

The conversion function INTEGER provided by Ada computes an integer from a floating-point value by rounding to the nearest integer.

The existence of coercion rules in a language has both advantages and disadvantages. The advantage is that many desirable conversions are automatically provided by the implementation. The disadvantage is that since implicit transformations happen behind the scenes, the language becomes complicated and programs may be obscure. In addition, coercions weaken the usefulness of type checking, since they override the declared type of objects with default, context-sensitive transformations. For example, Algol 68 consistently applies the principle of implicit conversions to the extreme. The type of the value required at any given point in an Algol 68 program can be determined from the context. But the way coercions interact with other constructs of the language can make programs hard to understand. In particular, difficulties arise because of the interaction between coercions and overloading of operators and routines.

3.4.5 Types and subtypes

If a type is defined as a set of values with an associated set of operations, a subtype can be defined to be a subset of those values (and, for simplicity, the same operations). In this section we explore this notion in the context of conventional languages, ignoring the ability to specify user-defined operations for subtypes. The concept of subtype will have a richer semantics in the context of object-oriented languages, as will be discussed in Chapter 6.

If ST is a subtype of T, T is also called ST's supertype (or parent type). We assume that the operations defined for T are automatically inherited by ST. A language supporting subtypes must define the following:

1 A way to define subsets of a given type.
2 Compatibility rules between a subtype and its supertype.

Pascal was the first programming language to introduce the concept of a subtype as a subrange of any discrete ordinal type (i.e., integers, boolean, character, enumerations, or subranges). For example, in Pascal one may define subtypes of integer type as follows:

```
type   natural = 0..maxint;
       digit = 0..9;
       small = -9..9;
```

where maxint is the maximum integer value representable by an implementation.

A Pascal program can only define a subset of contiguous values of a discrete type. For example, it cannot define a subtype EVEN consisting of all even integers, or MUL_10 consisting of all multiples of 10 in the range −100..100. Different subtypes of a given type are considered to be compatible among themselves and with the supertype. However, type-safe operations may cause run-time errors. No error arises if an object of a subtype is provided in an expression that expects an object of its supertype. For example, if an expression requires an integer, one may provide a natural; if it expects a natural, one might provide a digit. If, however, a small is provided where a digit is expected, an error arises if the value provided is not in the range expected. That is, if an argument of type T is provided to an operation expecting an operand of type R, the expression is type safe if either R or T is a subtype of the other, or both are subtypes of another type Q. No value error will occur at run time if T is a subtype of R. In all other cases, the operation must be checked at run time and an error may arise if the value transmitted does not belong to the expected type.

Ada provides an explicit construct for, and a richer notion of, subtype than Pascal. A subtype of an array type can constrain its index; a subtype of a variant record type can freeze the variant; a subtype of a discrete ordinal type is a finite subset of contiguous values. Examples of Ada types and subtypes are shown in Figure 3.9.

```
type Int_Vector is array (Integer range < >) of Integer;
type Var_Rec(Tag: Boolean) is
    record X: Float;
        case Tag of
            when True =>  Y: Integer;
                          Z: Real;
            when False=>  U: Char;
        end case;
    end record;
subtype Vec_100 is Int_Vector(0..99);
    --this subtype constrains the bounds of the array to 0..99
subtype Var_Rec_True is Var_Rec(True);
    --this subtype freezes the variant where Tag = True;
    --objects of the subtype thus have fields X, Y, and Z;
subtype SMALL is Integer range -9..9;
    --this subtype defines a small set of integers
```

FIGURE 3.9   Examples of Ada types and subtypes

Ada subtypes do not define new types. All values of all subtypes of a certain type T are of type T. The subtype construct can be viewed as a way to signal that certain run-time checks must be inserted by the compiler to ensure that objects of a given subtype always receive the specified restricted set of values.

3.4.6 Generic types

As we have seen in this chapter, modern languages allow parameterized (generic) routines and abstract data types to be defined. A typical example is a stack of elements of a parameter type T, whose operations have the following signatures:

```
push: stack(T) × T → stack(T)   --pushes an element on top of the stack
pop: stack(T) → stack(T) × T    --extracts the topmost element from the stack
length: stack(T) → int          --computes the length of the stack
```

An implementation of this example was illustrated in Section 3.3 for C++ and Eiffel. In the example, the abstract data type being defined is parametric with respect to a type, and the operations of the generic type are therefore defined as generic routines. The operations defined for the type stack(T) are supposed to work uniformly for any possible type T. However, since the type is not known, how can such routines be type-checked to guarantee type safety?

Such type checking is supported by languages such as Ada, C++, and Eiffel through the instantiation at compile time, by binding generic type parameters to a concrete type. These languages differ in their specific treatment of generic types, as we will see in later chapters. For example, Ada and Eiffel require explicit instantiation of both generic routines and generic abstract data types, while C++ only requires explicit instantiation of generic classes, and not of generic routines. Compile-time instantiation binds each instance to known types and thus allows each instance to be statically checked to ensure type safety. The solution adopted by ML will be explained in Chapter 7.

3.4.7 Summing up: Monomorphic versus polymorphic type systems

A simple strong type system can be provided by a statically typed language where every program entity (constant, variable, routine) has a specific type, defined by a declaration, and every operation requires operands of exactly the type that appears in the operation definition. For such a language, it is possible to verify at compile time that any occurrence of a constant, variable, or routine is type correct. Such a type system is called *monomorphic* (from ancient Greek, "single shape"): every object belongs to one and only one type. By contrast, in a *polymorphic* ("multiple shape") programming language objects can belong to more than one type. Routines (e.g., functions) can accept as formal parameters actual parameters of more than one type.

Having examined in the previous sections traditional programming languages such as C, Pascal, and Ada, we have seen that all deviate from strict monomorphism in one way or another. Compatibility, discussed in Section 3.4.3, is a first departure from strict monomorphism, since it allows any compatible type to be accepted where a certain type is needed. Coercion, discussed in Section 3.4.4, is also a deviation from strict monomorphism. In fact, it allows an operand of one type to be used when an object of a different type is expected. Subtyping, discussed in Section 3.4.5, provides yet another example of deviation, since an element of the subtype also belongs to the supertype. As yet another example, overloading (introduced in Section 3.4.2) allows operators, such as + or *, to be applied to both integer operands and real operands.

Since polymorphic features creep in into most—if not all—existing languages, a distinction between monomorphic and polymorphic languages is of no practical use. All practical languages have some degree of polymorphism. Consequently, to differentiate among languages, we would need to differentiate among different kinds and levels of polymorphism. It is also interesting to see the degree to which polymorphism and strong typing may be combined. Understanding the possible different forms of polymorphism can help us appreciate the sometimes profound semantic differences among them. Moreover, it will help us organize concepts such as coercion, subtyping, and overloading, which were examined in previous sections separately, into a coherent conceptual framework.

The different facets of polymorphism can be classified as shown in Figure 3.10. For the sake of simplicity and abstraction, let us discuss Figure 3.10 in the case of polymorphic functions, i.e., mathematical functions whose arguments (domain and range) can belong to more than one type.

A first distinction is between universal polymorphism and ad hoc polymorphism. *Ad hoc polymorphism* does not really add to the semantics of a monomorphic language. Ad hoc polymorphic functions work on a finite and often small set of types and may behave differently for each type. *Universal*

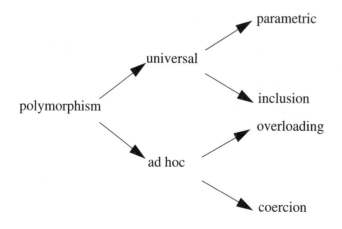

FIGURE 3.10   A classification of polymorphism

polymorphism characterizes functions that work uniformly for an infinite set of types, all of which have some common structure. An ad hoc polymorphic function can be viewed as a syntactic abbreviation for a small set of different monomorphic functions, whereas a universal polymorphic function executes the same code for arguments of all admissible types.

The two major cases of ad hoc polymorphism are overloading and coercion. In *overloading*, the same function name can be used in different contexts to denote different functions, and in each context the function actually denoted by a given name is uniquely determined. A *coercion* is an operation that converts the argument of a function to the type expected by the function. In such a case, polymorphism is only apparent: the function actually works for its prescribed type only, although the argument of a different type may be passed to it, but the argument is automatically transformed to the required type prior to function evaluation. Coercions can be provided statically by code inserted by the compiler in the case of statically typed languages, or they can be determined dynamically by run-time tests on type descriptors in the case of dynamically typed languages.

Overloading and coercion can be illustrated by the C example of the arithmetic expression a + b. In C, + is an ad hoc polymorphic function, whose behavior is different depending on whether it is applied to float values or int numbers. In the two cases, the two different machine instructions float+ (for real addition) or int+ would be needed. If the two operands are of the same type—say, float—the + operator is bound to float+; if both are bound to int, + is bound to int+. The fact that + is an overloaded operator is a purely syntactic phenomenon. Since the types of the operands are known statically, one might eliminate overloading statically by substituting the overloaded + operator with float+ or int+, respectively. If the types of the two operands are different (i.e., integer plus real or real plus integer), however, the float+ operator is invoked after converting the integer operand to real.

Figure 3.10 defines two kinds of universal polymorphism: parametric and inclusion polymorphism. Subtyping, discussed in Section 3.4.5, is an example of *inclusion polymorphism*. A function is indeed applicable to a given type and any of its subtypes. This concept is applicable not only to the case of subtyping of Section 3.4.5, but also to the more general concept that will be discussed in the context of object-oriented languages in Chapter 6.

Parametric polymorphism is perhaps the most genuine form of universal polymorphism. In this case the polymorphic function works uniformly on a range of types. An implicit or explicit type parameter determines the type of the arguments for each application of the function. Generic routines, as in the case of ML functions, are examples of parametric polymorphic functions. In languages such as Ada and C++ for which, as anticipated in Section 3.4.6, generic routines are instantiated at compile time, with full binding of type parameters to specific types, genericity is only an apparent kind of polymorphism; that is, it can be viewed as a case of ad hoc polymorphism.

The term *dynamic polymorphism* is also used frequently to denote the case where the binding between language entities and the form they can take varies dynamically. Languages that support unrestricted forms of dynamic polymorphism cannot provide a strong type system. By providing suitable forms of inclusion and/or parametric polymorphism, however, languages can preserve a strong type system. We will discuss this in Chapter 6 for object-oriented languages, which can support inclusion polymorphism, and in Chapter 7 for the functional language ML, which supports parametric polymorphism.

3.5 The type structure of representative languages

In this section we review the type structure of a number of existing programming languages. The description provides an overall hierarchical taxonomy of the features provided for data structuring by each language. For a full understanding of language semantics, such a description must be complemented by a precise understanding of the rules of the type system (strong typing, type compatibility, type conversion, subtyping, genericity, and polymorphism), according to the concepts discussed in Section 3.4. Our discussion will touch on the main features of type structures. Other comments were given in previous parts of this chapter. Moreover, the reader is urged to refer to language manuals for a discussion of all details and subtleties that cannot be addressed in this general treatment.

3.5.1 Pascal

The type structure of Pascal is described in Figure 3.11. In this figure, we have divided unstructured types into three classes: built-in types, enumerations, and subranges. A different decomposition of unstructured types would be in terms of ordinal types and the real type. *Ordinal types* comprise integers, booleans, characters, enumerations, and subranges. Ordinal types are characterized as consisting of a discrete set of values, each of which has (at most) a unique predecessor and (at most) a unique successor, evaluated by the built-in functions pred and succ, respectively.

Figure 3.11 shows how structured types can be built in Pascal. Recursive data structures are defined via pointers. Cartesian products are defined by *records*. Unions and discriminated unions are described by *variant records*. Comments on these constructs, and particularly on their possible insecurities,

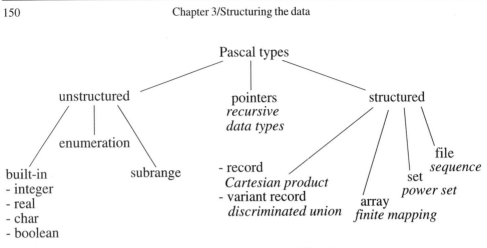

FIGURE 3.11   The type structure of Pascal

were given earlier. Finite mappings are described by *arrays*, whose index type must be an ordinal type. The size of an array is frozen when the array type is defined and cannot change during execution. Pascal regards arrays with different index types as different types. For example, a1 and a2 below are different types.

```
type a1 = array[1..50] of integer;
     a2 = array[1..70] of integer;
```

This was a serious problem in Pascal as originally defined. Because procedures require formal parameters to have a specified type, it was not possible, for example, to write a single procedure capable of sorting both arrays of type a1 and of type a2. During the standardization of Pascal by ISO, a new feature was added to solve this problem. This feature, called the *conformant array*, allows the formal array parameter of a procedure to conform to the size of the actual array parameter. The actual and formal parameters are required to have the same number of indexes and the same component type. The example in Figure 3.12 illustrates the use of conformant arrays.

When the procedure sort is called with a one-dimensional array parameter, low and high assume the values of the lower and upper bounds of the actual parameter, respectively.

Another solution, not available in Pascal, could have been based on genericity (i.e., allowing a procedure to be generic with respect to the array bounds). More generally, Pascal provides only limited forms of ad hoc polymorphism. Some built-in operators, such as + or succ, are overloaded. In fact, succ is applicable to operands of any ordinal type. Similarly, + can be applied to integer operands, real operands, or even sets (in which case it denotes the union operator). The language also defines some cases of coercion. For example, if

```
procedure sort(var a: array[low..high: integer] of CType);
var i: integer;
    more: boolean;
    temp: CType;
begin
    more := true;
    while more do begin
        more := false;
        for i := low to high - 1 do begin
            if a[i] > a[i + 1] then begin {move down element}
                temp := a[i];
                a[i] := a[i + 1];
                a[i + 1] := temp;
                more := true
            end
        end
    end
end
```

FIGURE 3.12 An example of conformant arrays in Pascal

an integer is added to a real, the integer is coerced to a real, and the addition is performed as real addition.

As we mentioned earlier, Pascal is not a strongly typed language. For example, its original definition did not carefully define the concept of type compatibility. Moreover, subtypes are defined by the language as new types, and thus the type of an expression may in general depend on the values of the operands at run time.

3.5.2 C++

The type structure of C++ is given in Figure 3.13. C++ distinguishes between two categories of types: *fundamental types* and *derived types*. Fundamental types are either *integral* or *floating*. Integral types comprise char, short int, int, and long int, which can be used for representing integers of different sizes. Floating-point types comprise float, double, and long double. New integral types may be declared via enumerations. For example,

```
enum my_small_set {low = 1, medium = 5, high = 10};
```

Arrays are declared by providing a constant expression, which defines the number of elements in the array. For example,

```
float fa[15];
```

declares an array of floating-point numbers that can be indexed with a value in the range 0..14.

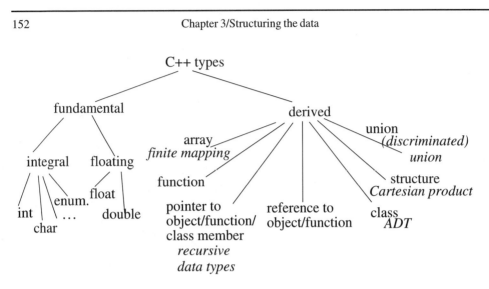

FIGURE 3.13 The type structure of C++

C++ distinguishes between pointers and references. A *reference* is an alias for an object. Therefore, once a reference is bound to an object, it cannot be made to refer to a different object. For example, having declared

```
int i = 5;
int& j = i;
```

i and j denote the same object, which contains the value 5.

When the reference's lifetime starts, it must be bound to an object. Thus, for example, one cannot write the following declaration:

```
int& j;
```

It is possible, however, to bind a reference to an object through parameter passing. This is actually the way C++ supports parameter passing by reference. For example, according to the following routine declaration,

```
void fun(int& x, float y)
```

x represents a by-reference parameter, which is bound to its corresponding actual parameter when the routine gets called.

Pointers are quite different from references. A pointer is a data object whose value is the address of another object. A pointer can be made to refer to different objects during its lifetime. That is, it is possible to assign a new value to a pointer, not only to the object referenced by the pointer. Of course, it is possible to use pointers also in the case where a reference would do. In fact, references are not provided by C, but were added to the language by C++. As we mentioned, however, pointers are extremely powerful but difficult to manage and often dangerous to use. They should be used only when necessary. References should be used in all other cases.

Another major distinctive feature of the C++ type system is the ability to define new types through the class construct. As we discussed, this allows the implementation of abstract data types.

Finally, two other kinds of types can be derived in C++ by using the function and the union constructs. As we already observed, the function construct defines a new data object. But C++ functions are not first-class objects. Thus, even though programs may declare pointers to functions and pass these pointers as parameters, variables of type function are not supported and functions may not be passed as parameters. The union construct defines a structure that is capable of containing objects of different types at different times.

3.5.3 Ada

The type structure of Ada is described in Figure 3.14. This structure is discussed and evaluated in this section, except for concurrency-related types, which are discussed in Chapter 4, and tagged types, which are discussed in Chapter 6.

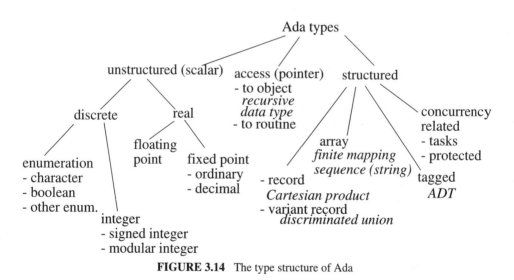

FIGURE 3.14 The type structure of Ada

Unstructured (scalar) types can be both numeric (i.e., integers and reals) and enumerations. All scalar types are ordered; i.e., relational operators are defined on them. Enumeration types are similar to those provided by Pascal. *Integer* types comprise a set of consecutive integer values. An integer type may be either signed or modular. Any *signed* integer type is a subrange of

System.Min_Int..System.Max_Int, which denote the minimum and maximum integer representable in a given Ada implementation. A *modular* integer is an absolute value, greater than or equal to zero. The Ada language predefines a signed integer type, called Integer. Other integer types, such as Long_Integer or Short_Integer, may also be predefined by an implementation. Programmer-defined integer types may be specified as shown by the following examples:

```
type Small_Int is range -10..10; -- range bounds may be any static expressions
type Two_Digit is mod 100; --the values range from 0 to 99;
                           --the bound must be a static expression
```

As we mentioned, Ada allows *subtypes* to be defined from given types. Subtypes do not define a new type. They conform to the notion of sub-type we discussed in Section 3.4.5. Two subtypes of Integer are predefined in Ada:

```
subtype Natural is Integer range 0..INTEGER'LAST;
subtype Positive is Integer range 1..INTEGER'LAST;
```

Ada provides a rich and elaborate set of facilities for dealing with *real* values; only the basic aspects will be reviewed here. Real types provided by the language are just an approximation of their mathematical counterpart (universal real, in the Ada terminology). In fact, the fixed number of bits used by the implementation to represent real values makes it possible to store the exact value of only a limited subset of the universal reals. Other real numbers are approximated. Real types in Ada come in two forms: floating point and fixed point. A *floating-point* real type approximates a universal real with an error that is relative to the number's absolute value. A *fixed-point* real approximates a universal real with an error that is independent of the value being represented. The language predefines one floating-point real type, called Float. It is left to the implementation whether additional real types, such as Short_Float or Long_Float, should be provided. The programmer can define additional floating-point real types, such as

```
type Float_1 is digits 10;
```

The digits clause specifies the minimum number of significant decimal digits required for the type. This minimum number of digits defines the relative error bound in the approximate representation of universal reals. Given a floating-point real type, attribute Digits gives the minimum number of digits associated with the type. Thus, Float_1'Digits yields 10, whereas Float'Digits yields an implementation dependent value.

Fixed-point real types provide another way of approximating universal reals, where the approximation error is independent of the value being represented. This error bound is specified as the delta of the fixed-point real. An ordinary fixed-point real type is declared in Ada as

type Fix_Pt **is delta** 0.01 **range** 0.00..100;

The declaration defines both the delta and the range of values.

A decimal fixed-point type is specified by providing the delta and the number of decimal digits. For example,

type Dec_Pt **is delta** 0.01 **digits** 3;

includes at least the range −9.99..9.99

Ada's *structured* (or *composite*) types comprise arrays and records. *Arrays* can have statically known bounds, as in Pascal. For example,

type Month **is** (Jan, Feb, Mar, Apr, May, Jun, Jul, Aug, Sep, Oct, Nov, Dec);
type Yearly_Pay **is array** (Month) **of** Integer;
type Summer_Pay **is array** (Month **range** Jul..Sep) **of** Integer;

Such array types are also said to be constrained. Constraints, however, do not need to be statically defined; that is, Ada supports dynamic arrays, as we show next. First, one can declare unconstrained array types by stating an unspecified range, indicated by the symbol <> (called box):

type Some_Period_Pay **is array** (Month **range** <>) **of** Integer;
type Int_Vector **is array** (Integer **range** <>) **of** Integer;
type Bool_Matrix **is array** (Integer **range** <>, Integer **range** <>) **of** Boolean;

In Ada, array types are characterized by the types of the components, the number of indices, and the type of each index; the values of the bounds are not considered to be a part of the array type and thus may be left unspecified at compile time. The values of the bounds must, however, become known when an object is created. For example, one can declare the following variables:

Spring_Salary: Some_Period_Pay (Apr..Jun);
Z: Int_Vector (-100..100);
W: Int_Vector (20..40);
Y: Bool_Matrix (0..N, 0..M);

Notice that the values of the bounds need not be given by a static expression. It is only required that the bounds be known at run time when the object declarations are processed.

An interesting way of instantiating the bounds of an array is by parameter passing. For example, the function in Figure 3.15 receives an object of type Int_Vector and sums its components.

```
function Sum(X: Int_Vector) return Integer;
Result: Integer := 0; --declaration with initialization
begin
    for I in X'First..X'Last loop
        --First and Last provide the lower and upper bounds of the index
        Result := Result + X(I);
    end loop;
    return Result;
end Sum;
```

FIGURE 3.15   A sample Ada function

The function can thus be called with array parameters of different sizes; for example,

```
A := Sum(Z) + Sum(W);
```

Ada views *strings* as arrays of characters of the following predefined type:

```
type String is array (Positive range <>) of Characters;
```

A line of 80 characters, initialized with all blanks, can be declared as follows:

```
Line: String(1..80) := (1..80 => ' ');
```

Similar to Pascal, Ada records can support both Cartesian products and (discriminated) unions. An example of a *Cartesian product* is

```
type Int_Char is
    X: Integer range 0..100;
    Y: Character;
end record;
```

Ada provides a safe version of *discriminated unions* through variant records. An example, corresponding to what we discussed in Section 3.2.3, is shown in Figure 3.16.

Type Safe_Address has a discriminant Kind that defines the possible variants of an address. The default initial value of the discriminant is declared in the example to be Absolute. Thus an object declared as

```
X: Safe_Address;
```

```
type Address_Type is (Absolute, Offset);
type Safe_Address is record (Kind: Address_Type := Absolute)
   case Kind is
      when Absolute =>
         Abs_Addr: Natural;
      when Offset =>
         Off_Addr: Integer;
   end case;
end record;
```

FIGURE 3.16 An example of a discriminated union in Ada

is an absolute address by default. The discriminant of a variable initialized by default can be changed only by assignment of the record as a whole, not by assignment to the discriminant alone. This forbids the producing of inconsistent data objects and makes variant records a safe representation of discriminated unions.

The discriminant of a variable can also be initialized explicitly when a variable is declared, as in the following:

```
Y: Address(Offset);
```

In such a case, the variant for the object is frozen and cannot be changed later. The compiler can reserve the exact amount of space required by the variant for the constrained variable. The following assignments,

```
X := Y;
X := (Kind => Offset, Off_Addr => 10);
```

are legal and change the variant of variable X to Offset. The following assignment, which would change the variant for Y, is illegal:

```
Y := X;   --illegal
```

Access to the variant of an object whose discriminant is initialized by default, such as

```
X.Off_Addr := X.Off_Addr + 10;
```

requires a run-time check to verify that the object is accessed correctly according to its current variant. In the example, if the address is not an offset, the error exception Constraint_Error is raised.

Access types (*pointers*) are used mainly to allocate and deallocate data dynamically. As an example, the declarations in Figure 3.17 define a binary

```
type Bin_Tree_Node; --incomplete type declaration
type Tree_Ref is access Bin_Tree_Node;
type Bin_Tree_Node is
   record
      Info: Character;
      Left, Right: Tree_Ref:
   end;
```

FIGURE 3.17 Binary tree declaration in Ada

tree. (Note that an incomplete type declaration is needed in Ada when recursive types are being defined.)

If P and Q are two pointers of type Tree_Ref, the Info component of the node referenced by P is P.Info. The node itself is P.all. Thus, assignment of the node pointed to by P to the node pointed to by Q is written as

```
Q.all := P.all;
```

If T is a pointer of type TREE_REF, allocation of a new node pointed to by T can be accomplished as follows:

```
T := new Bin_Tree_Node;
```

The assignment

```
T.all := (Info => 0, Left => null, Right => null);
```

initializes the object pointed to by T to have null Left and Right pointers and field info to contain zero. The language-defined value null denotes a null pointer value, which does not refer to any object.

Ada allows pointers to refer also to routines. For example, the following declaration defines type Message_Routine to be any procedure with an input parameter of type String:

```
type Message_Routine is access procedure(M: String);
```

If Print_This is a previously defined procedure with an input parameter M of type String, one can write

```
Give_Message: Message_Routine; --declares a pointer to a routine
...
Give_Message := Print_This'Access;
            --attribute Access yields a reference to the routine
...
Give_Message.all("This Is A Serious Error");
            --invokes Print_This; ".all" (dereferencing) is optional
```

Finally, it is also possible in Ada to define pointers that refer to named objects, fields of records, or array elements. Such referenceable objects (or parts of an object) must be declared aliased (dynamically allocated data are aliased). As the name indicates, such elements are accessible via several possible names (aliases). If an element is declared aliased, the attribute Access can be applied to provide a pointer to the element, as in the above example. Further examples are

```
Structure: array (1..10) of aliased Component;
                          --Component is a previously defined type
type ComponentPtr is access all Component;
Mine, Yours: ComponentPtr;
...
Mine := Structure (1)'Access; --Mine points to the first element of the array
Yours := Structure (2)'Access; --Yours points to the second element of the array
```

As we discussed in Section 3.2.6, allowing pointers to refer to named data objects (or parts thereof) can generate dangling references. This is avoided in Ada by checking at run time that an object referenced by a pointer is allocated in an activation record that is allocated more recently than the activation record of the unit in which the access type is declared. This check ensures that the object will live at least as long as the access type, which, in turn, ensures that the access values cannot refer to objects that do not exist.

The Ada type system is largely based on Pascal but is richer, more complex, and more systematic. It also solves several of the problems and insecurities of the original Pascal definition. As a result, the language gets close to the goal of strong typing. Type compatibility (based on name compatibility) is specified explicitly. The notion of subtype and the necessary run-time checks are defined precisely. If a new type is to be defined from an existing type, a derived type construct is provided. For example,

```
type Celsius is new Integer;
type Farenheit is new Integer;
```

define two new types; Integer is their parent type. New types inherit all properties (values, operations, and attributes) from their parent type, but they are considered to be different types.

Overloading and coercion are widely available in Ada. The language also provides for inclusion polymorphism in the case of subtypes and type extensions (see Chapter 6).

Finally, Ada makes extensive use of *attributes*. Attributes are used to designate properties of data objects and types. As we saw in many examples so far, the value of an attribute is retrieved by writing the name of the entity whose attribute is being sought, followed by a ' and the name of the attribute. Ada predefines a large number of attributes; more can be defined by an implementation.

3.6 Implementation models

This section reviews the basic implementation models for data objects. The description is language independent. It is intended to complement the conceptual model of programming language processing provided in Chapter 2, by showing how data can be represented and manipulated in a machine. It is not, however, intended to provide a detailed account of efficient techniques for representing data objects within a computer, which can be highly dependent on the hardware structure. We present straightforward solutions along with some comments on alternative, more efficient representations.

Following Chapter 2, data will be represented by a pair consisting of a *descriptor* and a *data object*. Descriptors are repositories that contain the attributes of the data. The items to be kept in the descriptors and their lifetime depend on the semantics of the programming language. Often, descriptors contain attributes that are used during translation to perform checks and to generate code. Only a subset of such attributes, in general, has a longer lifetime that extends to run time. Again, we will pay little attention to the physical layout of descriptors, which depends on the overall organization of the symbol table. We will mostly concentrate on their logical structure.

3.6.1 Built-in primitive types and enumerations

Integers and reals are hardware-supported on most conventional computers, which provide fixed- and floating-point arithmetic. Existing computers may also provide different lengths for the supported arithmetic types. In a language like C, these are reflected by long and short prefixes of int and float data declarations. If the language provides different lengths for arithmetic types and the underlying hardware does not, an implementation is usually free to ignore the prefixes. If, for simplicity, we ignore the issue of different lengths for arithmetic types, integer and real variables may be represented as shown in Figure 3.18 and Figure 3.19.

Values of an enumeration type ENUM can be mapped, one-to-one, to integer values in the range 0..n–1, n being the cardinality of ENUM. This mapping does not introduce any possibility of mixing up values of type ENUM with values of any other enumeration type, if all run-time accesses are routed via a descriptor containing the type information. The use of the descriptor is of

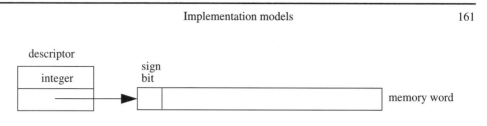

FIGURE 3.18 Representation of an integer variable

course not necessary for statically typed languages. In a language like C, the mapping of enumeration types to integers is not just part of the implementation of the type (and as such, invisible to the programmer), but it is explicitly stated in the language definition. This allows the programmer to take advantage of this knowledge and find ways to break the protection shield provided by the type to access the representation directly.

Booleans and characters can be viewed as enumeration types and implemented as above. To save space, characters and booleans can be stored in storage units smaller than a word (e.g., bits or bytes), which might be addressable by the hardware, or may be packaged into a single word and then retrieved by suitable word manipulation instructions that can disassemble the contents of a word. In such a case, accessing individual characters or booleans may be less efficient, but it would save memory space. Thus the choice of the implementation model depends on a trade-off between speed and space.

3.6.2 Structured types

In this section we review how to represent structured types, built via the constructors discussed in Section 3.2. Our discussion will not be dependent on the specific syntax adopted by an existing language. Rather, it will refer to a hypothetical, self-explaining, programming notation. For simplicity, we will assume that variables are declared by providing an explicit type name. This means that a declaration of, say, a finite mapping X,

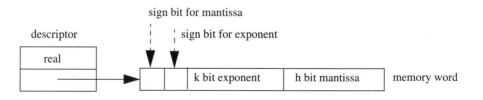

FIGURE 3.19 Representation of a floating-point variable

```
float array[0..10] X;
```

is a shorthand for a declaration of a type followed by a declaration of an array variable:

```
type X_type is float array[0..10];
X_type X;
```

Similarly, we assume that if a type declaration contains a structured component, that component is separately defined by a type declaration. For example, if a field of a Cartesian product is a finite mapping, there are two type declarations: the declaration of an array type T and the declaration of a structure, with a field of type T. As a consequence of these assumptions, each component of a structured type is either a built-in type or a user-defined type.

As for built-in types, each variable is described by a descriptor and its storage layout. The descriptor contains a description of the variable's type. In an actual implementation, for efficiency reasons, all variables of a given type might point to a separately stored descriptor for that type.

3.6.2.1 Cartesian product

The standard representation of a data object of a Cartesian product type is a sequential layout of components. The descriptor contains the Cartesian product type name and a set of triples (name of the selector, type of the field, reference to the data object) for each field. If the type of the field is not a built-in type, the type field points to an appropriate descriptor for the field.

Let us consider the following declarations:

```
type another_type is struct {
    float A;
    int B;
};
type sample_type is struct {
    int X;
    another_type Y;
};
sample_type Z;
```

The variable Z is represented as shown in Figure 3.20. Note that each component of the Cartesian product occupies a certain number of addressable storage units (e.g., words). In a statically typed language, if each component is guaranteed to occupy a fixed memory size, known by the compiler, the descriptor is not needed at run time, and the reference to each field can be

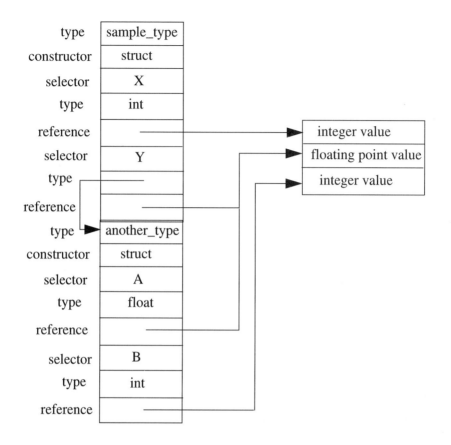

FIGURE 3.20 Representation of a Cartesian product

evaluated statically by the compiler as a fixed offset with respect to the initial address of the composite object.

3.6.2.2 Finite mapping

A conventional representation of a finite mapping allocates a certain number of storage units (e.g., words) for each component. The descriptor contains the finite-mapping type name; the name of the domain type, with the values of the lower and upper bound; the name of the range type (or the reference to its descriptor); and the reference to the first location of the data area where the data object is stored.

For example, given the declarations

```
type X_type is float array[0..10];
X_type X;
```

the corresponding representation is given in Figure 3.21.

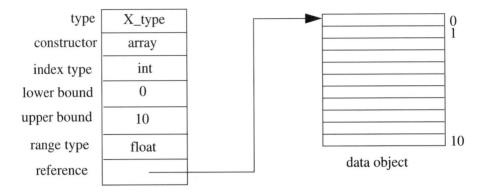

FIGURE 3.21 Representation of a finite mapping

A reference to X[I] is computed as an offset from the address A_X of the first location of the array. Let the domain type be the integer subrange M..N. Let K be the number of words occupied by each element of the array (this is known from the type of the range, but might be stored in the descriptor to avoid computing the value each time it is necessary). The offset to be evaluated for accessing A[I] is K(I - M).

In a statically typed language with arrays of statically known index bounds, the descriptor does not need to be saved at run time. The only exceptions are index bounds, which may be used to check at run time that the index value belongs to the stated range.

As we discussed in Chapter 2 (Section 2.6.5), in a language that supports dynamic arrays, the value of the array in the activation record is composed of two parts. The first part (often called *dope vector*) contains a reference to the data object (which, in general, can only be evaluated at run time) and the values of the bounds (to be used for index checking). The second part is the array itself, which is accessed indirectly through the dope vector.

3.6.2.3 Union and discriminated union

The representation of union types does not require any special new treatment. A variable of a union type has a descriptor that is a sequence of the descriptors of the component types. Instances of the values of the component types share the same storage area.

Discriminated union types are an extension of the Cartesian product. The variant record can be viewed as the conjunction of several fields plus a disjunction of fields, prefixed by the definition of a tag field. When the conjunction of fields is empty, we obtain a discriminated union. As an example, consider the following Pascal fragment. Since all variants share the same storage area, a variable Z of type Z_type can be represented as in Figure 3.22.

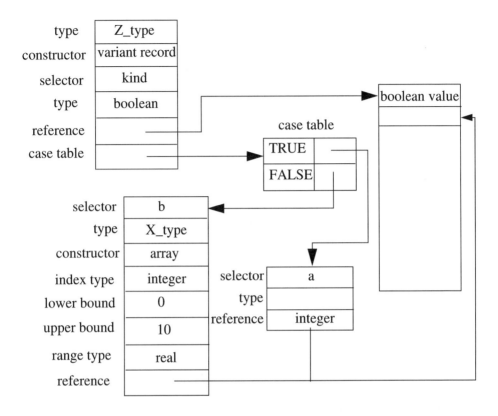

FIGURE 3.22 Representation of a discriminated union

Note that the various variants are accessible via a case table, according to the value of the tag field.

```
type X_type =  array [0..10] of real;
type Z_type =  record
                    case kind: boolean of
                        TRUE: (a: integer);
                        FALSE: (b: X_type)
               end
```

3.6.2.4 Powerset

Powersets can be implemented efficiently in terms of access time, manipulation time, and storage space, provided that a machine word has at least as many bits as there are potential members of the set (i.e., the cardinality of the base type). The presence of the i-th element of the base type in a certain set S is denoted by a "1" as the value of the i-th bit of the word associated with S. The empty set is represented by all zeros in the word. The union between sets is easily performed by an OR between the two associated words, and the intersection by an AND. If the machine does not allow bit-level access, test for membership requires shifting the required bit into an accessible word position (e.g., the sign bit) or using a mask. The existence of such an appealing representation for powersets is responsible for the implementation-defined limits on the cardinality of sets, which is normally equal to the size of a memory word.

3.6.2.5 Sequence

Sequences of elements of arbitrary length on a secondary storage are represented as files. File management is out of the scope of this book. Strings, as supported by many languages, are just arrays of characters. In other languages, such as SNOBOL4 and Algol 68, strings may vary arbitrarily in length, having no programmer-specified upper bound. This kind of array with dynamically changing size must be allocated in the heap (see Chapter 2, Section 2.5.2.6).

3.6.2.6 Classes

User-defined types specified via the simple class construct introduced in Section 3.3 are easy to represent as extensions of structures. The differences are:

1 Only public fields are visible outside the construct. Such fields must be tagged as public in the descriptor.
2 Some fields may be routines. It is thus necessary to be able to store routine signatures in descriptors.

The representation scheme presented in Section 3.6.2.1 can be extended easily to keep these new requirements into account. Since the code of the routines encapsulated in a class is shared by all class instances, routine fields are represented as pointers to the routines.

Objects that are instances of a new type defined by a class are treated as any other data object. Some languages allow the programmer to choose whether class-defined objects must be allocated on the stack or on the heap. For example, in C++, after class point is declared as in Figure 3.3, the following declarations are possible in some function f:

```
point x(1.3, 3.7);
point* p = new point(1.1, 0.0);
```

In the first case, x is a named variable that is allocated in f's activation record on the stack. In the second, p is allocated in f's activation record, while the data structure for the point is allocated on the heap. Heap management is discussed next.

3.6.2.7 Pointers and garbage collection

A pointer holds as a value the address of an object of the type bound to the pointer. Pointers usually can have a special null value (e.g., they have value nil in Pascal; they belong to type void in C and C++). To catch an inadvertent reference via a pointer with null value, such a null value can be represented by an address value that would cause a hardware-generated error trap. For example, the value might be an address beyond the physical addressing space into a protected area.

Pointer variables are allocated as any other variable in the activation record stack. Data objects that are allocated via the run-time allocation primitive new are allocated in the heap. Heap management is a crucial aspect of a programming language implementation. In fact, the free storage might quickly be exhausted unless there is some way of returning allocated storage to the free area.

The memory allocated to hold a heap object can be released for later reuse if the object is no longer accessible. Such an object is said to be *garbage*. Precisely, an object is said to be *accessible* if some variable in the stack points to it or, recursively, some accessible object points to it. An object is *garbage* if it is not accessible. There are two main aspects involved in heap management. One is the recognition that some portion of allocated memory is garbage; the other is to recycle such memory for new memory allocation requests issued by the user.

Garbage recognition often relies on the programmer, who is required to notify the system when a given object becomes useless. For example, in order to state that the object pointed by p is garbage, in C++ one would write delete(p) and in Pascal one would write dispose(p). As we mentioned, there is no guarantee that only objects that become unreferenced are defined as garbage: the correct use of delete (or dispose) is entirely the programmer's responsibility. Should the programmer inadvertently mark an object as garbage, the pointer to it becomes dangling.

Another strategy is to let the run-time system take care of discovering garbage by means of a suitable automatic *garbage collection* algorithm. Automatic garbage collection is vital for languages, such as LISP, that make heavy use of dynamically generated variables. In fact, garbage collection was invented for implementing the first LISP systems. Eiffel and Java, which uniformly treat all objects as referenced by pointers, provide an automatic garbage collector. Although the subject is usually treated in courses on data structures, we provide a brief and simplified view of possible strategies for automatic garbage collection here.

Garbage collection can be performed incrementally by using a *reference counting* scheme. Under such a scheme, each heap-allocated object is supposed to have an extra descriptor field, to store the current number of pointers to it. Whenever a pointer variable is deallocated from the stack, the reference count of the heap object it pointed to is decreased by 1. When the reference count becomes 0, the object is declared to be garbage, and the reference count of any objects pointed to is decreased by 1. This method thus releases an object as soon as it is found to become unreferenced. The problem with this method, however, is that it does not work for circular heap data structures (see Figure 3.23). If a pointer to the head of a circular list is deallocated, the nodes of the list are inaccessible, but they are not found to be garbage, because the reference count for each node is 1.

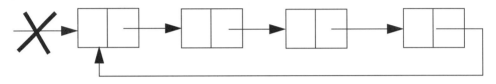

FIGURE 3.23   A circular heap data structure

A nonincremental strategy for automatic garbage collection consists of allocating free cells from the heap until the free space is exhausted. At that point the system enters a garbage collecting phase. We describe one such scheme under the simplifying assumption that

- The heap data objects have fixed size,
- It is known apriori which fields of a heap object contain pointers to other heap data objects, and
- It is possible to find all the pointers from the stack into the heap.

The following method for garbage collection allows all accessible heap data objects to be distinguished from garbage objects. To accomplish this, a working set of pointers T may be used. Initially, T contains the stack values that point into the heap. An element E is repeatedly extracted from T, the objects referenced by E are marked, and E is replaced by the pointers to the node(s) contained in E, if they are not marked. When T becomes empty, all accessible heap data objects have been marked. All other objects are garbage.

A number of variations have been proposed in the literature to make this garbage collection method more efficient. Its main problem, however, is that "useful" processing time is lost when the garbage collector is invoked. In an interactive system, this may be perceived by the programmer as an unexpected slow-down of the application, which occurs at unpredictable times. In a real-time system, this can be particularly dangerous, because an urgent request for service might arrive from the environment just after the garbage collector has started its rather complex activity. Garbage collection time is distributed more uniformly over processing time by using the reference-counting scheme, but unfortunately such a scheme works only partially. An appealing solution is based on a parallel execution scheme, where the garbage collector and the normal language processor execute in parallel.

Having discovered which heap data objects are garbage (either by explicit notification by the programmer or by running a garbage collector), one should decide how to recycle them by adding them to the free storage. One possibility is to link all free areas in a free list. In such a case, each block would contain at least two cells: one for the block size and one for the pointer to the next block. It is convenient to keep the list ordered by increasing block address, so that as a block is ready to be added to the list, it can be merged with possible adjacent blocks in the list. As a new storage area is to be allocated, the free list is searched for a matching block, according to some policy.

3.7 Bibliographic notes

The systematic view of data aggregates and the classification of type constructors presented in Section 3.2 is taken from a paper by C. A. R. Hoare in [Dahl72].

Programming language research in the 1970s emphasized the need for taming (or eliminating) insecure constructs, which can cause programs to be difficult to write and evaluate and therefore potentially unreliable. Several works concentrated on evaluating the type structure of existing languages to find insecurities. For example, [Welsh77] and [Tennent78] provide critical assessments of the original Pascal definition. Another research direction concentrated on new language constructs that could solve the insecurities that were found in existing languages. The work on Euclid [Lampson77] is a notable example of this research stream. Other language experiments emphasized the need to support program reliability through language constructs that favor modularity and information hiding. The concept of abstract data type was introduced, and languages such as CLU [Liskov81], [Liskov86] were designed and implemented to support program decomposition through abstract data types. CLU, as we mentioned, is based on the early seminal work on SIMULA 67 [Birtwistle73]. The SIMULA 67 experience, as well as the language experiments made in the 1970s, can be viewed as the origin of later developments both in the direction of modular languages (such as

Modula-2 and Ada) and object-oriented languages (e.g., C++, Smalltalk, Java, and Eiffel). More on these concepts will be discussed in Chapters 5 and 6.

Language experiments and developments have proceeded in parallel with more theoretical work that laid the semantic foundations of the concepts of type, subtype, polymorphism, strong typing, etc. We gave a cursory introduction to such work in Section 3.4. The interested reader should refer to [Cardelli85] for a deeper treatment of the subject. [Abadi96] is another good source for many of these concepts.

For a detailed understanding of the type systems of different languages, the reader should refer to the language manuals referenced in the Appendix "Language References." Implementation models for data objects are analyzed in the aforementioned paper by Hoare in [Dahl72] and in most compiler textbooks, such as [Aho86] and [Fischer91]. Garbage collection is surveyed in [Knuth69], [Cohen81], and [Wilson96]. It is also briefly discussed in most textbooks on data structures, such as [Wood93].

3.8 Exercises

1. List all the reasons you can find to justify why variables should be typed. Distinguish, where appropriate, between static and dynamic typing.
2. Discuss the possible strategies adopted by a programming language to bind a finite mapping to a specific finite domain (i.e., to bind an array to a specific size). Give examples of languages adopting each different strategy.
3. Show how a variant record type in Pascal or Ada can be used to define a binary tree of either integer or string values.
4. Write a short report illustrating how array manipulation facilities are richer in Ada than in Pascal (or C).
5. What is a dangling reference? How can it arise during execution? Why is it dangerous?
6. Consider the C++ class in Figure 3.4. What happens if the size of the array used to store the stack is exceeded by the push operation?
7. Add assertions to the Eiffel program in Figure 3.7. Discuss what happens when the length of the array is exceeded by a call to push, and what happens when pop is called for an empty stack.
8. Eiffel, unlike C, does not provide destructors. What does the language do when an object should be destroyed? When does this happen in Eiffel?
9. Define a C++ or an Eiffel implementation for a generic abstract data type defining a first-in/first-out queue, whose operations have the following signatures:

enqueue: fifo(T) x T → fifo(T)	adds an element to the queue
dequeue: fifo(T) → fifo(T) x T	extracts an element from the queue
length: fifo(T) → int	computes the length of the queue

10. Discuss the truth or falsity of the following statement and discuss its relevance: "A program can be unsafe and yet execute without type errors for all possible input data."

11. An index check verifies that the index of an array is in the bounds declared for the array. Can an index check be performed statically? Why? Why not?

12. What is a strong type system? Why is it useful?

13. Is a static type system strong? Conversely, is a strong type system static?

14. What kind of type compatibility does the typedef construct of C introduce?

15. In Section 3.4.4, we stated, "Unexpected difficulties, in particular, arise because of the interaction between coercions and overloading of operators and routines." Provide examples that justify this statement.

16. Define monomorphic and polymorphic type systems.

17. Compare genericity in Ada (or C++) and in ML. Which can be defined as an example of parametric polymorphism?

18. Check in the Pascal manual if procedures and functions can be overloaded.

19. Justify through examples the following statement on Pascal: "Since subtypes are defined by the language as new types, strong typing is not strictly enforced by the language."

20. In C++, what is the difference between assigning a value to a pointer and to a reference?

21. In C++, what is the difference between taking the address (via operator &) of a pointer and of a reference?

22. Figure 3.13, which describes the C++ type system, shows the existence of pointers to class members. Study the language manual and provide an example that shows the use of this feature.

23. In C++, each class has an associated default assignment operator that does a memberwise copy of the source to the target. But when a new object of class T is declared this way,

```
T x = y;
```

the copy constructor of x is used to construct x out of y. Why can the assignment operation not be used? What is the difference between assignment and copy construction?

24. C++ has a default assignment operation defined for classes. If the user does not define the assignment operation for a new class, the language uses a memberwise copy by default. Is this a good decision? When is memberwise copy desirable? (Hint: Consider a stack object implemented as an array and a stack object implemented as a linked list.)

25. In Eiffel, each object has a feature called copy that is used for assignment to the object. For example, a.copy(b) assigns the value of object b to a. What is the difference between

```
a.copy(b) and a := b?
```

26. Write a short report comparing variant records in Pascal, C++, and Ada.

27. Discuss how storage is allocated for class instances in C++ and Eiffel.

28. Justify or refute the following statement: "Ada attributes support program portability."

29. Following the schemes presented in Section 3.6, how can the following union variable X be represented?

```
type X_type is union Y_type, W_type;
type Y_type is float array[0..10];
type W_type is struct{
    float A;
    int B;
};
X_type X;
```

30. Instead of having only one free list for unused heap storage areas, one could keep several free lists, one for each object type. Discuss advantages and disadvantages of this alternative implementation.

31. Write a recursive algorithm to do the marking of all reachable heap objects, under the assumptions listed in Section 3.6.2.7.

32. Write a short report on potential policies for extracting a block from the heap free list as a new storage area needs to be allocated. In order to survey the possible solutions, you may refer to books on data structures.

33. The simplest possible reaction of the run-time system to a statement like dispose (in Pascal) is to ignore it. That is, storage is not freed for later reuse. How would you design an experiment to check what a language implementation actually does? Perform the experiment on an available implementation of Pascal.

34. Referring to the implementation schemes discussed in Section 3.6, write an abstract algorithm to perform structural type compatibility. (Hint: Be careful to avoid infinite loops in the algorithm.)

Structuring the
computation

C H A P T E R   4

This chapter is devoted to a detailed analysis of how computations are structured in a programming language in terms of the flow of control among the different components of a program. We start in Section 4.1 with a discussion of the elementary constituents of any program: expressions (which play a fundamental role in all programming languages, including functional and logic) and statements (which are typical of conventional statement-based languages). Our discussion will then focus primarily on conventional programming languages. We will first analyze *statement-level control structures* (Section 4.2), which describe how individual statements can be organized into various patterns of control flow to construct program units. Programs are often decomposed into units. For example, routines provide a way of hierarchically decomposing a program into units representing new complex operations. Once program units are constructed, it becomes necessary to structure the flow of computation among such units. We will address different kinds of *unit-level control structures* in Section 4.3 through Section 4.8.

The simplest kind of unit-level control regime is the *routine call* and *return* (Section 4.3). Another kind of control regime is *exception handling* (Section 4.4), which supports the ability to deal with anomalous situations that may arise, even asynchronously, as the program is being executed. Features supporting advanced control regimes are then introduced in Section 4.5 (*pattern matching*, which supports case-based analysis), Section 4.6 (*nondeterminism* and *backtracking*), and Section 4.7 (*event-driven* control structures). Such features are quite common in nonprocedural languages, such as

ML and PROLOG, and will in fact be taken up in the presentation of such languages in Chapters 7 and 8. Finally, Section 4.8 provides an introduction to the control structures needed for concurrent programming, where units execute largely independently.

4.1 Expressions and statements

Expressions define how a value can be obtained by combining other values with operators. The values from which expressions are evaluated either are denoted by a literal (e.g., 57.73) or are the r-value of a variable.

Operators appearing in an expression denote mathematical functions. They are characterized by their *arity* (i.e., the required number of operands) and are invoked using the function's signature. A unary operator is applied to only one operand. A binary operator is applied to two operands. In general, an n-ary operator is applied to n operands. For example, "–" can be used as a unary operator to transform, say, the value of a positive expression into a negative value. In general, however, it is used as a binary operator to subtract the value of one expression from the value of another expression. Functional routine invocations can be viewed as n-ary operators, where n is the number of parameters.

Regarding the operator's notation, one can distinguish between infix, prefix, and postfix. *Infix notation* is the most common notation for binary operators: the operator is written between its two operands, as in x + y. Postfix and prefix notations are common especially for nonbinary operators. In *prefix notation*, the operator appears first, and the operands follow. This is the conventional form of function invocation, where the function name denotes the operator. In *postfix notation* the operands appear first and are followed by the corresponding operator. Assuming that the arity of each operator is fixed and known, expressions in prefix and postfix forms may be written without resorting to parentheses to specify subexpressions that are to be evaluated first. For example, the infix expression

a * (b + c)

can be written in prefix form as

* a + b c

and in postfix form as

a b c + *

In C, the increment and decrement unary operators ++ and -- can be written both in prefix and in postfix notation. The semantics of the two forms, however, is different; that is, they denote two distinct operators. Both expressions ++k and k++ increment by 1 the value of k as a side effect. In the former case, the value of the expression is the value of k incremented by 1 (i.e., first the stored value of k is incremented, and then the new value of k is provided as the value of the expression). In the latter case, the value of the expression is the value of k before being incremented.

Infix notation is the most natural one to use for binary operators, since it allows programs to be written as conventional mathematical expressions. Although the programmer may use parentheses to explicitly group subexpressions that must be evaluated first, programming languages complicate matters by introducing their own conventions for operator associativity and precedence. Indeed, this is done to facilitate the programmer's task of writing expressions by reducing redundancy, but often this can cause confusion and make expressions less understandable, especially when switching from one language to another. For example, the convention adopted by most languages is such that

a + b * c

is interpreted implicitly as

a + (b * c)

i.e., multiplication has precedence over binary addition (as in standard mathematics). However, consider the Pascal expression

a = b < c

and the C expression

a == b < c

In Pascal, operators < and = have the same precedence, and the language specifies that application of operators with the same precedence proceeds left to right. The meaning of the above expression is that the result of the equality test (a=b), which is a boolean value, is compared with the value of c (which must be a boolean variable). In Pascal, FALSE is assumed to be less than TRUE, so the expression yields TRUE only if a is not equal to b, and c is TRUE; it yields FALSE in all other cases. For example, if a, b, and c are all FALSE, the expression yields FALSE.

In C, the operator "less than" (<) has higher precedence than "equal" (==). Thus, first b < c is evaluated. The result is then compared for equality with the value of a. For example, assuming a = b = c = false (represented in C as 0), the evaluation of the expression yields 1, which in C stands for true.

Some languages, such as C++ and Ada, allow programmer-defined operators. For example, having defined a new type Set, one can define the operators + for set union and – for set difference. Programmer-defined operators, as any other feature that causes overloading, can in some cases make programs easier to read, and in other cases make it harder. Readability is improved since the programmer is allowed to use familiar operators and the infix notation for newly defined types. The effect of this feature, however, is such that several actions happen behind the scenes when the program is processed. This is good whenever what happens behind the scenes matches the programmer's intuition; it is bad whenever the effects are obscure or counterintuitive to the programmer.

Some programming languages support conditional expressions, i.e., expressions that are composed of subexpressions, of which only one is to be evaluated, depending on the value of a condition. For example, in C one can write

```
(a > b) ? a : b
```

which could be written in a perhaps more conventional form as

```
if (a>b) a else b;
```

or in ML as

```
if a > b then a else b
```

to yield the larger of the values of a and b.

ML allows for more general conditional expressions to be written using the "case" constructor, as shown by the following simple example.

```
case x of
    1 => f1(y)
|   2 => f2(y)
|   _ => g(y)
```

In the example, the value yielded by the expression is f1(y) if x = 1, f2(y) if x = 2, and g(y) otherwise (the value "_" denotes a catch-all case not covered by any previous cases).

Functional programming languages are based heavily on expressions. In such languages, a program is itself an expression, defined by a function applied to operands, which may themselves be defined by functions applied to operands. Conventional languages, on the other hand, make the values of expressions visible as a modification of the computation's state, through assignment of expressions to variables. An *assignment statement*, such as x := y + z in Pascal, changes the state by associating a new r-value with x, computed as y + z. To evaluate the expression, the r-values of variables y and z are used. The result of the expression (an r-value) is then assigned to a memory location by using the l-value of x. Since the assignment changes the state of the computation, the statement that executes next operates in the new state. Often, the next statement to be executed is the one that textually follows the one that just completed its execution. This is the case of a *sequence* of statements, which is represented in C as

```
statement_1;
statement_2;
...
statement_n;
```

The sequence can be made into a *compound statement* by enclosing it between the pair of brackets { and }. In other languages, such as Pascal and Ada, the keywords begin and end are used instead of brackets.

In many conventional programming languages, such as Pascal, the distinction between assignment statements and expressions is sharp. In others, such as C, an assignment statement is just an expression with a side effect. The value returned by an assignment statement is the one that is stored in the left operand of the assignment operator "=". A typical example is given by the following loop, which reads successive input characters until the end of file is encountered:

```
while ((c = getchar()) != EOF);
    /* assigns the input character to c and yields the read value, which is compared
    to the end of file symbol */
    ...
```

Furthermore, in C the assignment operator associates from right to left. That is, the statement

```
a = b = c = 0;
```

is interpreted as

```
a = (b = (c = 0));
```

Many programming languages, such as Pascal, require the left-hand side of an assignment operator to be a simple denotation for an l-value. For example, it can be a variable name, an array element, or the cell pointed to by some variable. More generally, other languages, such as C, allow any expression yielding an l-value to appear on the left-hand side. Thus, it is possible to write the following kind of statement:

```
(p > q) ? *p : *q = 0;
```

which sets to zero the element pointed to by the larger of p and q.

As another example, one can write

```
*p++ = *q++;
```

The right-hand side expression yields the value pointed to by q. The left-hand side is an expression that provides the r-value of p, which is a reference, i.e., an l-value. So the overall effect is that the value of the object pointed to by q is copied into the object pointed to by p. Both pointers are also incremented as a side effect. Since the above assignment is an expression, the value of the expression is that of the object pointed to by q. For example, the following concise piece of code copies a sequence of integers terminated by zero pointed to by q into a sequence pointed to by p.

```
while ((*p++ = *q++) != 0) { };
```

Sequences, as shown before, are the simplest form of compound statements. Often, the syntax of the language requires each statement in a sequence to be separated from the next by a semicolon. For example, in Pascal a sequence can be written as

```
begin
    stat_1;
    stat_2;
    ...
    stat_n
end
```

Other languages instead require each statement to be terminated by a semicolon, and therefore do not need any special separator symbol. For example, in C we would write

```
{
    stat_1;
    stat_2:
    ...
    stat_n;
}
```

Although the choice between the two syntactic forms has no deep implications, pragmatically the latter can be more convenient, because one does not need to distinguish between the last statement of a sequence (which does not require the separator) and any other statements, since all are terminated by a semicolon.

4.2 Conditional execution and iteration

Programming languages provide different constructs to organize the flow of control among statements. We review them in this section, concentrating implicitly on conventional languages.

4.2.1 Conditional execution

Conditional execution of different statements can be specified in most languages by the *"if" statement*. Languages differ in several important syntactic details concerning the way such a construct is offered. Semantically, however, they are all alike. Syntactic details are not irrelevant: as we mentioned in Section 2.1, the syntactic appearance of a program may contribute to its readability, its ease of change, and, ultimately, its reliability.

Let us start with the example of the "if" statement as originally provided by ALGOL 60. Two forms are possible, as shown by the following examples:

```
if i = 0                        if i = 0
    then i := j;                    then i := j
                                    else  begin i := i + 1;
                                                j := j - 1
                                          end
```

In the first case, no alternative is specified for the case $i \neq 0$, and thus nothing happens if $i \neq 0$. In the latter, two alternatives are present. Since the case where $i \neq 0$ is described by a sequence, it must be made into a compound statement by bracketing it with **begin** and **end**.

The selection statement of ALGOL 60 raises a well-known ambiguity problem, illustrated by the following example:

```
if x > 0 then if x < 10 then x := 0 else x := 1000
```

It is unclear if the "else" alternative is part of the innermost conditional (**if** x < 10...) or the outermost conditional (**if** x > 0...). The execution of the above statement with x = 15 would assign 1000 to x under one interpretation, but leave it unchanged under the other. To eliminate ambiguity, ALGOL 60 requires an unconditional statement in the "then" branch of an "if" statement. Thus the above statement must be replaced by either

if x > 0 **then begin if** x < 10 **then** x := 0 **else** x := 1000 **end**

or

if x > 0 **then begin if** x < 10 **then** x := 0 **end else** x := 1000

The same problem is solved in C and Pascal by automatically matching an "else" branch to the closest conditional without an "else." Even though this rule removes ambiguity, nested "if" statements remain difficult to read, especially if the program is written without careful indentation (as shown above).

A syntactic variation that avoids this problem is adopted by Algol 68, Ada, and Modula-2, which use a special keyword as an enclosing final bracket of the "if" statement (**fi** in the case of Algol 68, **end if** in the case of Ada, and **end** in the case of Modula-2). Thus, the above examples would be coded in Modula-2 as

```
if i = 0
    then  i := j
    else  i := i + 1;
          j := j - 1
    end
```

and

if x > 0 **then if** x < 10 **then** x := 0 **else** x := 1000 **end end**

or

if x > 0 **then if** x < 10 **then** x := 0 **end else** x := 1000 **end**

depending on the desired interpretation.

Choosing among more than two alternatives using only "if-then-else" statements may lead to awkward constructions, such as

```
if a
    then S1
    else
```

```
if b
    then S2
    else
        if c
            then S3
            else S4
        end
    end
end
```

To solve this syntactic inconvenience, Modula-2 has an "else-if" construct that also serves as an end bracket for the previous "if." Thus the above fragment may be written as

```
if a
    then S1
else if b
    then S2
else if c
    then S3
else S4
end
```

Ada provides a similar abbreviation.

Most languages also provide an ad hoc construct to express multiple-choice selection. For example, C++ provides the switch construct, illustrated by the following fragment:

```
switch (operator) {
    case '+':
        result = operand1 + operand2;
        break;
    case '*':
        result = operand1 * operand2;
        break;
    case '-':
        result = operand1 - operand2;
        break;
    case '/':
        result = operand1 / operand2;
        break;
    default:
        break; //do nothing
};
```

Each branch is labeled by one (or more) constant values. Based on the value of the switch expression, the branch labeled by that value is selected. If the value of the switch expression does not match any of the labels, the (optional) default branch is executed. If the default branch is not present, no action takes place. In the above example, an explicit break statement is used to terminate each branch; otherwise execution would fall into the next branch.

The same example may be written in Ada as

```
case OPERATOR is
   when '+' =>     result := operand1 + operand2;
   when '*' =>     result := operand1 * operand2;
   when '-' =>     result := operand1 - operand2;
   when '/' =>     result := operand1 / operand2;
   when others => null;
end case
```

In Ada, after the selected branch is executed, the entire case statement terminates.

4.2.2 Iteration

Iteration constructs allow a number of actions to be executed repeatedly. Most programming languages provide different kinds of *loop constructs* to define an iteration of certain actions (called the *loop body*). Often, they distinguish between loops where the number of repetitions is known at the start of the loop and loops where the body is executed repeatedly as long as a condition is met. The former kind of loop is usually called a *"for" loop*; the latter is often called the *"while" loop*.

"For" loops are named after a common statement provided by languages of the Algol family. They define a *control variable*, which takes on all values of a given predefined sequence, one after the other. For each value, the loop body is executed.

Pascal allows iterations where control variables can be of any ordinal type: integer, boolean, character, enumeration, or subranges of them. A loop has the following general appearance:

```
for loop_ctr_var := lower_bound to upper_bound do statement
```

A control variable assumes all of its values from the lower to the upper bound. The language prescribes that the control variable and its lower and upper bounds must not be altered in the loop. The value of the control variable is also assumed to be undefined outside the loop.

As an example, consider the following fragment:

```
type day = (sun, mon, tue, wed, thu, fri, sat);
var week_day: day;
```

```
...
for week_day := mon to fri do...
```

As another example, let us consider how "for" loops can be written in C++ by examining the following fragment, where the loop body is executed for all values of i from 0 to 9:

```
for (int i = 0; i < 10; i++) {...}
```

The control part of the statement is clearly composed of three parts: an initialization and two expressions. The initialization provides the initial state for the loop execution. The first of the two expressions specifies a test, made before each iteration, which causes the loop to be exited if the expression becomes zero (i.e., false). The second expression specifies the incrementing that is performed after each iteration. In the example, the statement also declares a variable i. This variable's scope extends to the end of the block enclosing the "for" statement.

In C++, the initialization and the expressions in a "for" loop can be omitted. For example, an endless loop can be written as

```
for ( ; ; ) {...}
```

"While" loops are also named after a common statement provided by languages of the Algol family. "While" loops describe any number of iterations of the loop body, including zero. They have the following general form:

```
while condition do statement
```

For example, the following Pascal fragment describes the evaluation of the greatest common divisor of two variables a and b using Euclid's algorithm:

```
while a ≠ b do
   begin
      if a > b then
         a := a - b
      else
         b := b - a
   end
```

The loop condition (a ≠ b) is evaluated before execution of the body of the loop. The loop is exited if a is equal to b, since in this case a is the greatest common divisor. Therefore, the program works also when it is executed in the special case where the initial values of the two variables are equal.

In C++, "while" statements are similar. The general form is:

```
while (expression) statement
```

Another way to write an endless loop in C++ is therefore

```
while (1) {...}
```

Often, languages provide another, similar kind of loop, where the loop control variable is checked at the end of the body (i.e., the loop body is executed at least once). In Pascal, the construct has the following general form:

```
repeat
    statement
until condition
```

In a Pascal "repeat" loop, the body is iterated as long as the condition evaluates to false. When it becomes true, the loop terminates.

C++ provides a "do-while" statement that behaves in a similar way:

```
do statement while (expression);
```

In this case the statement is executed repeatedly until the value of the expression becomes zero (i.e., the condition is false).

Ada has only one general loop structure, with the following form:

```
Iteration_Specification loop
    Loop_Body
end loop;
```

where Iteration_Specification is either

```
while Condition
```

or

```
for Counting_Var in Discrete_Range
```

or

```
for Counting_Var in reverse Discrete_Range
```

An example is provided by the following fragment:

```
for K in Index_Range while A(K) /= 0 loop
    B(K) := B(K) / A(K);
end loop;
```

Endless loops are easy to write since Iteration_Specification is optional. In addition, loops can be terminated by an unconditional exit statement,

exit;

or by a conditional exit statement,

exit when Condition;

If the loop is nested within other loops, it is possible to exit an inner loop and any number of enclosing loops.

```
Main_Loop:
   loop
      ...
      loop
         ...
         exit Main_Loop when A = 0;
         ...
      end loop;
      ...
   end loop Main_Loop;
   -- after the exit statement execution continues here
```

In the example, control is transferred to the statement following the end of Main_Loop when A is found to be equal to zero in the inner loop. The exit statement is used to effect a premature termination of a loop.

C++ provides a break statement which causes termination of the smallest enclosing loop and passes control to the point following the terminated loop statement. It also provides a continue statement, which causes the termination of the current iteration of a loop and continuation from the next iteration (if there is one). A continue statement can appear in any kind of loop ("for" loop and both kinds of "while" loops).

In some cases, it is useful to allow the programmer to define a mechanism to step through the elements of a given collection. To do so, a programming language might provide support for user-defined control structures, in much the same way as it provides support for user-defined types and operations. For example, having defined a set, the programmer might need to step through all elements in the set. User-defined control structures that sequence through elements of user-defined collections are sometimes called *iterators*. Languages providing constructs for the implementation of abstract data types allow iterators to be defined naturally. For example, in C++ let the generic "collection of elements of type T" be defined by a template. To define an iterator, we can design three operations that are exported by the template:

start(), which initializes the loop by positioning a cursor on the first element of the collection (if any); more(), which yields true if there are elements left to examine in the collection; and next(), which yields the current element and positions the cursor on the next element of the collection (if any). A typical iteration on an instantiated collection X of elements of type T would be

```
T y;
... ;
X.start();
while (X.more()) {
    y = X.next();
    ... // manipulate y
};
```

This solution works for user-defined types, provided they define the operations start, more, and next. It does not work for collections defined by built-in constructors (such as arrays), for which these operations are not defined. In Chapter 5, we will see a more general way of defining iterators that work for any kinds of collections.

4.3 Routines

A routine is a program decomposition mechanism that allows programs to be broken into several units. Routine calls are control structures that govern the flow of control among these program units. The relationships among routines defined by calls are asymmetric: the caller transfers control to the callee by naming it explicitly, and the callee transfers control back to the caller without naming it. The unit to which control is transferred when a routine R terminates is always the one that was executing immediately before R. Routines are used to define abstract operations. Most modern languages allow such abstract operations to be defined recursively. Moreover, many such languages allow generic operations to be defined.

Chapter 2 presented the basic run-time modeling issues of routine activation, return, and parameter passing. In this section we review how routines can be written in different languages and what style issues arise in properly structuring programs.

Most languages distinguish between two kinds of routines: procedures and functions. A *procedure* does not return a value: it is an abstract command that is called to effect some desired state change. The state may change because the values of some parameters transmitted to the procedure get modified, because some nonlocal variables are updated by the procedure, or because some actions are performed on the external environment (e.g., reading or writing). A *function* corresponds to its mathematical counterpart: its activation is supposed to return a value, which depends on the value of the transmitted parameters.

Pascal provides both procedures and functions. It allows formal parameters to be either by value or by reference. It also allows procedures and functions to be parameters, as shown by the following example of a procedure header:

procedure example(**var** x: T; y: Q; **function** f(z: R): integer);

In the example, x is a by-reference parameter of type T; y is a by-value parameter of type Q; f is a function parameter that takes one by-value parameter z of type R and returns an integer.

Ada provides both procedures and functions. Parameter passing mode is specified in the header of an Ada routine as either **in**, **out**, or **in out**. If the mode is not specified, **in** is assumed by default. A formal **in** parameter is a constant which only permits reading of the value of the corresponding actual parameter. A formal **in out** parameter is a variable and permits both reading and updating of the value of the associated actual parameter. A formal **out** parameter is a variable and permits updating of the value of the associated actual parameter. In the implementation, parameters are passed either by copy or by reference. Except for cases that are explicitly stated in the language standard, it is left to the implementation to choose whether a parameter should be passed by reference or by copy. As we discussed in Section 2.7.7, in the presence of aliasing, the two implementations may produce different results. In such a case, Ada defines the program to be *erroneous*, but, unfortunately, the error can only be discovered at run time.

In C all routines are functional, i.e., they return a value, unless the return type is void, which states explicitly that no value is returned. Parameters can only be passed by value. It is possible, however, to achieve the effect of call by reference through the use of pointers. For example, the routine

```
void proc(int* x, int y);
{
    *x = *x + y;
}
```

increments the object referenced by x by the value of y. If we call proc as follows,

```
proc(&a, b);  /* &a means the address of a */
```

x is initialized to point to a, and the routine increments a by the value of b.

C++ introduced a way of directly specifying call by reference. This frees the programmer from the lower-level use of pointers to simulate call by reference. The previous example would be written in C++ as follows.

```
void proc(int& x, int y);
{
    x = x + y;
}

proc(a, b); // no address operator is needed in the call
```

4.3.1 Style issues: Side effects and aliasing

In Section 2.5 we defined side effects as modifications of the nonlocal environment. Side effects are used principally to provide a method of communication among program units. Communication can be established through nonlocal variables. However, if the set of nonlocal variables used for this purpose is large and each unit has unrestricted access to such nonlocal variables, the program becomes difficult to read, understand, and modify. Each unit can potentially reference and update every variable in the nonlocal environment, perhaps in ways not intended for the variable. The problem is that once a global variable is used for communication, it is difficult to distinguish between desired and undesired side effects. For example, if unit u1 calls u2 and u2 inadvertently modifies a nonlocal variable x used for communication between units u3 and u4, the invocation of u2 produces an undesired side effect. Such errors are difficult to find and remove because the symptoms are not easily traced to the cause of the error. (Note that a simple typographical error could lead to this problem.) Another difficulty is that examination of the call instruction alone does not reveal the variables that can be affected by the call. This reduces the readability of programs because, in general, the entire called unit must be scanned to understand the effect of a call.

Communication via unrestricted access to nonlocal variables is particularly dangerous when the program is large and composed of several units that have been developed independently by several programmers. One way to reduce these difficulties is to use parameters as the only means of communication among units. The overhead caused by parameter passing is almost always tolerable, except for critical applications whose response times must be within severe bounds. Alternatively, it must be possible to restrict the set of nonlocal variables held in common by two units to exactly those needed for the communication between the units. Also, it can be useful to specify that a unit can read but not modify some variable.

The modification of an actual parameter that is passed by reference to a routine is also a side effect, which may produce undesired results. The same problem arises with call by name. A more substantial source of obscurity in call by name is that each assignment to the same formal parameter can affect different locations in the environment of the calling unit. Such problems do not arise in call by copy.

Languages that distinguish between functions and procedures suggest a programming style in which the use of side effects should be restricted to procedures: this should be the way a procedure sends results back to the caller. Side effects should not be used in functions. In fact, functions are invoked as constituents of expressions, as in

```
v := x+ f(x, y) + z
```

In the presence of side effects—in Pascal, for example—the call to f might produce a change to x or y (if they are passed by reference) or even z (if z is global to the function) as a side effect. This reduces the readability of the program, since a reader expects a function to behave like a mathematical function. Also, one cannot rely on the commutativity of addition in general. In the example, if f modifies x as a side effect, the value produced for v is different if x is evaluated before or after calling f.

Besides affecting readability, side effects can prevent the compiler from generating optimized code for the evaluation of certain expressions. In the example

```
u := x+ z+ f(x, y) + f(x, y) + x+ z
```

the compiler cannot evaluate function f and subexpression x+ z just once and reuse their values later in the expression.

Ada prohibits such undesirable side effects on function parameters, by allowing only **in** formal parameters for functions.

In Chapter 2 we defined two variables as *aliases* if they denote (*share*) the same data object in a unit activation. A modification of the data object under one variable name is automatically visible through its aliases. An example is provided by the FORTRAN EQUIVALENCE statement. For instance, the statements

```
EQUIVALENCE(A, B)
A = 5.4
```

bind the same data object to A and B and set its value to 5.4. Consequently, the statements

```
B = 5.7
WRITE (6, 10) A
```

print 5.7, even though the value explicitly assigned to A was 5.4. The assignment to B affects both A and B.

As we observed in Section 2.7.7, aliasing may arise during the execution
of a procedure when parameters are passed by reference. Consider the following C++ procedure, which is supposed to interchange the values of two integer variables without using any local variables.

```
void swap(int& x, int& y) {
    x = x + y;
    y = x - y;
    x = x - y;
}
```

Before proceeding, examine the procedure and decide whether it works
properly.

The answer is "generally yes"; in fact, the procedure works properly
except when the two actual parameters are the same variable, as in the call

```
swap(a, a);
```

In this case, the procedure sets a to 0, because x and y become aliases and thus
any assignments to x and y within the procedure affect the same location. The
same problem may arise from the call

```
swap(b[i], b[j]);
```

when the index variables i and j happen to be equal.

Pointers can cause the same problem. For example, the call

```
swap(*p, *q)
```

does not interchange the values pointed at by p and q if p and q happen to
point to the same data object.

The above cases of aliasing occur because of the following two conditions.

- Formal and actual parameters share the same data objects; and
- Procedure calls have overlapping actual parameters.

Aliasing also may occur when a formal (by-reference) parameter and a
global variable denote the same or overlapping data objects. For example, if
procedure swap is rewritten as

```
void swap(int& x) {
    x = x + a;
    a = x - a;
    x = x - a;
}
```

where a is a global variable, the call

```
swap(a)
```

generates an incorrect result, because of the aliasing between x and a. Aliasing does not arise if parameters are passed by value-result; such parameters act as local variables within the procedure and the corresponding actual parameters become affected only at procedure exit. This is the basis for the semantic difference between call by reference and call by value-result.

The disadvantages of aliasing affect programmers, readers, and language implementers. Subprograms can become hard to understand because, occasionally, different names denote the same data object. This problem cannot be discovered by inspecting the subprogram: rather, discovery requires examining all the units that may invoke the subprogram. As a consequence of aliasing, a subprogram call may produce unexpected and incorrect results.

Aliasing also impairs the possibility of generating optimized code. For example, in the case

```
a := (x - y * z) + w;
b := (x - y * z) + u;
```

the subexpression x - y * z cannot be evaluated just once and the result used in the two assignments if a is an alias for x, y, or z.

Although side effects and aliasing can cause difficulties and insecurities, programmers using conventional languages must learn how to live with them. In fact, it is not possible to eliminate from a language all features that can cause side effects and aliasing, such as pointers, reference parameters, global variables, and arrays. This would leave us with a very lean and impractical language. The Java language took a major step by not supporting pointers, thus removing a major cause of aliasing and side effects. Other approaches have been taken in experimental languages (such as Euclid—see sidebar on page 192), but they did not become practically accepted.

Euclid

Euclid restricts the use of such features as pointers, reference parameters, global variables, and arrays to rule out the possibility of aliasing. For reference parameters, the problem arises if actual parameters are overlapping. If the actual parameters are simple variables, it is necessary to ensure that they are all distinct. Thus the call p(a, a) is considered illegal. Passing an array and one of its components (e.g., p(b[1], b)) is also prohibited. These forms of illegal aliasing can be caught statically. However, the call p(b[i], b[j]) causes aliasing only if i is equal to j. In such a case the compiler generates the *legality assertion* i ≠ j. Legality assertions can either be checked at run time or they can be proven with the aid of a program verifier.

To detect aliasing caused by pointers, Euclid introduces the notion of a *collection*. Dynamically allocated objects must be declared to belong to a collection, and pointers are allowed to point to the data in only one collection. Pointer assignment is legal only if the two pointers point into the same collection. Detecting illegal aliasing between pointers caused by procedure calls is now similar to the case of arrays. In fact, a collection C and a pointer bound to C are similar to an array and a variable used as an index. Dereferencing is exactly like indexing within an array. For example, if p and q point into the same collection, and *p and *q are both passed, the nonoverlapping rule requires the test p ≠ q to be produced as a legality assertion.

Aliasing also can occur between global variables and formal parameters of a routine. In Euclid, global variables must be explicitly imported by a routine if they are needed, and they must be accessible in every scope from which the routine is called. For each imported variable, it is also necessary to indicate whether it can be read or written or both. Thus, modifiable global variables can be treated by the aliasing detection algorithm as implicit additional parameters passed by reference. In addition, Euclid functions are not allowed to have by-reference parameters and can import only read-only variables. Thus, they cannot cause side effects.

An important consequence of disallowing aliasing in routines is that passing parameters by reference is equivalent to passing them by value-result. Therefore, the choice of how to implement parameter passing can be made by the translator based exclusively on efficiency considerations.

4.4 Exceptions

Programmers often write programs under the optimistic assumption that nothing will go wrong when the program executes. Unfortunately, there are many factors that may invalidate this assumption. For example, it may happen that under certain conditions an array is indexed with a value that exceeds the declared bounds. An arithmetic expression may cause a division by zero, or the square root operation may be executed with a negative argument. A request for new memory allocation issued by the run-time system might exceed the amount of storage available for the program execution. Or, finally, an embedded application might receive a message from an external sensor that overrides a previously received message, before the old message has been handled by the program.

When they enter an erroneous state, programs often fail unexpectedly, maybe simply displaying some obscure message. This behavior is unacceptable in many situations. To improve reliability, it is necessary that such erroneous conditions can be recognized by the program, and certain actions are executed in response to the error. Conventional control structures, however, are simply inadequate to do that. For example, to check that an index never exceeds the array bounds, one would need to explicitly test the value of the index before any indexing takes place and insert appropriate response code in case the bounds are violated. Alternatively, one would like the run-time machine to be able to trap such anomalous conditions, and let the programmer program the response to the condition. This would be more efficient under the assumption that array bounds violations are the exceptional case.

To cope with this problem, programming languages provide features for exception handling. According to the standard terminology, an *exception* denotes an undesirable, anomalous behavior that supposedly occurs rarely. The language can provide facilities to define exceptions, recognize their occurrence, and specify the response code (*exception handler*) that must be executed when the exception occurs.

Exceptions have a wider meaning than merely computational errors. They refer to any kind of anomalous behavior that, intuitively and informally, corresponds to a deviation from the expected course of actions, as envisioned by the programmer. The concept of "deviation" cannot be stated in absolute and rigorous terms. It represents a design decision taken by the programmer, who decides that certain states are "normal" and "expected," whereas others are "anomalous." Thus, the occurrence of an exception does not necessarily mean that we are facing a catastrophic error. It simply means that the unit being executed is unable to proceed in a manner that leads to its normal termination as specified by the programmer. For example, consider a control system that processes input messages defined by a given protocol. The normal course of action consists of parsing the input message and performing some actions that depend on its contents. The arrival of a message which does not match the expected syntax might be considered an exception to be handled by an *exception handler*, a clearly identifiable piece of code that is separate from the rest of the program that is responsible for the normal case.

Earlier programming languages (except PL/I) offered no special help in properly handling exceptional conditions. Most modern languages, however, provide systematic exception-handling features. With these features, the concern for anomalies may be moved out of the main line of program flow, so as not to obscure the basic algorithm.

To define exception handling, the following main decisions must be taken by a programming language designer:

1 What are the exceptions that can be handled? How can they be defined?
2 What units can raise an exception and how?
3 How and where can a handler be defined?
4 How is the binding between an exception and its handler defined and how does control flow from a raised exception to its handler?
5 Where does control flow after an exception has been handled?

The answers provided to such questions, which can differ from language to language, affect the semantics of exception handling, its usability, and its ease of implementation. In the following, we will analyze the solutions provided by Ada, C++, Java, Eiffel, and ML. The exception-handling facilities of PL/I and CLU are presented in sidebars on page 202 and on page 203.

4.4.1 Exception handling in Ada

Ada provides a set of four predefined exceptions that can be automatically trapped and raised by the underlying run-time machine:

- Constraint_Error: failure of a run-time check on a constraint, such as array index out of bounds, zero right operand of a division, etc.
- Program_Error: failure of a run-time check on a language rule. For example, a function is required to complete normally by executing a return statement that transmits a result back to the caller. If this does not happen, the exception is raised.
- Storage_Error: failure of a run-time check on memory availability; for example, it may be raised by invocation of new.
- Tasking_Error: failure of a run-time check on the task system (see Section 4.8).

A program unit can declare new exceptions such as

Help: **exception**;

A unit that has visibility to Help may raise it explicitly as

raise Help;

Once raised, built-in and programmer-defined exceptions behave in exactly the same way. Exception handlers can be attached to a subprogram body, a package body, or a block, after the keyword **exception**. For example,

```
begin --this is a block with exception handlers
    ... statements ...
    exception   when Help =>handler for exception Help;
                when Constraint_Error => handler for exception
                    Constraint_Error, which might be raised by a
                    division by zero;
                when others => handler for any other exception that is neither
                    Help nor Constraint_Error;
end;
```

In the example, a list of handlers is attached to the block. The list is prefixed by the keyword **exception** and each handler is prefixed by the keyword **when**.

If the unit that raises the exception provides a handler for it, control is transferred immediately to that handler: the actions following the point at which the exception is raised are skipped, the handler is executed, and then the program continues execution as if the unit that raised the exception had completed normally, that is, from the point after **end** of the block. If the currently executing unit U does not provide a handler, the unit terminates and the exception is *propagated*. Propagation means that the exception is reraised in another context. The precise effect of propagation depends on the kind of unit U that raises the exception:

- If U is a block, its termination reraises the exception in the immediately enclosing unit.
- If U is a procedure, its termination causes the routine to return to the caller and the exception to be reraised at the point of call.
- If U is a package body (see Section 5.3.4), its termination causes the exception to be reraised in the unit that contains the package declaration.
- If U is a task body (see Section 4.8), the exception is not propagated further; that is, the task terminates abnormally.

In general, if a propagated exception is not handled at the point to which it was transferred, it is further propagated, and propagation might eventually lead to the end of the program. If a handler is found for an exception, it is executed and further processing proceeds from the statement that follows the handler textually. Exceptions can also be explicitly reraised via the statement **raise**. For example, an exception handler that can handle the exception partially might perform some recovery actions and then explicitly reraise the exception.

As an example, consider the program sketched in Figure 4.1. The figure shows the overall structure of the program, ignoring all internal details. In particular, the scope defined by procedures is shown by using solid lines, while blocks' scopes are shown by dashed lines. Suppose that the following sequence of unit activations occurs:

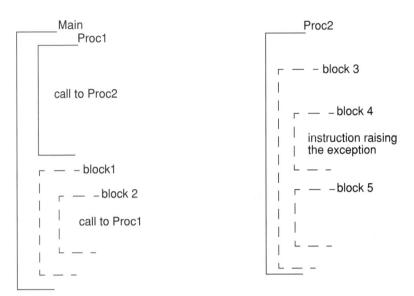

FIGURE 4.1 An example of an Ada program that raises an exception

- Main is activated
- block 1 is entered
- block 2 is entered
- Proc1 is called
- Proc2 is called
- block 3 is entered
- block 4 is entered

If an exception is raised at this point, execution of block 4 is abandoned and a check is performed to see if the block provides an exception handler for the exception. If a handler is found, the handler is executed and, if no further exceptions are raised, execution continues from the statements that follow block 4. If not, the exception is propagated to the enclosing block 3. That is, execution of block 3 is abandoned, and a check for an exception handler provided by block 3 is performed. If a handler is located, it is executed and further processing continues normally in the body of procedure Proc2. If not, the exception is propagated to the body of Proc2, which may or may not provide a handler. If it provides a handler, Proc2 returns normally to its caller after the handler is executed. If not, the exception is propagated to the caller. If no exception handlers are provided by procedure Proc1, block 2, block1, and by Main, eventually the program terminates abnormally.

To provide an implementation model of Ada's exception handling in SIM-PLESEM, each declared exception (including built-in ones) can be bound to an internal exception name at compile time. The internal exception name should distinguish between two identically named exceptions in different scopes. At run time, the binding between an exception raised by a unit and the corresponding handler is dynamic and follows the chain of unit activations. A possible implementation consists of having in each activation record a fixed-contents *handler table*, which contains the descriptors of all the handlers that appear in the unit. (For simplicity, let us assume an implementation model of blocks that allocates a new activation record on the stack as the block is entered—see Section 2.7.4.) Each descriptor in the table contains

1 The internal exception name handled by the handler.
2 A pointer to the handler body.

When an exception is raised, its internal exception name is used to search for a handler in the handler table. If it is found there, control is transferred to its body. If not, the activation record is deleted from the stack, and the search is continued in the caller's handler table.

By unwinding the dynamic chain in the propagation process, an exception can be propagated outside its scope. In such a case, it can only be handled by a catch-all handler (**when others** …). The static scope rules of the language ensure that it cannot be handled by any other locally declared exception that, by coincidence, has the same name. The implementation scheme sketched above ensures this by giving them different internal exception names.

4.4.2 Exception handling in C++

In C++, exceptions either may be generated by the run-time environment (e.g., due to a division by zero) or raised explicitly by the program. An exception is raised by a throw instruction, which transfers an object to the corresponding handler. A handler may be attached to any piece of code (a block) that needs to handle faults. To do so, the block must be prefixed by the keyword try. As an example, consider the simple case in Figure 4.2.

Suppose that the try block in Figure 4.2 contains the statement

```
throw Help(MSG1);
```

A throw expression causes the execution of the block to be abandoned and control to be transferred to the appropriate handler. In the example, Help(MSG1) actually invokes the constructor of class Help passing a parameter that is used by the constructor to initialize field kind. The temporary object so created is used to initialize the formal parameter msg of the matching catch, and control is then transferred to the first branch (case MSG1) of the switch in the first handler attached to the block.

```
class Help {...};
    // objects of this class have a public attribute "kind" of type enumeration,
    // describing the kind of help requested, and other public fields which carry
    // specific information about the point in the program where help is requested
class Zerodivide {};
    // assume that objects of this class are generated by the run-time system
...
try {
    // fault tolerant block which may raise Help or Zerodivide exceptions
    ...
}
catch(Help msg) {
    // handles a Help request transmitted by object msg
    switch(msg.kind) {
        case MSG1:
            ...;
        case MSG2:
            ...;
        ...
    }
    ...
}
catch(Zerodivide) {
    // handles a division by 0
...
}
```

FIGURE 4.2 An example of exception handling in C++

The above block might call routines that may, in turn, raise exceptions. If one such routine raises, say, a Help request and does not provide a handler for it, the routine's execution is abandoned and the exception is propagated to the point of call within the block. Execution of the block is, in turn, abandoned, and control is transferred to the handler as in the previous case. In other words, C++, like Ada, propagates unhandled exceptions. Like Ada, a caught exception can be propagated explicitly by simply saying throw. Also, as in Ada, after a handler is executed, execution continues as if the unit to which the handler is attached had completed normally.

Unlike Ada, any amount of information can be transmitted with an exception. To raise an exception, in fact, one can throw an object, which contains data that can be used by the handler. For example, in the previous example, a help request was signaled by providing an object that contained specific information on the kind of help requested. If the data in the thrown object are not used by the handler, the catch statement can simply specify a type without naming an object. This happens in our example for the division by zero.

C++ routines may list in their interface the exception they may raise. This feature allows a programmer to state the intent of a routine in a precise way, by specifying both the expected normal behavior (the data it can accept and return) and its exceptional behaviors. For example,

```
void foo() throw(Help, Zerodivide);
```

might be the interface of a function foo that is called within the above fault-tolerant block. Knowing that the used function foo may raise exceptions, the client code may guard against anomalous behaviors by providing appropriate exception handling facilities, as we did.

What happens if foo terminates by raising another exception that is not listed in its interface? This might happen, for example, because an error other than a division by zero is caught by the run-time machine (e.g., an underflow). In such a case, there is no propagation: A special function unexpected() is called automatically. The default behavior of unexpected(), which may be redefined by the programmer, eventually causes abort() to be called, which terminates the program execution.

The list of possible exceptions raised by a routine, however, is not required to be stated in the routine interface. If no list is provided, it means that any possible exception can be propagated. Instead, if the empty list throw() is provided, this means that no exception is propagated by the routine.

If an exception is repeatedly propagated and no matching handler is ever found, the special function terminate() is called automatically. Its default behavior, which can be redefined by the programmer, eventually aborts the program execution.

Since the exceptions that can be raised in C++ are expressions of a given type, one can use the general facilities available to structure types (and abstract data types) to organize exceptions. For instance, one can use enumerations to structure and classify exceptions in groups. In the previous examples, if only the specific kind of needed help must be provided to handle exceptions of type Help, the following definition would suffice,

```
enum Help {MSG1, MSG2, ...};
```

and the corresponding catch statement would be rewritten as

```
catch(Help msg) {
    switch(msg) {
        case MSG1:
            ...;
```

```
        case MSG2:
            ...;
        ...
    }
    ...
}
```

Other interesting ways of organizing exceptions can be achieved by organizing the corresponding classes according to subtype hierarchies, by means of subclasses (see Section 6.1.2).

Intuitively, an abstract implementation of the C++ mechanism can be similar to what we outlined for Ada. When an exception is raised, the dynamic chain is unwound until the appropriate handler is found. Further comments will be provided in Section 4.4.6.

4.4.3 Exception handling in Java

As in C++, Java exceptions are objects that can be thrown and caught by handlers attached to blocks. The main differences introduced by Java are

1 All exceptions that can be thrown explicitly by a routine—other than the exceptions RuntimeException and Error, which may be raised by the run-time support—must be listed in the routine's interface, for example,

```
void foo() throws Help;
```

The rationale is that users of the routine need to know which exceptions the routine may throw so that they can properly react in their code by

  – catching the exception and handling it, or
  – catching the exception and mapping it into one of their throwable exceptions, or
  – listing the exception in their declaration and letting the exception propagate.

2 A fault-tolerant block that can handle exceptions is called a *"try" block*. "Try" blocks have the following form:

```
try
    block;
catch(exception_type_1)
    handler_1;
    ...
catch(exception_type_n)
    handler_n;
finally
    final_block;
```

The section final_block, if present, performs any needed finalization actions. It is always executed at the end of the "try" block, whether an exception is thrown or not, unless the "try" block raises an exception that is not caught by its handlers, in which case the exception is propagated.

4.4.4 Exception handling in Eiffel

The features provided by Eiffel to support exception handling have been influenced strongly by a set of underlying software design principles that programmers should follow. A key notion of such design principles is called the *contract*. Each software component has obligations with respect to other components, since such components may rely on it to provide their own services. Syntactically, such obligations are described by the interface of the component (a class), i.e., by the features exported to the other classes. Semantically, they are specified by the preconditions and postconditions of all exported routines and by the invariant condition. Once the program compiles correctly, syntactic obligations are guaranteed to hold. What may happen, however, is that semantic obligations are not fulfilled during execution. This is how exceptions occur in Eiffel.

Thus, exceptions are raised in Eiffel because an assertion is violated (assuming that the program has been compiled under the option that sets run-time checking on). They can also arise because of anomalous states caught by the underlying abstract machine (memory exhausted, dereferencing an uninitialized pointer, etc.). Finally, they can arise because a called routine terminates signaling a failure (see below for what this means).

To respond to an exception, an exception handler (rescue clause) may be attached to any routine. There are two possible approaches to exception handling, which comply with the contract-based methodology underlying Eiffel programming. The first approach is called *organized panic*. Following this approach, the routine raising the exception fails; that is, as an exception is raised, the routine's execution is abandoned, and control is transferred to the corresponding rescue clause, if any. The handler performs some cleanup of the object's state and then terminates signaling failure. The cleanup should leave the object in a consistent state; i.e., the invariant should be true when the handler terminates. If no rescue clause is attached to the routine, it is as if a rescue clause with an empty list of cleanup statements were attached to it. When a routine terminates by signaling a failure, an exception is propagated to the caller. Thus, if all exceptions are handled according to organized panic, all routines eventually fail; that is, any failure causes an orderly shutdown of the executing program. As an example, consider the abstract data type NON_AXIAL_INT_POINT that was defined in Figure 3.6 and suppose that the program is compiled with the option "check assertion" on. If any of the operations is called by a client module with parameters that do not satisfy the corresponding precondition (e.g., one of the parameters of make_point is zero), control is transferred to the implicit empty rescue clause that is attached to all

Exception handling in PL/I

PL/I was the first language to introduce exception handling. Exceptions are called CONDITIONS. Exception handlers are declared by ON statements: ON CONDITION (exception_name) exception_handler, where exception_handler can be a simple statement or a block. An exception is raised by the statement SIGNAL CONDITION (exception_name).

The language also defines a number of built-in exceptions and provides system-defined handlers for them. Built-in exceptions are automatically raised by the execution of some statements (e.g., ZERODIVIDE is raised when a divide by zero is attempted). The action performed by a system-provided handler is specified by the language. This action can be redefined, however, as with user-defined exceptions:

```
ON ZERODIVIDE BEGIN;
   ...
END;
```

Handlers are bound to exceptions dynamically. When an ON unit is encountered during execution, a new binding takes place between an exception and a handler. Such binding remains valid until it is overridden by the execution of another ON statement for the same exception, or until termination of the block in which the ON statement appears. If more than one ON statement for the same exception appears in the same block, each new binding overrides the previous one. When control exits a block, the bindings that existed prior to block entry are reestablished. When an exception is raised, the handler currently bound to the exception is executed as if it were a subprogram invoked explicitly at that point. Therefore, unless otherwise specified by the handler, control subsequently will return to the point that issued the SIGNAL.

Built-in exceptions can be explicitly *enabled* and *disabled*. Most built-in exceptions are enabled by default and bound to a predefined handler. Enabling an exception can be specified by prefixing a statement, block, or procedure with (exception_name). An enabled exception can be explicitly disabled by using the prefix (NO exception_name), for example,

```
(ZERODIVIDE): BEGIN          (NOZERODIVIDE): BEGIN
   ...                          ...
END;                         END;
```

---

exported operations. This causes propagation of the failure to the object that called the operation with improper arguments. To explain the reason for the failure to the programmer, one might attach rescue clauses to the routines of the class in Figure 3.6 that print out a message describing the reason for the failure, i.e., violation of the precondition.

An alternative approach to organized panic is called *retrial*. This means that the handler can find an alternative way to fulfill the object's contract. This is achieved by a statement retry that may appear in the rescue clause and would cause reexecution of the routine's body. In such a case, if reexecution

Exception handling in CLU

In CLU, exceptions can only be raised by procedures. That is, if a statement raises an exception, the procedure containing the statement returns abnormally by raising the exception. A procedure cannot handle an exception raised by its execution: its caller is responsible for handling it. The exceptions that a procedure may raise are to be declared in the procedure's header. As we saw, this choice was adopted by Java later. Its motivation is that the exceptions that an operation may raise are part of the definition of the operation's behavior, and thus should be known to the caller. Exceptions may be raised explicitly by means of a **signal** instruction. Built-in exceptions are raised automatically; for example, an exception is raised if the value of the denominator is zero in a division operation.

Exception handlers can be attached to statements by **except** clauses having the following syntactic form:

<statement> **except** *<handler_list>* **end**

where *<statement>* can be any (compound) statement of the language. If the execution of a procedure invocation within *<statement>* raises an exception, control is transferred to *<handler_list>*. A *<handler_list>* has the following form:

when *<exception_list_1>*: *<statement_1>*
...
when *<exception_list_n>*: *<statement_n>*

If the raised exception belongs to *<exception_list_i>*, then *<statement_i>* (the handler body) is executed. When the execution of the handler body is completed, control passes to the statement that follows the one to which the handler is attached. If *<statement_i>* contains a call to a unit, another exception may be raised. In such a case, control flows to the **except** statement that encloses *<statement>*. If the raised exception is not named in the exception list that should handle it, it is propagated to the enclosing statements. If no handler is found within the procedure that issued the call, the procedure implicitly signals a language-defined exception **failure** and returns.

does not raise an exception, the routine does not terminate with failure and the object's contract would be fulfilled. As an example, suppose that several methods are available to solve a specific task, so that if one of them fails, another can be tried instead; the task fails only if none of the available methods succeeds. This strategy can be described in Eiffel according to the scheme shown in Figure 4.3.

It is easy to verify that routine try_several_methods fails only if all possible methods fail. Otherwise, if one of the methods succeeds, the routine returns normally to its caller.

```
try_several_methods is
local
    i: INTEGER;
    --it is automatically initialized to 0
do
    try_method(i);
rescue
    i := i + 1;
    if i < max_trials then
        --max_trials is a constant
        retry
    end
end
```

FIGURE 4.3   A "retrial" strategy in Eiffel

4.4.5 Exception handling in ML

The functional language ML allows exceptions to be defined, raised, and handled. There are also exceptions that are predefined by the language and raised automatically by the run-time machine during program execution.

The following example shows the declaration of an exception,

```
exception Neg
```

which can be raised subsequently in the following function declaration:

```
fun fact(n) =
    if n < 0 then raise Neg
    else if n = 0 then 1
        else n * fact(n - 1)
```

A call such as fact(-2) would cause the evaluation of the function to be abandoned and the exception raised, and, since no handler is provided, the program will stop by writing the message "Failure: Neg."

Suppose we wish to handle the exception by returning 0 when the function is called with a negative argument. This can be done, for example, by defining the following new function:

```
fun fact_0(n) =
    fact(n) handle Neg => 0;
```

which uses fact as a subsidiary function.

Exceptions that are not handled in a chain of function calls are implicitly propagated. That is, suppose that function fact is called by some function f that does not provide a handler for Neg; function f is, in turn, called by function g, which provides a handler for Neg in the same way that function fact_0 does. In such a case, the evaluation of the expression

    g(f(fact(-33)))

yields 0.

4.4.6 A comparative evaluation

The languages we surveyed in the previous sections are representative of the different approaches followed by programming languages to provide exception handling. Although the field has matured in recent years and the main design decisions to be faced by language designers are now basically restricted to a limited number of choices, there are still differences and there is no consensus on a standard scheme that languages should adopt. The question is influenced by how software should be structured to handle exceptional conditions. We will compare and evaluate the different solutions adopted by existing languages by examining the questions we posed at the beginning of our discussion, that is,

1 What are the exceptions that can be handled? How can they be defined?
2 What units can raise an exception and how?
3 How and where can a handler be defined?
4 How is the binding between an exception and its handler defined and how does control flow from a raised exception to its handler?
5 Where does control flow after an exception has been handled?

Regarding questions 1 and 2, all languages (except Eiffel) are quite similar. They all allow both built-in and programmer-defined exceptions. The main differences are whether an exception can carry information and how it can do so. In Ada (and PL/I) an exception is basically a named signal, and thus it does not allow any additional information to be passed to the handler along with it. In C++ and Java any data may be passed along with the exception.[1]

The Eiffel approach to exception handling has been designed to fit a particular program development discipline. According to this discipline, an exception arises only if a routine fails because of some error. The language also explicitly and precisely defines what may cause a routine to fail. Thus, in most cases there is no need for naming exceptions or for providing a raise

---

1. Actually, in Ada it is possible to pass to the handler information about the exception occurrence, and a number of predefined operations are provided to extract some limited information from the exception occurrence.

statement. All that matters is whether a failure that would violate the object's contract occurred in a routine.[2]

Exception handlers in both Ada and C++ can be attached to any block. In Eiffel they can be attached to any routine. As an exception is raised, control is transferred to the appropriate handler. To match the raised exception with the corresponding handler, Ada and C++ unwind the run-time stack by following the dynamic chain until the relevant handler (if any) is found. In Eiffel, each routine provides its own handler (either explicitly or implicitly), and the stack is unwound only if the routine terminates and signals a failure.

The combination of static scope rules for exception declarations (adopted by languages Ada and C++) dynamic binding between an exception raised by some unit and its handler makes programs hard to read. We illustrate the point in the case of C++ in order to show how different language features may interfere with each other, thus making language semantics and language implementation more complex.

Consider two separate files that contain parts of a program (see Figure 4.4). If when f is called by foo the exception is thrown and not handled by f, propagation reaches the catch point in file F2. The scope rules of the language, however, are such that the parameter of the catch and the object thrown are bound to different types. Therefore, the match does not occur, and the exception is further propagated. In addition to understandability, ease and efficiency of the implementation are also affected. Suitable information, in fact, must be kept to perform the required run-time binding.

File F1	File F2
``class A {};
void f() {

    ...
    throw A();
    ...
}``` | ```extern void f();
class A {};
void foo() {

    ...
    try {
        ...
        f();
        ...
    }
    catch(A a) {
        ...
    }
}``` |

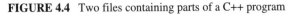

FIGURE 4.4 Two files containing parts of a C++ program

---

2. To provide finer control over the handling of exceptions, Eiffel also provides a kernel library class EXCEP-TIONS, through which exceptions may be named and raised explicitly.

The last important point about exception handling is where control should flow after an exception is handled. There are essentially two possible solutions, which correspond to different styles of handling exceptions: *termination* and *resumption*. The resumption scheme implies that the handler's code may cause control to return to the point where the exception was raised, whereas the termination scheme does not allow that. Of the languages discussed here, only PL/I fully supports the resumption scheme. Ada and C++ support termination. Although for many years the debate on termination versus resumption gave no clear indication of which approach is superior, termination has now gained wider acceptance. Practical experience with languages providing resumption has shown that the resumption mechanism is more error prone. Furthermore, it can promote the unsafe programming practice of removing the symptom of an error without removing the cause. For example, the exception raised for an unacceptable value of an operand could be handled by arbitrarily generating an acceptable value and then resuming the computation. CLU is even stricter than the other languages in that it does not allow the unit that raises an exception to try to handle it. Rather, the unit (a procedure) terminates abnormally and places the burden of handling the exception upon its caller. The caller expects the exception to be possibly raised, since it is listed in the called unit's interface definition.

Eiffel is different from other languages with respect to termination and resumption. Termination in Eiffel is stronger than in other languages. In fact, after control is transferred to a rescue clause that does not contain a retry, completion of the clause implies that the routine fails, and the failure is notified to the caller. In C++, on the other hand, if a catch clause terminates without raising another exception, execution continues normally from the statement that follows the one to which the currently completed handler is attached. Furthermore, Eiffel provides an explicit way of describing a disciplined form of resumption (retry). The retry statement provided by Eiffel does not fully correspond to the above definition of resumption, since the statement executed after the handler terminates is not the one that caused the exception. Rather, retry allows a routine that failed to be retried as a whole.

4.5 Pattern matching

Pattern matching is a high-level way of stating conditions based on which different actions are specified to occur. Pattern matching is the most important control structure of the string manipulation programming language SNOBOL4 (see the sidebar on page 209). Pattern matching is also provided by most modern functional programming languages (such as ML and

Miranda) and is also provided by the logical language PROLOG and by rule-based systems.

Let us start by discussing the following simple definitions of a data type and a function in ML:

```
datatype day = Mon | Tue | Wed | Thu | Fri | Sat | Sun
fun day_off (Sun) = true
   | day_off(Sat)= true
   | day_off ( _ ) = false
```

In the example, the function day_off is defined by a number of *cases*. Depending on the value of the parameter with which the function will be invoked, the appropriate case will be selected. Cases are checked sequentially, from the first one on. If the first two cases are not matched by the value of the parameter with which the function is called, the third alternative will be selected, since the so-called wild card "_" matches any argument.

As another example, consider the following function definition:

```
fun reverse(nil) = nil
   | reverse(head::tail) = reverse(tail) @ [head]
```

In this case, if the argument is an empty list, then reverse is defined to return the empty list. Otherwise, suppose that the argument is the list [1, 0, 5, 99, 2]. As a result of pattern matching [1, 0, 5, 99, 2] with head::tail, head is bound to 1 and tail is bound to [0, 5, 99, 2]. Thus the result of reverse is the concatenation (operator @) of reverse([0, 5, 99, 2]) with the list [1].

As a final example, suppose that a new operation to reverse lists is to be defined, such that a (sub)list remains unchanged if its first element is zero. The following function rev would do the job:

```
fun rev(nil) = nil
   | rev(0::tail) = [0] @ tail
   | rev(head::tail) = rev(tail) @ [head]
```

In this case, since pattern matching examines the various alternatives sequentially, if the function is invoked with a nonempty list whose first element is zero, the second alternative would be selected. Otherwise, for a nonempty list whose first element is not zero, the third alternative would be selected.

As the example shows, pattern matching has a twofold effect. On the one hand, it chooses the course of action based on the argument; on the other, since the pattern can be an expression with variables, it binds the variables in

Pattern matching in SNOBOL4

A *pattern* is a data structure that specifies a *set of strings*. A pattern is used in *pattern-matching statements* to examine a subject string for the presence of a pattern. For example, the statement

```
MESSAGE PAT
```

means "search the string MESSAGE for the occurrence of the pattern PAT." If, previous to this statement, we had executed the two assignment statements

```
MESSAGE = 'THERE ARE NO ERRORS HERE'
PAT = 'ERROR'
```

then the above pattern-matching statement would have succeeded. The notion of success and failure of statements is used in SNOBOL4 to control the flow of execution in a program. Each statement can specify labels of target statements for *success*, *failure*, or *unconditionally*. For example,

```
MESSAGE PAT : S(OK)  F(NOTFOUND)
```

will transfer control to the statement labeled OK if the pattern matching succeeds and to NOTFOUND otherwise. The pattern PAT is the simplest kind of pattern we can have—simply one string. We may specify a pattern as a choice among a number of patterns:

```
ADVERB = 'MAYBE' | 'PERHAPS' |...
```

Now ADVERB will match any string that contains 'MAYBE', 'PERHAPS', ... A pattern may also be defined as a concatenation of other patterns:

```
SENTENCE = ADVERB SENTENCE '.'
```

The pattern SENTENCE will match any string that contains the patterns ADVERB, MESSAGE, followed by a period. It is also possible to define *recursive patterns*, such as,

```
SENTENCE = ADVERB *SENTENCE | MESSAGE '.'
```

At pattern-matching time, pattern *SENTENCE will match either MESSAGE followed by a period (i.e., 'THERE ARE NO ERRORS HERE.') or ADVERB *SENTENCE, i.e., any sequence of ADVERB followed by 'THERE ARE NO ERRORS HERE.'

the pattern (if any) with the values that match. The same bound variables can then be used in the expression that defines the value of the function. Pattern matching can thus be viewed as a generalization of conventional parameter passing. The value of actual parameters is used to match the pattern appearing in the formal parameter part. Thus the case selected by pattern matching can vary from call to call.

More will be said on pattern matching for ML in Chapter 7. Chapter 8 addresses pattern matching in PROLOG.

4.6 Nondeterminism and backtracking

Problem solutions can often be described via and/or decompositions into sub-problems. For cxamplc, to solve problem A, one needs to solve either B, C, or D; to solve, say, C, one needs to solve E, F, and G. This can be represented as an *and/or tree* (see Figure 4.5). Node A, which has no incoming arcs, is called a *root node*; nodes B, D, E, F, and G, which have no exiting arcs, are called *leaf nodes*. And/or decompositions can also be described—in the syntax of some hypothetical programming language—as

```
A if B or
   C or
   D;
C if E and
   F and
   G;
D if I or
   H;
```

The solution of A is described as a *disjunction* of subproblems; the solution of C is described as a *conjunction* of subproblems. We can further assume B, D, E, F, and G to be problem-solving routines, which can terminate in either a success or a failure state.

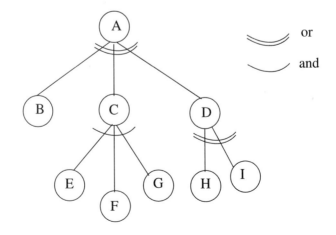

FIGURE 4.5 An and/or tree

If the order in which subproblems are solved is unspecified (and irrelevant as far as the problem statement is concerned), we say that the program is *nondeterministic*. In the example, this means that the order in which B, C, and D are tried does not matter. Similarly, the way in which E, F, and G are tried does not matter. What matters is that a solution be found, if it exists, or a notification of failure be returned, if no solution exists. The latter happens if all three subproblems in the disjunct fail, which implies that at least one of the subproblems of the conjunction failed.

An and/or problem decomposition can be viewed as a high-level design of a problem solution, which is then implemented in any programming language using the conventional constructs it provides. However, there are programming languages (such as logic languages of the PROLOG family or the string manipulation language Icon) that support this way of decomposing problems directly. Since features of this kind are very high-level, a programming language incorporating them is extremely powerful. As one can imagine, however, these features are hard to implement efficiently. Abstractly, this is the theme of problem solving by exploring a large search space for solutions. Possible strategies to deal with it are described in textbooks on artificial intelligence and computer algorithms.

A classical strategy to search a solution examines one node of the tree at a time. At each branch of the tree, one must choose which subgoal to examine next. The choice can be fixed (e.g., always choose the leftmost subgoal), arbitrary, or based on some heuristic knowledge of the problem being solved. If a subproblem solution fails, an alternative subproblem solution must be tried, if one exists. For example, to solve A, one might choose to solve C, and to solve C, one might first choose to solve B. If the solution of B fails, one might try to solve C instead. If any of C's subproblems fails (e.g., F), C (being an "and" node) fails. Thus, as F fails, one needs to go back to try another solution for the "or" node A, for example, trying to solve D. If D fails, because both H and I fail, one needs to go back to try to solve B. The mechanism that goes back on the tree trying to identify unexplored paths that were left behind in this *depth-first* search is called *backtracking*. This mechanism ensures that the overall problem solution fails only if there is no way of solving the problem without failure. That is, backtracking guarantees completeness of the search.

Another solution strategy might explore all descendants of a node in a *breadth-first* manner. Even more interesting would be to explore the and/or tree in *parallel*, in order to shorten the search time for the solution. In such a case, subproblems B, E, F, G, H, and I would be solved in parallel.

More on backtracking will be said in Chapter 8 in the case of logic and rule-based languages.

4.7 Event-driven computations

In some cases, programs are structured conveniently as *reactive* systems, i.e., systems where given *events* occurring in the environment cause certain program fragments to be executed. An example is provided by modern user interfaces, where a number of small graphical devices (called *widgets*) are displayed to mediate human-computer interaction. By operating on such widgets (e.g., by clicking the mouse on a push-button) the user generates an event. The event in turn causes a certain application fragment to be executed. Execution of such a fragment may cause further screen layouts to be generated with a new context of available widgets on it. The events that can be generated in any given state are defined by the context. The entire application can be viewed as a system that reacts to events by dispatching them to the appropriate piece of code that is responsible for handling the event. This is shown pictorially in Figure 4.6.

This conceptual view of an application suggests a way of structuring its high-level design, which can then be detailed into a conventional implementation. There are languages, however, that directly support this conceptual view by providing the necessary abstractions. For example, languages or toolkits such as Visual Basic, Visual C++, or Tcl/Tk allow one to separately design the widgets and the code fragments and to bind events on a widget to the fragments that respond to the event.

Another common event-driven control paradigm is based on so-called *triggers*. Triggers became popular with new developments in the field of active databases. Since there is no precise and universal definition of a trigger, we will give examples based on a hypothetical language syntax. An *active database* consists of a conventional underlying (passive) database and

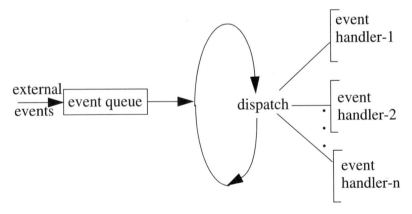

FIGURE 4.6 Structure of an event-driven computation

a set of *active rules* (or triggers) of the following form:

```
on event
when condition
    do action
```

When the event associated with the rule occurs, we say that the rule is *triggered*. A triggered rule is then checked to see if the condition holds. If this is the case, the rule can be executed.

For example, the following trigger specifies that the total number of employees should be updated whenever a new employee record is inserted in the database.

```
on insert in EMPLOYEE
when TRUE
    do emp_number ++
```

As another example, in a database application, triggers may be used to specify some constraints that must be verified as new elements are inserted or existing elements are updated or deleted from the database. For example, a constraint might be that no employee can have a salary that is more than the average salary of managers. A trigger might watch that no insertion, update, or deletion violates the constraint; if that happens, some appropriate action would be undertaken.

A trigger-based problem solution can be viewed as a high-level design, which may be implemented in a programming language using the conventional constructs it provides. In the above example, the check that trigger conditions become true might be explicitly associated with the start and the end of each class member routine, along with the execution of the corresponding code fragment.[3] However, there are languages where triggers are available as a built-in language construct; i.e., they are implemented by the underlying run-time machine. For example, the forthcoming SQL standard supports triggers.

4.8 Concurrent computations

Sometimes it is convenient to structure the software as a set of *concurrent units* which execute in parallel. This can occur when the program is executed on a computer with multiple CPUs (multiprocessor) or on a distributed system composed of several cooperating computers. In such cases, when different processors execute different concurrent units at the same time, we say

---

3. We are implicitly assuming that intermediate states of the routines may not cause the violation of a constraint.

that the underlying machine that executes the program provides *physical* parallelism: each unit is in fact executed by its dedicated processor. Parallelism, however, may be only *logical*. For example, if the underlying machine is a uniprocessor, the logical view of parallel execution may be provided by switching the CPU from one unit to another in such a way that all units appear to progress simultaneously. The switching of the execution of the uniprocessor among the various units can be performed by a software layer, implemented on top of the physical machine, which provides the programmer with a view of an abstract parallel machine where all units are executed simultaneously. Once such an abstract machine is in place, one can in fact abstract away from the physical architecture of the underlying hardware, where components are actually executed. The hardware structure might provide a dedicated processor for each unit, or it might be a multiprogrammed uniprocessor. Allowing for the possibility of different underlying machines means that the correctness of a concurrent system cannot be based on an assumption of the speed of execution of the units. Indeed, the speed can differ greatly if every unit is executed by a dedicated processor, or if a single processor is shared by several units. Moreover, even if the architecture is known, it is difficult to design a system in such a way that its correctness depends upon the speed of execution of the units. Both the design of the software and the programming language constructs must make it possible to reason about the correctness without reference to relative speeds of execution. We will return to these points in the discussion of implementation models for concurrency.

Concurrency is an important area of computer science studied in different contexts: machine architectures, operating systems, distributed systems, databases, etc. In this section we give an overview of how programming languages support concurrency. Concurrent programs consist of a number of units (called *processes*) that execute in parallel (logically or physically). The term *thread* is used when the concurrent units share a single address space, i.e., have access to the same global environment. We will use the term "process" in the sequel. The distinction between thread and process is more important in operating systems and systems programming.

If the abstract machine that executes the program does not support concurrency, it is possible to simulate it by transferring control explicitly from one unit to another. This low-level approach is supported by *coroutines*, reviewed in the following sidebar.

To support correct interaction among processes, a language should provide suitable *synchronization statements*. We introduce this concept through an example. Suppose that a certain system contains concurrent activities of

Coroutines

Coroutines are low-level constructs for describing pseudo-concurrent units. They can be used to simulate parallelism on a uniprocessor by explicitly interleaving the execution of a set of units. Thus coroutines do not describe a set of concurrent units, but a particular way of sharing the processor to simulate concurrency.

Coroutines are program units that activate one another explicitly, via a resume primitive. Only one unit is executing at a given time. The executing unit may explicitly transfer control to another unit (via resume), which resumes execution at the place where it last terminated. Consequently, units activate each other explicitly in an interleaved fashion, according to a pattern of behavior that is explicitly described by the program.

As an example, consider the two coroutines client and give_me_next shown in Figure 4.7, written in a self-explaining C-like notation. Unit client repeatedly activates unit give_me_next to get the next value of a variable. Each reactivation of unit give_me_next produces a new value that depends on the previously generated value. The two units resume one another. There is a global variable i, which is shared by client and give_me_next. Unit main, which is activated initially, resumes client.

An abstract implementation model of coroutines differs from that of routines. When a coroutine A issues a resume to a coroutine B, the pointer to the instruction following resume B is saved in A's activation record. Moreover, A's activation record is not deallocated, so that A's execution can later be resumed in the state where it left off. If coroutines can have nested units that may be activated recursively, each coroutine requires an activation record stack that can grow and shrink independently of the other stacks. In addition, as in the example, they may access the global environment.

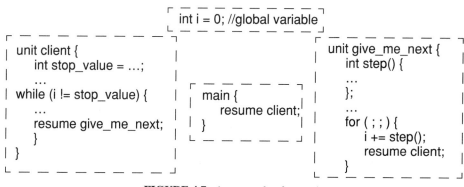

FIGURE 4.7 An example of coroutines

the following two kinds: producers and consumers. A *producer* produces a stream of values and places them into a suitable data structure (a *buffer* of a certain size, N). A *consumer* reads these values from the buffer in the same order as they are produced and then processes those values according to some policy. This example is a classic problem that exhibits many relevant issues of concurrency. An abstract description of two producer and consumer processes is shown in Figure 4.8. A given system might contain many such processes, all interacting through the same buffer.

The two processes in Figure 4.8 are described by cyclic and, ideally, nonterminating program units, which cooperate to achieve the common goal of transferring data from the producer (which could be reading them from an input device) to the consumer (which could be storing them in a file). By smoothing the effect of their different speeds, the buffering mechanism allows the two processes to proceed independently. To guarantee the correctness of the cooperation, however, the programmer must ensure that no matter how quickly or slowly the producer and the consumer progress, there will be no attempts to write into a full buffer or to read from an empty buffer. This can be accomplished by the use of synchronization statements. In general, synchronization statements delay the execution of an operation by a process, whenever that is necessary for correct cooperation with other concurrent units. In the example, when the buffer is full, the producer is delayed if it tries to append an element until the consumer removes at least one element. Similarly, when the buffer is empty, the consumer is delayed if it tries to remove an item, until the producer appends at least one new element.

Process Producer	Process Consumer
repeat forever { produce an element; append it to the buffer; }	repeat forever { remove an element from the buffer; operate on it; }

FIGURE 4.8 Sample processes: producer and consumer

Another, more subtle, need for synchronization may arise when several activities can legally have access to the same buffer. For example, suppose that append and remove are implemented by the fragments in Figure 4.9, where t represents the total number of elements stored in the buffer, and next_in and next_out are two operations that yield the value of the buffer index where the next element can be stored and where the next element is to be read from, respectively. Let us assume that the individual statements in Figure 4.9 are elementary, indivisible instructions of the executing machine. The sequences, however, cannot be assumed to be indivisible; i.e., the execution

Append	Remove

t++;
i = next_in();
buffer[i] = x;
	t--;
	j = next_out();
	x = buffer[j];

FIGURE 4.9 Operations to append and remove from a buffer

of their constituent actions may be interleaved by the underlying machine. For example, suppose that the buffer is initially empty. A producer might start depositing into the buffer by performing the first two actions. The total number of buffered items becomes 1 and the index of the position where the item should be deposited is evaluated. Suppose that at this point another producer gets access to the buffer (since the buffer is not full). If this producer completes all three actions, the value will be deposited in the second buffer slot (since the first one was acquired by the first producer that did not complete its own deposit). At this point, a consumer might access the buffer (which is not empty, since t = 2). This is an error, however, because the consumer would read its value from the position which was assigned to the first producer, but no assignment was ever performed to this position. To avoid this error, we must ensure that the operation Append or Remove (Figure 4.9), once started, completes its execution before another such operation is allowed to start. We say that Append and Remove must be executed in *mutual exclusion*; synchronization primitives must allow mutual exclusion to be specified.

In general, synchronization primitives may be viewed as mechanisms that constrain the order in which operations performed by different processes are executed. Let $\{P_1, P_2, ..., P_n\}$ be a set of concurrent processes. Each process can be assigned for execution to an abstract machine, such as SIMPLESEM, which was discussed in Chapter 2. Let ip_i be the value of the instruction pointer of the i-th abstract machine that executes P_i; ip_i yields the address of the instruction $C_i[ip_i]$ that is to be executed next in each process i. If the processes are logically independent, at any instant, all machines can execute $C_i[ip_i]$. Synchronization, however, may force some abstract machines to remain idle until some condition is met that allows them to resume execution.

Besides synchronization, programming languages must provide facilities to describe *communication* among processes. Communication allows information to flow from one process to another. Processes cooperate in problem solving through synchronization and communication. Communication can be achieved in different ways, depending on the underlying computation model. The traditional way to achieve communication is via a *shared memory*. According to such a model, all concurrent processes have access to a common set of variables. This model reflects an abstract multiprocessor architecture with a common memory area where all processors can read and write. Another paradigm for communication is *message passing*. In such a case, the model reflects more closely an underlying decentralized architecture where processors are connected by a network through which messages can flow. Both logical paradigms, of course, can be implemented on any underlying architecture, although implementation of, say, the shared memory paradigm on a physically distributed architecture is less natural and requires considerably more support than implementing the message-passing paradigm.

The rest of this chapter is organized as follows. Section 4.8.1 illustrates how processes may be defined in programming languages, using the Ada language as a case study. In Section 4.8.2 we review two kinds of synchronization mechanisms—semaphores and signals—and discuss communication via shared memory. We also discuss communication via message passing and the rendezvous mechanism. Finally, Section 4.8.3 discusses implementation models. Our presentation of this last point does not go into details, which go beyond the scope of this book and are usually discussed in textbooks on operating systems. A discussion of concurrency in Java is delayed until Chapter 6, after the presentation of the necessary background on object-oriented programming languages.

4.8.1 Processes

A concurrent programming language must provide constructs to define processes. Processes can belong to a type, of which several instances can be created. The language must define how and by what a process is initiated; i.e., a new independent execution flow is spawned by an executing unit. The language also needs to address the issue of process termination, i.e., how can a process be terminated, what happens after a process terminates, etc.

In this section we will briefly review the main concepts and solutions provided by Ada. In Ada, processes are called *tasks*. The execution of an Ada program consists of the execution of one or more tasks, each representing a separate computation that proceeds concurrently with other tasks, with which it may interact through synchronization statements.

Tasks can be defined by a *task type*, of which many instances can be declared. It is also possible to declare a task object (shortly, a task) directly. The *declaration* of a task, or a task type, specifies how the task, or all instances of the type, can interact with other tasks. As we will see shortly, interaction with a task is achieved by calling one of its *entries*, which must appear in its declaration. Thus, the declaration of a task type is a declaration of an abstract data type; entries represent the operations available for interaction with task objects. In Ada, the *body* of the task, or a task type, which describes the implementation of the task's internal code, can be described separately from its declaration.

This is an example of a task type declaration:

```
task type SERVER is
    entry NEXT_REQUEST(NR: in REQUEST);
    entry SHUT_DOWN;
end SERVER;

type SERV_PTR is access SERVER;  --declares a pointer to a SERVER
```

These are examples of task object declarations:

```
MY_SERVER: SERVER;

task CHECKER is
    entry CHECK(T: in TEXT);
    entry CLOSE;
end CHECKER;

HIS_SERVER_PTR: SERV_PTR := new SERVER;
```

The execution of a task consists of executing its body. A task is allocated implicitly when storage is allocated to the task object. For example, consider the following fragment:

```
procedure P is
    A, B: SERVER;
    HER_SERVER_PTR: SERV_PTR;
begin
    ...
    HER_SERVER_PTR := new SERVER;
    ...
end P;
```

Tasks A and B are activated as the block in which they are locally declared is entered at run time, that is, when procedure P is called. The task pointed to by HER_SERVER_PTR is activated by the execution of the **new** operation.

The concept of task *termination* is more complex, and we will not describe it in all its subtleties. For simplicity, let us assume that a task can terminate when it reaches the last statement of its body and that (1) all of the locally declared task objects have terminated and (2) tasks allocated by a **new** statement and referenced only by pointers local to the task have terminated.

4.8.2 Synchronization and communication

In this section we present some elementary mechanisms for process synchronization and interprocess communication: semaphores, signals and monitors, and rendezvous. Semaphores are low-level synchronization mechanisms that are mainly used when interprocess communication occurs via shared variables. Monitors are higher-level constructs that define abstract objects used for interprocess communication; synchronization is achieved via signals. Finally, the rendezvous is a mechanism that combines synchronization and communication via message passing.

4.8.2.1 Semaphores

A semaphore is a data object that can assume an integer value and can be operated on by the primitives P and V. The semaphore is initialized to a certain integer value when it is declared.

The definitions of P and V are

```
P(s):  if s>0 then s = s - 1
       else suspend current process

V(s):  if there is a process suspended on the semaphore
       then wake up process
       else s = s + 1
```

The primitives P and V are assumed to be indivisible, atomic operations; that is, only one process at a time can be executing P or V operations on the same semaphore. The atomicity must be guaranteed by the underlying implementation, which should make P and V behave like elementary machine instructions.

The semaphore has (1) an associated data structure where the descriptors of processes suspended on the semaphore are recorded and (2) a policy for selecting one process to be awakened when required by the primitive V. Usually, the data structure is a queue served on a first-in/first-out basis. However, it is also possible to assign priorities to processes and devise more complex policies based on such priorities.

The simple producer-consumer example of Figure 4.8 can be solved using semaphores as shown in Figure 4.10 (as usual, we adopt an arbitrary, self-explanatory C++-like notation).

The keyword process starts the segments of code that can proceed concurrently. Three semaphores are introduced. Semaphores spaces and in are used to guarantee the logical correctness of the accesses to the buffer. In particular, spaces (number of available free positions in the buffer) suspends the producer when it tries to insert a new item into a full buffer. Similarly, in (number of items already in the buffer) suspends the consumer if it tries to remove an item from an empty buffer. Semaphore mutex is used to enforce mutual exclusion

```
buffer buf;                    // object of class buffer, with member functions
                               // append, remove, and size
semaphore mutex = 1;    // semaphore used to guarantee mutual exclusion
        in = 0;                // semaphore to control the reading from the buffer
        spaces = buf.size(); // semaphore to control the writing into the buffer
process producer {
    int i;
    for ( ; ; ) {
        produce(i);
        P(spaces);         // wait for free spaces
        P(mutex);          // wait for buffer availability
                           // the buffer must be used in mutual exclusion
        buf.append(i);
        V(mutex);          // buffer is now available
        V(in)              // one more item in buffer
    };
};
process consumer {
    int j;
    for ( ; ; ) {
        P(in);             // wait for item in buffer
        P(mutex);          // wait for buffer availability
                           // the buffer must be used in mutual exclusion
        j = buf.remove();
        V(mutex);          // buffer is now available
        V(spaces)          // one more free space in buffer
    };
}
```

FIGURE 4.10 Producer-consumer example with semaphores

of accesses to the buffer. We can see that semaphores are used both for pure synchronization, as in mutex, to ensure that only one process may use the buffer at a time, and for communicating control information among processes. For example, by executing V(spaces) the consumer communicates to the producer that it has consumed an item and that more space is now available in the buffer.

Programming with semaphores requires the programmer to associate one semaphore with each synchronization condition. Our example shows that semaphores are a simple but low-level mechanism; their use can be awkward in practice, and the resulting programs are often difficult to design and understand. Therefore, semaphores require considerable discipline on the part of the programmer. For example, one should not forget to execute a P before accessing a shared resource, or neglect to execute a V to release it. Moreover,

Concurrency in PL/I and Algol 68

PL/I was the first language to allow concurrent units, called *tasks*. A procedure may be invoked as a task, in which case it executes concurrently with its caller. Tasks also can be assigned priorities. Synchronization is achieved by the use of *events*, which are binary semaphores that can assume only one of two values: '0'B and '1'B (Boolean constants 0 and 1). A P operation on a semaphore is represented by a WAIT operation on the completion of an event E: WAIT(E). A V operation is represented by signaling the completion of the event: COMPLETION(E) = '1'B. PL/I extends the notion of semaphores by allowing the WAIT operation to name several events and an integer expression e. The process will be suspended until any e events have been completed. For example, WAIT(EI, E2, E3) (1) indicates the waiting for any one of the events EI, E2, and E3.

Algol 68 supports concurrent processes in a parallel clause whose constituent statements are elaborated concurrently. The language supports semaphores with the built-in type sema.

little checking can be done statically on programs that use semaphores. For example, a compiler would not be able to catch the incorrect use of a semaphore, such as one resulting from a change of V(mutex) into P(mutex) in the producer process (see also Exercise 16). Catching such an error is impossible because it requires the translator to know the correctness requirements of the program—the operations on the buffer are to be executed in mutual exclusion—that mutex is supposed to guarantee.

Using semaphores for synchronization purposes other than mutual exclusion is even more awkward. In the producer-consumer example, the process consumer suspends itself by executing P(spaces) when the buffer is full. It is the responsibility of some other piece of code—the consumer in this case—to provide the matching V operation. If the programmer forgets to write a V(spaces) after each consumption, the producer will become blocked forever.

Semaphores are often provided by operating systems to support systems programming. They have also been integrated into a number of existing programming languages, such as PL/I and Algol68 (see sidebar above).

4.8.2.2 Monitors and signals

Concurrent Pascal introduced the signal and monitor constructs into programming languages. *Signals* are synchronization primitives; *monitors* describe abstract data types in a concurrent environment. The operations that manipulate the data structure are guaranteed to be executed in mutual exclusion by the underlying implementation. Cooperation in accessing the shared data structure must be programmed explicitly by using the monitor signal primitives delay and continue.

Using the notation of Concurrent Pascal, the program in Figure 4.11 illustrates the use of monitors in the producer-consumer example.

```
type fifostorage =
monitor
    var contents: array[1..n] of integer; {buffer contents}
        tot: 0..n; {number of items in buffer}
        in, {position of item to be added next}
        out: 1..n; {position of item to be removed next}
        sender, receiver: queue;
    procedure entry append (item: integer);
    begin if tot = n then delay(sender);
        contents[in] := item;
        in := (in mod n) + 1;
        tot := tot + 1;
        continue(receiver)
    end;
    procedure entry remove (var item: integer);
    begin if tot = 0 then delay(receiver);
        item := contents[out];
        out := (out mod n) + 1;
        tot := tot - 1;
        continue(sender)
    end;
  begin {initialization part}
    tot := 0; in := 1; out := 1
  end
```

FIGURE 4.11   Producer-consumer example with monitor

An instance of the monitor (i.e., a buffer) can be declared,

var buffer: fifostorage

and can be created by the statement **init** buffer. Monitor instances are abstract objects through which interprocess communication and synchronization are coordinated.

The **init** statement allocates storage for the variables defined within the monitor definition (i.e., contents, the contents of the buffer; tot, the total number of buffered items; and in and out, the positions at which the next items will be appended and removed, respectively) and executes the initialization part (which sets tot to 0, and in and out to 1). The monitor defines the two procedures append and remove. They are declared with the keyword **entry**, which means that they are exported procedures that can be used to manipulate monitor instances. Cooperation between the producer and the consumer is achieved by using the synchronization primitive signals delay and continue. The operation delay(sender) suspends the executing process (the producer) in the queue sender. The process loses its exclusive access to the monitor's data structure and its execution is delayed until another process (the consumer) executes the operation continue(sender). Similarly, with delay(receiver) a consumer process is delayed in the queue receiver if the buffer is empty, until the producer resumes it by executing the instruction continue(receiver). The execution of the continue(q) operation makes the calling process return from the monitor call and, additionally, if there are processes waiting in the queue q, one of them immediately resumes the execution of the monitor procedure that previously delayed it.

The structure of a Concurrent Pascal program that uses the above monitor to represent cooperation between a producer and a consumer is given in Figure 4.12. The program in Figure 4.12 implements processes as nonterminating, cyclic activities (**cycle**...**end**). It declares two particular process instances (meproducer and youconsumer), binds them to an instance of the resource type fifostorage, and then activates them as concurrent processes by the **init** statement.

The examples given so far have used shared memory for interprocess communication. A globally accessible buffer was used by producer and consumer processes, and suitable synchronization primitives were introduced to allow them to proceed safely. In the example using semaphores, synchronization and communication features were separate. Semaphores are used for synchronization; shared variables are used for communication. In the monitor example, the two issues were more intertwined, and the resulting construct is higher level. One can view the monitor construct as defined by two logical components: an abstract object that is used for communication among processes in mutual exclusion, and a signal mechanism that supports synchronization (e.g., the ability to delay and resume processes based on some logical condition). Note that while the first component is intrinsically based on a shared-memory computation paradigm, the second is not, and might be used also in a decentralized scheme for concurrent computation.

```
const n = 20;
type fifostorage =  ...as above...
type producer =
    process (storage: fifostorage);
    var element: integer;
    begin cycle
            ...
            storage.append(element);
            ...
        end
    end;
type consumer =
    process(storage: fifostorage);
    var datum: integer;
    begin cycle
            ...
            storage.remove(datum);
            ...
        end
    end;
var meproducer: producer;
    youconsumer: consumer;
    buffer: fifostorage;
begin
    init buffer, meproducer(buffer), youconsumer(buffer)
end
```

FIGURE 4.12 A Concurrent Pascal program with two processes and one monitor

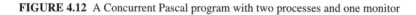

4.8.2.3 Rendezvous

In this section we illustrate the *rendezvous* construct introduced by the Ada programming language. The construct can be viewed as a high-level mechanism that combines synchronization and communication, where communication is based on the *message-passing* paradigm. This makes the rendezvous natural to use in the design of software for distributed architectures, although its possible interaction with other features in Ada can make this more difficult. Here we concentrate on the basic properties of rendezvous; for the sake of simplicity, additional features and the interaction with other facilities provided by the language (such as scope rules and exception handling) will be ignored.

The Ada task object in Figure 4.13 describes a process that handles requests to append and remove elements of a buffer.

The declaration of task Buffer_Handler specifies Append and Remove as entries. An entry can be viewed as a *port*, or a *mailbox*, through which a task

```
task Buffer_Handler is   --task declaration
   entry Append(Item: in Integer);
   entry Remove(Item: out Integer);
end;
task body Buffer_Handler is --task implementation
   N: constant Integer := 20;
   Contents: array (1..N) of Integer;
   In_Index, Out_Index: Integer range 1..N := 1;
   Tot: Integer range 0..N := 0;
begin loop
   select
      when Tot < N =>
         accept Append(Item: in Integer) do
            Contents(In_Index) := Item;
         end;
         In_index := (In_Index mod N)+1;
         Tot := Tot+ 1
   or
      when Tot > 0 =>
         accept Remove(Item: out Integer) do
            Item := Contents(Out_Index);
         end;
         Out_Index := (Out_Index mod N) + 1;
         Tot := Tot - 1;
   end select;
end loop;
end Buffer_Handler;
```

FIGURE 4.13 An Ada task that manages a buffer

can send a message to another task, which can then accept it. The task can indicate its willingness to accept a message if it is an owner of the corresponding entry (i.e., the entry is declared in it). It does so by executing the **accept** statement. At this point, the sender and the receiver tasks can be viewed as meeting together (that is, they *rendezvous*).

If the sender calls the entry (i.e., sends the message) before the receiver issues an **accept**, the sender is suspended until the rendezvous occurs. Similarly, a suspension of the receiver occurs if an **accept** statement is executed before the corresponding entry is called (i.e., before the message is sent). A task can accept messages from more than one task; consequently, each entry potentially has a queue of tasks that have sent messages to it.

The **accept** statement is similar to a routine. After a repetition of the header of the entry, the **do...end** part (*accept body*) specifies the statements to be executed at the rendezvous. Once a match between an entry call and the corresponding accept occurs, the sender is suspended until the **accept** body is executed by the called task. The **accept** body is the only place at which the parameters of the entry are accessible. Possible **out** parameters (as in the case of Remove) are passed back to the sender at the end of the rendezvous, that is, when the execution of the **accept** body is completed. Thereafter, the two tasks that met in the rendezvous can proceed in parallel.

The bodies of tasks PRODUCER and CONSUMER, which interact with Buffer_Handler in the producer-consumer example, are sketched in Figure 4.14.

PRODUCER	CONSUMER
loop	**loop**
produce a new value V;	Buffer_Handler.Remove(V);
Buffer_Handler.Append(V);	**exit when** V is the end-of-stream
exit when V is the end-of-stream	value;
value;	consume V;
end loop;	**end loop**;

FIGURE 4.14 Sketch of the producer and consumer tasks in Ada

In the example of Figure 4.13, **accept** statements are enclosed within a **select** statement. The **select** statement specifies several alternatives, separated by **or**, that can be chosen in a nondeterministic fashion. The Ada selection is specified by an **accept** statement, possibly prefixed by a **when** condition (as in our example). Execution of the select statement proceeds as follows.[4]

1 The conditions of the **when** parts of all alternatives are evaluated. Alternatives with a true condition, or without a **when** part, are considered open; otherwise, they are considered closed. In the example, both alternatives are open if $0 < \text{Tot} < N$.

2 An open alternative can be selected if a rendezvous is possible (i.e., an entry call has already been issued by another task). After the alternative is selected, the corresponding **accept** body is executed.

3 If there are open alternatives but none can be selected immediately, the task waits until a rendezvous is possible.

4 If there are no open alternatives, an error condition is signaled by the language-defined exception Program_Error.

4.8.2.4 Summing up

Semaphores, monitors, and rendezvous provide different constructs to model concurrent systems. As we pointed out, semaphores are rather low-level mechanisms: programs are difficult to read and write, and no checks on their correct use can be done automatically. Monitors, on the other hand, are a higher-level structuring mechanism. Using monitors, a typical system

---

4. This is a simplified view of Ada. We are ignoring a few features that would complicate our presentation.

structuring proceeds by identifying (1) shared resources as abstract objects with suitable access primitives (*passive entities*), and (2) processes (*active entities*) that cooperate through the use of resources. Resources are encapsulated within monitors. Mutual exclusion on the access to a shared resource is guaranteed automatically by the monitor implementation, but synchronization must be enforced explicitly by suspending and signaling processes via delay and continue statements. The distinction between active and passive entities (processes and monitors, respectively) disappears in a scheme based on rendezvous. Resources to be used cooperatively are represented by tasks, that is, by active components representing resource managers. A request to use a resource is represented by an entry call, i.e., by sending a message that must be accepted by the corresponding resource manager.

A system structured via monitors and processes can be restructured via tasks and rendezvous, and vice versa; the choice between the two schemes is largely dependent on personal taste. As we mentioned, the latter scheme mirrors more directly the behavior of a concurrent system in a distributed architecture, where remote resources are actually managed by processes that behave as guardians of the resource. However, it can be somewhat awkward in case processes need to communicate via shared objects. In fact, early experience with the Ada programming language, which initially provided only the rendezvous, showed that the need for additional tasks to manage shared data often led to poor performance. Therefore, Ada 95 introduced a kind of monitor construct—*protected types*—in addition to the rendezvous.

The use of an Ada protected type to implement our running example of a buffer type (Fifo_Storage) is shown in Figure 4.15.

Similar to the monitor, operations defined for a protected type are executed by the underlying abstract machine in mutual exclusion. There are two kinds of possible operations: routines (i.e., procedures and functions) and entries. *Entries* (shown in the above example) have an associated *barrier* condition that is used for synchronization. *Routines* have no associated barriers. The difference with the monitor is that no explicit signals are issued. Rather, when an entry is called its barrier is evaluated; if the barrier is false, then the calling process is suspended and queued. At the end of the execution of an entry (or a routine) body, all barriers that have queued tasks are reevaluated, thus possibly allowing a suspended task whose barrier became true to be resumed. The absence of explicit signals to be exchanged for synchronization purposes makes the construct simpler to use and the corresponding abstraction easier to understand than in the case of monitors.

Ada is an example of a programming language that provides a coherent set of integrated features supporting concurrency, including facilities for real-

```
protected type Fifo_Storage is
    entry Append (Item: in Integer);
    entry Remove (Item: out Integer);
private
    N: constant Integer := 20;
    Contents: array (1..N) of Integer;
    In_Index, Out_Index: Integer range 1..N := 1;
    Tot: Integer range 0..N := 0;
end Fifo_Storage;

protected body Fifo_Storage is
    entry Append (Item: in Integer) when Tot < N is
    begin
        Contents(In_Index) := Item;
        In_Index := (In_Index mod N) + 1;
        Tot := Tot + 1
    end Append;

    entry Remove (Item: out Integer) when Tot > 0 is
    begin
        Item := Contents(Out_Index);
        Out_Index := (Out_Index mod N) + 1;
        Tot := Tot - 1;
    end Remove;
end Fifo_Storage;
```

FIGURE 4.15 A protected Ada type implementing a buffer

time programming (ignored here for space reasons). Java is another example that will be discussed in Chapter 6. Most other languages do not. Such languages often provide support for concurrent programming either via calls to low-level operating system primitives or via libraries added to language implementations.

4.8.3 Implementation models

In a concurrent system, processes are either suspended (waiting on some synchronization condition) or are ready to run; that is, there are no logical obstacles to their execution. In general, only a subset of ready processes can be running, unless there are as many processors as there are ready processes. In the common case of a uniprocessor, only one of these processes can be running at a time. It is thus customary to say that processes can be in one of the following states (see also Figure 4.16):

- Waiting
- Ready (i.e., potentially active, but presently not running)
- Running

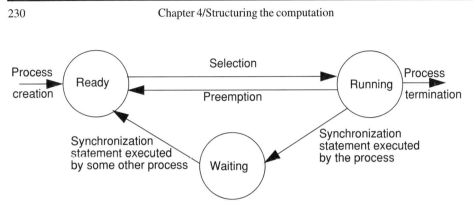

FIGURE 4.16 State diagram for a process

The state of a process changes from running to waiting if there is some logical condition that prevents the process from continuing its execution. That is, the process is suspended by the execution of some synchronization statement (e.g., the buffer is full for the producer process). The state can later change from waiting to running if some other process performs a suitable synchronization statement (e.g., a consumer process signals that the buffer is not full anymore).

In concurrent programming, the programmer does not have direct control over the speed of execution of the processes. In particular, the user is not responsible for changing the state of a process from ready to running (operation *selection* in Figure 4.16), which is done by the underlying implementation. Figure 4.16 shows that a process can leave the running state and enter the ready state as a consequence of the action of *preemption.*

Preemption is an action performed by the underlying implementation; it forces a process to abandon its running state even if, from a logical point of view, it could safely continue execute. A process can be preempted either after it performs a synchronizing statement that makes another suspended process enter the ready state (e.g., a V on a semaphore) or when some other condition occurs, such as the expiration of a specified amount of time (*time slice*).

After the preemption of one process, one of the ready processes can enter the running state. This kind of implementation allows the programmer to view the system as a set of activities that proceed in parallel, even if they are all executed by the same processor. Only one process at a time can be executed by the processor, but each process runs only for a limited amount of time, after which control is given to another process. It is also possible to have nonpreemptive implementation of concurrency. In this case, execution switches to another process only when the currently executing process deliberately suspends itself or requires the use of an unavailable resource.

The portion of run-time support of a concurrent language responsible for the implementation of the state transitions shown in Figure 4.16 is called the *kernel*. To illustrate the basic features of a kernel, consider a single processor shared by a set of processes. For the sake of simplicity, we will ignore the problems of synchronizing processes with input/output devices and concentrate our attention on the interactions among internal processes. More complete discussions of these issues are addressed in textbooks on operating systems. Here we provide only a glimpse of the basic problems that are relevant to understanding concurrency features of programming languages.

The information about a process needed by the kernel is represented in a *process descriptor*—one for each process. The descriptor for a process is used to store all the information needed to restore the process from a waiting or ready state to the running state. This information (called *process status*) includes the value of the instruction pointer, of machine registers, and so on. Saving the status of the process when it becomes suspended and restoring the status when the process becomes running is one of the kernel's jobs.

The kernel can be viewed as an abstract data type; it hides a private data structure and provides operations to manipulate it. All of the kernel's operations are assumed to be executed in a *noninterruptible way*; i.e., all interrupts are disabled during execution of kernel operations. In our abstract implementation, the kernel's data structures are organized as queues of process descriptors. The descriptors of ready processes are kept by the kernel in READY_QUEUE. There is also one CONDITION_QUEUE for each condition that might suspend a process; that is, there is one queue for each semaphore and one for each object declared to be of type queue in a monitor. In Ada, there would be a CONDITION_QUEUE for each entry of a protected type. Each such queue is used to store the descriptors of all processes suspended on the semaphore or delayed in the queue. We will use the notation CONDITION_QUEUE(c) where c is a semaphore, a condition, or a monitor queue to represent the queue associated with c. A variable RUNNING denotes the descriptor of the running process. A typical snapshot of the kernel's data structures is shown in Figure 4.17. The queues used by the kernel can be considered instances of an abstract data type whose operations are defined by the following signatures:

enqueue:Queue x Descriptor → Queue *inserts a descriptor into the queue*
dequeue:Queue → Queue x Descriptor *extracts a descriptor from the queue*
empty: Queue → Boolean   *true if the queue is empty; false otherwise*

In what follows, we discuss the basic operations performed by the abstract machine to execute concurrency constructs. The notation we use is a

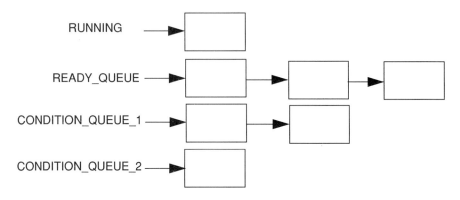

FIGURE 4.17   Data structures of the kernel

self-explaining pseudocode based on C++. Whenever necessary, additional comments are added to the pseudocode.

Time slicing is implemented by a clock interrupt. Such an interrupt activates the following kernel operation Suspend-and-Select, which suspends the most recently running process into READY_QUEUE and transfers a ready process into the running state.

```
Operation Suspend-and-Select()

RUNNING = process_status;
                    -- save status of running process into RUNNING
READY_QUEUE.enqueue(RUNNING);
                    -- enqueue RUNNING into READY_QUEUE
RUNNING = READY_QUEUE.dequeue();
                    -- move a descriptor from READY_QUEUE into RUNNING
process_status = RUNNING;
                    -- activate the new process
```

4.8.3.1 Semaphores

If semaphores are provided by the language, primitives P and V can be implemented as calls to kernel procedures. A suspension on a condition c caused by a P operation is implemented by the following kernel operation:

```
Operation Suspend-on-Condition(c)
RUNNING = process_status;
CONDITION_QUEUE(c).enqueue(RUNNING);
RUNNING = READY QUEUE.dequeue();
process_status = RUNNING;
```

Awakening a process waiting on condition c, caused by a V operation, is implemented by the following private operation of the kernel:

```
Operation Awaken(c)
RUNNING = process_status;
READY_QUEUE.enqueue(RUNNING);
READY_QUEUE.enqueue(CONDITION_QUEUE(c).dequeue());
    -- move a descriptor from CONDITION_QUEUE(c) into READY_QUEUE
RUNNING = READY_QUEUE.dequeue();
process_status = RUNNING;
```

This implementation guarantees indivisibility of primitives P and V, since we assumed that kernel operations are noninterruptible.

4.8.3.2 Monitors and signals

In the case of monitors and Ada's protected types, a simple way to implement the required mutual exclusion consists of disabling interrupts when a monitor procedure is called and enabling them on return from the call. Thus, a process cannot be preempted while it is executing a monitor procedure. We assume that interrupts are enabled and disabled by a single machine instruction, and that a special machine register determines whether interrupts are enabled or disabled. This register is part of the process status and must be saved in the process descriptor when the process is suspended. For the sake of simplicity, we also assume that monitor procedures do not contain calls to other monitor procedures. When a process calls a monitor procedure, the value of the return point from the call is saved in an entry of the process descriptor. Operations delay and continue can be implemented by kernel procedures. In particular, delay is implemented by operation Suspend-on-Condition(c), and Continue(c) (where c is a condition queue) is implemented by the following operation:

```
Operation Continue(c)

RUNNING = process_status (with interrupts enabled and program counter set to
            the return point from the monitor call);
READY_QUEUE.enqueue(RUNNING);
if not CONDITION_QUEUE(c).empty()
    READY_QUEUE.enqueue(CONDITION_QUEUE(c).dequeue());
RUNNING = READY_QUEUE.dequeue();
process_status = RUNNING;
```

Note that we do not state the policies for the management of queues in this abstract implementation. Queues might be handled according to a first-in/first-out policy, or one may even use sophisticated strategies that take into account waiting times and priorities. The part of the kernel responsible for choosing such policies is called the *scheduler*. In our scheme, the scheduler is a hidden part of the implementation of the abstract data type that defines queues.

4.8.3.3 Rendezvous

In this section, we discuss some implementation issues of Ada's rendezvous. There is one queue of ready tasks (READY_QUEUE). Each entry has a descriptor that contains the following fields:

- A boolean value O describing whether the entry is open (O = true indicates that the task owning the entry is ready to accept a call to this entry).
- A reference W to a queue of descriptors of tasks whose calls to the entry are pending (waiting queue).
- A reference T to the descriptor of the task owning the entry.
- A reference I to the first instruction of the accept body (to simplify matters, we assume that no two **accept** statements for the same entry can appear in a **select** statement). This reference is significant only if the task owning the entry is ready to accept a call to the entry (that is, O = true). For simplicity, we can assume that the value of this field is a constant, statically associated with the entry.

As usual, we assume that the implementation of the synchronization statements is done by kernel operations that are noninterruptible; that is, interrupts are disabled and enabled by the kernel before and after executing such statements. The problem of passing parameters across tasks is ignored for simplicity.

Let e be an entry that is called by a task, and let DESCR(e) be e's descriptor. The implementation of a call to entry e can be done by the kernel as follows:

```
RUNNING = process_status;
(DESCR(e).W).enqueue(RUNNING);   -- status of caller process is saved in the
                                 -- queue associated with the entry
if DESCR(e).O {                  -- if the entry is open
    for all open entries oe of the task DESR(e).T do
        oe.O = false;            -- close all open entries
    RUNNING = DESCR(e).T;        -- task owning the entry becomes running
    RUNNING.ip = DESCR(e).I;
            -- ip is the field containing the value of the program counter
            -- which is set to the value stored in field I of the entry's descriptor
else
    RUNNING = READY_QUEUE.dequeue();
}
```

When the end of the body of an accept statement for entry e is reached, the following kernel actions complete the rendezvous.

```
RUNNING = process_status;
READY_QUEUE. enqueue(dequeue(DESCR(e).W));
        -- move descriptor of caller referenced by field W of e's descriptor
        -- into READY_QUEUE
```

```
READY_QUEUE.enqueue(RUNNING);
      -- move descriptor of the task owning the entry e into RUNNING
RUNNING = READY_QUEUE.dequeue();-- select a ready task
process_status = RUNNING;
```

The actions to be executed as a consequence of an **accept** statement for entry e (not embedded in a **select** statement) are

```
if (DESCR(e).W).empty() {        -- if there are no pending requests
    DESCR(e).O = true;           -- the task issuing accept is suspended
    save process status in DESCR(e).T;
    RUNNING = READY_QUEUE.dequeue()
    process_status = RUNNING;
}   -- if waiting queue is not empty, then simply continue executing the accept body
```

To execute a select statement, a list LOE of the open entries involved in the selection is first constructed. If LOE is empty, then the exception PROGRAM_ERROR is raised. Otherwise, the following kernel actions are required:

```
if for all e in LOE (DESCR(e).W).empty() = true {
    -- i.e, there are no pending requests on the entries
    for all e in the list {
        DESCR(e).O = true;
        save process status in DESCR(e).T;
    };
    RUNNING = READY_QUEUE.dequeue()
    process_status = RUNNING;
else
    choose an e with (DESCR(e).W).empty() = false;
    -- i.e., e has a pending request
    proceed execution from instruction DESCR(e).I;
}
```

This completes our model implementation for concurrency features in programming languages. In practice, implementing such features requires the exploitation of machine features to reduce overheads due to process switching and unnecessary delays on synchronization conditions. However, our purpose in this section was not to describe detailed implementation techniques, but rather to provide a view of the operational semantics of concurrency, which complements what we saw in Chapter 2 for sequential constructs.

4.9 Bibliographic notes

Statement-level control structures were the subject of active research in the late 1960s and early 1970s. E.W. Dijkstra was the first to stress the need for discipline in programming and the influence of control structures on program understanding. He showed that unconstrained jumps (**goto** statements) should be avoided because they are responsible for the production of obscure, unstructured programs [Dijkstr68a]. Much of the subsequent research on "structured programming" was aimed at uncovering suitable control structures that could promote the writing of well-organized, readable programs. For a comprehensive retrospective view of this work, the reader may refer to [Knuth74].

Research on exception handling began in the 1970s [Goodenough75]. The main directions of investigations were design methods and language constructs to deal with exceptions. For a comprehensive survey of the field, the reader may refer to [Cristian95]. The discussion reported in the exception handling chapter of [Stroustrup94] is an excellent account of the trade-offs that must be considered by a language designer in the definition of certain programming language features. For a detailed understanding of the different choices made by different programming languages, the reader should refer to the specific bibliographic sources (see the "Language References" appendix).

Backtracking and and/or graphs are presented in most textbooks on computer algorithms, such as [Horowitz78]. Event-driven control structures in the context of database applications are surveyed in [Fraternali95].

An extensive study of coroutines is reported by [Marlin80]. This includes a survey of languages, a semantic description of the concept, and a discussion of programming language methodologies.

Concurrency in programming languages is often studied either as part of an operating systems course or as a separate course on concurrent programming. [Tanenbaum87] is a reference textbook on operating systems. [Andrews91] and [Ben-Ari90] provide an in-depth coverage of concurrent and distributed programming. The concept of semaphore was introduced in [Dijkstra68b]. Monitors were introduced by [Hoare74] and [BrinchHansen75]. [Hoare78] is a classic in the literature on message passing. It strongly influenced the rendezvous concept of Ada.

4.10 Exercises

1. Study the case statement of Pascal and compare it to the C++ switch statement and the Ada case statement.
2. What is the minimum possible number of iterations of the body of a Pascal "while" loop? How about a "repeat" loop?
3. It can be shown that, in principle, any program can be written using just these control structures:
   - grouping statements into a block;

- if...then...else...
- while...do...

Show how other control structures (such as the case statement or a repeat loop) can be represented using the above minimal set. Discuss why in practice a richer set of control structures is provided by a programming language.

4. Show how pointers to procedures (or functions) can be used in Ada to pass procedures (or functions) as parameters.

5. Ada, as originally defined, did not allow procedures or functions to be passed as parameters to a procedure (or function). Can this drawback be overcome by the use of generics? How? What are the differences with respect to passing a routine as a parameter?

6. Explain why aliasing makes the effects of implementing parameter passing by reference and by value-result different. Give an example.

7. Check in the Ada manual how the language specifies what happens when the effects of passing parameters by reference and by value-result are different.

8. What are the strings matched by the following SNOBOL4 pattern?

```
OPERATOR = '+' | '-'
EXPRESSION = *EXPRESSION OPERATOR *EXPRESSION | IDENTIFIER
```

9. Ada provides features to transfer specific information from the point where an exception is raised to the corresponding handler. Check in the language manual how this can be accomplished and show how these features can be used during debugging.

10. Compare the feature provided by Ada to disable exceptions (see the language manual) with the disabling mechanism provided by PL/I.

11. How can the exception-handling facilities of C++ be used to achieve the same effect as that described by the Eiffel fragment of Figure 4.3?

12. Suppose you have a program unit U that calls a function fun, which may raise exceptions and propagates them back to U. There are five kinds of exceptions that can be propagated: V, X, Y, Z, and W. An exception of kind V allows U to do some fixing and then re-invoke fun. An exception of kind X allows U to do some cleanup of the local state and then proceed normally. An exception of kind Y allows U to simply propagate the same exception. An exception of kind Z allows U to perform some action and then turn the received exception into another exception that is raised. Finally, an exception of kind W forces U to terminate the entire program. Provide an implementation of this scheme in C++, Ada, and Eiffel.

13. Write a short assessment of exception handling in ML, according to the style of the assessment we did in Section 4.4.6.

14. Examine the manuals of a few languages of your choice to find out what happens if an exception is raised while an exception is being handled.

15. Discuss how memory is managed for coroutines, assuming a block-structured language where coroutines can be declared locally inside (co)routines. (Hint: The creation of a set of coroutines can be viewed as the creation of a new execution stack—one for each coroutine.)

16. In the producer-consumer example implemented with semaphores in Section 4.8.3.1, suppose that V(mutex) is written incorrectly as P(mutex) in process Producer. How does the system behave?

17. When semaphores are used to implement mutual exclusion, it is possible to associate a semaphore SR with each resource R. Each access to R can then be written as

```
P(SR);
access R;
V(SR)
```

What should the initial value of SR be?

18. Some computers provide an indivisible machine instruction *test and set* (TS) that can be used for synchronization purposes. Let X and Y be two boolean variables. The execution of the instruction TS(X, Y) copies the value of Y into X and sets Y to false. A set of concurrent processes that must execute some instructions in mutual exclusion can use a global boolean variable PERMIT, initialized to true, and a local boolean variable X in the following way:

```
repeat TS(X, PERMIT)
until X;
instructions to be executed in mutual exclusion;
PERMIT:= true
```

   – In this case, processes do not suspend themselves; they are always executing (this is called *busy waiting*). Compare this solution to one based on semaphores in which P and V are implemented by the kernel.
   – Describe how to implement P and V on semaphores by using the test-and-set primitive in a busy wait scheme.

19. Define an Ada protected type to implement a shared protected variable that can be read and written in mutual exclusion.

20. How can you define task types in Ada? What are the main differences between protected types and task types?

21. We implemented mutual exclusion of monitor procedures by disabling interrupts. An alternative solution uses a semaphore for each monitor and performs a P on the semaphore before entering a monitor procedure, and a corresponding V upon exit. Detail this implementation and compare the two solutions.

22. Show how an Ada task can be used to implement a semaphore.

23. Show how an Ada protected type can be used to implement semaphores.

24. Design an Ada package that implements the abstract data type queue that is used in the abstract implementation of concurrency in Section 4.8.3.

25. Design a C++ class that implements the abstract data type queue that is used in the abstract implementation of concurrency in Section 4.8.3.

Structuring the program

C H A P T E R   **5**

The basic mechanisms described in previous chapters for structuring data (Chapter 3) and computation (Chapter 4) may be used for writing limited-size programs. In Chapter 4, we also discussed the use of control structures for structuring large programs. This chapter deals strictly with issues of programming large systems. We describe the basic concepts for structuring large programs (encapsulation, interfaces, information hiding) and the mechanisms provided by languages to support it (packaging, separate compilation). We also consider the concept of genericity in building software component libraries. Another approach that helps with writing large-scale programs is object-oriented programming, which is the subject of the next chapter.

The production of large programs—those consisting of more than several thousand lines—presents challenging problems that do not arise in developing smaller programs. The same methods and techniques that work well with small programs just don't "scale up." To stress the differences between small and large systems production, we refer to "programming in the small" and "programming in the large."

Two fundamental principles—*abstraction* and *modularity*—underlie all approaches to programming in the large. Abstraction allows us to understand and analyze the problem by concentrating on its important aspects and ignoring irrelevant details. Modularity allows us to design and build the program from smaller pieces called *modules*. During problem analysis, we discover and invent abstractions that allow us to understand the problem. During program design and implementation, we try to discover a modular structure for the program. In general, if modules that implement the program correspond closely to abstractions discovered during problem analysis, the program will be easier to understand and manage. The principles of modularity and abstraction help us apply the well-known problem-solving strategy known as "divide and conquer."

The concept of a "large program" is difficult to define precisely. We certainly do not want to equate the size of a program (e.g., the number of source statements) with its complexity. Largeness relates more to the "size" and complexity of the problem being solved than to the final size of a program in terms of the number of source lines. Often, however, the size of a program is a good indication of the complexity of the problem being solved.

Consider, as an example, the task of building an airline reservation system. The system is expected to keep a database of flight information. Reservation agents working at remote sites may access the database at arbitrary times and in any order. They may inquire about flight information, such as time and price; make or cancel a reservation on a particular flight; and update existing information, such as the local telephone number for a passenger. Certain authorized personnel can access the database to do special operations, such as adding or canceling a flight, or changing the type of the airplane assigned to a flight. Others may access the system to obtain statistical data about a particular flight or all flights. A problem of this magnitude imposes severe restrictions on the solution strategy and the following key requirements:

- The system has to function correctly. A seemingly small error, such as assignment to the wrong pointer, may lead to losing a reservation list or interchanging two different lists and be extremely costly. To guarantee correctness of the system, virtually any cost can be tolerated.
- The system is "long-lived." The cost associated with producing such a system is so high that it is not practical to replace the system with a totally new system. It is expected that the cost will be recouped only over a long period of time.
- During its lifetime, the system undergoes considerable modification. For our example, because of completely unforeseen new government regulations, changes might be required in price structure, a new type of airplane might be added, and so on. Other changes might be considered because experience with the system has uncovered new requirements. We might find it desirable to have the system find the best route automatically by trying different connections.
- Because of the magnitude of the problem, many people—tens or hundreds—are involved in the development of the system.

The study of these problems and their solutions—which are both technical and managerial—is outside the scope of this book: they are studied in software engineering. This chapter deals with requirements that these issues place on the programming language. Thus, this chapter is about issues of program organization. Section 5.1 reviews software design methods. Design methods provide guidelines for applying divide-and-conquer in software design. In Section 5.2 we discuss the concepts of encapsulation, interface, separate compilation, and module libraries. These concepts provide the bases for the application of modularity in programming languages. Case studies of different languages are provided in Section 5.3. Section 5.4 covers language support for *generic* units, which are highly flexible and general units that may be used in many contexts.

5.1 Software design methods

To combat the complexities of programming in the large, we need a systematic design method that guides us in composing a large program out of smaller units—which we call *modules*. A good design is composed of modules that interact with one another in well-defined and controlled ways. Consequently, each module can be designed, understood, and validated independently of the other modules. Once we have achieved such a design, we need programming language facilities that help us in implementing these independent modules, their relationships, and their interactions.

The goal of software design is to find an appropriate modular decomposition of the desired system. Indeed, even though the boundaries between programming in the large and programming in the small cannot be stated rigorously, we may say that programming in the large addresses the problem of modular system decomposition, and programming in the small refers to the production of individual modules. A good modular decomposition is one that is based on modules that are as independent from each other as possible. There are many methods for achieving such modularity. A well-known approach is *information hiding*, which uses the distribution of "secrets" as the basis for modular decomposition. Each module hides a particular design decision as its secret. The idea is that if a design decision has to be changed, only the module that "knows" the secret design decision needs to be modified and the other modules remain unaffected.

In Chapter 1 we discussed the importance of software design. If a design is composed of highly independent modules, it supports the requirements of large programs:

- Independent modules form the basis of work assignment to individual team members. The more independent the modules are, the more independently the team members can proceed in their work.

- The correctness of a complete program depends on the correctness of each individual module with respect to its expected behavior and on the correct interaction among the modules.
- Defects in the system may be repaired and, in general, the system may be enhanced more easily because the effects of modifications may be isolated to individual modules.

5.2 Concepts in support of modularity

We can summarize the discussion of the last section by saying that the key to software design is modularization. A good module represents a useful abstraction; it interacts with other modules in well-defined and regular ways; it may be understood, designed, implemented, compiled, and enhanced with reference to only the specification (not the implementation secrets) of other modules. Programming languages provide facilities for building programs in terms of constituent modules. In this chapter, we are interested in programming language concepts and facilities that help the programmer in dividing a program into modules, the relationships among those modules, and the extent to which program decompositions can mirror the decomposition of the design.

We have already seen some units of program decomposition in Chapters 3 and 4. *Procedures* and *functions* are an effective way of breaking a program into two modules: one which provides a service and another which uses the service. We may say that the procedure is a *server* or *service provider* and the caller is a *client*. Even at this level we can see some of the differences between different types of modularization units. For example, if we provide a service as a function, then the client has to use the service in an expression. On the other hand, if we provide the service in a procedure, then the client may not use it in an expression and is forced to use an imperative style.

Procedures and functions are units for structuring small programs, perhaps limited to a single file. Sometimes, we may want to organize a set of related functions and procedures together as a unit. For example, we saw in Chapter 3 how the *class* construct of C++ lets us group together a data structure and related operations. Ada and Modula-2 provide other constructs for this purpose. Before we delve into specific language facilities, we will first look at some of the underlying concepts of modularity. These concepts clarify the need for the language facilities and help us compare the different language approaches.

5.2.1 Encapsulation, interface, and implementation

As we have seen, a program unit provides a service that may be used by its clients. The unit is said to *encapsulate* the service. Encapsulation mechanisms provide two benefits: to group together the program components that combine to provide a service, and to make only the relevant aspects visible to clients. Information hiding is a design method that emphasizes the importance of concealing information as the basis for modularization. Encapsulation mechanisms are linguistic constructs that support the implementation of information-hiding modules. Through encapsulation, a module is clearly described by two parts: the *interface* and the *implementation*. The interface describes what services are provided by the module and how they can be accessed by clients. The implementation describes the module's internal secrets that provide the desired services.

The interface of a module describes a set of entities that are *exported* by the module. A client module *imports* those entities to be able to use the services of the provider module. Languages differ with respect to the kinds of entities they allow to be exported. For example, some languages allow a type to be exported and others do not.

For example, assume that a program unit implements a dictionary data structure that other units may use to store and retrieve pairs of the form <name, id>. This dictionary unit makes available to its clients operations for inserting a pair, such as <"Mehdi", 46>; retrieving elements by supplying the string component of a pair; and deleting elements by supplying the string component of a pair. The unit uses other helper routines and data structures to implement its service. The purpose of encapsulation is to ensure that the internal structure of the dictionary unit is *hidden* from the clients. By making visible to clients only those parts of the dictionary unit that they need to know, we achieve two important properties:

- The client is simplified: clients do not need to know how the unit works in order to be able to use it; and
- The service implementation is independent of clients and may be modified if necessary without affecting the clients.

Different languages provide different encapsulation facilities. Based on what we have seen in Chapter 3, we may say that the built-in types of a language are examples of encapsulated types. They hide the representation of the instances of those types and allow only legal operations to be performed on those instances.

We have also seen that the class construct of C++ makes only a subset of the defined entities—those declared as public—available to clients. All other class information is hidden. Figure 5.1 is a C++ class that declares the dictionary service mentioned above.

This program declares five publicly available functions. As we know from Chapter 4, the first two functions, dict() and ~dict(), may be used to create and

```
class dict {
public:
    dict();              //constructor for dictionary
    ~dict();             //destructor for dictionary
    void insert (char* c, int i);
    int lookup(char* c);
    void remove (char* c);
private:
    struct node {
        node* next;
        char* name;
        int id};
    node* root;
};
```

FIGURE 5.1 Definition of a dictionary module in C++

clean up a dictionary object, respectively. The other three functions may be used to access the dictionary object. The private part of the class defines the representation of a node of a dictionary and the root of the dictionary. This part of the declaration is not visible to the users of the class. The class encapsulates the dictionary service—both providing access and hiding unnecessary details.

To use the dictionary class, a client module may declare several instances of dictionaries and apply the allowed operations on them. The program fragment below shows a sample client of the dictionary class.

```
...
dict games();                        // create a dictionary object called games
games.insert("volleyball", 1);
games.insert("basketball", 2);
games.insert("football", 3);
...
cout << games.lookup("football") << "football." << endl;
```

The client may not access the elements of the games dictionary object directly through the pointer root. The only way to access the elements in the dictionary is through the public operations of the class.

5.2.2 Separation of interface and implementation

We have seen that a module may be thought of as having two components: an interface and an implementation. The services exported by a module are described in its interface; the clients need the interface to import those services. In fact, ideally, the interface is all that the client needs to know about the provider's unit. The implementation of the unit should be hidden from the client. Such a clean separation of the interface from the implementation contributes to the independence of the client and the server from one another. Languages differ in the amount of support that they provide to achieve independence of clients from servers.

The simplest interface—one that we have already seen in Chapter 4—is a *procedure* or *function interface*. A function declaration such as

```
int max (int& x, int& y)
```

specifies to the clients that the function max may be called by passing to it two integers; the function will return an integer result. We introduced the term *signature* to refer to these requirements on input and output for procedures and functions. Procedure signatures form the basis of type checking across procedures. The name of the function, max, is intended to convey something about the semantics of the function, namely, that the integer it will return is the maximum of the two integer input parameters. Ideally, the interface would specify the semantics and the requirements on parameters (for example, that they must be positive integers). Most programming languages do not support such facilities, however, and it is left as the task of the designer to document them in the design documents. An exception is the Eiffel language. In Chapter 3, we saw the use of preconditions and postconditions to specify such semantic requirements for procedures, functions, and classes.

In C++, where the unit of encapsulation is a *class*, the interface to the class consists of the interfaces of all the member functions of the class that are available to clients, as well as any other entities, such as types and variables, that are made public by the unit. The public entities defined in Figure 5.1 constitute the interface of the dictionary unit. Strictly speaking, a class definition represents more than the pure interface because it also lists some of the hidden secrets.

Ada treats the separation of interface and implementation quite strictly. In Ada, the unit of encapsulation is a *package*. A package encapsulates a set of entities such as procedures, functions, variables, and types. The package interface consists of the interfaces provided by each of those entities. The interface of a package (called *package specification*) is declared separately from the implementation of the package (called *package body*). Figure 5.2

```
package Dictionary is
    procedure Insert (C:String; I: Integer);
    function Lookup(C:String): Integer;
    procedure Remove (C: String);
end Dictionary;
```

FIGURE 5.2 Package specification in Ada

shows the Ada package specification for our Dictionary unit. The body of the dictionary package is shown in Figure 5.3. The package body contains all the implementation details that are hidden from the clients. This separation helps achieve both of the goals stated for encapsulation in Section 5.2.1. The package body, as can be seen in the figure, defines both the implementation of the entities defined in the package interface and the implementation of other entities internal to the module. These entities are completely hidden from the clients of the package. The package specification and the package body may appear in different files and may even be compiled separately. To write and compile a client module, only the service's package specification is necessary. Figure 5.4 shows the sketch of a client module that uses the Dictionary package.

The **with** clause serves as an import clause: it indicates the dependence of the client unit on the Dictionary unit. This clause is used by the compiler to select all the specification units required for the compilation of the client. The **use** clause gives visibility to the Dictionary package. Without the **use** clause, imported entities from Dictionary will have to be accessed using the dot

```
package body Dictionary is
    type Node;
    type Node_Ptr is access Node;
    type Node is
        record
            Name: String;
            Id: Integer;
            Next: Node_Ptr;
        end record;
    Root: Node_Ptr;
    procedure Insert (C:String; I: Integer) is
    begin
        --implementation...
    end Insert;
    function Lookup(C:String) return Integer is
    begin
        --implementation...
    end Lookup;
    procedure Remove (C: String) is
    begin
        --implementation...
    end Remove;
begin
    Root := null;
end Dictionary;
```

FIGURE 5.3 Package body in Ada

```
with Dictionary; use Dictionary;
procedure Main is
    Code: Integer;
begin
    Insert ("volleyball", 1);
    Insert ("basketball", 2);
    Insert ("football", 3);
    ...
    Code := Lookup ("basketball");
    ...
end;
```

FIGURE 5.4 Fragment of a client of the dictionary package of Figure 5.2

notation (e.g., Dictionary.Insert(...)). The **use** clause opens the scope of the package so that the imported entities can be accessed directly.

The example of Figure 5.2 and Figure 5.3 defines a module that provides a single dictionary, in contrast to the C++ example of Figure 5.1, which provides a class that can instantiate any number of dictionary objects. We will show later, in Section 5.3.4, how this can be done in Ada as well.

5.2.3 Separate and independent compilation

The idea of modularity is to enable the construction of large programs out of smaller parts that are developed independently. At the implementation level, independent development of modules implies that they may be compiled and tested individually—independently of the rest of the program. This is referred to as *independent* compilation. The term *separate* compilation is used to refer to the ability to compile units individually but subject to certain ordering constraints. For example, C supports independent compilation and Ada supports separate compilation. In Ada, as we will see later, some units may not be compiled until other units have been compiled. The ordering is imposed to allow checking of interunit references. With independent compilation, there is normally no static checking of entities imported by a module. That is, there is no *intermodule checking*.

To understand this point, consider the program sketch in Figure 5.5, written in a hypothetical programming language. Separate compilation means that unit B, which imports routine X from unit A, must be compiled after A. This allows any call to X issued by B to be checked statically against X's definition in A. If the language allows module interfaces to be compiled separately from their bodies, only A's interface must be compiled before B; its body can be compiled at any time after its corresponding interface has been compiled.

An independent or separate compilation capability is a necessity in the development of large programs because it allows different programmers to

Unit A
    export routine X (int, int);
    ...
end A

Unit B
    import from **Unit** A
    ...
    call X (...);
    ...
end B

FIGURE 5.5 Sketch of a program composed of two units

work concurrently on different parts of the program. Independent compilation does not constrain the order in which modules are developed. This gives the programmer the freedom to choose any order in the development of modules. Unfortunately, however, many linkers that are used to combine independently compiled modules into an executable program are unable to check intermodule errors. Both independent and separate compilation support the ability to limit the number of modules needed to be recompiled after some changes are made in a module. This is quite important in practice because it would be impractical to recompile thousands of modules when only a few modules have changed. Some language concepts and features support the limiting of the number of units that must be recompiled.

In general, programming languages need to define

- The *unit of compilation*: what may be compiled independently?
- The *order of compilation*: are compilation units required to be compiled in any particular order?
- The *amount of checking* between separately compiled modules: are interunit interactions checked for validity?

The issue of separate compilation is at the border of language definition and implementation. Clearly, if the language requires interunit checking to be performed, this implies a programming environment that is able to check module implementations against the interfaces of compilation units from which they import services. Interface checking of separately compiled modules is analogous to static type checking for programming in the small: both are aimed at the development of safe and reliable programs.

5.2.4 Libraries of modules

We have seen that the C++ class and Ada's package make it possible to group related entities into a single unit. But large programs consist of hundreds or even thousands of such units. To control the complexity of dealing with the large number of entities exported by all these units, it is essential to be able to organize these units into related groups. For example, it is difficult to ensure that all the thousands of units have unique names! In general, we can always find groupings of units that are related closely and avoid name clashes within those units, but not necessarily across all units.

A common example of a grouping of related services is a *library* of modules, such as a library of matrix manipulation routines. A library collects a number of related and commonly used services. Clients typically need to make use of different libraries in the same program and, since libraries are written by different people, the names in different libraries may conflict. For example, a library for manipulating lists and a library for manipulating dictionaries may both export procedures named insert. Mechanisms are needed for clients to conveniently distinguish between such identically named services. We have seen that the dot notation helps with this problem at the module level. But consider trying to use two different releases of the same library at the same time. How can you use some of the entities from one release and some from the other? Two major issues arise in the development and use of such libraries. One is how to deal with the increasing likelihood of name clashes when the number of units increases. The other is how to avoid the necessity of recompiling a client when a library that it uses has changed but the changes are in parts of the library not used by the client. Both C++ and Ada 95 have features to deal with these issues. We will describe these facilities when we discuss specific languages: namespaces of C++ in Section 5.3.3.3 and child libraries of Ada in Section 5.3.4.6.

5.3 Language features for programming in the large

We have so far discussed the concepts of programming in the large with isolated examples from programming languages. In this section we look at some interesting ways that existing programming languages support—or do not support—the concepts of programming in the large. All programming languages provide features for decomposing programs into smaller and largely autonomous units. We refer to such units as *physical* modules; we will use the term *logical* module to denote a module identified at the design stage. A logical module represents an abstraction identified by the designer. A logical module may be implemented by one or more physical modules. The closer the relationship between the physical modules and logical modules is, the better the physical program organization reflects the logical design structure.

We will discuss the relevant aspects of each language based on the following points:

- Module encapsulation: What is the unit of modularity and encapsulation supported by the language?

- Separation of interface from implementation: How does a client module gain access to a service provided by a server module? What entities may be exported and imported by a module?
- Program organization and module groupings: How independently can physical modules be implemented and compiled? What are the visibility and access control mechanisms supported by the language?

We will discuss Pascal, C, C++, Ada, and ML. Pascal and C are viewed here as representatives of the class of traditional, minimalist, procedural languages. Our conclusions about them hold, with minor changes, for other members of the class, such as older versions of FORTRAN. C++ is a representative of class-based languages. Ada is a representative of module-based languages, although the 1995 version of the language supports some level of object orientation. ML is reviewed as a representative of functional languages. A few comments on other languages will be given in Section 5.3.6.

Our discussion in this chapter touches on the subject of programming paradigms. Two specific paradigms, object-oriented and functional programming, will be covered in detail in Chapters 6 and 7, respectively.

5.3.1 Pascal

In this section we provide an assessment of Pascal's features for programming in the large. Since many dialects and extensions of Pascal exist, here we consider the original version of the language. Most of the inconveniences discussed here have been corrected by the enhancements provided by modern implementations.

The only features provided by Pascal for decomposing a program into modules are procedures and functions, which can be used to implement procedural abstractions. The language thus only supports procedural programming. Some later versions of the language have modified the original version of Pascal extensively by adding module-based and object-oriented programming features.

A Pascal program has the structure shown in Figure 5.6. A program consists of declarations and operations. The operations are either the built-in ones provided by the language or those declared as functions and procedures. A procedure or function itself may contain the declaration of constants, types, variables, and other procedures and functions. The organization of a Pascal program is thus a *tree structure of modules* (see the discussion of the static nesting tree in Section 2.7.4). The tree structure represents the textual nesting of lower-level modules. Nesting is used to control the scope of names declared within modules, according to the static binding rule presented in Section 2.7.4.

```
program program_name (files);
declarations of constants, types, variables, procedures and functions;
begin
    statements (no declarations)
end.
```

FIGURE 5.6 Structure of a Pascal program

To assess the structure of Pascal programs, consider the following example. Suppose that the top-down modular design of a module A identifies two modules, B and C, providing subsidiary procedural abstractions. Similarly, module B invokes two private procedural abstractions provided by modules D and E. Module C invokes a private procedural abstraction provided by module F. Figure 5.7 shows a nesting structure for a program that satisfies the design constraints.

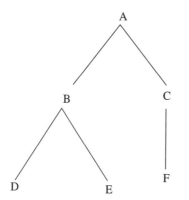

FIGURE 5.7 Static nesting tree of a hypothetical Pascal program

A basic problem with the solution of Figure 5.7 is that the structure does not enforce the restrictions on procedure invocations found at the design stage. Actually, the structure allows for the possibility of several other invocations. For example, E can invoke D, B, and A; C can invoke B and A; and so on. On the other hand, the structure of Figure 5.7 imposes some restrictions that might become undesirable. For example, if we discover that module F needs the procedural abstraction provided by module E, the current structure is no longer adequate. Figure 5.8 shows a rearrangement of the program structure that is compatible with this new requirement. The problem with this new organization is that the structure no longer displays the hierarchical decomposition of abstractions. Module E appears to be a subsidiary abstraction used by A, although the only reason for its placement at that level in the tree is that both modules B and F need to refer to it. Similar problems occur

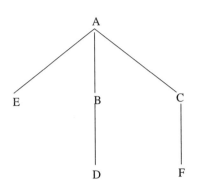

FIGURE 5.8 A rearrangement of the program structure of Figure 5.7.

for variables, constants, and types. The tree structure provides indiscriminate access to variables declared in enclosing modules. In addition, if any two modules M and N need to share a variable, this variable must be declared in a module that statically encloses both M and N; thus the variable becomes accessible to any other modules enclosed by this module.

Further problems are caused by the textual layout of a Pascal program. The entire program is a single monolithic text. If the program is large, module boundaries are not immediately visible, even if the programmer uses careful conventions for indentation. A routine heading can appear well before its body, because of intervening inner routine declarations. Consequently, programs can be difficult to read and modify.

The problems with Pascal discussed in this section stem from block structure and, therefore, hold for other ALGOL-like languages. Block structure is adequate for programming in the small because it supports stepwise refinement quite naturally. It is not so valuable for structuring large programs. The program structure resulting from nesting may interfere with the logical structure found during design. This can impair the writability, readability, and modifiability of programs.

Another important question regarding Pascal is the support of the separate compilation of modules. The original Pascal Report, which provides the official language definition, does not address the issue at all. For example, the original Report leaves unanswered the following questions:

- What program entities can a separate compilation unit export?
- How is a unit interface specified?
- What amount of type checking is performed across unit interfaces?

Different implementations have adopted different solutions to these points. As a result, Pascal programs developed on different platforms may be incompatible. For example, some implementations allow outer-level procedures and functions to be compiled independently. Independently compiled units are assembled via a standard linker, which resolves the bindings between the entities imported by each module and the corresponding entities exported by other modules. No intermodule checks are performed, however, to verify if, say, a call to an external procedure is consistent with the corresponding procedure declaration. Errors of this kind might thus remain uncaught. Other implementations of Pascal provide safer separate-compilation facilities based on the notion of a module that encapsulates a set of constants, procedures, and types.

5.3.2 C

C provides function definitions as the units for decomposing a program into procedural abstractions. Functions may not be further decomposed via locally nested functions. In addition, C relies on a minimum of language features and a number of conventions to support programming in the large. These conventions are well recognized by C programmers and are even reflected in tools that have been developed to support the language. Indeed, a major portion of the programming in the large support is provided by the file-inclusion commands of the C preprocessor.

5.3.2.1 Encapsulation

The unit of encapsulation in C is a file. Typically, the entities declared at the head of a file are visible to the functions in that file and are also made available to functions in other files if those functions choose to declare them. The declaration

```
extern int max;
```

states that the variable max to be used here is defined—and storage for it allocated—elsewhere. Variables declared in a C function are local and known only to that function. Variables declared outside of functions are assumed to be available to other units if they declare them using the extern specifier. But a unit may decide to hide such variables from other units by declaring them static.

5.3.2.2 Interface and implementation

The C unit of physical modularity is a file. There is no language support for the separation of a module's interface from its implementation. Instead, by convention, a logical module is implemented in C by two physical modules (files), which we may roughly call the module's interface and its implementation. The interface, called a *header* or an *include* file, declares all symbols exported by the module and thus available to the clients of the module. The header file contains the information necessary to satisfy the type system when the client modules are compiled. The implementation file of the module contains the private part of the module and implements the exported services. A client module needing to use the functionality of another module "includes" the header file of the provider module and links to the implementation file. A header file may declare constants, type definitions, variables, and functions. Only the signature of the function—called *prototype* in C—is given by the declaration; the function definition appears in the implementation file. Any names defined in the outer level of a file—that is, not inside functions—are known throughout that file and may also be known outside of that file.

The header files included by a module enable the compiler to compile the module separately from other implementation files. The object module generated by the compiler includes unresolved references to those variables and functions imported via the header files. The linker combines several such separately compiled modules into an executable module, resolving the intermodule references in the process. The header file is usually named with a .h extension and the implementation file is named with a .c extension. These conventions have largely overcome the lack of any explicit support for program organization.

Figure 5.9 shows the header and implementation files for a module providing a stack data structure. As we can see, within the file the language provides no encapsulation facilities. For example, the main program in Figure 5.9 has complete access to the internal structure of the stacks s1 and s2. In fact, this property is used by the main program to initialize the stacks s1 and s2 by setting their stack pointers (top) to 0. There are ways to implement this program to reduce this interference between client and server, but all depend on the care taken by the programmer. There is no control over what is exported: by default, all entities in a file are exported. Files may be compiled separately and interfile references are resolved at link time with no type checking. A file may be compiled as long as all the header files it includes are available.

5.3.2.3 Program organization

The general structure of a C program is shown in Figure 5.10. All files have similar structure except that only one of the files must contain a function named main, which is used to start the program's execution. Because functions are not allowed to be nested in C, the nesting problems of Pascal do not occur.

```
/* file stack.h */
/* header (include) file exporting declarations to clients*/
typedef struct stack {
    int elments[100];    /* stack of 100 ints */
    int top;             /* number of elements*/
};
void push(stack, int);
int pop(stack);
/*****---------------------end of file        ****/

/*file stack.c */
/*implementation of stack operations*/
#include "stack.h"
void push(stack s, int i) {
    s.elements[s.top++] = i;
};
int pop (stack s) {
    return s.elements[--s.top];
};
/*****---------------------end of file        ****/

/* file main.c */
/* a client of stack*/
#include "stack.h"
void main(){
    stack s1, s2;            /* declare two stacks */
    s1.top = 0; s2.top = 0; /* initialize them */
    int i;
    push (s1, 5);    /* push something on first stack */
    push (s2, 6);    /* push something on second stack*/
    ...
    i = pop(s1);     /* pop first stack */
    ...
}
```

FIGURE 5.9 Separate files implementing and using a stack in C

```
#include ...various files...
global declarations
function definitions
void main (parameters)
{
...one main function needed
...in a program
}
```

FIGURE 5.10 Structure of a C module

There are no explicit import or export facilities. There are two facilities for controlling the scope of names across files, extern and static:

- All functions defined in a file are available for import by default. Variables may be imported by explicitly declaring them as being externally defined (using extern).
- To prevent the importation of an entity—thus limiting the scope of the entity to be local to itself only—a module may declare such an entity (function or variable) to be static.

The following two lines import the integer variable maximum_length and hide the integer variable local_size from other modules.

```
extern int maximum_length;
static int local_size;
```

The static designation affects the exported symbols at link time. A compiled module exports the names of its (nonstatic) routines and variables as symbols defined to the linker. A compiled module will have unresolved references for any symbols designated as extern in the module. The linker attempts to match such unresolved references with the symbols defined by other modules.

5.3.3 C++

C++ is based on C and it shares C's reliance on conventions. It also uses a file as the unit of physical modularity. Like C, C++ provides functions as a decomposition construct to implement abstract operations. Nevertheless, C++'s most important enhancements to C are in the area of programming in the large. In particular, the class construct of C++ provides a unit of logical modularity that supports the implementation of abstract data types. Combined with templates, classes may be used to implement generic abstract data types. The class provides encapsulation and control over interfaces. Actually, classes have many uses in C++. In this chapter, we review the use of classes as modules. We will examine the use of classes to support object-oriented programming in Chapter 6.

5.3.3.1 Encapsulation

The unit of logical modularity in C++ is the class. A class serves several purposes, including

- Definition of a new (user-defined) data type.
- Encapsulation of a group of entities into a unit.

Entities defined by a class are either *public*—exported to clients—or *private*—hidden from clients. There are also *protected* variables, which will be discussed in the next chapter.

The class defines a user-defined type; to use the services offered by a class, the client must first create an instance of the class, called an *object*. We saw an example of this with the dictionary example in Section 5.2.1.

Classes may be nested. But as we saw in the case of Pascal, nesting may be used only for programming in the small and is of limited utility for programming in the large.

Both classes and functions may be generic, supporting a generic programming style. We will discuss generic units in Section 5.4.

5.3.3.2 Program organization

Classes define the abstractions from which the program is to be composed. The main program or a client creates instances of the classes and calls on them to perform the desired task. Figure 5.11 shows a class implementing a stack of integers.[1] By convention, the interface and implementation of a class are separated into two files, a header file and an implementation file.

The :: operator used in stack::push is used to resolve the scope of names. In this case, it indicates that the push operation is an operation of the class stack. In general, X::x refers to x in the scope X; ::x refers to x in the global environment.

Some points to observe about this program are as follows:

- In the main program, stacks are declared in the same way that variables of language-defined types are declared.
- The operations exported by stack—push and pop—are called in the main program by using the dot notation and accessing the desired operation of the appropriate stack object (s1 or s2).
- The definitions of the operations push and pop may appear in the class body or outside of it.
- Finally, in some cases, the compiler will try to expand the code of the member functions in-line, if possible, to avoid the overhead of a function call.

In summary, C++ supports the development of independent modules (but does not enforce it):

1 A class's *interface* and *implementation* may be separated and even compiled separately from each other. The implementation must "include" the interface definition and therefore has to be compiled after the interface file exists.
2 The separation between a class interface and its definition is not complete. A class definition, which we have equated to its interface, contains not only the exported entities, but also private entities of the class. Even though these entities appear in the interface file, they are invisible to the clients. They are included in the interface to enable the

---

1. The same problem can, of course, be solved by instantiating a generic class, such as the one defined by the template in Figure 3.4.

```
// ********** file stack.h
//header file containing declarations exported to clients
class stack {
public:
    stack();
    void push(int);
    int pop();
private:
    int elements[100]; // stack represented as array
    int top = 0;          // number of stored elements
};
// **********end of file stack.h
// **********file stack.c
// the implementation of stack member functions
#include "stack.h"
void stack::push(int i) {
    elements[top++] = i;
};
int stack::pop() {
    return elements[--top];
};
// **********end of file stack.c
// ********** file main.c
// a client of stack
#include "stack.h"
main(){
    stack s1, s2;  // declare two stacks
    int i;
    s1.push(5);  // push something on first stack
    s2.push(6);  // push something on second stack
    ...
    i = s1.pop();  // pop first stack
    ...
}
// ********** end of file main.c
```

FIGURE 5.11 Stack class in C++, and a client

compiler to compile the clients of the class without access to the implementation of the
class. Section 5.3.4.5 contains a detailed explanation of this point.

3 Client modules may be compiled with access only to the interface modules of the service providers, and not to their implementation modules.

4 Any names defined in a class are local to the class unless explicitly declared to be public. Client modules must use the object name to gain access to the names internal to the
class.

5.3.3.3 Grouping of units

C++ has several mechanisms for relating units to each other. First, classes may be nested. As we have said before, this is a programming-in-the-small feature. Two other mechanisms, "friend" functions and namespaces, are discussed next.

Friend functions

A class in C++ defines a user-defined type. As a result, the operations it defines as public are operations on objects of that type. But sometimes we may encounter operations that do not naturally belong to one object or another. For example, if we define a class for complex numbers, it may have a data part that stores the real and imaginary parts of the number, along with exported operations that let clients create and manipulate objects of type complex. But what about an addition operation that takes two complex objects to add together? To which of the two complex objects does the operation belong as a member? As another example, consider defining a function that multiplies a vector with a matrix. Should this function be a member of the vector class or the matrix class? For such functions to be implemented efficiently, they need to have access to the private parts of the objects they manipulate, but they do not really belong to a particular object. Module-based languages such as Ada and Modula-2 allow these related entities to be packaged together in a single textual unit. A class-based language such as C++ must adopt a different solution. In C++, a class can grant access to its private parts by declaring certain functions as its "friends." Friend functions have the same rights as member functions of the class but are otherwise normal global functions or methods of other classes.

Figure 5.12 shows the definition of a complex number class. The class defines the type complex, which is internally composed of two doubles, rep-

```
class complex {
public:
    complex(double r, double i ){re = r; im = i;}
    friend complex operator+ (complex, complex);
    friend complex operator- (complex, complex);
    friend complex operator* (complex, complex);
    friend complex operator/ (complex, complex);
private:
    double re, im;
};
```

FIGURE 5.12 Illustration of the use of friend declarations in C++

resenting the real and imaginary parts of a complex number. These are hidden from clients. The class exports a method of constructing a complex number out of two doubles. Thus, the following declaration creates two complex numbers:

```
complex x(1.0, 2.0), y(2.5, 3.5);
```

The other declarations in Figure 5.12 state that the operator functions to be defined later (+, −, *, and /) are friends of the class complex and thus may access the private parts of the class. They are not member functions of the class and they are not exported by the class. They are simply given preferential treatment by the class. Of course, friend functions do not need to be exported to clients if they are global functions.

Defining these operators as friend functions allows the clients to naturally use these functions as binary operations, such as

```
complex c = c + x;
```

If the addition operation were a member of the class, the notation for clients would be quite awkward. For example, we might have had to write something like

```
c.add(x)
```

in order to add the complex x to complex c.

The need for friend functions is a consequence of C++'s use of classes both as user-defined types and as the encapsulation mechanism. In a language like Ada, where the package is used not to implement types but to group related entities, we would naturally group type definitions for complex and its "friend" functions in the same package. The functions automatically gain access to the private parts of the package because they are part of the package. In both cases, any changes to the representation of the data may require changes to the functions, whether they are part of a package or they are friend functions. We will see in Section 6.3.5 that Java combines classes and packages and thus resolves this dichotomy.

Namespaces

In C and in C++, the unit of global naming is a file. The names defined at the outer level of a file are known globally by default. For example, the names of all classes defined in a file implementing a library are known to any client that "includes" that file. As we asked in Section 5.2.4, how can we handle the situation when two libraries provide two classes with the same name? How can a client use both of those classes? How can a library provider add a new service to its library and be sure that the new name of the service does not conflict with any existing uses of the clients? Since names are created by independent people, a single global name space is a serious problem in the development of large programs. The solution of C++ is to partition the global name space into smaller spaces called *namespaces*. The names defined in a namespace are independent of those in any other namespace and may be referenced by supplying the name of the namespace. This mechanism enables library writers to provide their libraries in their own namespaces with a guarantee of independence from other library providers. Of course, it is necessary for the names of the namespaces themselves to be unique.

For example, consider the XYZ Corp., which provides a library of classes for manipulating turbine engines. It might provide its library in a namespace XYZCorp:

```
namespace XYZCorp {
    typedef turbodiesel ...;
    void start(turbodiesel);
    //...other definitions
}
```

A client wanting to use the turbodiesel definition has several options. One is to directly name the definition. The :: operator is used to qualify the namespace in which the compiler should look for the desired object.

```
XYZCorp::turbodiesel t;
```

Another option is to first create a synonym for the name so that the namespace name does not need to be repeated:

```
using XYZCorp::turbodiesel; //creates a synonym turbodiesel
// ...
turbodiesel t;
XYZCorp::start(t);
```

The final option is for a client that wants to import all the definitions from a namespace. The namespace may be opened by importing it:

```
using namespace XYZCorp; //this opens the namespace completely
turbodiesel t;
start(t);
```

The namespace mechanism is intended to help library providers become independent of other library providers, enable them to update their libraries without danger of interfering with client code, and even provide new releases of libraries that coexist with older releases (each release lives in a different namespace).

The :: operator is used generally to deal with scope resolution. X::x refers to x in the scope X, which may be a namespace or a class whose name, X, is known in the current referencing environment.

5.3.4 Ada

Ada was designed specifically to support programming in the large. It has elaborate facilities for the support of modules, encapsulation, and interfaces. Rather than relying on convention as in C and C++, Ada makes an explicit distinction between specification and implementation of a module. A file may be compiled if the specifications of the modules it uses are available. Thus, Ada naturally supports a software development process in which module specifications are developed first and implementation of those modules may proceed independently. Because Ada requires strict type checking across modules, the usual Ada implementation is based on a compile-time library with which module specifications are compiled. Each time a module specification is compiled, all relevant type information is stored in the library. A module may be compiled if all the module specifications it needs are already in the library. This library supports the checking of intermodule references at compile time (Section 3.5.3).

5.3.4.1 Encapsulation

The package is Ada's unit of modularity. An Ada module encapsulates a group of entities and thus supports module-based programming. We have already seen that the language's explicit distinction between module specification and module body forces the programmer to separate what is expected by the module from what is hidden within the module. All units in Ada may also be generic. We will discuss generic units in Section 5.4.

5.3.4.2 Interface and implementation

We have already seen in Section 5.2.2 that Ada's package supports the separation of the specification and body of a module. The interface of an Ada unit consists of the **with** statement, which lists the names of units from which entities are imported, and the *unit specification* (enclosed within an **is...end** pair), which lists the entities exported by the unit. For example, the following unit, T, lists unit X (a subprogram) in its **with** statement. Consequently, it is legal to use X within T's body.

```
with X;
package T is
    C: Integer;
    procedure D (...);
end T;
package body T is
    ...
    ...
    ...
end T;
```

Similarly, the following procedure U can legally call procedure T.D and access variable T.C. On the other hand, unit X is not visible to U.

```
with T;
procedure U (...) is
    ...
    ...T.D...
    ...T.C...
    ...
end U;
```

To make it possible to refer to imported entities more conveniently, Ada has a **use** clause that serves to open the scope of the used unit. With the **use** clause, the dot notation may be avoided. For example, the same program as above may be written as

```
with T;
use T;
procedure U (...) is
    ...
    ...D... --no need for T.
    ...C... --no need for T.
    ...
end U;
```

The **with** clause applies to the specification part of a package. That is, only the entities listed in the specification part are made available to the importing unit. The package body is the implementation of the module and is hidden from the importing module.

The clean separation between interface and implementation breaks down if a unit wants to export a type. We will discuss this issue in Section 5.3.4.5 after we look at the separate compilation facility of Ada.

5.3.4.3 Program organization

Ada's support for programming in the large consists not only of features that support modular programs but also features that support separate development

and compilation of modules. An Ada program is a linear collection of modules
that can be either subprograms or packages. These modules are called *units*.
One particular unit that implements a subprogram is the main program in the
usual sense.

Module declarations may be nested. Consequently, a unit can be organized
as a tree structure of modules. Overuse of nesting within a unit causes the
same problems as were discussed for Pascal (see Section 5.3.1). These problems can be mitigated by the use of the *subunit* facility offered by Ada. This
facility permits the body of a module embedded in the declarative part of a
unit (or subunit) to be written separately from the enclosing unit (or subunit).
Instead of the entire module, only a *stub* need appear in the declarative part of
the enclosing unit. The program in Figure 5.13 illustrates the concept of the
subunit.

```
procedure X ( ... ) is                --unit specification
    W: Integer;
    package Y is                      --inner unit specification
        A: Integer;
        function B (C: Integer) return Integer;
    end Y;
    package body Y is separate;       --this is a stub
begin                                 --uses of package Y and variable W
    ...
    ...
    ...
end X;
-----------------------------------next file--------------
separate (X)                          --subunit's body
package body Y is
    procedure Z (...) is separate;    --this is a stub
    function B (C: Integer) return Integer is
    begin                             --use procedure Z
        ...
        ...
        ...
    end B;
end Y;
-----------------------------------next file--------------
separate (X.Y)
procedure Z (...) is
begin
    ...
end Z;
```

FIGURE 5.13 The use of stubs in Ada

The prefix **separate** (X) specifies package body Y as a subunit of unit X. Similarly, **separate** (X.Y) specifies procedure Z as a subunit of package Y nested within X. The subunit facility not only can improve the readability of programs, but also supports top-down programming. When writing a program at a certain level of abstraction, you may want to leave some details to be decided at a lower level. Suppose you realize that a certain procedure is required to accomplish a given task. Although calls to that procedure can be immediately useful when you want to test the execution flow, the body of the procedure can be written at a later time. For now, all you need is a *stub*. The subunit facility, however, does not overcome the problems caused by the tree nesting structure. The textually separate subunit body is still considered to be logically located at the point at which the corresponding stub appears in the enclosing (sub)unit. It is exactly this point that determines the entities visible to the subunit. In the example, both subunits Y and Z can access variable W declared in unit X.

Each logical module discovered at the design stage can be implemented as a unit. If the top-down design has been done carefully, logical modules should be relatively simple. Consequently, there should be little or no nesting within units. Of course, Ada does not prevent the abuse of nesting within units. Actually, the entire program could be designed as a single unit with a deeply nested tree structure. It is up to the designer and programmer to achieve a more desirable program structure.

5.3.4.4 Separate compilation

The separate compilation facility of Ada supports an incremental rather than a parallel development of programs, because units must be developed according to a partial ordering. This ordering reflects Ada's support for a particular discipline of program development. A unit can be submitted for compilation only after the interfaces of all used units are frozen. Consequently, the programmer is forced to postpone the design of a unit body until the imported interfaces have been designed.

In the previous section, we have seen how the **use** and **with** clauses are used to import services from packages. The **with** clause is also used to support separate compilation by establishing a partial ordering on the sequence in which modules may be compiled. The set of units and subunits that make up a program can be compiled in one or more separate compilations. Each compilation translates one or more units and/or subunits. The order of compilation must satisfy the following constraints.

- A unit can be compiled only if all units mentioned in its **with** statement have been compiled previously.

- A subunit can be compiled only if the enclosing unit has been compiled previously.

In addition, unit specifications can be compiled separately from their bodies. A unit body must be compiled after its specification. The **with** clause only
establishes an order based on specification units. That is, the specification of
a unit U mentioned in the **with** statement of a unit W must be compiled before
W. On the other hand, U's body may be compiled either before or after W.
These constraints ensure that a unit is submitted for compilation only after the
compilation of unit specifications, from which it can import entities. The
compiler saves in a library file the descriptors of all entities exported by units.
When a unit is submitted for compilation, the compiler uses this library file to
perform the same amount of type checking on the unit, whether the program
is compiled in parts or as a whole.

5.3.4.5 Ada's private type

Ada's choice of the package as an encapsulation mechanism, together with its
support for the separate compilation of the package specification and its body,
create an interesting issue when a package exports a type. This issue has motivated the **private** type feature of Ada.

In Figure 5.2, we declared a dictionary module that exports procedures
and functions only. The package body included the implementation of the
dictionary data structures. When the package is declared in the program, the
data structures necessary for the package, in this case the Root pointer, are
allocated. Therefore, with such a module, we get exactly one dictionary
object in the program. In this case, we have achieved a clean separation
between the client module and the dictionary module because the representation of the dictionary object is completely hidden from the client and appears
only in the body of the Dictionary module.

But suppose that we want a solution similar to the C++ example of Figure
5.1, which allows clients to create as many dictionaries as they need. In this
case, the Dictionary module must export a dictionary type. To support information hiding, we want the representation of the type to be hidden from clients.
As we saw in the C++ program, the representation of the dictionary was
declared in the private section of the class definition. In Ada, this can be done
using the private type. Figure 5.14 shows a package specification for our
modified Dictionary module.

The beginning part of the package specification, the part between **is** and
private, are the exported entities. The type Dict is declared to be **private**. At the
end of the package specification, there are a series of declarations after the

```
package Dictionary is
    type Dict is private;
    procedure Insert (D: in out Dict; C:String; I: Integer);
    function Lookup(D: Dict; C: String) return Integer;
    procedure Remove (D: in out Dict; C: String);
private
    type Node;
    type Node_Ptr is access Node;
    type Node is
        record
            Name: String;
            Id: Integer;
            Next: Node_Ptr;
        end record;
    type Dict is new Node_Ptr;
end Dictionary;
```

FIGURE 5.14 An Ada package specification exporting a (private) type

keyword **private**. These declarations are not exported by the package and are secrets of the package implementation. They are similar to the private members in a C++ class declaration. In this example, we wanted to implement the Dict type as a linked list. To do so, we needed some auxiliary type definitions for dictionary entries. Following these auxiliary type definitions, we finally define the type Dict as a pointer to dictionary entries. Thus, the representation for the exported type Dict appears in the private part of a package specification.

The information in the private part of a package specification is not part of the module interface and is invisible to the client. Therefore, the private information X should logically be placed in the body of the package. Indeed, the information did appear in the body of the package in our previous solution when we did not export a Dict type. Why is it required in the package specification now? The answer has to do with Ada's support of separate compilation. As we have seen, to support programming in the large, Ada allows the separate compilation of clients and providers. In particular, a client using the Dictionary package may be compiled separately after the Dictionary package specification has been compiled. Let us look at such a client.

Figure 5.15 shows a sample client using the Dictionary package. This client declares two objects of type Dict. The compiler needs to know how much storage to allocate for these variables. To do that, it needs to know the size of the Dict type. But if the provider module is exporting a type and not its representation, the size of the type cannot be determined from the specification. Ada's solution to this problem is the **private** type. Placing the representation in the

```
with Dictionary;
use Dictionary;
procedure Main is
    People, Things: Dict;
    ...
begin
    Insert (Things, "Table", 20);
    Insert (People, "Bill", 45);
    ...
end;
```

FIGURE 5.15 A client of package Dictionary

private part of a package specification makes it available to the compiler but hides it from the programmers of client modules. This solution enables the compiler to generate code to allocate variables for imported types. The drawback of this solution is that if we decide to change the representation of an exported type, the clients will have to be recompiled even though the type representation is not logically part of the module interface. The recompilation is necessary because a change is made in the module specification.

In conclusion, the private type in a package specification solves the practical problem of separate compilation but, by mixing implementation and interface, suffers from the following consequences:

- It violates the principle of top-down design. The representation must be determined at the same time as the specification of the data type, and both appear in the same textual unit.
- It limits the power of the language to support libraries of reusable modules, unless special care is taken in the implementation. For example, a client module using FIFO queues may be compiled and validated with respect to a FIFO queue package providing a specific representation for FIFO queues (e.g., arrays). The client module must be recompiled if we want to reuse it in a different program in which FIFO queues are implemented using a different data representation, even though the interfaces for manipulating FIFO queues are the same in both cases.

These comments also hold for C++ because of the appearance of private entities in a class definition. Modula-2 and Java solve these problems in different ways. Their approaches are discussed in Section 5.3.6.

5.3.4.6 Grouping of units

Developers of large programs consisting of thousands of modules face two kinds of practical challenges. One is to deal with the proliferation of names and the increasing likelihood of naming conflicts. The other is to reduce the amount of recompilation required when one or more units change. These issues arise in particular when we try to build libraries of reusable modules. *Child library units* of Ada address these issues by allowing the programmer to group packages together in a hierarchical organization.

Child libraries

The Ada package groups a set of related entities. The package may seem to be an ideal mechanism for building program libraries such as libraries of mathematical functions. Clients may import either selected services from a package or all the services provided by the package by using the **use** clause. The package, however, is inadequate as a structural mechanism for grouping a collection of library modules. Here are some deficiencies in the use of a package as a structuring mechanism for libraries:

- Suppose a client uses two different libraries, encapsulated in packages A and B. Since the client expects to make extensive use of both libraries, it uses the **use** clause to import all the library services. But if libraries A and B export entities with the same name, the client would encounter name clashes at compile time. Ada provides a renaming facility to get around this problem. Renaming solves initial name clash problems but does not solve the serious problem, which we discuss next.

- More serious is the case where there are no name clashes. The client code compiles and works properly. But suppose that a new version of library B is released with new functionality. It happens that one of the new functions introduced in B has a name identical to a name provided by A. The next time that the client code is compiled, compilation errors will show up due to name clashes. These errors would be particularly confusing because the previously working client code appears not to work even though it may not have been changed at all.

- In the previous case, after the release of the new version of the library B, the client code has to be recompiled even though it does not make use of the new functionality of the library B. The recompilation is necessary due to Ada's rules on the order of compilation, because in this case the specification of the library module has changed.

Ada 95 has addressed these problems by introducing the notion of child libraries, which allow packages to be hierarchically organized. The idea is that if new functionality is added to an existing package that implements a library, the new functionality may itself be organized as a new package that is a child of the original package. The child package has visibility to the parent package. But the clients of the original library are not affected by the introduction of a child package. The child package makes it possible to add functionality to a package without disturbing the existing clients of the package.

In general, a library developer may provide a number of packages organized as a tree. Each package other than the root package has a parent package. An existing library may be extended by adding a child library unit to one of its existing nodes. Neither the parent library unit nor any clients of the parent need to be recompiled. For example, if the library Root exists, we may add Root.Child without disturbing Root or clients of Root. Root.Child may be compiled separately. It has visibility to Root and to Root's siblings.

```
package Root is
    --specification of Root library
    --...
end Root;
-----------
package Root.Child is
    --specification of a child library unit
    --...
end Root.Child;
-----------
package body Root.Child is
    --implementation of Root.Child
    --...
end Root.Child;
-----------
```

Each of the above segments may be compiled separately. The clients of Root need not be recompiled if they do not use Root.Child.

Ada's child libraries and C++ namespaces are two different solutions to the same problem.

5.3.5 ML

Modularity is not only the province of imperative languages. The notion of module is important in any language that is to be used for programming in the large. For example, ML is a functional programming language with extensive support for modularity and abstraction. In Chapter 7, we will study the basics of functional programming and ML. There we will see ML's support for defining new types and abstract data types, which also help in programming in the large. In this section we give a brief overview of ML's support for modules and interfaces.

5.3.5.1 Encapsulation

The ML module system provides three main constructs for building modules and interfaces. These are *structures*, *signatures*, and *functors*. Structures and functors are used to build modules. Structures make it possible to group a set of entities together but do not hide any of the entities. A signature is used to define an interface. It consists of a set of types and signatures of individual functions, without any implementations. We can achieve information hiding by attaching a signature to a structure. Only the entities listed in the signature will be available to the clients of the structure when it is constrained by the signature. Thus, the structure corresponds somewhat to an Ada package body and the signature to a package specification. But a difference with Ada is that the interface and the structure are independent of each other. We may attach the same signature to different structures and use the same structure with different signatures.

Functors are used to build a new structure out of an existing structure. It is an operation for combining structures to produce new structures. For example, if a structure S provides a sort routine that uses a less-than operation, and a structure Math provides a less-than operation, we can define a functor to specialize S with Math to build a particular sort structure that uses the less-than operation from Math. We will discuss structures and signatures more in Chapter 7. Here, we examine these constructs only as support for encapsulation.

We start by looking at structures. Figure 5.16 shows a Dictionary structure in ML that corresponds to our dictionary example package of Figure 5.3. Recall the syntax and case analysis style of programming from Chapter 5. We will describe the details of the functions in Chapter 7. Here, we are interested only in what is exported to clients by the module.

This Dictionary structure exports an exception, NotFound; a variable, create; and two functions, insert and lookup. The create variable is declared to have the type (string * int) list. This type denotes a "list of pairs." The pairs, denoted

```
structure Dictionary =
struct
    exception NotFound;

    val create: (string * int) list = nil;  (*create an empty dictionary*)

(* insert (c, i, D) inserts pair <c,i> in dictionary D*)
    fun insert (c:string, i:int, nil:(string * int) list) = [(c,i)]
    |   insert (c, i, (cc, ii)::cs) =
            if c=cc then (c,i)::cs
            else (cc, ii)::insert(c,i,cs);

(* lookup (c, D) finds the value i such that pair <c,i> is in dictionary D *)
    fun lookup(c:string, nil:(string * int) list) = raise NotFound
    |   lookup (c, (cc,ii)::cs) =
            if c = cc then ii
            else lookup(c,cs);
end;
```

FIGURE 5.16 Dictionary module in ML

by (string * int), are defined as a Cartesian product of strings and integers. The list will represent the elements of the dictionary. A nil list indicates an empty dictionary. The insert function is defined in terms of two cases: when the dictionary is empty and when it is not. In both cases, the function takes an integer, a string, and a list as parameters and returns a new list. The function lookup takes a string and a list and returns an integer. It is also defined in terms of two cases. In this example, we have declared explicit types for all variables and functions. We will see later that theses type are not strictly necessary. By removing them, the structure becomes generic.

As in a package body, this structure gives the implementation for the entities being defined and it provides no hiding: it exports all the entities that it defines. To use the entities exported by the structure, a client uses the dot notation.

The fragment of a client of the Dictionary structure is shown in Figure 5.17. In the first line, the client uses a variable D to hold the dictionary being created. This is analogous to constructing a new dictionary. Since we are not exporting a type, we are simply representing the dictionary by a pointer. In the next line, we insert a new pair into the dictionary. We also need to pass a dictionary to the insert function. In this case we pass the empty dictionary that we created in the previous line. The result of this call is assigned to variable newD, which represents our current dictionary. The final line does a lookup in the dictionary. This is a functional program and works by computing values rather than by producing side effects, as we did in the Ada and C++ programs for the same task. That is, the result of inserting into a dictionary is a *new* dictionary, not the old dictionary that has been modified somehow.

```
val D = Dictionary.create;  (*create an empty dictionary *)
val newD = Dictionary.insert ("Mehdi", 46, D);  (*insert a pair*)
...
Dictionary.lookup("Mehdi", newD); (*produces value 46*)
```

FIGURE 5.17 Fragment of client of Dictionary structure of Figure 5.16

5.3.5.2 Interface and implementation

In the last section, we defined a Dictionary structure that exported several entities. The structure also included the implementation of the entities it exported. So a structure can be viewed as including a module's interface and its implementation in the same unit. But ML provides an elegant way to define interfaces for modules separately from the module's implementation.

For example, Figure 5.18 gives the signature of a module that exports an exception called NotFound and a function called lookup. A signature has no

```
signature DictLookupSig = sig
    exception NotFound;
    val lookup : string * (string * int) list -> int
end
```

FIGURE 5.18 A signature definition for a specialized dictionary

implementation. It merely defines an interface, or a specification, for a service. We can combine a signature and a structure to build a new module that presents the interface defined in the signature and the implementation defined in the structure. That is, the signature may be used to provide information hiding. For example, we may use the signature of Figure 5.18 to restrict the exported entities of the structure of Figure 5.16. The system will do type checking to ensure that the structure provides at least what the signature requires. In Figure 5.19 we create such a structure, called LookupDict.

In the first line of the program, we create a new structure called LookupDict, with the "type" DictLookupSig. This structure is assigned the Dictionary structure defined before. The assignment is checked to see that the signature DictLookupSig matches the Dictionary structure. This means that any signatures provided in DictLookupSig must be matched with an implementation in Dictionary. Any use of LookupDict must comply with the signature DictLookupSig. Therefore, only the operation lookup is allowed by this new structure. For example, the second line attempts to create a new dictionary but, since create is not exported, the attempt will be disallowed. In the next two lines, we use Dictionary to create an empty new dictionary, and insert a pair into it. The resulting dictionary is assigned to newD. The next two lines show that LookupDict supports the operation lookup but not insert.

```
structure LookupDict: DictLookupSig = Dictionary;
val L = LookupDict.create; (* not allowed by the LookUp interface *)
val D = Dictionary.create; (*create a new empty dictionary *)
val newD = Dictionary.insert ("Mehdi", 46, D);(* insert something *)
val age = LookupDict.lookup("Mehdi", newD);
val L2 = LookupDict.insert("Carlo", 50, newD); (*error, insert not available*)
```

FIGURE 5.19 A structure constrained by a signature

We may say that the signature—or interface—of a structure definition consists of the signatures and types of all the entities defined in the structure. We may use signatures to constrain the interface of a structure definition.

Another use of signatures is in combination with generic modules or structures. For example, if we define a dictionary module in terms of an arbitrary type for pairs inserted in a dictionary, we may use a signature to construct a new dictionary that works only with <string, integer> pairs. Indeed, if we remove the occurrences of the terms string and int from Figure 5.16, we will have a generic dictionary. We can then use the signature DictLookupSig to constrain both the types and the operations exported to clients. We will see an example of this in Section 5.4.3.

5.3.6 Abstract data types, classes, and modules

We have discussed an abstract data type as a program modularization concept. Languages that provide a class construct, such as C++, support the implementation of abstract data types directly. For example, Figure 5.11 shows a class that implements an abstract data type stack and a client that declares instances of the stack and uses them. The name of the class is used as the type name when instantiating the objects. Operations are performed directly on the instantiated objects, e.g., s1.push(...).

Module-based languages such as original Ada or Modula-2, however, do not support objects directly and are operation oriented. We use a module to implement an abstract data type by packaging the type and its operations together. But the client creates instances of the abstract data type and passes them to operations as necessary, rather than calling the operations associated with the object. That is, rather than calling s1.push(...) the client calls push(s1, ...). In object-based languages, the object is an implicit first parameter automatically passed to the operation. We can see the differences between the two approaches by examining the Ada client given in Figure 5.15 and the C++ client given in Figure 5.2.

As this example shows, the separation of client and server is cleaner in an object-based language. On the other hand, in a module-based language, the need for a construct such as a friend function disappears: we simply put all the related functions and types in the same module and they gain visibility to each other. In an object-based language, the requirement to package a single type and its operations together makes it difficult to deal with operations that do not belong clearly to a single type. We generally have to make such operations global. Java resolves this dichotomy by supporting both modules and classes. Classes defined in the same module have visibility to one another's internal structure.

A final comparison of Ada and C++ styles concerns the export of types. In both languages, a client may instantiate a variable of a type defined by another module (or class). Given a declaration of the form s: T in a client, an important question for the compiler is how much storage to allocate for the instance of s. Even though this information logically is part of the implementation of the module that implements the type, and not part of its specification, the compiler needs the information at the time it compiles the client. This is the reason, as we have seen, that Ada requires the private clause in the specification part of a package. The information in the private part is there only for the compiler. C++ also requires the same information in the class definition.

Requiring the data representation in the specification of a module means that if the representation changes, the clients will have to be recompiled. This is a serious cost in large system development. To address this problem, Modula-2 introduced the notion of *opaque* export, which allows types to be exported without the details of their representation. Variables of such types are constrained to be accessible via pointers; therefore, there is no need to have the equivalent of Ada's private clause in the interface. In fact, the amount of storage to be allocated in client modules for such data objects is known to be the size of a pointer. The restriction that abstract data types be accessible via pointers means that every access incurs the cost of a pointer dereference but ensures intermodule decoupling. Changing the data representation for an abstract data type does not affect client modules from either a logical or an implementation viewpoint. The client modules do not need to be recompiled. In Java, CLU, and Eiffel, all objects are accessed through pointers, and there is therefore no need to have the representation of a type in its specification.

5.4 Generic units

In this chapter, we have considered the issue of modularity as support for developing large programs. One important approach to developing large programs is to build them from existing modules. Traditional software libraries offer examples of how such existing modules may be packaged and used. One of the criteria for evaluating the suitability of a language for programming in the large is whether it provides language mechanisms that enable the construction of independent components, the packaging together of related components, the use and combination of multiple libraries by clients, etc. We have seen the namespaces of C++ and the libraries and child libraries of Ada 95 as language mechanisms explicitly developed for the support of such packaging of related and independent software components. In this section, we concentrate on genericity as a mechanism for building individual modules that are general and thus usable in many contexts by different clients.

5.4.1 Generic data structures

Let us first consider the development of libraries of standard data structures, for example, stacks and queues. What should be the types of elements stored in these structures? Early typed languages such as Pascal and C require the designer to define one structure for every data type to be supported. This is an unsatisfactory solution for two reasons: first, the solution only works for the types the library designer knows about and not for any types that may be defined by the user of the library; second, the solution forces the library designer toward code duplication. C++ templates and Ada generics allow us to avoid such code duplication by defining a template data structure that is independent of the type of the element to be stored in it. For example, in Figure 5.20, we define a generic *pair* data structure in C++. The definition is followed by samples of its use by a client. The template parameters T1 and T2 stand for any type. We may "instantiate" a particular pair by supplying concrete types for T1 and T2. For example, in the figure, we create a pair of integers, a <string, integer> pair, and a pair of employees.

```
template <class T1, class T2>
class pair {
    public:
        T1 first;
        T2 second;
        pair (T1 x, T2 y) : first(x), second(y) { }
                        // first(x) initializes first with x;
                        // second(y) initializes second with y;
};
...
pair<int, int> intint(2, 1456);
pair<string, int> stringint("Mehdi", 46);
pair<employee_t, employee_t> employees(jack, jill);
                        //pair of user-defined type employee_t
```

FIGURE 5.20 Definition and use of a generic pair data structure in C++

We may refer to pair as a parameterized or generic type. The template of C++ allows us to define such a parameterized type, which may later be used to create concrete types such as pair<int, int>. Class parameters to templates represent types uniformly: they may be instantiated with either user-defined or primitive types. Eiffel supports a similar scheme for generic classes, with which, for example, we can define a class stack[T] and then instantiate an intstack from stack[integer]. In Chapter 3 we saw examples of generic stacks in both C++ and Eiffel.

5.4.2 Generic algorithms

Generic routines allow us to parameterize algorithms and achieve a higher level of generality by capturing an algorithm in a type-independent way. In

C++ templates may also be used to define generic routines. For example, in Chapter 2, we saw the following generic function swap, which interchanges the values of its two parameters:

```
template <class T>
void swap(T& a, T& b)
{
    T temp = a;
    a = b;
    b = temp;
}
```

This function may be used for any two parameters of the same type that support the "=" operation. Therefore, we can use it to swap integers, reals, and even user-defined types such as pairs. This facility gives us the possibility to write higher-level generic functions such as sort that encapsulate an algorithmic abstraction independent of the data types on which it operates. Unlike generic data structures, generic functions do not have to be instantiated before they are used.

To use a template data structure, C++ requires explicit instantiation of the structure, as we saw, for example, in pair<int,int>. For functions, on the other hand, explicit instantiation is not necessary. The compiler will infer the instance required and instantiate it automatically. For example, the following program fragment is a valid use of swap:

```
int i, j;
char x, y;
pair<int,string> p1, p2;
...
swap(i, j);        //swap integers
swap(x, y);        //swap characters
swap(p1, p2);   //swap pairs
```

The compiler will generate three different swap functions: for integers, strings, and pairs of <int, string>. To generate an appropriate function, the compiler checks at generation time to ensure that the parameters meet the expected requirements. Examination of the body of swap shows that the parameters passed must support assignment, that is, be able to be passed and be able to be assigned. (Exercise 21 asks you to explain why pairs meet this requirement.)

The implicit parameter requirements in C++ are made explicit in Ada generic functions. The same swap function is defined in Ada as

```
generic
    type T is private;
procedure Swap(X, Y: T) is
begin
    Temp: T = X;
    X = Y;
    Y = Temp;
end Swap;
```

The generic function is explicitly stated to be based on a type T that is **private**. The **private** indication means that the type supports assignment and equality. In general, if other operations are required of the type, they have to be stated explicitly. For example, a generic max function will require its operands to support an order operation such as "<":

```
generic
    type T is private;
    with function "<" (X, Y: T) return Boolean is (<>);
                    -- <> says the type must be discrete
function Max (X, Y: T) return Boolean is
begin
    if X<Y
        then return X;
        else return Y;
    end if;
end Max;
```

To use the function, we have to first create an instance of it:

```
function Int_Max is new Max (Integer);
```

The type parameters passed at instantiation time are checked to ensure that they support the required operations. After instantiation, we have a new function that we may call:

```
m := Int_Max (3, 6);
```

The Ada view is that different functions are generated and used, whereas the C++ view is that there is just one function, max, which is generic. It is the compiler's job to generate as many instances as it needs to satisfy all the calls to the function. The C++ approach is more flexible and is more supportive of generic programming because generic functions are not treated any differently than nongeneric functions: you simply call them. Ada treats generic functions as a special type of function that you must instantiate before you call it.

Recalling the discussion on polymorphism in Section 3.4.7, genericity in both C++ and Ada can be considered as ad hoc polymorphism, since the binding of type parameters to specific types is performed at compile time. We will examine the solution adopted by ML, which supports parametric polymorphism, in Chapter 7.

5.4.3 Generic modules

Collections of data and algorithms may also be packaged together and collectively made to depend on some generic type parameter. Both C++ classes and Ada packages may be defined as generic in the types they use. We saw a generic stack class in Chapter 3.

The ML support for generic modules is particularly interesting because of the separation of structures and signatures. Recall the ML dictionary module in Section 5.3.5. The structure definition of Figure 5.16 can be defined in a generic way by not making any mention of specific types such as int and string. We define such a generic or polymorphic structure in Figure 5.21. The signature of this module is independent of specific types. Can we apply the signature of Figure 5.18 to this structure? That signature definition indeed *matches* this structure, because the structure is more general than the signature. By applying the signature, we are restricting the view of the structure. Applying a signature to a polymorphic structure accomplishes the same purpose as instantiating a generic Ada package with a concrete type parameter.

```
structure Dictionary =
struct
    exception NotFound;
    val create = nil;  (*create an empty dictionary*)
(* insert (c, i, D) inserts pair <c,i> in dictionary D*)
    fun insert (c, i, nil) = [(c,i)]
    |    insert (c, i, (cc, ii)::cs) =
            if c=cc then (c,i)::cs
            else (cc, ii)::insert(c,i,cs);
(* lookup (c, D) finds the value i such that pair <c,i> is in dictionary D *)
    fun lookup(c, nil) = raise NotFound
    |    lookup (c, (cc,ii)::cs) =
            if c = cc then ii
            else lookup(c,cs);
end
```

FIGURE 5.21 A polymorphic Dictionary module in ML

5.4.4 Higher levels of genericity

We have seen that we may define a generic algorithm that works on any type of object passed to it. For example, the max algorithm may be applied to any ordered type. This facility allows us to write one algorithm for n different data types rather than n algorithms. It leads to great savings for writers of libraries. But consider a higher level of generality. Suppose we want to write an algorithm that works on different types of data *collections*, not just different data types. For example, we may want to write one algorithm to do a linear search in any "linear" data structure. Of course, we have to capture the notion of linearity somehow, but, intuitively, we want to be able to find an element in a collection regardless of whether the collection is implemented as an array or a list. The goal of the generic programming paradigm is to develop exactly these kinds of units. In Chapter 3, we saw one kind of iterator for stepping through a collection. Here we will examine a more general kind of iterator that helps in achieving our goal.

A high level of genericity is usually associated with functional languages, and we will see it in the context of ML in Chapter 7. Conventional languages, such as Ada and C++, do not have any particular language facilities for this kind of programming. C++ templates can be combined with overloading of operators, however, to support a high degree of generic programming. For example, consider the function find in Figure 5.22.

```
template<class Iter, class T>
Iter find (Iter first, Iter last, T x)
{
    while (first != last && *first != x)
        ++first;
    return first;
}
```

FIGURE 5.22 A generic algorithm find

We might think of this function as accepting two pointers into a sequence of elements. It sequences through the elements by using the ++ on the first pointer until either the value x is found or the sequence is exhausted. Checking that the list is exhausted relies on the assumption that the two pointers passed to find point to the first element of the sequence and to one element past the end of the sequence, respectively. So the following code fragment looks through the first half of an integer array:

```
int a[100];
int x;
int *r;
...
```

```
r= find(&a[0], &a[50], x);
if (r == &a[50])
    // not found
...
```

Here we have used two integer pointers as the template parameters. However, the function is quite abstract: nothing in its description constrains us to use it with pointers and arrays! It is based on an abstract object that we have called Iter (for *iterator*). We can think of an iterator as a generalization of a C++ pointer. From the definition of the function find we can see that such an object is required to support the following operations: * to return a value, ++ to step to the next position, and == and != for comparison with another Iter. Certainly, pointers meet these requirements. But we might imagine writing a list object that also provides an Iter type object that supports ++, *, ==, and != operations with the same semantics as those of pointers into arrays. More importantly, any time a library writer provides a new linear structure, he or she can also provide it with such iterators. In this way, any generic operations will be immediately usable with the library's new data structures. What we have done is to treat operations such as !=, *, and ++ as generic operations and write a higher-level operation, find, in terms of them. This style of generic programming is possible in C++ and likely will be the way standard libraries are provided. The advantage of such an approach for programming in the large is the reduction of the amount of code that needs to be written, because one generic unit may be customized automatically depending on the context of its use. It is a form of modularity in which we form modules that encapsulate common properties of a family of units. We can build increasingly specific units that encapsulate more and more secrets of the family of units. Object-oriented programming is another approach to achieving this same kind of modularity. That will be the subject of the next chapter.

5.5 Final remarks

Appropriate abstractions and proper modularization help us confront the inherent complexities of large programs. Even with appropriate modularization, however, writing all the modules from scratch is a tedious and time-consuming task. Rather than inventing new abstractions and implementing new modules for each new program, we can improve software productivity by using previously developed abstractions and modules. In this chapter, we have studied linguistic mechanisms that help in the building of modules and libraries of modules that may be used by others. But where do such useful modules come from, and how can we build them? Different programming paradigms provide different answers to these questions. In the next chapter, we see how the object-oriented paradigm answers these questions.

5.6 Bibliographic notes

The problems of programming in the large and techniques for addressing them are covered in software engineering textbooks such as [Ghezzi91]. An informal but insightful and entertaining account of problems arising in the production of large software systems may be found in [Brooks95]. The distinction between programming in the small and programming in the large is pointed out in [DeRemer76]. The methodology of stepwise refinement is described by Dijkstra in [Dahl72]. Information hiding was introduced in [Parnas72a] and [Parnas72b]. The approach to generic programming using iterators was pioneered by the STL library, which is now part of the C++ standard library [ISO95b], [Musser96], [Nelson95]. [Koenig96] contains essays on C++, including a good discussion of generic programming. [Jazayeri95] discusses the construction and use of generic components in C++ based on this new style.

5.7 Exercises

1. Discuss the effect of global variables on the writability and readability of large programs.
2. Study and present the main features of FORTRAN's separate compilation.
3. Why is a pure ALGOL-like program structure inadequate for programming in the large?
4. Complete the implementation of the package body in Figure 5.3.
5. Design the interface of an Ada module that provides a symbol table for a translator (e.g., an assembler), and show how a separately compiled procedure can access the symbol table. The data structure representing the symbol table should be hidden from the procedure, and all accesses to the symbol table should be routed through abstract operations provided by the symbol table module. Can you compile the procedure before implementing a representation for the symbol table? Why? What is wrong if you cannot?
6. Do the same as in Exercise 5 but in C++. Do you run into the same problems?
7. Suppose two Ada units U1 and U2 must use the same procedure P. Can P be embedded in a single subunit? Can P be embedded in a single unit? In the latter case, what are the constraints on the order of compilation?
8. In this exercise, we compare nested packages and child libraries. In particular, answer the following questions:
   - Can nested packages be compiled separately? Can child libraries be compiled separately?
   - Can a package have both a child package and a nested package with the same name? Why not? What can you conclude about the utility of nested packages?
9. Describe the tools that an ideal program development system should provide to support independent development of modules, system structuring from independently developed modules, and complete intermodule type checking.

10. The C language has three storage classes, called automatic, extern, and static. These determine whether and how memory is allocated for variables. But the same storage classes are used to control visibility of entities. Discuss the use of storage classes for import and export of entities.

11. This exercise is about achieving visibility in C units. If a variable is declared in a function, which units have access to it? If a variable is declared outside of functions, which units have access to it? If a variable is declared as extern, where is it defined? If a variable is defined as static, which units have access to it?

12. We have seen in Chapter 2 that the scope rules of the language provide for the control of names and their visibility. Discuss the relationship between name scopes in block-structured languages and the child libraries of Ada and the namespaces of C++.

13. In this chapter, we have discussed the need for a unit to give access to its private parts to some units but not export it to all units. Ada and C++ have two different ways of satisfying this requirement. What is the solution provided by each language? Compare the two facilities.

14. Solve the problem of Figure 5.11 by instantiating the generic class defined in Figure 3.4.

15. Write a C++, an Ada, and an Eiffel program for a generic abstract data type defining a first-in/first-out queue that can contain an unbounded number of items. The operations provided by queues have the following signatures:

enqueue: fifo (T) x T $\rightarrow$ fifo (T)   adds an element to the queue
dequeue: fifo (T) $\rightarrow$ fifo (T) x T   extracts an element from the queue
length: fifo (T) $\rightarrow$ int   computes the length of the queue

   – Show how instances can be created.
   – Next, provide fixed-length queues, such that an exception is raised if one tries to enqueue an element in a full queue.
   – Write a short description of the rationale for your implementation.

16. Assume that I buy a software library from a vendor. The library contains the specification of an abstract object stack. I write a program in which I create an instance of type stack.
   – Assume the stack object is written in Ada and the vendor decides to change the implementation of its push operation. Do I need to recompile my program? Assume the vendor decides to change the representation of the stack. Do I need to recompile my program? Explain your answers.
   – Explain the same two problems if the language used is C++.
   – Explain the same two problems if the language used is Eiffel. (This requires you to study the Eiffel manual.)

17. Consider a generic function swap(x,y) that interchanges the values of its two arguments. Write a bubble sort in C++ that uses swap to interchange the elements. How would your solution be different if you try the same approach in Ada?

18. Without generics, if we have m data types, n algorithms, and p data structures, we need to write on the order of m*n*p library components to support all possible algorithms on all possible data structures for all possible data types. For example, we need a sort routine for arrays of integers and a sort routine for lists of reals. Explain how the use of generics reduces the number of library components that need to be written. Assuming that we could write all the m*n*p components without using generics, what other problems do we face in terms of documentation, use, and maintenance of these routines?

19. Ada defines two kinds of types: private type and limited private type. (Check these features in the language manual.) What is the difference between these two? Is there a similar concept in C++? If not, why not? Does their absence imply a lack of functionality in C++?

20. What is the difference between overloaded functions and generic functions in C++?

21. We did not define an assignment operator for the template type pair in Section 5.4.1. Yet, in Section 5.4.2 we used swap with pair. The function swap requires the assignment operator for its operands. Is the assignment operator defined for pair? (Hint: Check the C++ rule for class definitions.)

22. Compare the possible implementation of Ada generics versus C++ templates. Does the source of a C++ template function need to be available to be able to compile the client code? Is this necessary for an Ada generic function? If there are two different calls to swap(x,y), will a C++ compiler generate two instances of swap? What about Ada?

23. Suppose we want to write a generic sort routine to sort elements of type T. We might use our swap routine from Section 5.4.2. A fragment of the C++ routine might look like this:

```
template<class T>
sort (...)
{
    ...
    swap (x, y);
    ...
}
```

If we were to write sort in Ada, we would have to instantiate swap first. What type should we use to instantiate swap? Explain the problem you encounter. Check the Ada manual to find a solution to this problem.

24. In Section 5.4.4, we saw a generic function called find. We said that this function may be applied to a list data structure if the list provides an appropriate iterator. Write a class list that provides such an iterator. That is, the class list provides a type called iterator. (Hint: The type must provide operations ++, *, and =.)

Object-oriented languages

Objects contain the possibility of all situations. (Wittgenstein)

C H A P T E R **6**

In the last chapter, we discussed the problems of programming in the large and the solutions offered by different programming languages. Modularity and abstraction are the two most important principles for building large programs. In the "pure" object-oriented style of programming, the unit of modularity is an abstract data type implementation. We have seen that classes may be used to define abstract data types. Another important principle of object-oriented programming is that you may define new classes of objects by extending or refining existing classes.

Some programming languages have been designed expressly to support this style of programming. These languages, namely, Smalltalk, Eiffel, and Java, are called object-oriented programming languages. Other languages, such as C++ and Ada 95, while not exclusively object-oriented, support the paradigm through features that enable the programming of extensible abstractions. All object-oriented languages trace their roots to the language Simula 67, which introduced the concept of class and subclass in 1967. In this chapter we examine the essential programming language features for the support of object-oriented programming and look at some representative object-oriented programming languages.

The starting point for object-oriented programming is abstract data types, which we examined in Chapters 3 and 5. We have seen, for example, that the class construct of C++ directly supports the definition of abstract data types. We may design classes Chair and Table if our application deals with such entities and then create as many instances of the specific Chairs and Tables that we need. Next comes the notion of *inheritance*. For example, rather than designing a class DiningTable and another class Desk, we might first design a class Table, which captures the common properties of different kinds of tables, and then "derive" DiningTable and Desk as new classes that "inherit" properties of Table and add their own unique attributes. This is a linguistic issue but it also requires a supporting design style. For our example, instead of considering the problem domain to consist of chairs and tables and desks, we might decide that the problem domain deals with *furniture*; some particular kinds of furniture are tables and chairs; particular kinds of tables are desks and dining tables; particular kinds of chairs are lounge chairs and sofas. Some concepts such as furniture are abstract and exist only as descriptions. Any particular piece of furniture is actually an instance of a more concrete class, such as the chair class. By factoring the common properties of individual concrete objects at the abstract level, we need to describe them only once rather than many times. The individual kinds of objects such as chairs need to be described by simply stating their specific features that make them unique as pieces of furniture. We say that a chair *inherits* the properties of furniture and may extend or modify these properties as necessary. Figure 6.1 shows the inheritance hierarchy for the furniture classes we have just described.

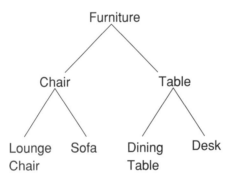

FIGURE 6.1 Sample inheritance hierarchy for furniture classes

Object-oriented programming is an attractive methodology because it promises the ability to package a whole set of related concepts tied together through their inheritance relationships. It aims to enable the production of libraries of related components that are

- Easy to understand by users because of the relationships among the components, and
- Easy to extend by the use of inheritance.

Many languages have been or are being extended to support object-oriented programming. This chapter examines the concepts underlying object-oriented programming and the implementation of these concepts in several programming languages. In Section 6.1 we introduce the basic concepts of object-oriented programming. In Section 6.2 we examine the relationship between inheritance and the type system of the language. In Section 6.3 we review the support of object orientation in C++, Eiffel, Ada 95, Smalltalk, and Java. Object orientation has affected not only the implementation phase of the software process but most other phases as well. In a sidebar on page 328, we briefly review this impact on the design and analysis phases of the software process.

6.1 Concepts of object-oriented programming

There are several definitions of object-oriented programming. Many people refer to an object-oriented program as any program that deals with entities that may be informally called "objects." In contrast to traditional procedural languages, in which the programs consist of procedures and data structures, objects are entities that encapsulate data and related operations. For example, as we observed in Chapter 5, given a stack data structure s, in a procedural language we would call a push operation, passing it a stack and the element to be added, as in

```
push (s, x);
```

Working with objects, in contrast, we tell the stack object to push an element onto itself, as in

```
s.push(x);
```

We have seen that in C++ and Eiffel we can use classes to define and create objects. We call a programming language that supports the definition and use of objects *object-based*. *Object-oriented* programming languages support additional features. In particular, object-oriented programming languages are characterized by their support of four facilities:

- Abstract data type definitions,
- Inheritance,
- Inclusion polymorphism, and
- Dynamic binding of function calls to functions bodies.

We have already discussed abstract data types extensively. They are used in object-oriented programming to define the properties of classes of objects. Inheritance is a mechanism that allows us to define one abstract data type by *deriving* it from an existing abstract data type. The newly defined type "inherits" the properties of the *parent type*. Inclusion polymorphism allows the use of polymorphic variables that may refer to an object of a class or an object of any of its derived classes. Dynamic binding supports the use of polymorphic functions; the identity of a function applied to a polymorphic variable is resolved dynamically based on the type of the object referred to by the variable.

The pure terminology of object-oriented languages refers to *objects* that are *instances* of *classes*. An object contains a number of *instance variables* and supports a number of *methods*. A *message* is sent to an object to request the invocation of one of its methods. For example, s.push(5) is interpreted as sending the message push(5) to object s. The message is a request to s to invoke its method push with the parameter 5. The syntax of Smalltalk reflects this interpretation directly without any appearance of function calls. In Smalltalk, the same statement would be written as s push 5. Using only the message metaphor, this expression sends the message push 5 to the object s; the object s uses the message to select its push method and send the message 5 to it.

Such method invocation or function calls are polymorphic because the actual method to invoke depends on the identity of the object at run time. In a dynamically typed language such as Smalltalk, the object that receives a message first checks to see that it can perform the method requested. If not, it reports an error. Other languages, such as Eiffel and C++, allow polymorphic function calls but restrict the polymorphism to enable static type checking. Thus, such languages combine polymorphism with strong typing.

We begin our detailed study of the concepts of object-oriented programming in Sections 6.1.1 through 6.1.4, using C++ as the example language. Following C++ terminology, we will call methods *member functions* and messages simply *function calls*. In Section 6.2, we examine the relationship between inheritance and the type system of a programming language. In Section 6.3, we will review more specific concepts of C++, Eiffel, Ada 95, Smalltalk, and Java. For Java, we will see how the concepts of object and thread have been combined to support concurrent execution.

6.1.1 Classes of objects

The first requirement for object-oriented programming is to be able to define abstract data types. We have already seen that this can be done using the class construct. As an example, recall the following definition of a stack class from

Section 5.3.3.2:

```
class stack{
    public:
        void push(int) {elements[top++] = i;};
        int pop() {return elements[--top];};
    private:
        int elements[100];
        int top=0;
};
```

This class is a particular implementation of a fixed-size stack abstraction. Clients may create objects of this class just as they may create variables of language-defined types. In fact, classes are user-defined types. They share most properties of language-defined types, including storage properties. For example, we can create stacks s1 and s2 as automatic variables:

```
stack s1, s2;
```

We may also create stacks in the free store (C++'s term for the heap):

```
stack* sp = new stack;
```

To access member functions (e.g., pop), the following notations denote equivalent expressions,

```
(*sp).pop();
```

and (more commonly)

```
sp -> pop();
```

While useful, the class facility only addresses the question of how to encapsulate useful abstractions. What we have seen so far does not address the need to create new abstractions based on existing ones. Inheritance is the mechanism used for this purpose.

6.1.2 Inheritance

In the last section, we defined a stack class. Now suppose that we are writing an application in which we need a stack but we also need to know how many elements have already been pushed on the stack. What should we do? Write a new counting_stack class? Take the code of the above class and modify it? Use the same stack and keep track of the number of push operations externally in the client? All of these solutions are deficient in a programming-in-the-large context. The first does not take advantage of work already done. The second creates two similar code modules that need to be maintained independently. Therefore, if a defect is found in the code or an optimization to the code is discovered, the changes must be applied to both copies of the code. The third alternative improperly separates the concerns of the client and the server and complicates the client code. The basic issue is that we already have a stack abstraction and what we need should be a simple extension of it.

Inheritance is a linguistic mechanism that allows us to do just that by defining a new class that "inherits" the properties of a parent class. We may then add new properties to the child class or redefine inherited properties. The terminology in C++ is to *derive* a class from a *base* class. In this case, we want to derive a counting_stack from stack as shown below:

```
class counting_stack: public stack {
    public:
        int size(); //return number of elements on the stack
};
```

This new class simply inherits all the functions of the class stack.[1] All public member functions of stack become public member functions of counting_stack (that's what the public before stack specifies). We have also specified that there will be a new public function size(), which is intended to return the number of elements stored in the stack. The class stack is called a *base class* or the parent class of counting_stack. The class counting_stack is said to be derived from its base class. The terms *subclass* and *superclass* are also used to refer to derived and base classes, respectively.

Even this simple example demonstrates that inheritance is a fundamental concept for supporting programming in the large in that it enables us to develop modules based on existing ones, without any modifications to the existing modules. This is the property that makes object-oriented programming an attractive paradigm for software engineering.

6.1.3 Polymorphism

The next feature of object-oriented programming languages is the support of polymorphism. All classes derived from the same base class may be viewed informally as specialized versions of that base class. Object-oriented languages provide polymorphic variables that may refer to objects of different classes. Object-oriented languages that adopt a strong type system limit the

---

1. Actually, in C++ and Java this cannot be done so simply. A way to implement size() is to return the value of top, but top is hidden to the subclass. As we will see in Section 6.3.1.4, to do this in C++ or Java we have to declare top in class stack as protected rather than private. In other languages, such as Eiffel, our current definition of stack would be sufficient with no changes.

polymorphism of such variables: usually, a variable of class T is allowed to refer to objects of type T or any classes derived from T.

In the case of our example, using stack and counting_stack in the previous section, this means that a variable of type stack may also refer to an object of type counting_stack. In strictly object-oriented languages such as Smalltalk, Eiffel, and Java, *all* objects are referred to through references and references may be polymorphic. In C++, only pointers, reference variables, and by-reference parameters may be polymorphic. That is, a stack pointer may also point to a counting_stack object. Similarly, a formal by-reference parameter expecting an actual parameter of type stack can refer to an actual parameter of type counting_stack. As an example, if we have two pointer variables declared:

```
stack* sp = new stack;
counting_stack* csp = new counting_stack;
...
sp = csp; //okay
...
csp = sp; //statically not sure if okay--disallowed
```

The assignment sp = csp; makes a pointer to a class to point to an object of a subclass. That is, the type of the object that is currently pointed at by sp can be of any of its derived types, such as counting_stack. The assignment csp = sp; is not allowed in C++ because C++ has a strong type system. If this assignment were allowed, then a later call to csp->size() would be statically valid but might lead to a run-time error because the object pointed at by sp may not support the member function size(). A language with a weak type system, such as Smalltalk, would allow such an assignment and defer error checking to run time. We will return to the typing issues raised by inheritance in Section 6.2.

According to the concepts developed in Chapter 3, a pointer to a class stack is a polymorphic variable that can refer to an object of class counting_stack. Assignments among objects of such types may be checked statically. The assignment of a counting_stack object to a variable of type stack is considered to be legal because a counting_stack object fulfills all the requirements of a stack object, whereas an assignment in the other direction should not be allowed, because a stack object does not have a size() component. In C++, if we do not use pointers, then we do not get inclusion polymorphism, which is a necessity for object-oriented programming:

```
stack s;
counting_stack cs;
...
```

```
s = cs; //okay, object is coerced to a stack (no more size operation available)
cs = s; //not allowed because a later cs.size() would look syntactically okay but
        //not work at run time
```

The assignment s = cs; is legal and is an example of coercion (i.e., a kind of ad hoc polymorphism). In fact, what happens is that the values stored in object cs are copied into the corresponding elements of s. This kind of coercion, of course, loses some of the values stored in cs, just as coercion from float to int loses some information.

6.1.4 Dynamic binding of calls to member functions

A derived class may not only add to the functionality of its base class, it may also add new private data and *redefine* or *override* some of the operations provided in the base class. For example, in counting_stack we may decide to provide a new implementation of the push function because we want to keep track of the number of times push has been called. Now, if sp is a reference to a stack variable and csp is a reference to a counting_stack variable, we expect that csp->push(...) will call the push of a counting_stack object. But what about sp->push(...)? Since sp is a polymorphic variable, it may be pointing at a counting_stack object or a stack object. This raises an issue of proper binding of operations. Consider the following example:

```
stack* sp = new stack;
counting_stack* csp = new counting_stack;
...
sp->push(...); // stack::push
csp->push(...); // counting_stack::push
...
sp = csp; //assignment is okay
...
sp->push(...); //which push?
```

Which is the push operation invoked in the last statement, stack::push or counting_stack::push? Because the assignment sp = csp is allowed, at run time sp may be pointing to a stack object or to a counting_stack object. Should the choice of which routine to call be made statically—based on the class type—in which case stack::push(...) would be called, or dynamically—based on the object type—in which case counting_stack::push(...) would be called? So-called purely object-oriented languages, such as Smalltalk and Eiffel, bind the choice dynamically based on the type of the object. In fact, as stated, dynamic binding (often called *dynamic dispatching* in object-oriented terminology) is one of the tenets for object-oriented programming languages. C++, however, not being a purely object-oriented language, provides features for both static and dynamic binding. Section 6.3.1 presents the C++-specific features.

The combination of dynamic binding and inheritance enables a new programming technique. For example, we may define a class polygon and derive various specialized versions of polygons, such as square and rectangle. Suppose that polygon defines a function perimeter to compute the perimeter of a general polygon. Some of the derived classes may define their own special perimeter functions because they are presumably more efficient. We may maintain a list of various types of polygons. Every time we select an element p from the list, the use of dynamic binding ensures that a call p.perimeter for a variable p of type polygon will call the "right" perimeter function based on the type of the object currently assigned to p.

Clearly, dynamic binding is more flexible than static binding. In languages that do not support such dynamic binding directly, we may have to use case statements (as in Pascal) or function pointers (as in C) to achieve the same result, but with code that is more verbose and harder to maintain. For example, in Pascal we might implement polygon as a variant record and explicitly call the right perimeter function based on the tag of the variant record. In C, we could take advantage of pointers to functions and represent each polygon as a record, with one field being a pointer to an appropriate perimeter function; the call then would have to be made indirectly through this pointer. Both of these solutions are more verbose, less secure, and less maintainable than the solution using inheritance and dynamic binding.

As we have seen in Chapter 3, dynamic binding of the function call may create possibilities of type violations. Indeed, in dynamically typed languages such as Smalltalk, this type of error may occur easily. A call to member function f of an object v may fail at run time because the object bound to v belongs to a class that does not provide function f, or, if it does, because the types of the actual parameters (or the result type) are incompatible with those of the formal parameters. Several languages, such as Eiffel and C++, as we shall see later, combine polymorphism and dynamic binding with static type checking.

6.2 Inheritance and the type system

In the previous section, we have described the basic components of object-oriented programming languages. The interaction between inheritance and type consistency rules of the language raises a number of interesting issues. In this section, we consider some of these issues.

6.2.1 Subclasses versus subtypes

In Chapter 3, we introduced the concept of subtype for defining a new type as a subset of an existing type. For example, we defined week_day as a subrange of day. Subtyping introduces a relationship among objects of the subtype and objects of the parent type such that objects of a subtype may also be viewed as objects of the parent type. For example, a week_day is also a day. This relationship is referred to as the *is-a* relationship: week_day *is-a* day. The subtype relationship is generalizable to user-defined types such as those defined by classes. If the *is-a* relationship holds between a subclass S and a class C (S *is-a* C) then we may say that the type defined by the subclass is a subtype of the type defined by the parent class. For example, a counting_stack *is-a* stack but not vice versa.

To make this notion precise, we need to state the conditions under which the *is-a* relationship holds between a subclass and a class, so that the subclass can be viewed as defining a subtype. In fact, not all subclasses create subtypes. If a derived class only adds member variables and functions or redefines existing functions in a *compatible* way, then the derived class defines a subtype. If it hides some of the parent's member variables and functions or modifies them in an incompatible way, then it does not create a subtype. Therefore, whether a derived class defines a subtype depends on the definition of the derived class and may not be guaranteed by the language.

What does it mean for a function f in a derived class to override a function f in a base class in a *compatible* way? Semantically, this would require the definition of some notion of *behavioral equivalence*. More pragmatically, we can say that it means that an occurrence of base::f(x) may be replaced by derived::f(x) without risking any type errors. For example, if the signature of the function derived::f is identical to the signature of base::f, no type errors will be introduced as a result of the replacement. Several languages, including C++, adopt exactly this rule for function redefinitions. We will examine this issue more deeply in the next subsection.

6.2.2 Strong typing and polymorphism

In Chapter 3 we defined a strong type system as one that guarantees type safety. Strong type systems have the advantage of enabling type errors to be caught at compile time. Statically typed languages provide a strong type system. In this section we discuss how object-oriented languages can rely on dynamic dispatch as a fundamental principle and yet adopt a strong type system.

Let us assume that we have a base class base and a derived class derived and two objects derived from them:

```
class base {...};
class derived: public base {...};
...
base* b;
derived* d;
```

We have seen that we may assign d to b but not b to d. The question is: under what circumstances can we guarantee that an assignment

```
b = d;
```

will not lead to a type violation at run time? We may ask this question in terms of *substitutability*: can an object of class derived be substituted for an object of class base in every context? Or, in general, can an object of a derived type be substituted for an object of its parent type in every context, and is such a kind of polymorphism compatible with strong typing? If substitutability is ensured, the derived type can be viewed as a subtype of the parent type.

To answer this question we need to examine the contexts under which objects are used. By imposing some restrictions on the use of inheritance, the language can ensure substitutability. Below we examine several sufficient (but not necessary) restrictions.

6.2.2.1 Type extension

If the derived class is allowed to only extend the type of the parent class, then substitutability is guaranteed. That is, if derived does not modify any member functions of base and does not hide any of them, then it is guaranteed that any call b.f(...) will be valid whether b is holding a base object or a derived object. The compiler may do type checking of any uses of base variables solely based on the knowledge that they are of type base. Therefore, static type checking can guarantee the lack of run-time violations. Type extension is one of the mechanisms adopted in Ada 95.

6.2.2.2 Overriding of member functions

Restricting derived classes to only extend the parent type is a severe limitation on an object-oriented language. In fact, it rules out dynamic dispatch completely. Many languages allow a derived class to redefine an inherited member function. For example, as in our previous example, we may derive a square class from a polygon class. The square class may redefine the general perimeter function from the base class and replace it with a more efficient version. In C++, the base class must specify the function perimeter as a virtual function, giving derived classes the opportunity to override its definition. That is,

```
class polygon {
    public:
        polygon (...) {...} //constructor
        virtual float perimeter () {...};
        ...
};
class square: public polygon {
    public:
        square (...) {...} //constructor
        ...
        float perimeter() {...}; //overrides the definition of perimeter in polygon
};
```

The typing question is: under what conditions can we guarantee that a use of a square object may substitute the use of a polygon object? That is, under what conditions can we guarantee that a call p->perimeter() will be valid whether *p is a polygon or a square object? C++ requires that the signature of the overriding function must be *exactly* the same as the signature of the overridden function. This rule ensures that the compiler can do the type checking based only on the static type of p and the signature of the function polygon::perimeter. If at run time p happens to hold a square object or any other derived type object, a function other than polygon::perimeter will be called, but that function will have exactly the same parameter requirements and no run-time type violations will occur.

Can we relax the C++ requirement and still ensure type safety? Again, we can analyze the semantic requirements of the relationship between an overridden function and the function it overrides in terms of substitutability. In general, the compiler must be able to do the type checking based on the parent class, knowing that a derived member function may be substituted for the overridden function. Clearly, we must require exactly the same number of parameters in the overriding function and the overridden function. What other relationship must hold between the signatures of the two functions?

Consider the following program fragment (we will use the syntax of C++ but we will take some liberty with its semantics):

```
//not C++
class base {
    public:
        void virtual fnc (s1 par) {...} //s1 is the type of formal parameter
        ...
};
```

```
class derived: public base {
    public:
        void fnc (s2 par) {...} //C++ requires that s1 is identical to s2
        ...
};
...
base* b;
derived* d;
s1 v1;
s2 v2;
...
if (...) b = d;
...
b->fnc(v1); // okay if b is base but what if it is derived?
```

To ensure substitutability, the call b->fnc(v1) must work at run time whether b holds a base object or a derived object. That is, the parameter v1 must be acceptable to both base::fnc() and derived::fnc(). This, in turn, means that derived::fnc() must be able to accept v1, which is of type s1. In other words, type s1 must be substitutable for type s2. That is, class s1 either simply extends class s2 (Section 6.2.2.1) or redefines member functions of s2, but redefinitions satisfy the constraints we are discussing in this section. Informally, this rule means that the overriding function must not impose any more requirements on the input parameters than the overridden function does.

Now let us consider a member function with a result parameter.

```
//not C++
class base {
    public:
        t1 virtual fnc (s1 par) {...};//s1 is the type of formal parameter;
                                      // t1 is the type of result parameter
        ...
};
class derived: public base {
    public:
        t2 fnc (s2 par) {...};        //C++ requires that s1 is identical to
                                      //s2 and t1 is identical to t2
        ...
};
...
base* b;
derived* d;
s1 v1;
s2 v2;
t0 v0;
...
if (...) b = d;
```

```
...
v0 = b->fnc(v1);                 // okay if b is base but what if it is derived?
```

Again, substitutability means that if b holds a derived object, the call fnc(...) will work at run time and a proper result will be returned to be assigned to v0 without any type violations. That means that the result type of the overriding function (t2) must be substitutable for the result type of the overridden function (t1), which must be substitutable for the type of v0, if the last assignment of the fragment is to be considered legal by the compiler. In other words, t2 must be a subtype of t1, which must be a subtype of t0. Combining the rules on input parameters and result parameter, we can state intuitively that an overriding function must not impose any stronger requirements on input parameters but may satisfy stronger requirements on result parameters.

Stated more precisely,

- The input parameters of the overriding function must be supertypes of the corresponding parameters of the overridden function.
- The result parameter of the overriding function must be a subtype of the result parameter of the overridden function.

These two type-checking rules are known respectively as the *contravariance* rule on input parameters and the *covariance* rule on result parameters. We have stated them here as syntactic rules that ensure type safety. However, the contravariance rule on input arguments is rather counterintuitive and can be impractical. It says that even though we may define a more specialized function in a derived class, the input parameters of the specialized function may not impose any more specific requirements.

Few programming languages enforce these rules completely. Emerald is one language that does. C++, Java, Object Pascal, and Modula-3 follow neither: they require the exact identity of the two functions. Eiffel and Ada require covariance of both result and input arguments.

The example in Figure 6.2 shows the counterintuitive nature of the contravariance requirement on input parameters and the basic difficulty of equating subtyping as an abstract concept and inheritance as a language construct that implements it. We have defined a class point characterized by x and y coordinates and a member function equal that can compare itself for equality with another point. We then derive a colorPoint, which inherits x and y from class point, adds another instance variable color, and redefines the equal member function. The member function must be redefined because the colorPoint equality test must compare two colorPoints. For this reason, the input parame-

```
class point{
    public:
        x: float;
        y: float;
        bool equal (point p) //bool is defined as a boolean type
            {return (x == p.x && y == p.y);}
};
class colorPoint: public point{
    public:
        color: float;
        bool equal (colorPoint p) //bool is defined as a boolean type
            {return (x == p.x && y == p.y && color == p.colorPoint);}
};
```

FIGURE 6.2 Classes point and colorPoint

ter to colorPoint::equal must be of type colorPoint. But if we allow such a redefinition, colorPoint may not be considered a subtype of point if we want to guarantee type safety. This redefinition, although intuitively necessary, goes against our rule of contravariance of input arguments, which requires the parameter to colorPoint::equal() to be a supertype of the input parameter of point::equal(). We can see the problem by considering a call p1.equal(p2). This call works if p1 and p2 are both of type point. But the call will fail if we substitute a colorPoint for p1 because the equality test will attempt to access the non-existent color variable of p2.

In conclusion, if inheritance is constrained by requiring that either (a) the derived class only provides extensions or (b) redefinitions are also allowed, but contravariance and covariance are required for input and output parameters, respectively, then substitutability is ensured and derived classes can be considered to define subtypes of their parent class. The resulting type system would be polymorphic (inclusion polymorphism) and yet it would be strong. The price to pay for this conceptual integrity of the language, however, is that the restrictions imposed on inheritance are severe and counterintuitive.

6.2.3 Inheritance hierarchies

Hierarchical organization is an effective method of controlling complexity. The inheritance relationship provides a mechanism for the development of a family of abstractions organized as a hierarchy of classes. In this section we discuss several issues raised by inheritance hierarchies.

6.2.3.1 Single and multiple inheritance

In Simula 67, Ada, Java, and Smalltalk, a new class definition is restricted to have only one base class: a class has at most one parent class. These languages have a *single-inheritance* model.

C++ and Eiffel have extended the notion of inheritance to allow a subclass to be derived from more than one base class. This is called *multiple inheritance*. For example, if we have a class displayable and a class bank_account, we might inherit from both to define a displayable_bank_account:

```
class displayable_bank_account: public displayable, bank_account {
    ...
}
```

Multiple inheritance can support the combination of independent abstractions represented by the base classes.

To provide multiple inheritance, a language must resolve several issues. For example, there may be *name clashes* among the parents of a subclass. If both parents in our example provide a member function draw(), which draw() function is exported by the class displayable_bank_account? The derived class needs a way to refer uniquely to all parent entities to be able to export the desired members. Another complication occurs if several of the parents are themselves derived from the same base class. This situation, referred to as *diamond inheritance*, is shown in Figure 6.3. The members of the parent (root) will be repeated multiple times in the child class (grandchild). This may or may not be desirable. Some languages provide features to resolve such anomalies. For example, Eiffel has a construct to **undefine** an inherited feature; it also has a construct to **rename** an inherited feature.

The successful use of multiple inheritance requires not only well-designed inheritance hierarchies but also orthogonally designed classes that may be combined without clashing. In practice, the use of multiple inheritance

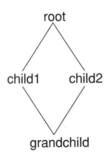

FIGURE 6.3 An example of diamond inheritance

requires care. Whether its benefits outweigh its complexity is an open question. Java, which adopts many features of C++, uses only single inheritance but introduces separate interfaces and supports the idea of inheriting from multiple interfaces. We cover Java in Section 6.3.5.

6.2.3.2 Implementation and interface inheritance

One of the promises of object-oriented programming is that new software components may be constructed from existing software components. This would be a significant contribution towards resolving programming-in-the-large problems. To what extent does inheritance support a methodology for such incremental building of components?

In the last chapter, we discussed the importance of encapsulation in achieving independent modules whose internals may be modified without affecting their interfaces and thus their *clients*, who *use* the resources specified in the interface. Inheritance complicates the issue of encapsulation because the derived classes of a class are a different type of client for the class. On one hand, they may want to extend the facilities of a parent class and may be able to do so solely by using the public interfaces of the parent class; on the other hand, the facilities they provide to their clients may often be implemented more efficiently if they access the internal representations of their parent classes. An inheritance construct which restricts derived classes to access a parent class only through its public interface is called *interface inheritance*. *Implementation inheritance*, on the other hand, allows a derived class to access also the private part (i.e., implementation) of a parent class. The default mode in C++ is interface inheritance, but, since pure interface inheritance is overly restrictive, C++ introduces protected members (see Section 6.3.1.4) to support implementation inheritance. Eiffel, on the other hand, is based on implementation inheritance.

There is a trade-off. If the derived class uses the internal details of the parent class, by inheriting the implementation of the parent it will be affected any time the implementation of the parent class is modified. This means that, at the very least, it will have to be recompiled; but most likely it will also have to be modified, leading to familiar maintenance problems. This is not a major problem if the base class and the derived class are part of the same package produced and maintained by the same organization. It is a serious problem, however, if the base class is supplied by a library and a different organization creates the derived class.

From a software engineering view, interface inheritance is a clean methodology because it forces the derived class to depend only on the interface of the parent, not its implementation. But interface inheritance is limited in power and leads to inefficiencies. For example, consider the counting_stack example of Section 6.1.2. If counting_stack "knows" that the implementation of its parent stack is an array, then size() may be implemented by simply returning the value of top. But this means that counting_stack works only with this representation of stack. On the other hand, not making use of top will lead to an inefficient implementation of the function size(). Exercise 8 asks you to develop such an implementation.

Regardless of the mode of inheritance, a well-designed inheritance hierarchy is a requirement for the successful use of object-oriented programming. Any hierarchy implies that the nodes closer to the root of the hierarchy affect a larger number of the leaf nodes of the hierarchy. If a node close to the root needs to be modified, all of its children are affected. As a result, even though inheritance supports the incremental creation of software components, it also creates a tightly dependent set of components. Modifications of base classes may have far reaching impact.

6.3 Object-oriented features in programming languages

The way different languages support object-oriented programming is related to the philosophy of the language and, more specifically, to the language's object and encapsulation models. Smalltalk, Eiffel, and Java are exclusively object-oriented, with classes as the basic encapsulation mechanism. C++ supports different paradigms; its class construct may be used to implement object orientation but it is possible to program in C++ using a purely procedural style. Ada's package is simply an encapsulation mechanism for packaging a set of related entities and is not restricted to building only objects. Ada 95 has some object-oriented features, but the language remains a module-oriented language. In this section, we examine these languages more closely from an object-oriented view.

6.3.1 C++

C++ supports object-oriented programming by providing classes for abstract data types, derived classes for inheritance, and virtual functions for dynamic binding. This support is provided with static type checking.

As we have seen, a C++ class defines a user-defined type. Indeed, the programmer can create first-class types because the language allows the definition of initialization, assignment, and equality test for the type being defined. As a result, objects of user-defined types may behave quite like objects of language-defined types: they may be created on the stack or in free store, passed as parameters, and returned by functions as results.

The language supports both single and multiple inheritance for defining new classes.

6.3.1.1 Classes

We have already seen the use of C++ classes as a definition mechanism for abstract data types. C++ provides the programmer with control over the creation, initialization, and cleanup of objects of such abstract data types. In particular, one or more *constructors* may be defined for a class. Such constructors are invoked automatically to initialize objects of the class at creation time. A constructor has the same name as the class. By analogy to a constructor, a *destructor* is invoked automatically when the object is destroyed—either explicitly through a call to delete or implicitly when the object goes out of scope. The ability to control what happens when an object is destroyed is critical for complex data types that may have allocated substructures in the heap. For example, simply deleting a pointer to the head of a list may leave the entire list inaccessible in the free store. A destructor gives the programmer the possibility to program the actions that are needed to deallocate the entire structure and perform the necessary cleanup.

We have seen in Chapter 3 that garbage collection is an important issue in programming languages that support dynamic object allocation. C++ does not provide an automatic garbage collector, but the programmer may redefine the operators new and delete for each class to provide object-specific storage allocation and garbage collection policies. For example, to implement garbage collection within a class, the delete operator associated with a class might link the released object in a free list managed by the class. The new operator included in the same class would first try to extract space from the free list and, if the free list is empty, would allocate a new object from the system's free store. This policy would be similar to a garbage collection service that collects and recycles different kinds of garbage (paper, plastic, etc.) separately.

The constructor for a derived class is invoked after that of its base class. This order guarantees that the derived class constructor may rely on the availability of its inherited variables. The destruction of a derived class proceeds in the opposite direction: first the destructor of the derived class is invoked, followed by that of its parent.

Besides construction and destruction, there are two other operations of user-defined types for which programmer control is important: assignment and equality comparison. These two operations are related semantically. In general, we expect that after assignment of an object a to object b, the two objects are equal. By default, C++ uses memberwise copy and memberwise comparison for assignment and comparison of class objects. This is often inadequate if the structure of the object involves heap-allocated components. For example, the equality function for stacks represented as lists should actually compare the values stored in the lists rather than comparing the two pointers to the heads of the lists. In these cases, the programmer may define class-specific assignment and equality operations. C++ does not provide any specialized features for this: as with any other operators, = and == may be overloaded.

Other languages treat these operations in a special way. For example, in Ada, declaring a type **private** indicates that it supports the language-defined assignment and equality operators; if a type is declared **limited private**, on the other hand, it means that it does not.

6.3.1.2 Virtual functions and dynamic binding

By default, a function call is bound to a function definition statically. If the programmer wants a function to be selected dynamically, the function must be declared virtual in the base class and then redefined in any derived classes. For example, suppose we define a class student that supports some operations, including a print() operation. We expect to derive different types of students from this class, such as college_student and graduate_student. First we define the student class and define a default print() function:

```
class student{
public:
    ...
    virtual void print(){...};
};
```

The virtual qualifier on print() says that classes derived from student may redefine the function print(). For a heap object that redefines print(), the appropriate print() function will be selected dynamically. For example,

```
class college_student: public student{
    void print() {
    ... // specific print for college_student
    }
};
```

defines a derived class that inherits all its operations from student but supplies a new definition for print(). Now, the following code sequence shows the effect of dynamic binding of function calls:

```
student* s;
college_student* cs;
```

```
...
s->print();    // calls student::print()
s = cs;        // okay
s->print();    // calls college_student::print()
```

Remember that in C++ the binding is normally static. The virtual function and pointers are used to effect dynamic binding.

Two rules ensure the type safety of programs in the presence of virtual functions and function redefinitions. First, the virtual function must be defined the first time it is declared, that is, in the base class. This ensures that the function will be available in any derived classes even if the derived class does not define it. Second, any redefinition of a virtual function along the inheritance chain may not change the signature of the function. This ensures that no matter which function is invoked, it is guaranteed to have the same signature. We have discussed this second rule in Section 6.2.2.2. The combination of these rules ensures that even though the compiler cannot know the identity of the function being called if the function is declared as virtual, it can still ensure that the function will exist at run time and it will have the correct signature.

6.3.1.3 Pure virtual functions for specification

Virtual functions may be used to define abstract classes. For example, we may specify that a shape must have three functions named draw, move, and hide, without providing an implementation for these functions. A virtual function that does not have an implementation is called a *pure virtual function*. To write a pure virtual function, its body is written as = 0;. If one or more member functions of a class are pure virtual, the class is called *abstract*. We may not create objects of an abstract class. In the example, objects of type shape cannot be created because such a class does not have an implementation. The pure virtual designation for a function says that a derived class based on shape must define such functions concretely. Figure 6.4 shows the outline of the class shape and a class rectangle derived from it.

We may view abstract classes as a specification for a set of derived classes. The abstract class specifies the interface, and the derived classes must provide the implementation. It is also possible to create an abstract derived class by defining only some of the pure virtual functions of the parent class.

6.3.1.4 Protected members

Let us go back to the example of counting_stack in Section 6.1.2. We want counting_stack to provide an additional function called size(). How are we

```
class shape {
public:
    void draw() = 0;      // this and the others are pure virtual functions
    void move(...) = 0;
    void hide() = 0;
    point center;
};

class rectangle: public shape {
private:
    float length, width;  // specific data for rectangle
public:
    void draw() {...};     // implementation for the derived pure virtual function
    void move(...) {...};
    void hide() {...};
};
```

FIGURE 6.4 A C++ abstract class using pure virtual functions

going to implement size()? The simplest way to do it is to return the value of top. That is, define size() as

```
counting_stack::size(){return top;}; //not quite right!
```

But there is a problem here. The variable top was declared to be private in stack. This means that it is only known within stack, and not within classes derived from stack. If we make top public, then that would make it available not only to derived classes but to all clients. For this reason, C++ has a third class of visibility for class entities: *protected* entities are visible within the class and any derived subclasses but are not visible to normal clients of the class. So if we declare top to be a protected variable of stack, rather than a private variable, the above implementation of size() will work properly. We show in Figure 6.5 the code for both stack and counting_stack.

Thus the general form of a C++ class is

```
class C {
    public:
        // accessible to the general public
    protected:
        // accessible to members and friends and
        // to members and friends of derived classes only
    private:
        // accessible to members and friends only
};
```

In summary, C++ provides three levels of protection. Entities defined in a class may be *private* (default case), in which case they are only accessible

```
class stack{
    public:
        stack(); {top = 0;} //constructor
        void push(int) {s[top++] = i;};
        int pop() {return s[--top];};
    protected:
        int top;
    private:
        int s[100];
};

class counting_stack : public stack {
    public:
        int size(){return top;};  //return number of elements on the stack
};
```

FIGURE 6.5 Example of class inheritance (derivation) in C++

inside the class itself; they may be defined as *protected*, in which case they are accessible inside the class and inside any classes derived from it; or they may be defined as *public*, in which case they are accessible generally to all clients. *Friends* have the same rights as the class itself. The public entities define the services provided by the class and constitute its interface. The private entities deal with the internal details of the class, such as the representation of data structures. The protected entities are not of interest to users of the class; they may be used by derived classes to provide services based on the services already provided by the class.

Using the terminology of Section 6.2.3.2, we can say that protected members support the use of implementation inheritance, whereas public members support the use of interface inheritance.

6.3.1.5 Overloading, polymorphism, and genericity

In Chapter 3 we discussed several kinds of polymorphism. Now we have seen that all the forms exist in C++. First, we have seen the use of ad hoc polymorphism in the support of overloading of operators and functions, in which case the binding of a name to an operator or function is done at compile time based on the types of the arguments. If a derived class redefines a virtual function f of a base class b, the base class defines a polymorphic type, and the function call b.f() is a call to a polymorphic function resolved dynamically on the basis of the type of the object referred to by b. Since the object must belong to a subclass of the class of b, this is a case of inclusion polymorphism. If the function is not declared to be virtual in the base class, then the two functions in the base and derived classes are treated as simply overloading the same function name: the proper function to call is selected at compile time based on the types of arguments passed to the function. Finally, we have seen that C++ also supports generic functions. If a function f(a,b) is generic, the types of a and b are used at compile time to instantiate a function that matches the types of the parameters a and b. There is no dynamic dispatch in this case.

6.3.2 Ada 95

The original version of the Ada language, introduced in 1983, was an object-based language. The package construct may be used to create objects that encapsulate both data—possibly private—and related operations. The package could export types, operations, variables, and other entities. We have seen that the programmer could use a package to implement abstract data types as in the dictionary example of Section 6.3.3.1. In this way, the original Ada supported object-*based* programming. Since the introduction of Ada, however, the concepts of object-oriented programming have become better understood. As a result, a number of features were added to Ada 95 to support object-*oriented* programming techniques such as inheritance and dynamic binding. In particular, *tagged types* support derivation of a new type from an existing type, and a technique called *classwide programming* combined with tagged types supports dynamic dispatch. Another feature of Ada 95 is the ability to define abstract types that may be associated with multiple implementations. Such flexibility is sometimes associated with object-oriented programming. We discuss these features below.

6.3.2.1 Tagged types

In Chapter 3 we saw how new types may be derived based on existing types. We have also seen how subtypes of discrete types may be defined that inherit the operations of the parent type but restrict the range of values of the type. In Chapter 5 we saw that we can use a package to group together a type and its associated operations, thus creating a user-defined type. With Ada 95, a type declaration may be designated as **tagged**, in which case it is possible to derive new types from it by extending it. This facility allows us to define a hierarchy of related types. For example, Figure 6.6 defines a tagged type named Planar_Object as having a certain set of basic properties, such as X and Y coordinates of its center, three routines: one to compute its Distance from the origin, another to Move it to a new position, and another to Draw it as a predefined icon on the screen. We might then derive other types, such as Point, Rectangle, and Circle, which each extend the basic tagged type in their own ways.

```
package Planar_Objects is
    type Planar_Object is tagged
    record
        X: Float := 0.0; --default initial value of the center's x coordinate
        Y: Float := 0.0; --default initial value of the center's y coordinate
    end record;
    function Distance (O: Planar_Object) return Float;
    procedure Move (O: inout Planar_Object; X1, X2: Float);
    procedure Draw (O: Planar_Object);
end Planar_Objects;
```

FIGURE 6.6 An Ada 95 package that defines a tagged type Planar_Object

We assume that the body (implementation) of the package Planar_Objects is given elsewhere. With this definition we may declare objects of type Planar_Object and apply Distance, Move, and Draw operations to them. Next we can define new types Point, Rectangle, and Circle that inherit the properties of the type Planar_Object. For a Point, the X and Y coordinates are enough; thus the data representation of Planar_Object does not need to be extended. But for a Circle we will add a Radius field, and for a Rectangle we will add the sizes of the two edges. Finally, it is necessary to redefine Draw for all of them. These shapes are defined in the package in Figure 6.7.

First, note that we may only *extend* a type, not remove any properties. Therefore, the new types are guaranteed to have all the fields of the parent type. As a result, the derived types can be coerced to the parent type by ignoring the additional fields. Thus, the following statements are valid:

```
with Planar_Objects; use Planar_Objects;
package Special_Planar_Shapes is
    type Point is new Planar_Object with null record; --indicates no additions
    procedure Draw (P: Point);
    type Circle is new Planar_Object with
        record
            Radius: float;
        end record;
    procedure Draw (C: Circle);
    type Rectangle is new Planar_Object with
    record
        Length, Width: Float; --sizes of edges of the rectangle
    end record;
    procedure Draw (T: Rectangle);
end Special_Planar_Shapes;
```

FIGURE 6.7 Extending tagged types in Ada 95

```
O1: Planar_Object; -- basic object at origin
O2: Planar_Object (1.0, 1.0); -- on the diagonal
C: Circle:= (3.0, 4.5, 6.7); --circle with radius 6.7 centered at (3.0,4.5)
...
O1:= Planar_Object(C); -- coercion by ignoring the radius field of C
```

What if we want to do the assignment in the opposite direction? We know that C++ does not allow this. It can be done in Ada, but, since the object on the right-hand side does not have all the necessary fields, they must be provided by the programmer explicitly. For example,

```
C:= (O2 with 4.7); --circle with radius 4.7
```

In our example, the three newly defined types inherit the operations Distance and Move from Planar_Objects. When they need to redefine (that is, override) an operation such as Draw, the rule on redefinition is similar to that in Eiffel; that is, the parameters of the overriding operations must be subtypes of (more specific than) the parameters of the overridden operations.

Thus, the tagged types of Ada 95 support the development of a tree of types through the use of inheritance, overriding, and extension. Type coercion is supported when an object of a derived type is assigned to an object of a parent type. One of the major goals of Ada in adopting the type extension model of inheritance has been to ensure that extension of a type does not force the recompilation of either the package declaring the type being extended or the client modules of that package. Recall that this was the same goal that motivated the definition of child libraries discussed in Section 5.3.4.6.

6.3.2.2 Dynamic dispatch through classwide programming

The tagged types of Ada 95 are also used to support dynamic binding of function calls. The tag is an implicit field of an object and is used at run time to identify the object's type. For example, suppose that we want to write a procedure Process_Shapes that will process a collection of objects that may be Points, Rectangles, or Circles. We need to declare this procedure as accepting a polymorphic type that includes all these types. The 'Class attribute of Ada 95 constructs exactly such a class. That is, the expression T'Class applied to a tagged type T is the union of the type T and all the types derived from T. It is called a *classwide* type. In our example, we can write our procedure as

```
procedure Process_Shapes(O: Planar_Object'Class) is
  ...
begin
  ...
  ... Draw(O) ...;  --dispatch to appropriate Draw procedure based on type of O
```

...
end Process_Shapes;

Since it is often useful to access objects through pointers, it is also possible to declare polymorphic pointers such as

type Planar_Object_Ptr **is access** Planar_Object'Class;

This type defines a pointer type that may point to objects of any of the types contained in the classwide type Object.

6.3.2.3 Abstract types and routines

As in C++ and Eiffel, Ada 95 supports the notion of top-down design by allowing tagged types and routines (called *subprograms* in Ada) to be declared abstractly as a specification to be implemented by derived types. For example, we might have declared our Planar_Object type before as an abstract type, as in Figure 6.8.

```
package Planar_Objects is
    type Planar_Object is abstract tagged null record;
    function Distance (O: Planar_Object'Class) return Float is abstract;
    procedure Move (O: inout Planar_Object'Class; X, Y: Float)  is abstract;
    procedure Draw (O: Planar_Object'Class) is abstract;
end Objects;
```

FIGURE 6.8 An abstract type definition in Ada 95

This package will not have a body. It is only a specification. By applying derivation to the type Planar_Object, we can build more concrete types. As before, we may derive a tree of related types. Once concrete entities (records and subprograms) have been defined for all the abstract entities, we obtain a concrete entity that may be instantiated.

6.3.3 Eiffel

Eiffel was designed as a language to support systematic design of type-safe programs. It provides classes for defining abstract data types, inheritance, and dynamic binding. Classes may be generic based on type parameters.

6.3.3.1 Classes and object creation

An Eiffel class is an abstract data type. As we saw in Chapter 3, it provides a set of *features*. In the initial versions of Eiffel, as opposed to C++, all objects were accessed through references. They could not be allocated on the stack. Later versions of Eiffel introduced a new type of object, called *expanded*, which is allocated on the stack and need not be accessed through a reference. Again in contrast to C++, object creation is an explicit, separate step from object declaration. In one statement a reference is declared, and in a following statement the object is created. For example,

```
b: BOOK;    --declaration of a reference to BOOK objects
!!b;        --allocating and initializing an object that b points to
```

The language provides a predefined way of creating and initializing objects based on their internally defined data representation. It is also possible to provide user-defined "creator" routines for a class that correspond to constructors of C++. Automatic garbage collection is provided to deallocate objects when they are no longer accessible.

6.3.3.2 Inheritance and redefinition

A new class may be defined by inheriting from another class. An inheriting class may *redefine* one or more inherited features. We saw that C++ requires that the redefining function must have exactly the same signature as the function that is redefined. Eiffel, like Ada, has a different rule: the signature of the redefining feature must conform to the signature of the redefined feature. This means that the parameters of the redefining routine must be assignment compatible with the parameters of the redefined routine.

Consider the following Eiffel code fragment:

```
class A
feature
    fnc (t1: T1): T0 is
        do ... end -- fnc
end --class A

class B
inherit
    A redefine fnc
feature
    fnc (s1: S1): S0 is
        do... end -- fnc
end --class B
...
a: A;
b: B;
...
a:= b;
```

...
... a.fnc (x)...

The signature of B.fnc must conform to the signature of A.fnc. This means that S0 and S1 must be assignment compatible with T0 and T1, respectively. Referring to the discussion of Section 6.2.2.2, the Eiffel rule follows the covariance rule on both input and output arguments. This is a loophole in the type system that inhibits complete static type checking. Its adoption in Eiffel is based on the recognition that the covariance rule, which would guarantee strong typing, is impractical.

Eiffel has a different view of inheritance from what we described in Section 6.1.2. In particular, Eiffel views a subclass (*derived class* in C++ terminology) as either extending its parent class or specializing it. For example, a subclass may **undefine** a feature of the parent class. In such a case, the child class may no longer be viewed as satisfying the *is-a* relationship with its parent.

The **deferred** clause of Eiffel may be used as the pure virtual specifier of C++ to implement abstract classes.

Eiffel supports multiple inheritance. To resolve the name conflicts that may occur due to inheriting from more than one base class, the **undefine** construct may be used to hide some features and **rename** may be used to rename others.

6.3.4 Smalltalk

Smalltalk was the first language to make object-oriented programming popular among software practitioners. Unlike C++ and Ada, which support multiple paradigms, Smalltalk (like Eiffel) is a purely object-oriented language. This means that the only available program decomposition paradigm is based on the identification of classes of interacting objects that can be organized through the inheritance hierarchy. Unlike Eiffel, Smalltalk is a fully dynamic language: each object carries its type at run time. The type of a variable is determined by the type of the object it refers to at run time

The following sections provide a brief introduction to the Smalltalk language, highlighting some interesting aspects of the language, without aiming at a complete coverage of the language.

6.3.4.1 Classes and inheritance

The Smalltalk encapsulation mechanism is the *class*. A class describes an abstract data type, whose instances are *objects*. A class contains a description of the *instance variables*, which represent the data structure to be allocated at each instantiation, and the description of operations (called *instance methods*) used to manipulate objects. Instance variables are not visible to other objects; they can only be manipulated by instance methods. Instance methods are invoked by sending a *message* to the object. Sending a message to an object corresponds to calling an instance method, which is a routine exported by the object's class.

For example, suppose that a class point exists—similar to what we described in Section 3.3.1 for C++ and in Section 3.3.2 for Eiffel—providing an operation xMove to move a point horizontally. Let myPoint be an instance of class point. The expression myPoint xMove delta sends the message xMove to the object myPoint to move itself horizontally by a quantity denoted by variable delta. Syntactically, this is a method call, which consists of the object's name, followed by the method's name, followed by the method's parameter. For multiple parameters, the syntax of method calls is based on the use of named parameter associations (see Section 2.4). For example, if we define a class table, we might provide a method to count the number of elements in the table whose value falls within a range designated by a lower bound and an upper bound, where the lower and the upper bounds are method parameters. The method might be defined to have the header

lowerBound: low upperBound: high

The message requesting the method's execution for table T, lower bound 6 and upper bound 95, would be:

T lowerBound: 6 upperBound: 95

When this message is sent to the table object, the names of the parameters are used to select the method to invoke. The method itself does not have any specific name. Besides instance variables and methods, classes can also have *class variables* and *class methods*. There is a single instance of the class variables and methods available to all objects of the class. In contrast, a copy of each instance variable and method is created for each instance object.

Classes can be organized in a hierarchy, where each subclass has at most one superclass (*single inheritance*). A subclass inherits all of the instance variables and methods from its superclass. The subclass can have its own instance variables and can both define new methods that do not exist in its ancestor classes and redefine inherited methods. When a message is sent to an object, the object's class is searched (at run time) for a matching method. If a match is not found, the search continues in the superclass, and so on up the inheritance chain until either a class is found that provides the method or the system class Object, which does not have any ancestors, is reached. In this latter case, an error is reported.

6.3.4.2 Variables and dynamic typing

Smalltalk views variables uniformly as references to objects. For example, even in a simple assignment statement like

    x ← 0

variable x is set to refer to an object whose value is 0.

Unlike in Eiffel, references are untyped: a reference is not bound statically to a class but can refer to any class instance. A message sent to x is type correct if the class of the object currently bound to x provides a method for it, either directly, or indirectly through inheritance.

Objects are allocated dynamically under the programmer's control via the new statement. For example, myPoint can be generated by sending the message new to class point, i.e., by writing the expression myPoint ← point new. Deallocation of unused objects is done by a language-provided garbage collector.

Dynamic binding of types to variables makes Smalltalk instructions polymorphic. The meaning of an operation invoked for an object depends on the class of the object that is currently bound to the variable; it is an error if no matching method is found by traversing the inheritance hierarchy upwards. According to the discussion in Section 3.4.7, Smalltalk is an example of a language providing dynamic polymorphism.

6.3.4.3 The pervasive role of objects

As we mentioned, the primary concept of Smalltalk is that of an object. Everything in Smalltalk, including classes and control structures, is an object.

A class is an object of the predefined class Object and, in particular, it provides a method to respond to messages requesting an instantiation. For example, in the assignment statement myPoint ← point new, the message new sent to class point requests the creation of a new object. This object is then assigned to the left-hand-side variable of the assignment operator (←), myPoint, to make it refer to the newly allocated object.

Smalltalk programs can be viewed as data. For example, a block in Smalltalk is a sequence of statements separated by periods and enclosed within brackets [and]. They are instance objects of class Block. For example, the following block sets two variables to zero:

    [x ← 0 . y ← 0]

A block is not executed as it is encountered. To request its execution, it is necessary to send it the value message, as in

[x ← 0 . y ← 0] value

The value returned from the evaluation of a block is the value of the last expression in the block. Blocks can be assigned to variables, which can then be evaluated, as in the following fragment:

setZero ← [x ← 0 . y ← 0].
...
setZero value

Control structures for conditional execution and iteration are then defined based on the definition of blocks. For example, the if-then-else instruction

x > y
    ifTrue: [max ← x]
    ifFalse: [max ← y]

is interpreted as follows. The message ifTrue:ifFalse: is sent to the object resulting from the evaluation of x>y, i.e., a Boolean object. Such an object can respond to the ifTrue:ifFalse: message by evaluating one of the two block objects sent as parameters, depending on its own value.

Similarly, the iteration statement in the fragment

10 timesRepeat: [x ← x + a]

is interpreted as follows. The message timesRepeat: is sent to an integer object along with a block as a parameter. Such an object can respond to the message by repeating the evaluation of the block as many times as is its own value.

As a final example, the fragment

[x < b] whileTrue: [x ← x + a]

is interpreted as follows. The message whileTrue: is sent to the conditional block with a block as a parameter, representing the code to be executed repeatedly. The message whileTrue: sends the conditional block the value message and, if the result is true, evaluates the block parameter. The process is repeated until the result of the evaluation of the conditional block is false.

The above examples suggest that, besides providing a number of predefined control structures, Smalltalk allows new control structures to be defined. Because new data types can be defined using classes, Smalltalk can be considered an *extensible* language: all computational mechanisms of the language can be tailored by the programmer.

6.3.4.4 The Smalltalk environment

Smalltalk was developed for writing applications in a highly interactive single-user personal workstation environment. The language is strictly coupled with its environment, which provides an object-oriented user interaction style. Anything that the user is working on (e.g., documents being edited, documents being browsed) are visible as objects in screen windows. It is possible to send messages to one such object by selecting it (e.g., by using a pointing device) and then specifying the required operation. The tools of the environment are written in Smalltalk. As a result, the language and the environment can be personalized and extended by users to fit their needs.

6.3.5 Java

Java is an object-oriented language that brings together many of the concepts that we have studied in this book. It is a derivative of C++ with some features removed and new features added. The new features are added primarily to support object orientation and concurrency. Java serves as a good case study for us because of the way it integrates the notion of objects with other language design concepts we have studied. Some of the interesting ideas of Java are:

- Java has no pointers. All objects are allocated in the heap and are accessed implicitly through references. As a result, garbage collection is necessary and is provided by the language.

- Java achieves portability by being based on an interpretive implementation. Programs are first translated to an intermediate code called *bytecodes* that define the Java virtual machine. Any machine with a bytecodes interpreter can then execute the program. The concept of portability is extended to the notion of *mobility*: a bytecodes interpreter executing on a computer in a network may load and execute a program or a class from another computer on the network. This concept is also used to enable many Internet browsers to directly load and execute Java programs. Because of these capabilities, Java is referred to as a *network language*.

- Java supports a separate interface module similar to ML's signatures. Interfaces are used to support multiple interface inheritance. Only single inheritance of implementations (that is, classes) is supported.
- Concurrency is supported through a predefined Thread class. A new class that inherits from Thread may run concurrently with other threads. Synchronized methods of objects make it easy to implement monitor-like behavior.

In this section, we will examine some of these issues in more detail.

6.3.5.1 Classes and inheritance

Like other object-oriented languages, Java has a class construct to define
new object types. The class is similar to the C++ class and consists of *fields*
and *methods* (called *member functions* in C++). As in C++, an instance of a
class contains its own copy of the fields that make up the object. Figure 6.9
shows a class definition for Planar_Object, which we defined in Ada in Figure
6.6. This class defines the object as containing two protected fields and three
methods. The fields x and y are of type float and represent the coordinates of
the center of the object; the methods are intended for manipulating the
object. Contrasting this definition with the Ada package, we see that the
method definitions here have one fewer parameter than the corresponding
Ada methods. The reason is that, as we have seen before, in the object-
oriented style the object itself (Planar_Object here) is an implicit parameter
passed to the method.

```
class Planar_Objects {
    protected float x, y;        //protected to be available to subclasses
    public float distance ();    //return distance from origin
    public void move (float x, y); //move object to point x,y
    public void draw ();         //draw object on screen
}
```

FIGURE 6.9 A Java class for Planar_Object

It is also possible to have *class variables* as well as *class methods*, of
which there is only one copy per class. As in C++, a field declared to be *static*
is shared among all the objects of that class. For example, if we want to keep
track of how many objects of type Planar_Object have been created, we could
declare a field

```
public static int count;
```

in the class Planar_Object. It is, of course, not a good idea to make such a variable public because clients may then manipulate it directly.

Class methods may also be declared to be static. Such class methods generally are intended to perform class-specific operations and work on class
variables rather than manipulate object-specific variables. As an example of
the use of static methods, consider solving our problem of keeping track of
the number of objects that have been created. We could make the count variable private and define a *static* method called counter that increments the static
count field. This method does not need any access to the public fields of

Planar_Object. To complete the solution, we should also provide a method to return the value of the count field.

Subclasses may be defined in Java by *extending* an existing class. Continuing with our Ada example of Planar_Object, in Figure 6.10 we define two subclasses Circle and Rectangle by extending the Planar_Object class. Each of the subclasses inherits all the fields of its superclass, adds its own private fields, and redefines the Draw() method of the superclass. The rule on redefinition is similar to C++: the overriding method must have exactly the same signature as the method being overridden. Obviously, static methods may not be overridden because they are class-wide rather than object-specific.

```
class Circle extends Planar_Object {
    private float Radius;
    public void Draw()              // draw a circle
        {...};
};
class Rectangle extends Planar_Object {
    private float Length, Width;   // edge sizes of rectangle
    public void Draw()
        {...};
};
```

FIGURE 6.10 Extending a class in Java

A subclass may only extend a *single* class. A subclass inherits the implementation of its superclass. Therefore, we say that Java supports single inheritance of implementations. The interface mechanism, presented in the next section, supports the notion of multiple inheritance, but for interfaces, not implementations.

Java also has a way to restrict or prohibit subclassing. If a *method* is declared to be final, then that method may not be redefined in any subclasses. A *class* may also be declared to be final, in which case the class may not be extended at all. This feature is used to ensure that certain important classes are not tampered with. For example, users of a method declared as

```
final public void ValidateUser();
```

may be sure that a subclass does not redefine the ValidateUser() method.

All classes in Java are nodes in an overall inheritance tree. The root of the tree is the Object class predefined by the language. Therefore, as in Smalltalk, every class implicitly or explicitly extends the Object class. The Object class defines certain methods that are available for all classes. For example, two methods defined by Object are equals and clone, which are used to compare two objects for equality and to make a copy of an object, respectively. Any object of a subclass type may be assigned to a variable of the superclass type. In particular, any object may be assigned to a variable of type Object. This inclusion polymorphism is used to declare equals and clone in Object as

```
public boolean equals (Object obj)
protected Object clone() throws CloneNotSupportedException
```

6.3.5.2 Interface and inheritance

In Chapter 5, we saw that an Ada module has two parts: a specification and a body. The specification is used to define the interface of the module. We also saw the use of ML's signatures for defining module interfaces. Java's interface mechanism is similar to ML's signature in that it defines an interface, except with no implementation. The interface may be implemented by one or more classes.

In Figure 6.11 we show the interface definition for a dictionary module. This is the same interface we defined in Ada in Figure 5.2. All methods declared in a Java interface are public.

```
interface Dictionary {
    void Insert (String c; int i); //String type is defined by Java
    int Lookup (String c);
    void Remove (String c);
}
```

FIGURE 6.11 Interface definition in Java for a dictionary

The implementation of an interface is provided by a class. For example, we might implement the Dictionary interface using an array implementation or a list implementation. The following code fragment shows a class that implements the Dictionary interface:

```
class ArrayDict implements Dictionary {
    private String[] Names;
    private int[] Values;
    private int size = 0;
    public void Insert (String c; int i) {
        //code to insert (c,i) pair in dictionary
    }
    public int Lookup (String c) {
        //code to look up c and return i
    }
    public void Remove (String c) {
```

```
        // code to remove c from dictionary
    }
}
```

We may also decide to implement a dictionary using lists instead of arrays. We could then declare:

```
class ListDict1 implements Dictionary {
    //private implementation of list structures
    //code for implementing the methods Remove, Insert, Lookup
    ...
}
```

But, more interestingly, we may already have an implementation of lists in a class called SpecialList. We may then *implement* the interface and *extend* the class at the same time:

```
class ListDict2 extends SpecialList implements Dictionary {
    //declaration of lists from SpecialList
    //code for implementing the methods Remove, Insert, Lookup
    ...
}
```

We can see that this is a kind of multiple inheritance. The class ListDict2 inherits both from the class SpecialList and from the interface Dictionary. In fact, multiple inheritance is supported for interfaces. For example, given our interfaces for Dictionary and List, we may define a new interface PhoneList for managing phone numbers:

```
interface PhoneList extends Dictionary, List {
    ...
}
```

An interface in Java may contain only constants and method declarations. Therefore, an interface may not be used to define an abstract data type because it contains only declarations and no implementation that may be used to contain state. Classes, as usual, may contain both declarations and implementations.

6.3.5.3 Abstract classes and abstract methods

As in Ada and C++, Java supports the definition of abstract classes and methods. A class or method may be specified as abstract, leaving it to be implemented by a subclass. As we have seen, Ada supports this feature using the

abstract keyword and C++ supports it using *pure virtual* functions. As we have seen, abstract classes are useful for defining specifications. Exercise 16 asks you to compare the use of interfaces and abstract classes as specifications.

6.3.5.4 Packages and programming in the large

We have seen that C++ supports classes and Ada supports packages. In Section 5.3.6, we contrasted the differences between these two approaches. Java combines the two approaches by allowing classes and interfaces to be grouped together in a package. A package is an encapsulation unit for programming in the large: any classes and interfaces declared as public in a package are exported to other packages.

A package has a name. A client may use the package by providing the name of that package in an import clause. For example, given a package called PhoneList, another package may access all public entities in PhoneList by stating:

```
import PhoneList.*;
```

The * means that all public entities are to be imported. It is also possible to import selective classes or interfaces.

A client package can refer to names of other packages and to all exported classes and interfaces of the packages that it imports. In particular, it can use the public members of any imported class and it can define subclasses of an imported class—such subclasses can use the protected members of their superclass.

The Java environment is organized as a tree of packages with the root java. For example, the java.io package provides basic I/O functionality, and java.util provides basic utilities such as useful data structures.

Java does not support any generic units.

6.3.5.5 Package access

Just as in C++, class members in a Java class may be public, protected, or private. This designation defines the access rights to these entities. Java introduces a new access right called *package access*. The default access for entities is package access. Members of classes that are not declared to be private are available to all other code in the package. For example, a field of a class declared as protected, or without any access modifier at all, is accessible to code in other classes defined in the same package. Members of interfaces are all public.

Package access addresses one of the problems we discussed in connection with the grouping of related entities in Section 5.3.6. We saw there that a module-based language is convenient for such grouping of related entities. For example, an Ada package providing facilities for manipulating vectors may contain the type vector and related operations. Some of these operations, such as one for multiplying a vector and a matrix, may not be directly associated with a particular vector object but need access to the internals of vectors and matrices. A module supports the packaging of related entities that share such secrets. A class-based language such as C++, which relies only on the class as an encapsulation mechanism, does not have a natural way of sharing such secrets among classes. We saw that the "friend" feature of C++ addresses this problem by granting visibility to internals of a class. Java's package access solves this problem by placing the vector and matrix classes in the same package and thus letting them share each other's representations. In a package, classes have visibility to each other's nonprivate data. Therefore, we may say that classes in the same package are "friends" in a C++ sense.

The package access still does not solve the problem of associating operations with objects, which is necessary in a purely object-oriented language. Since we cannot define operations independently from objects, we still are faced with the problem of whether the multiplication operation is associated with the vector or the matrix.

6.3.5.6 Threads and synchronization

In Chapter 4 we saw different models of concurrent execution. As in Concurrent Pascal and Ada, Java supports concurrency at the language level, rather than through run-time libraries. Support for concurrency is integrated with objects. The run-time libraries provide two mechanisms that the programmer can use to create parallel threads of execution: a Runnable interface and a Thread class. We start with the Thread class.

The Thread class of Java supports several methods for controlling the execution of a thread object. In particular, invoking the start() method of a thread will execute the run() method associated with the object. To create an object that may run in an independent thread of execution, we can extend the Thread object and supply a run() method. For example, the code fragment in Figure 6.12 defines a class Consumer that may be run in a thread.

A thread object such as Consumer in the figure may be invoked in a thread by calling its start() method, which will invoke the run() method of the object. So to start the consumer thread, we simply construct a Consumer object and start it:

```
class Consumer extends Thread {
    private Buffer buff;
    //construct a consumer
    Consumer (Buffer b) {
        buff = b;
    }
    public void run () {
        //remove item from buffer
        x = buff.get(); // buffer is an object shared with a producer
        //...do something with x...
    }
}
```

FIGURE 6.12 A consumer object in Java, inheriting from the Thread object

```
Consumer C = new Consumer(aBuff); //construct a consumer attached to a buffer
C.start (); // start the thread, i.e. invoke C.run()
```

or simply

```
new Consumer (aBuff).start(); //construct a consumer with a buffer and start it
```

Another way to create a thread object is to extend the Runnable interface. Runnable defines a single abstract method called run(). Any class that implements Runnable must provide its own run() method (that is the meaning of abstract). Objects of such a class are capable of running in a thread concurrently with other threads. Such an object may be started in a thread by executing its run() method. The Runnable interface is defined as

```
public interface Runnable {
    abstract public void run();
}
```

In Figure 6.13, we define a class Producer that implements the Runnable interface. To use a runnable object such as Producer in an independent thread, we first need to use the Thread class to construct a thread object. We can create a thread and run our Producer in it in this way:

```
Producer P = new Producer (aBuff); //construct a producer attached to a buffer
Thread PT = new Thread (P); // create a thread object for producer P
PT.start (); // start the thread, i.e. invoke P.run()
```

One reason to use Runnable instead of Thread in defining thread objects is if we have an existing class that we want to make runnable. We can define a new class that inherits from the existing class and implement Runnable at the

```
class Producer implements Runnable {
    private Buffer buff;
    //construct a producer object
    Producer (Buffer b) {
        buff = b;
    }
    public void run() {
        //produce things and put them in buffer
        buff.put (...);      //buff is a shared buffer object
        ...
    }
}
```

FIGURE 6.13 A producer object in Java, implementing the Runnable interface

same time. This is an example of the use of multiple inheritance as supported by Java.

In the above producer and consumer programs, we used the put and get methods of a buffer object. The buffer object is shared by the producer and the consumer. As we discussed in Chapter 4, accesses by parallel threads to such shared objects must be synchronized. In Java, a method may be declared to be synchronized. Invocations of synchronized methods are done in mutual exclusion. That is, a thread that executes a synchronized method on an object effectively locks that object, and any other threads that attempt to invoke synchronized methods on that object are blocked until the lock is released.

Figure 6.14 shows the implementation of a synchronized buffer. We have defined the put and get methods as synchronized. This ensures that if a get or put is being executed on a particular buffer object, any other thread attempting to execute a put or get on that same object will be blocked. Two methods, wait() and notify(), are also used in this example. These two special methods are defined in the Object class and therefore available in all objects. A call to wait() blocks the caller. A call to notify() wakes up one of the blocked threads. In general, a wait() is used in conjunction with a *condition*. A notify() indicates that something has happened and wakes up one of the threads that are waiting on that condition. If there is more than one thread waiting, the programmer does not have control over which thread will be notified. Another method is notifyAll(), which wakes up all waiting threads.

In this program, the put method checks the value of total and, if it indicates that the buffer is full, it executes a wait(). Eventually, some get method will call notify(), which will wake up the blocked put. The get method similarly waits when the buffer is empty and notifies when it has taken something out of the buffer.

```
public class Buffer {
    private int n;                  // size of buffer
    private int [] contents;        // contents of buffer
    private int in, out = 0;        // indexes of where to read from/write to
    private int total = 0;          // number of items in the buffer
    Buffer (int size) {
        n = size;
        contents = new int [n];
    }
    public synchronized void put (int item) {
        while (!(total < n))
            try { wait(); }         // wait until there is space
            catch (InterruptedException e) { }
        contents [in] = item;
        System.out.println("Buffer: write at " + in + " item " + item);
        if (++in == n) in = 0;
        total++;
        notify();                   // wake up any blocked threads
    }
    public synchronized int get () {
        int temp;
        while (!(total > 0))
            try { wait(); }         // wait till there is something
            catch (InterruptedException e) { }
        temp = contents[out];
        System.out.println("Buffer: read from " + out + " item " + temp);
        if (++out == n) out = 0;
        total--;
        notify();                   // wake up any blocked threads
        return temp;
    }
}
```

FIGURE 6.14 A synchronized buffer in Java

Given the producer and consumer outlines in Figures 6.12 and 6.13 and
the buffer of Figure 6.14, a main program may be written as given in Figure
6.15. The difference between the ways we create the producer and the consumer is due to the fact that we defined one as a Runnable and the other as a
Thread.

The entry point for programs in Java is the main() method defined in some
object. As we can see, with synchronized methods, it is easy to build objects
that behave like monitors. This scheme is reminiscent of Concurrent Pascal,
described in Chapter 4.

```
public class Main {
    /** Entry point of the program */
    public static void main (String args[])
    {
        Buffer B = new Buffer (100);      // create shared buffer
        Consumer C = new Consumer (B);// create consumer
        Producer P = new Thread (new Producer (B));// create producer
        C.start();                        // start consumer thread
        P.start();                        // start producer thread
    }
}
```

FIGURE 6.15 Main program for the Java producer/consumer example

6.4 Final remarks

Object-oriented programming is an effective style of programming for many situations. In recent years, however, it has been advertised rather as a panacea to all software development problems. The design of large software systems is an inherently difficult activity. Programming language features may help in implementing good designs, but they do not remove the deficiencies of a bad design. More importantly, designs are not necessarily bad or good. For example, consider the task of developing several tree abstractions for use in a system. Suppose we need both general trees and binary trees. Should the two classes be related by an inheritance relationship? If so, which one should be the base class? Depending on how the rest of the design fits together, one or the other class would be the better choice as a base class.

In practice, the initial development of the design is not the major problem. The designer is often able to build an inheritance hierarchy that fits the problem at hand. Difficulties arise later during maintenance when new classes need to be defined, introducing new *is-a* relationships that are not compatible with previous such relationships. If the inheritance tree needs to be modified significantly, the impact on the rest of the software can be significant.

6.5 Bibliographic notes

Simula 67 [Birtwistle73] was the first object-oriented language. It introduced the notions of class and inheritance. It also had a coroutine facility for support of concurrent execution. All other object-oriented languages have their ancestry in Simula 67. Smalltalk was the first popular object-oriented language. It is a

Object-oriented analysis and design

In this chapter we have described programming language support for object-oriented programming. The object-oriented approach to software development has grown to encompass not just programming but most other phases of software development. Object-oriented analysis tries to analyze the application domain and identify objects and related operations in the application domain; the relationships among the identified objects is established using inheritance. Object-oriented design emphasizes design decomposition based on objects rather than modules. Such designs are implemented more easily in object-oriented languages. Indeed, the use of object-oriented languages is only effective if the design is object oriented. It is at the design stage that component objects and their relationships are identified. Constructs such as abstract classes that we have seen in Ada, Eiffel, and C++ may be used to document object-oriented designs that can then be implemented in programming languages.

In Section 6.2.1, we used the *is-a* relation to define the notion of subtypes. The substitutability property that we have discussed for programming languages is treated in terms of *is-a* relationship at the analysis and design stages. In our example, a counting_stack *is-a* stack and therefore may be substituted anywhere a stack is needed (for example, passed to a procedure that expects a stack). But not (stack *is-a* counting_stack), and therefore a stack may not be substituted for a counting_stack. A good design rule is to use inheritance to derive a new class when derived_class *is-a* base_class. This is consistent with the C++ rule on assignments among derived and base classes, which may also be defined using the *is-a* relationship. The assignment y = x is allowed if x *is-a* y. Although this rule is intuitive and simple to state, it is not always easy to determine whether two objects are related with the *is-a* relation. For example, we have seen that colorPoint is not necessarily a point (Section 6.2.2.2). Usually, the relationship that holds among objects is *is-a-kind-of*. It often takes great care to create *is-a* relationships.

Although object-oriented programming is promising, simply using an object-oriented programming language does not ensure a project's success. We have seen that it is possible, for example, to use both C++ and Ada without relying on object orientation. To be successful with object-oriented programming, not only must the language be used properly; the analysis and design phases must also produce properly designed objects and object hierarchies.

---

dynamically typed language and was initially developed on special hardware, but current implementations of the language are available on many computers, including personal computers. CLOS (Common LISP Object System) introduces objects in LISP [Bobrow88], [Keene89]. C++ added object-orientation support to an existing imperative language [Stroustrup92]. [Stroustrup94] gives a fascinating account of how C++ grew from "C with classes" to a full language on its own. It also explains the differences between an object-oriented language and a language that supports object-oriented programming. Java [Gosling96], [Arnold96], is an object-oriented language based on a subset of C++. It has become popular because of its use in Internet programming. [Meyer88] is a comprehensive treatment of object-oriented programming using the Eiffel language. The language itself is described fully in [Meyer92]. Objective C is another language that extended C for object-oriented programming. It took a dynamic approach similar to Smalltalk as opposed to the static approach of C++.

[Taivalsaari96] is a survey of the different ways that inheritance has been used in computer science. It presents four different uses for inheritance: classification, aggregation, generalization, and grouping. [Snyder86] points out the differences and trade-offs between implementation and interface inheritance with a comparison of languages. [Wegner87] is the source for the classification of languages into object-based and object-oriented.

[Bruce96] is the source of the example in Section 6.2.2.2. The type structure of strongly typed object-oriented languages has sparked a large amount of type-theoretic research in recent years. A number of papers have been written to clarify the rules of covariance and contravariance. Examples are [Liskov94], [Castagna95], and [Bruce96]. [Cardelli85] was the first of these papers. [Abadi96] is a comprehensive treatment of objects with supporting calculi.

[Barnes96] is the source for our treatment of Ada 95. [Wirth88] describes the idea of type extension, which is adopted in Ada. A large number of object-oriented languages have been created in the last decade. Among the popular ones are Dylan [Apple92], Beta [Madsen93], Self [Ungar87], Emerald [Raj91], Oberon-2 [Mössenböck93] and Modula-3 [Nelson91]. Self does not use classes. Instead, it is based on the concept of prototypes, which are instances. Thus, Self supports the definition of instances (not classes) that inherit from other instances. Both Oberon-2 and Modula-3 are object-oriented extensions of Modula-2 and include support for concurrency.

A number of approaches to object-oriented analysis and design are described in [Fowler97]. [Booch94] is an introduction to object-oriented analysis and design.

6.6 Exercises

1. Implement a C++ class employee that supports a virtual method print(), which prints the name and age of an employee object. Next derive a class manager that supplies its own print() method, which, in addition to the employee information, prints the group number for which the manager is responsible (this is an additional field of manager). Also derive another class from employee called part_time. The part_time class also supplies its own print(), which prints how many hours a week the employee works.

- Can you use the print() of employee in manager?
- Explain how you would implement the same program in Pascal or C.
- Compare the object-oriented and the procedural solutions in terms of maintainability. What changes are necessary in the two solutions if we need to add a new category of employee?
- In the C++ solution, how would you implement a part_time_manager? Does your solution allow you to implement this new class using multiple inheritance?

2. Consider the following C++ program fragment:

```
class point {
public:
    float x;
    float y;
    point (float xval, float yval): x(xval), y(yval) {}
    virtual int equal (point& p) {
        cout << "calling equal of point." << endl;
        return x == p.x && y == p.y;
    }
};

class colorPoint: public point {
public:
    int color;
    colorPoint (float xval, float yval, int cval): point(xval, yval), color(cval){}
    int equal (colorPoint& cp) {
        cout << "calling equal of colorPoint." << endl;
        return x == cp.x && y == cp.y && color == cp.color;
    };
    int equal (point& cp) {
        cout << "calling equal of colorPoint with point." << endl;
        return x == cp.x && y == cp.y;
    }
};

...
point p1 (2.0, 6.0);
colorPoint cp1 (2.0, 6.0, 3);
...
p1 = cp1;
```

- Which function will be called with the calls p1.equal (p1), p1.equal(cp1), and according to what rule (polymorphism or overloading)?
- After the execution of a statement point *pp = new colorPoint(...);, which functions will be called with the calls pp->equal (p1), pp->equal(cp1), and according to what rule (polymorphism or overloading)?
- After the execution of a statement colorPoint *cpp = new colorPoint(...);, which functions will be called with the calls cpp->equal (p1), cpp->equal(cp1), and according to what rule (polymorphism or overloading)?
- Explain the differences between the answers in the first three parts of this question.

3. In Exercise 2, what is the type of p1 after the assignment p1 = cp1? What is the type of pp after the assignment pp = &cp1? Explain the differences between the object held by p1 and the object pointed to by pp.

4. In an object-oriented language such as C++, define an abstract class furniture and two derived classes for chair and table. The chair and table classes each have their own method

price(), which returns the price of the object. Allocate a list of furniture to store some chair and table objects. Write a loop to go through the list and sum the prices of the objects in the list. Explain how this object-oriented solution is different from one written in C or Pascal.

5. In Section 6.1.4 we suggested that a language that does not support dynamic binding may use case statements or function pointers to achieve the same result. Explain how this can be done and discuss the drawbacks of such solutions.

6. Let us define a relation s ≤ t to mean that s is a subtype of t. We want to define a subtype relation for function signatures. First we represent a signature as f: t1→t2, indicating a function f that takes an argument of type t1 and yields a result of type t2. How would you state the covariance and contravariance requirements using the subtype relation? That is, complete the equivalence relation below by replacing the question marks with appropriate relations: Given (f1:s1 → t1) and (f2:s2 → t2), f1 ≤ f2 iff (s1 ? t1) ∧ (s2 ? t2). How would you describe the Eiffel rule on redefinitions?

7. In C++, it is possible for a derived class to hide the public members of its base class from its clients. Give an argument and example to show that this is not a good design practice. (Hint: substitutability.)

8. In Section 6.1.2, we considered a subclass counting_stack, which supports a size() function. How can you implement the size() function using only the public interface of the parent class stack?

9. Sometimes inheritance is used improperly. For example, consider defining an automobile class. We have an existing class window. Since automobiles have windows, we have two options: we can derive automobile from window, ensuring that the automobile will have a window, or we can define the class automobile and use window as a member of the class. Why is the second solution better? Explain the proper use of inheritance in terms of the *is-a* relation.

10. When a class b is derived from a class a, class b may add new properties, or it may redefine properties defined in a. How do addition of properties affect the subtyping relation between parent and child? How do redefinitions affect the relationship?

11. In Chapter 3, we defined two classes POINT and NON_AXIAL_POINT. Is NON_AXIAL_POINT a subtype of POINT?

12. From an implementation point of view, multiple inheritance introduces two issues:
    - If an operation is defined in more than one of the base classes, which one is inherited by the derived class?
    - If we pass an object of a derived class to an operation of the base class, what type does it have? For example, a displayable_rectangle object passed to an operation that expects a polygon object should appear as a polygon object, and one passed to an operation expecting a displayable object should look like a displayable object.

    Find out and explain how C++ and Eiffel handle the first issue. Devise an implementation to solve the second issue.

13. Section 6.3.2.2 introduced the class-wide types of Ada 95. Consider a tagged class Object and a class Circle derived from it. In the following code,

```
Poly: Object'Class;
Mono: Circle;
...
Poly:= Mono;
...
Mono:= Poly;
```

which of the two assignment statements are statically type-safe? Which one may raise a run-time exception? Based on what you know from this chapter, is Ada able to detect such an exception?

14. In Figure 6.6, we define a tagged type Planar_Object. To hide the internal details of the type, we may want to declare the type as **tagged private**. Is it possible to hide the details from normal clients but make them available to types that extend Planar_Object? (You will need to check the Ada reference manual.) How is the problem solved in C++?

15. Recall the classes point and colorPoint of Section 6.2.2.2. Given the procedure

```
void problem (point p)
{
    colorPoint n = new colorPoint(...);
    if p.equal(n) {...}
}
```

can we call the procedure with a colorPoint parameter? With a point parameter? Will the class definitions pass type checking in Eiffel? Will they pass type checking in C++? Will a call to procedure problem cause a run-time error in C++? Will it cause a run-time error in Eiffel? Can we modify the class definitions to avoid a run-time error?

16. Java supports both interfaces and abstract classes. Both may be used to define specifications. Compare these two concepts as supported in Java.

17. In the buffer example of Figure 6.14, explain why the constructor does not have to be synchronized.

18. In the buffer example of Figure 6.14, both the put and get methods have a statement of the form while (condition) wait();. Explain why we should not replace the "while" loop with an "if" statement.

19. In the buffer example of Figure 6.14, we use a notify() to wake up blocked threads. Could we use notifyAll() instead? Describe an example situation in which it is necessary to use notifyAll() and not notify().

20. Write a Java interface for our dictionary example of Figure 5.2. Implement a class that satisfies the interface and may be used by concurrent threads.

Functional programming languages

I see an expression as a function of the expressions contained therein. (Wittgenstein)

C H A P T E R 7

So far in this book we have been concerned primarily with languages that may be described as statement oriented or imperative. These languages are affected strongly by the architecture of conventional computers. Functional programming languages take as their basis not the underlying computing engine but rather the theory of mathematical functions. Rather than efficient execution, these languages are motivated by the questions: what is the proper unit of program decomposition, and how can a language best support program composition from independent components?

We have seen that procedural languages use procedures as the unit of program decomposition. Procedures may use side effects on global data structures to communicate with other procedures. Abstract data types attempt to modularize a program by packaging data structures and operations together in order to limit the scope of side effects within encapsulated units. Functional programs reduce the impact of side effects further, or even eliminate them entirely, by relying on mathematical functions, which operate on *values* and produce *values* and have no side effects.

We start by describing the basic elements of imperative programming. These elements help illustrate the main differences of functional programming. To highlight these differences further, we will then compare mathematical functions with programming language functions. In Section 7.3.2 we present *lambda calculus* as a model for function definition, evaluation, and composition. We then look at ML and LISP as examples of functional programming languages. We also look briefly at functional features of APL.

Early functional languages, starting with LISP, were dynamically typed and scoped. Scheme is a dialect of LISP that introduces static scoping into the language. Later functional languages, such as ML, include not only static scoping but also strong typing. Many functional languages, including both Scheme and ML, have also added a module construct to address programming in the large.

7.1 Characteristics of imperative languages

Imperative languages are characterized by three concepts: variables, assignment, and sequencing. The state of an imperative program is maintained in program variables. These variables are associated with memory locations characterized by an address (l-value) and by a stored value (r-value). We may access the value of a variable either directly, through its l-value, or indirectly, through the r-value of another variable that denotes its l-value. The value of a variable is modified using an assignment statement. The assignment statement introduces an order dependency into the program: the value of a variable is different before and after an assignment statement. Therefore, the meaning (effect) of a program depends on the order in which the statements are written and executed. Although this is natural if we think of a program being executed by a computer with a program counter, it is quite unnatural if we think of mathematical functions. In mathematics, variables are bound to values and, once bound, they do not change value. Therefore, the value of a function does not depend on such concepts as the order of execution. Indeed, a mathematical function defines a mapping from a value domain to a value range. It is a set of ordered pairs that relate each element in the domain uniquely with a corresponding element in the range. Imperative programming language functions, on the other hand, are described as algorithms that specify how to compute the range value from a domain value with a prescribed series of steps.

One final characteristic of imperative languages is that repetition—that is, loops—is used extensively to compute desired values. Loops are used to scan through a sequence of memory locations such as arrays, or to accumulate a value in a given variable. In contrast, in mathematical functions, values are computed using function application. Recursion is used in place of iteration. Function composition is used to build more powerful functions.

Because of their characteristics, imperative languages have been given labels such as *state based* and *assignment oriented*. In contrast, functional languages have been called *value based* and *applicative*.

7.2 Mathematical and programming functions

A function is a rule for mapping (or associating) members of one set (the *domain* set) to those of another (the *co-domain*, or *range*, set). For example, the function "square" might map elements of the set of integer numbers to the set of integer numbers. A function definition is composed of two parts: a signature and a mapping rule. A function's *signature* specifies the domain and the range. The *mapping rule* specifies the value of the range associated with each value of the domain. For example, the function definition

```
square: integer → natural        --signature
square(n) ≡ n x n                 --mapping rule
```

defines the function named "square" as the mapping from integer numbers to natural numbers. We use the symbol "≡" for "is defined as." In the definition, n is a *parameter*. It stands for *any* member of the domain set. By convention, in function definitions we omit the signature if the domain and range are implicit in the context.

Once a function has been defined, it can be *applied* to a particular element of the domain set: the application yields (or *results* in, or *returns*) the associated element in the range set. At application time, a particular element of the domain set is specified. This element, called the *argument*, replaces the parameter in the definition. The replacement is purely textual. If the definition contains any applications, they are applied in the same way until we are left with an expression that can be evaluated to yield the result of the original application. The application

```
square (2)
```

yields the value 4 according to the definition of the function square.

The parameter n is a mathematical variable, which is not the same as a programming variable. In the function definition, n stands for any member of the domain set. In the application, it is given a specific value—*one* value. Its value never changes thereafter. This is in contrast to a programming variable, which takes on different values during the course of program execution.

New functions may be created by combining other functions. The most common form of combining functions in mathematics is function *composition*. If a function F is defined as the composition of two functions G and H, written as

```
F ≡ G o H,
```

applying F is defined to be equivalent to applying H and then applying G to the result.

In conventional programming languages, a function is defined procedurally: the rule for mapping a value of the domain set to the range set is stated in terms of a number of steps that need to be executed in a certain order specified by the control structure. Mathematical functions, on the other hand, are defined applicatively—the mapping rule is defined in terms of combinations or applications of other functions.

Many mathematical functions are defined recursively; that is, the definition of the function contains an application of the function itself. For example, the standard mathematical definition of the factorial of a natural number is

n! ≡ **if** n = 0 **then** 1 **else** n * (n - 1)!

As another example, we may formulate a (recursive) function, from natural numbers to booleans, to determine if a number is a prime:

prime (n) ≡ **if** n = 2 **then** true **else** p(n, n **div** 2)

The auxiliary function p(n, i) yields true if n has no divisors in the range 2..i. It is defined as

p(n, i) ≡ **if** (n **mod** i) = 0 **then** false
       else   **if** i = 2 **then** true
              else p(n, i - 1)

Notice how the recursive call to p(n, i-1) takes the place of the next iteration of a loop in an imperative program. Recursion is a powerful problem-solving technique. It is used heavily in programming with functions.

7.3 Principles of functional programming

A functional programming language has three primary components:

  1 A set of *data objects*. Traditionally, functional programming languages have provided a single high-level data-structuring mechanism such as a list or an array.

  2 A set of *built-in functions* for manipulating the basic data objects. For example, LISP and ML provide a number of functions for building and accessing lists. APL provides functions for array manipulation.

  3 A set of *functional forms* (also called high-order functions) for building new functions.

A common example is function composition (o). Another common example is function reduction.The functional form reduce applies a binary function across successive elements of a sequence. For example, reducing + over an array yields the sum of the elements of the array and reducing * over the elements of an array yields the product of the elements of the array. In APL, / is the *reduction* functional form (called *operator* in APL) and it takes one operation as argument. The plus reduction can be accomplished by /+ and the multiplication reduction by /x. Functional forms allow programmers to define new operations as combinations of functions without the explicit use of low-level control structures such as iteration and conditional statements.

The execution of functional programs is based on two fundamental mechanisms: binding and application. *Binding* is used to associate values with names. Both data and functions may be used as values. Function *application* is used to compute new values.

In this section we will first review these basic elements of functional programs using the syntax of ML. We will then introduce lambda calculus, a simple calculus that can be used to model the behavior of functions by defining the semantics of binding and application precisely.

7.3.1 Values, bindings, and functions

As we said, functional programs deal primarily with values, rather than variables. Indeed, variables denote values. For example, 3 and "a" are two constant values. A and B are two variables that may be *bound* to some values. In ML we may bind values to variables using the binding operator =.[1] For example,

```
val A = 3;
val B = "a";
```

The ML system maintains an *environment* that contains all the bindings that the program creates. Function calls introduce new bindings between the value of the actual parameter and the name of the formal parameter.

Values need not be just simple data values as in traditional languages. We may also define values that are functions and bind such values to names:

```
val sq = fn(x:int) => x * x;
```

where fn is a reserved word for binding a function object. We may also define functions in the more traditional way:

```
fun square (n:int) = n * n;
```

---

1. There are several variations of ML. As is common, we will use the Standard ML syntax here.

We may also keep a function anonymous and just apply it without binding it to a name:

```
(fn(x:int) => x * x) 2;
```

We may, of course, use functions in expressions. For example,

```
2 * sq (A);
```

will print the value of the expression $2A^2$, where the value of A is looked up in the environment. For example, if the environment contains a binding for A to 3, the ML system will yield the value 18.

The role of iteration in imperative languages is played by recursion in functional languages. For example, Figure 7.1 shows the function factorial written in C++ using iteration and ML using recursion. In both programs, the function is implicitly assumed to operate on nonnegative values.

```
int fact (int n)                    fun fact (0) = 1
{   int i=1;                        |    fact (n) = n * fact (n-1);
    //assume n>=0
    for (int j=n;  j>1; --j)
        i= i*j;
    return i;
}
```

FIGURE 7.1 Definition of factorial in C++ and ML

As we saw in Chapter 4, functions in ML may be written using patterns and case analysis. The factorial program in the figure is written as being composed of two cases: when the argument is 0 and when it is not.

7.3.2 Lambda calculus: A model of computation by functions

In the previous section, we saw the essential elements of programming with functions: binding, function definition, and function application. As opposed to an imperative language, in which the semantics of a program may be understood by following the sequence of steps specified by the program, the semantics of a functional program may be understood more naturally in terms of function applications. Lambda calculus is a simple calculus that models the computational aspects of functions. Studying lambda calculus helps us understand the elements of functional programming and the underlying semantics of functional programming languages independently of the syntactic details of a particular programming language.

Lambda calculus takes its name from the Greek letter λ (lambda), which is used in the notation. The *expressions* of lambda calculus are of three kinds:

e1 An expression may be a *single identifier* such as x, or a constant such as 3 or *.

e2 An expression may be a *function definition*. Such an expression has the form $(\lambda x.e)$, which stands for the expression e with x designated as a *bound* variable. The expression e represents the body of the function and x the parameter of the function. The expression e may contain any of the three forms of lambda expressions. Our familiar square function may be written as $\lambda x.x^{*}x$.

e3 An expression may be a *function application*. A function application has the form (e1 e2), which stands for expression e1 applied to expression e2. For example, our square function may be applied to the value 2 in this way: $((\lambda x.x^{*}x)\ 2)$.

Parentheses may be dropped from (e1 e2) and $(\lambda x.e)$. In the absence of parentheses, function application associates from left to right. Thus e1 e2 e3 stands for ((e1 e2) e3). Also, function application has higher precedence than function definition. That is, $\lambda x.y\ z$ stands for $(\lambda x.(y\ z))$.

A variable appearing in a function definition F is said to be *free* in F if it is not bound in F. Bound variables are like formal parameters in a routine definition and act like local variables; free variables are like nonlocal variables that will be bound at an outer level. For example, the function definition

$\lambda x.x^{k}$

defines the k-th power function with x as a bound variable and k as a free variable.

The above syntax of lambda expressions shows that function application uses the prefix form but the usual notation

f(x)

is replaced by

f x

Moreover, we have implicitly assumed that functions have only one argument. Actually, lambda calculus uses an ingenious alternative to multiple-argument functions. All functions are reduced to single-argument functions by means of a conceptual device called *currying* (after the logician Haskell B. Curry, who introduced it). For example, to express the sum of 1 and 3, we normally write 1+3 or, in functional form, add (1, 3). Using the syntax of lambda calculus, we would write add 1 3, or, using the operator symbol +, + 1 3, which groups as (+ 1) 3. The expression (+ 1) denotes the function that adds 1 to its argument.

Currying is a common technique in functional programming to deal with a variable number of arguments. Each argument is handled in sequence through one function application. Each function application replaces one of the bound variables, resulting in a "partially evaluated" function that may be applied again to the next argument. In general, a function f(x, y, z) can be written in curried form as a new function g x y z, which corresponds to (((g x) y) z). In this form, g x yields a function that is applied to y. The result is a function that is applied to z. In the example we gave above, the expression x * x should be read as * x x, which, in turn, stands for (* x) x. ML uses currying to deal with functions of more than one argument.

Lambda calculus captures the behavior of functions with a set of rules for rewriting lambda expressions. The rewriting of an expression models a step in the computation of a function. To apply a function to an argument, we rewrite the function definition, replacing occurrences of the bound variable by the argument to which the function is being applied.

Thus, to define the semantics of function application in terms of rewriting, we first define the concept of *substitution*. Substitution is used to replace all occurrences of an identifier with an expression. This is useful for binding parameters to arguments and avoiding the name conflicts that arise if the same name appears in both the expression being applied and the argument expression to which it is applied. We will use the notation [e/x]y to stand for "substitute e for x in y." We will refer to variables as x_i. Two variables x_i and x_j are the same if i=j. They are not the same if i≠j. We can define substitution precisely with the following three rules, based on the form of the expression y:

s1 If the expression is a single variable:

$$[e/x_i]x_j \quad = e, \text{ if } i = j$$
$$= x_j, \text{ if } i \neq j$$

s2 If the expression is a function definition, we must do the substitution carefully:

$$[e_1/x_i](\lambda x_j.e_2)= \lambda x_j.e_2, \text{ if } i = j$$
$$= \lambda x_j.[e_1/x_i]e_2, \text{ if } i \neq j \text{ and } x_j \text{ is not free in } e_1 \text{ (otherwise, it would become newly bound)}$$
$$= \lambda x_k.[e_1/x_i]([x_k/x_j]e_2) \text{ otherwise, where } k \neq i, k \neq j, \text{ and } x_k \text{ is not free in either } e_1 \text{ or } e_2$$

The last case renames all occurrences of variable x_j with another fresh variable x_k to avoid name clashes and then substitutes e_1 for x_i.

s3 If the expression is a function application, we first do the substitution both in the function definition and in the argument, and then we apply the resulting function to the resulting argument expression:

$$[e_1/x](e_2\ e_3)= ([e_1/x]e_2)([e_1/x]e_3)$$

Using the substitution rules above, we can define the *semantics* of functional computations in terms of *rewrite rules*. That is, we define the result of a function application in terms of rewriting the definition of the function, replacing the bound variables of the function with corresponding arguments. The following three rewrite rules define the concept of function evaluation:

> **r1** *Renaming*, also called α-conversion in the functional programming jargon:
> $$\lambda xi.e \leftrightarrow \lambda xj.[xj/xi]e, \text{ where } xj \text{ is not free in } e$$
> The renaming rule says that we can replace all occurrences of a bound variable with another name without affecting the meaning of the expression. In other words, a function is abstracted over the bound variables.
>
> **r2** *Application*, also called β-conversion:
> $$(\lambda x.e1)e2 \leftrightarrow [e2/x]e1$$
> This rule says that function application means replacing the bound variable with the argument of the application.
>
> **r3** *Redundant function elimination*, also called η-conversion:
> $$\lambda x.(e\ x) \leftrightarrow e, \text{ if } x \text{ is not free in } e$$

The symbol $\leftrightarrow$ is used in the above rules to indicate that the rules may be used in both the forward and reverse directions. The β- and η-conversion rules may be used in the forward direction to reduce a lambda expression. In fact, any lambda expression may be reduced using these rules, possibly also using renaming (α-conversion) to eliminate name clashes, until no further reduction is possible. An expression that may no longer be reduced is said to be in *normal form*. The theory of lambda calculus proves that different reductions lead to a unique normal form (up to a renaming conversion). The following shows the application of the evaluation rules to reach a normal form for the original expression.

$$(\lambda x.(\lambda y.x + y)\ 5)\ ((\lambda y.y * y)\ 6) =$$
$$(\lambda x.x + 5)\ ((\lambda y.y * y)\ 6) =$$
$$(\lambda x.x + 5)\ (6 * 6) =$$
$$(6 * 6) + 5$$

The pure lambda calculus is untyped and only deals with symbols. The semantics of constants and operations is left to the domain of arithmetic. Other forms of lambda calculus exist that expand on pure lambda calculus, but these are beyond the scope of our treatment. In our examples, we informally assume the properties of mathematical constants and operations. In other words, we can reduce the last line of the above example to 41.

Even without arithmetic, pure lambda calculus can be used to define and analyze programming language concepts such as binding, function definition, and function application, which are the primitive elements of functional programming languages. The clear semantics of functional languages is due to the fact that the semantics of function definition and application can be defined with these three simple rules.

7.4 Representative functional languages

In this section, we examine pure LISP, APL, CLOS, and ML. LISP was the first functional programming language. The LISP family of languages is large and popular. LISP is a highly dynamic language, adopting dynamic scoping and dynamic typing and promoting the use of dynamic data structures. Indeed, garbage collection was invented to deal with LISP's heavy demands on dynamic memory allocation. One of the most popular descendants of LISP is Scheme, which adopts static scope rules. CLOS is an object-oriented extension of LISP, providing classes, generic functions, and multiple inheritance.

APL in an expression-oriented language. Although it is not generally considered a functional language, it has many functional features that are due to the value orientation of expressions. As opposed to LISP's lists, the APL data-structuring mechanism is the multidimensional array. ML is a more recent member of the family of functional programming languages that introduces a strong type system into functional programming. We will examine ML in more detail because of its interesting type structure.

Functional programming languages are designed especially to support the functional programming paradigm. In Section 7.5, we look at C++ to see how a conventional programming language may be used to implement some functional programming techniques.

Most functional programming languages are *interactive*: they are supported by an interactive programming system. The program is stored in an intermediate form and the user interacts with a virtual machine that evaluates user instructions immediately. The interactive nature of these languages is in line with their value orientation. The system maintains an environment of bindings that is updated by each command entered by the user. The system responds to user commands by printing out a value requested by the user or indicating the result of a new binding supplied by the user.

7.4.1 LISP

The original LISP, introduced by John McCarthy in 1960 and known as pure LISP, is a completely functional language. It introduced many new programming language concepts, including the uniform treatment of programs as data, conditional expressions, garbage collection, and interactive program execution. LISP used both dynamic typing and dynamic scoping. Later versions of LISP, including Scheme, decided in favor of static scoping. Common LISP is an attempt to merge the many different dialects of LISP into a single language. In this section, we take a brief look at the LISP family of languages.

7.4.1.1 Data objects

LISP is a language for symbolic computation. Values are represented by symbolic expressions (called *S-expressions*). An expression is either an *atom* or a *list*. An atom is a string of characters (letters, digits, and others). The following are atoms:

```
A
AUSTRIA
68000
```

A list is a sequence of atoms or lists, separated by space and bracketed by parentheses. The following are lists:

```
(PLUS A B)
((MEAT CHICKEN) (BROCCOLI POTATOES TOMATOES) WATER)
(UNC TRW SYNAPSE RIDGE HP TUV)
```

The empty list "()" is also called NIL. The list is the only mechanism for structuring and encoding information in pure LISP. Other dialects have introduced most standard data-structuring mechanisms such as arrays and records.

A symbol (an *atom*) is either a number or a name. A number represents a value directly—it is an r-value. A name represents a value bound to the name—it is an l-value.

There are different ways to bind a value to a name: SET binds a value globally and LET binds it locally. (SET X (A B C)) binds X to the list value (A B C).

SET is an example of a function application. A function application, as in lambda calculus, is written as a list: the first element of the list is the function name, and the rest of the elements are parameters to the function. For example, (PLUS A B) stands for A+B. Thus, functions and data have the same representation.

7.4.1.2 Functions

There are very few primitive functions provided in pure LISP. Existing LISP systems provide many functions in libraries. It is not unusual for such libraries to contain hundreds of functions.

QUOTE is the identity function. It returns its (single) argument as its value. This function is needed because a name is an l-value that represents an r-value. When we use the name, the name is evaluated and the r-value is returned. Using QUOTE prevents the evaluation, and the l-value is returned instead. Many versions of LISP use 'A instead of the verbose QUOTE A. We will follow this practice.

The purpose of the QUOTE function is to enable its argument to be treated as a constant. Thus, 'A in LISP is analogous to "A" in conventional languages. For example,

```
(QUOTE A) = 'A = A
(QUOTE (A B C)) = '(A B C) = (A B C)
```

All functional languages provide many functions to work with the supported data structures. In the case of LISP, there are many useful functions for list manipulations: CAR and CDR are selection operations, and CONS is a structuring operation. CAR returns the first element of a list; CDR returns the list with the first element removed; CONS adds an element as the first element of a list. For example,

```
(CAR '(A B C)) = A
```

The argument to CAR needs to be "quoted" to prevent its evaluation. The function application rule in LISP is that the arguments are evaluated first and then the function is applied to their results. In our case the evaluation of the argument '(A B C) yields the list (A B C), which is operated on by CAR. If QUOTE were missing, (A B C) would first be evaluated, which would result in using A as a function operating on arguments B and C. If A is not a previously defined function, this would result in an error. Other examples are as follows:

```
(CDR '(A B C)) = (B C)
(CDR '(A)) = ( ) = NIL
(CAR 'A) = error, CAR requires a list parameter
(CONS 'A '(B C)) = (A B C)
(CONS '(A B C) '(A B C)) = ((A B C) A B C)
```

A few predicates are also available. A true value is denoted by the atom T and a false value by NIL. The values of the atoms NIL and T are preset by the system and we do not need to "quote" them.

ATOM returns T if its argument is an atom, and () otherwise. NULL returns T if its argument is NIL. EQ compares its two arguments, which must be atoms, for equality. For example,

```
(ATOM 'A) = T
(ATOM '(A)) = NIL
(EQ 'A 'A) = T
(EQ 'A 'B) = NIL
```

The function COND serves as a "case" expression. It takes as argument a list of pairs of the form (predicate, expression). It is evaluated by examining the pairs in sequence, to find the first pair whose predicate evaluates to true. The value of the expression part of this pair is returned as the value of the COND expression. For example,

(COND ((ATOM '(X)) 'B) (T 'C)) = C

The first condition is false because (X) is not an atom. The second condition is identically true and works like an "else" clause in this case. The COND function, known as the *McCarthy conditional*, is the major building block for user-defined functions.

Function definition is based on lambda expressions. The function

$\lambda x,y.x+y$

is written in LISP as

(LAMBDA (X Y) (PLUS X Y))

Function application also follows lambda expressions. For example,

((LAMBDA (X Y) (PLUS X Y)) 2 3)

binds X to 2 and Y to 3, and applies PLUS, yielding 5.

The binding of a name to a function is done by the function DEFINE, which makes the function name known globally:

(DEFINE (ADD (LAMBDA (X Y) (PLUS X Y))))

Now the atom ADD can be used in place of the function above; that is, the atom ADD has value that is a function. Another function, LABEL, is used if we want to define the function to be known only locally.

Giving a name to a function is especially useful in defining recursive functions. For example, we can define a function REVERSE to reverse the elements of a list:

```
(DEFINE (REVERSE (LAMBDA (L)
        (REV NIL L))))
(DEFINE (REV (LAMBDA (OUT IN)
        (COND ((NULL IN) OUT)
        (T (REV (CONS (CAR IN) OUT) (CDR IN)))))))
```

The REVERSE function calls a subsidiary function REV, which works by picking the first element of a list and calling REV on the rest of the list. This simple program demonstrates two techniques used in functional programming. The first is *stepwise refinement*: we define REVERSE first in terms of another function, REV, to be defined later. LISP accepts the definition of REVERSE even though REV is undefined. The system simply binds the name REVERSE to its definition; the definition is not evaluated. Evaluation will be done when the function is applied. This property is used commonly to write the higher-level, more abstract functions first, to be followed by functions at increasing levels of detail.

The second technique used in the program above is the use of REV to do the computation. REV has two parameters and is called recursively. Initially, the second parameter holds the input value (the list to be reversed) and the first parameter holds the empty list. Each call to REV removes the first element from the second parameter and inserts it at the head of the first parameter. When the second parameter is exhausted (is the empty list), the first parameter holds the result of the reversal. The second parameter is initialized to NIL by the caller, the function REVERSE. Since REVERSE is a function called by clients, we cannot expect them to pass in the correct initial value for such a variable. On the other hand, since the function REV is called only by REVERSE, we can impose such a requirement on it. Auxiliary functions such as REV, which progressively accumulate the result, are quite common in functional programming. In fact, we saw an example of this technique already in the prime number computation in Section 7.2.

The use of DEFINE is one way to bind an atom to a value. Another way is through function application, which binds parameters to the arguments. The assignment statement, the conventional way of binding a value to a name, is not present.

The variables in pure LISP are more like the variables in mathematics than those in other languages. In particular, variables may not be modified: they can be bound to a value and they retain that value throughout a given scope (i.e., function application). Finally, because there are no pointers and no static scoping, there is no aliasing of variable names.

7.4.1.3 Functional forms

LISP systems do not provide many functional forms. One of the most common functional forms supported by all current LISP systems, however, is MAPCAR, which supports the application of a function to every element of a list. For example,

```
(MAPCAR SQUARE L)
```

squares every element of the list L. MAPCAR has been adopted in most other functional programming languages.

Rather than provide many functional forms, the choice in LISP has been to supply a large number of primitive functions in the library.

7.4.1.4 LISP semantics

One of the most remarkable points about LISP is the simplicity and elegance of its semantics. In less than one page, McCarthy was able to describe the entire semantics of LISP by giving an interpreter for LISP written in LISP itself. The interpreter is defined by a function called *eval*.

The simplicity of the interpreter is due to two points. The first is that pure LISP is built from only five primitive functions and predicates: ATOM, EQ, CAR, CDR, and CONS. The second is that LISP programs are structured as lists—the data structure that the language is designed to support. That is, programs and data have the same representation. A program consists of a list of expressions that are to be evaluated in order of occurrence. The interpreter simply applies CAR to the program to pick out the first expression to evaluate. The structure of the expression is similarly analyzed using appropriate CAR and CDR applications.

7.4.2 APL

APL was designed by Kenneth Iverson at Harvard University during the late 1950s and early 1960s. Even though APL relies heavily on the assignment operation, its expressions are highly applicative. We will look at these features here to see the use of functional features in a statement-oriented language.

7.4.2.1 Data objects

The objects supported by APL are *scalars*, which can be numeric or character, and *arrays* of any dimension. An array is written as a sequence of space-separated elements of the array. Numeric 1 and 0 may be interpreted as boolean values *true* and *false*, respectively. APL provides a rich set of functions and a few higher-order functions for defining new functions.

The assignment operation ($\leftarrow$) is used to bind values to variables. On assignment, the variable takes on the type of the value being assigned to it. For example, in the following, the variable X takes on the type integer, character, and array, in successive statements:

```
X ← 123;
X ← 'b';
X ← 5 6 7 8 9;
```

The assignment produces a value also. Therefore, as in C, it may be used in expressions. For example,

```
X ← (Y ← 5 6 7 8 9) × (Z ← 9 9 7 6 5);
W← Y − Z;
```

will set the value of Y to 5 6 7 8 9, Z to 9 9 7 6 5, X to 45 54 49 48 45, and W to −4 −3 0 2 4.

7.4.2.2 Functions

In contrast to pure LISP, APL provides a large number of primitive functions (called *operations* in APL terminology). An operation is either *monadic* (taking one parameter) or *dyadic* (taking two parameters).

All operations that are applicable to scalars also distribute over arrays. Thus, A x B multiplies A and B. If A and B are both scalars, the result is a scalar. If they are both arrays and of the same size, it is element-by-element multiplication. If one is a scalar and the other an array, the result is the multiplication of every element of the array by the scalar. If A and B are arrays of different sizes or dimensions, the result is undefined.

The usual arithmetic operations (+, −, ×, ÷, | [residue or remainder]) and the usual boolean and relational operations (∧, ∨, ~, <, ≤, =, >, ≥, ≠) are provided. APL uses a number of arithmetic symbols and originally required a special keyboard with all the special keys. Today, APL implementations use standard keyboards and key combinations.

There are a number of useful operations for manipulating arrays. The operation "ι" (the Greek letter iota) is a "generator" and can be used to produce a vector of integers. For example, ι5 produces

```
1 2 3 4 5
```

Combining objects and functional programming

The Common Lisp Object System (CLOS) is an object-oriented extension to Common LISP to enable object-oriented programming in a functional setting. Among other things, it provides classes, multiple inheritance, and generic functions. Generic functions support dynamic binding to function calls. A generic function contains a set of methods, some of which are selected for execution depending on the classes of the arguments supplied to the function. To enhance the support for generic programming, the concept of slot is used to represent both fields and members functions of classes.

CLOS grew out of previous experimental object-oriented extensions to LISP such as Flavors [Moon86] and CommonLOOPS [Bobrow86].

The operation ";" concatenates two arrays. So ι4; ι5 results in

1 2 3 4 1 2 3 4 5

The operation "ρ" uses its left operands as dimensions to form an array from the data given as its right operands. For example,

$$2\ 2\ \rho\ 1\ 2\ 3\ 4 \equiv \begin{bmatrix} 1 & 2 \\ 3 & 4 \end{bmatrix}$$

and

$$2\ 3\ \rho\ 1\ 2\ 3\ 4\ 5\ 6 \equiv \begin{bmatrix} 1 & 2 & 3 \\ 4 & 5 & 6 \end{bmatrix}$$

The *compress* operation "/" takes two arguments of the same dimension and selects elements of its right-hand argument, depending on whether the corresponding left-hand argument is a (boolean) 1 or 0. For example,

1 0 0 1 / ι4 ≡ 1 4

because / will select the first and fourth elements of the vector on its right-hand side. The left argument may consist of boolean expressions. For example,

A<B B<C C<D / X

will pick certain values from X, depending on the comparisons on the left. X must be a three-element vector in this case.

There are many other primitive operations in APL. They can be regarded as mathematical functions because they operate on operands and produce values without side effects. User-defined functions are similar to the primitive functions in that they also are either monadic or dyadic (niladic functions correspond to subroutines). They are used in infix notation and thus can be used in expressions, in the same way that built-in functions can.

7.4.2.3 Functional forms

As we have seen, functional forms give the programmer the ability to construct new functions. APL provides three functional forms (*operators* in the APL terminology) that may be used uniformly to combine the many built-in functions of the language. The functional forms are as follows:

1 The *reduction* operator "/" (same symbol as compress). For example, the sum of the elements of the vector A is given by +/A. Contrasting this with adding the elements of a

vector in an imperative language shows that the iteration and step-by-step computation are handled by the functional form. If the right operand of "/" is a matrix, the reduction operation applies to successive rows; that is, if A is the matrix

```
1  2
3  4
```

then +/A is

```
3
7
```

which is represented as 3 7. In general, a reduction applied to an n-dimensional array results in an (n – 1)-dimensional array. It is also possible to apply reduction along a particular dimension of a multidimensional array by providing the dimension. For example, if A is a two-dimensional array, +/[1]A sums the elements along the first dimension: it sums the columns of A. Similarly, +/[2]A sums the rows of A, by reducing along the second dimension.

2 The *inner product* operator "." takes two primitive binary operations as arguments and produces a binary operation as result. The operands of the resulting operation must be arrays that "conform" in size. For example, if they are matrices, the number of rows of the left operand must be the same as the number of columns of the right operand; the result will be a matrix with as many rows as the left operand and as many columns as the right operand. If f and g are two primitive binary functions, the effect of A f.g B is to apply g, element by element, to the corresponding rows of A and columns of B (i.e., first row of A with first column of B, and so on). This is followed by an f reduction (/f) on the resulting vector.

As an example of the power of inner product in building operations, matrix multiplication can be accomplished by using +.x. This time, the functional form accomplishes the equivalent of two nested loops necessary in a procedural way to do the same job.

3 The third functional form of APL is the outer product "∘", which takes one primitive operation as operand and results in a binary operation. The operation ∘.f applied to arrays A and B (i.e., A ∘.f B) has the effect of applying f between each element of A and every element of B. For example, if A has the value (1 2 3) and B has the value (5 6 7 8), the result of A ∘.x B is the matrix

```
 5  6  7   8
10 12 14  16
15 18 21  24
```

The effect can be seen as forming a matrix with the rows labeled with elements of A and columns labeled with elements of B. The entries of the matrix are the result of applying the operation to the row and column labels. So the above matrix was derived from

```
x  5  6  7  8
1  5  6  7  8
2 10 12 14 16
3 15 18 21 24
```

The outer product finds many applications in data processing, in producing tables of interest rates, taxes, and so on. It has other uses as well. As an example, to find which elements of A occur in B, A°.= B provides a map of boolean values, with a 1 in the position where an element of A equals the corresponding element of B.

The many operations of APL and its functional forms support an expression-oriented style of programming that reduces the reliance on loops and computation of intermediate values. The functional forms are used to build powerful operations that hide the internal details of the functions, which may in fact be accomplished using loops in a conventional statement-based language.

7.4.2.4 An APL program

As an example of the power of (expression-oriented) functional programming, in this section we will look at how we may derive an APL program to compute prime numbers in the range 1 to N. Despite the limited exposure to APL provided in this section, we have seen enough to construct the desired program.

The style of programming emphasizes exploiting arrays and expressions rather than scalars, assignments, and iteration. Because of this, we plan to produce a vector of prime numbers. We can start with a vector of numbers in the range 1 to N and, using the compress operator, remove the nonprimes from it. In other words, if we compute a vector of boolean values called mask, where position p is 1 only if p is a prime, then the following expression will yield the prime numbers of interest:

mask / ιN

We can start with the definition of a prime number: a positive integer that is divisible only by 1 and by itself. So, for each number in the range of interest, 1 to N, we can (a) divide it by all the numbers in the range and (b) select those that are divisible only by two numbers.

Step (a) can be done with the residue operation and an outer product:

(ιN) °.| (ιN)

This will yield a matrix where each entry is the remainder of the division operation between the row label and the column label. If the remainder is 0, the row label is divisible by the column label. If there are more than two 0's in the row, then the row label is not a prime. So we check first for 0's:

0 = (ιN) °.| (ιN)

Recall that operations such as the equality test—here applied to a scalar and an array—distribute over the array. That is, the equality test is performed between 0 and all the elements of the matrix on the right-hand side. Therefore, our expression yields a two-dimensional boolean matrix indicating whether the numbers were divisible (1) or not (0).

In step (b), we want to see how many times the number was divisible, that is, the number of 1's in each row. We sum the rows by doing a + reduction along the rows (the second dimension):

$$+/[2]\ 0 = (\iota N)\ ^{\circ}.|\ (\iota N)$$

Now we have a one-dimensional vector with each entry indicating how many times the row label was divisible by numbers in the range 1 to N. We are only interested in those rows that have a 2, that is, were divisible twice.

$$2 = (+/[2]\ 0 = (\iota N)\ ^{\circ}.|\ (\iota N))$$

The result is a boolean vector indicating whether the index is a prime (1) or not (0). This is the mask vector we are looking for. To get the actual prime numbers, we apply compression:

$$(2 = (+/[2]\ 0 = (\iota N)\ ^{\circ}.|\ (\iota N))) /\ \iota N$$

The prime number program is simply *one* expression. The essence of this solution is that it builds successively more complex expressions from simpler ones. We may compose parts easily because the parts do not interfere with one another. Lack of interference is due to the lack of side effects in expressions. This is indeed the promise of functional programming: functions are appropriate building blocks for program composition because they are independent units.

7.4.3 ML

ML starts with a functional programming foundation and adds a number of features found to be useful in the more conventional languages. In particular, it adopts polymorphism to support the writing of generic components; it adopts strong typing to promote more reliable programs; it uses type inference to free the programmer from having to make type declarations; and it adds a module facility to support programming in the large. The most notable contribution of ML has been in the area of type systems. The combination of polymorphism and strong typing is achieved by a "type inference" mechanism used by the ML interpreter to infer the static type of each value from its context.

7.4.3.1 The list data object and its operations

As in LISP, the *list* is the major data structuring mechanism of ML; it is used to build a finite sequence of values of the same type. Square brackets are used to build lists: [2, 3, 4], ["a", "b", "c"], [true, false]. The empty list is shown as [] or nil. A list has a recursive structure: it is either nil or it consists of an element followed by another list. The first element of a nonempty list is known as its *head* and the rest is known as its *tail*. Lists are homogeneous, consisting of elements of the same type. The type of a list of elements of type t is written as t list.

There are many built-in list operators. The two operators hd and tl return the head and tail of a list, respectively (like CAR and CDR of LISP). So hd([1,2,3]) is 1 and tl([1,2,3]) is [2,3]. Of course, hd and tl are polymorphic. The construction operator :: takes a value and a list of the same type of values and returns a new list (like CONS of LISP). The list consisting of head hd and tail tl can be denoted as hd::tl. For example, 1::[2,3] returns [1,2,3]. We can combine two lists by concatenation: [1,2]@[3] is [1,2,3].

The structure of lists is used in structuring a function. Let us look at some functions that work with lists. First, recall from Chapter 4 the function to reverse a list:

```
fun reverse([]) = []
|   reverse(x::xs) = reverse(xs) @ [x];
```

Let us write a function to sort a list of integers using insertion sort. First we define a function to insert an element into its proper position in a sorted list, then we use this function to do a sort.

```
fun insert(x,[]) = [x]
|   insert(x:int, y::ys) =
            if x < y then x::y::ys
                      else y::insert(x,ys);
fun sort([]) = []
|   sort(x::xs) = insert(x, sort (xs));
```

The recursive structure of lists makes them suitable for manipulation by recursive functions. For this reason, functional languages usually use lists or other recursive structures as a basic data-structuring mechanism in the language.

7.4.3.2 Bindings, values, and types

Establishing a binding between a name and a value is an essential concept in functional programming. In Section 7.3.1 we saw examples of how ML establishes bindings. Every value in ML has an associated type. For example, the value 3 has type int and the value fn(x:int) =>-x has type int ->int, which is the signature of the functional value being defined.

We may also establish new scoping levels and establish local bindings within these scoping levels. These bindings are established using let expressions. For example,

```
let
    val x = 5
in
    2*x*x
end;
```

evaluates to 50. The name x is bound only in the expression in the let expression. There is a similar construct for defining bindings local to a series of other declarations:

```
local
    val x = 5
in
    val sq  = x*x
    val cube = x*x*x
end;
```

Such constructs may be nested, allowing nested scoping levels. As opposed to LISP, ML is statically scoped. Therefore, a new name may mask out a variable of the same name in an enclosing scope, but each occurrence of a name may be bound statically to its declaration. Previous bindings of the name are remembered in the environment and become accessible again after the current scope is exited.

7.4.3.3 Functions

In ML, we can define a function without giving it a name, just as a lambda expression. For example, as we have seen,

```
fn(x:int) => -x;
```

is a value that is a function complementing its integer argument. It is the same as the lambda expression λx.-x with the additional type declarations. We may pass this value to another function as an argument or bind it to a name:

```
val intnegate = fn(x:int) => -x;
```

The type of this function is fn:int->int.

Similarly, fn(x:int, y:int) => x*y; is a function that multiplies its two arguments. Its type is fn: int*int -> int.

We have seen that functions are often defined by considering the cases of the input arguments. For example, we can find the length of a list by considering the case when the list is empty and when it is not:

```
fun length(nil) = 0
|    length(_::x) = 1+length(x);
```

The two cases are separated by a vertical bar. In the second case, the underscore indicates that we do not care about the value of the head of the list. The only important thing is that there exists a head, whose value we will ignore. That is, the second case applies a nonempty list.

We may also use functions as values of arguments. For example, we may define a higher-order function compose for function composition:

```
fun compose (f, g)(x) = f(g(x));
```

The type of compose is ('a->'b * 'c->'a)->('c->'a). The 'x stands for *any* type x. This type expression says that the domain of the function consists of a pair of functions, each of which takes a single argument and returns some type. The range of the function is also a function that takes a single argument. The names of the types in the type expressions are used to relate type equality requirements. For example, 'a and 'a denote the same type. We will discuss such type expressions in detail in Section 7.4.3.5.

7.4.3.4 Functional forms

ML provides some built-in functional forms. The classic one is the same as MAPCAR of LISP, here called map, which takes two arguments: a function and a list. It applies the function to each element of the list and forms the results of the applications into a new list. The function map is curried. For example, the result of

```
map length [[], [1,2,3],[3]]);
```

is [0,3,1].

Some ML implementations provide a function similar to the APL reduction operator /. We can define such a function, call it fold, which takes three parameters: a function f to apply, a list l to apply it to, and a "seed" value s to be used as the result if the input list is nil. This function can be defined by considering two cases:

```
fun fold (f, s, nil) = s
|    fold (f, s, (h::t)) = f (h, fold (f, s, t));
```

We can now sum the elements of a list by

```
fold((op+), 0, [1,2,3,4]);
```

which yields 10. Notice that to pass the + operator as argument, we have to package it as a function object. That is what we have done as the first parameter.

ML supports *curried functions*. For example, we can define the function to multiply two integers in curried form:

```
fun times (x:int) (y:int) = x * y;
```

The signature of this function is fn: int-> (int->int). We can build a new function, say, multby5, by binding one of the arguments of times:

```
fun multby5(x) = times 5;
```

7.4.3.5 Type system

Unlike LISP and APL, ML adopts a strong type system. Indeed, it has an interesting type system. It starts with a conventional set of *built-in types*: bool, int, real, and string. Strings are finite sequences of characters. There is a special type called *unit* that has a single value denoted as (). It can be used to indicate the type of a function that takes no arguments.

There are several built-in *type constructors*: lists, records, tuples, and functions. A *list* is used to build a finite sequence of values of a single type. The type of a list of T values is written as T list. For example, [1,2,3] is an int list and ["a","b","cdef"] is a string list. An empty list is written as nil or []. The type of an empty list is 't list. 't is a *type variable* that stands for any type. The empty list is a polymorphic object because it is not specifically an empty int list or an empty bool list. The expression 't list is an example of a polymorphic type expression (called *polytype* in ML).

Tuples are used to build Cartesian products of values of different types. For example, (5, 6) is of type int*int and (true, "fact", 67) is of type bool*string*int. We can of course use lists as elements of tuples: (true, []) is of type bool*('t list).

Records are similar to Pascal records: they are constructed from named fields. For example, {name="Darius", id=56789} is of type {name: string, id: int}. Tuples are special cases of records in which fields are implicitly labeled by integers starting with 1. The equality operation is defined for records based on comparing corresponding fields, that is, the fields with the same names.

As we have seen before, a *function* has a—possibly polymorphic—signature, which is the type of the function. For example, the built-in predicate null, which determines whether its argument is the empty list, is a polymorphic function of type 't list -> bool.

In addition to the built-in type constructors, the programmer may define new types using any of the following three ways: type abbreviation, data type definition, and abstract data type definition. The simplest way to define a new type is to bind a type name to a type expression. This is simply *type abbreviation*, which allows one to use a name rather than the type expression. As such, it does not really introduce a new type. Rather, it introduces a new name for an existing type. Some examples are

```
type intpair = int * int;
type 'a pair = 'a * 'a;
type boolpair = bool pair;
```

In the second line, we have defined a polymorphic type called pair that is based on a type 'a. The type pair forms a Cartesian product of two values of type 'a. We have used this type in the third line to define a monomorphic type boolpair.

The second way to define a new type is to specify how to construct values of the new type. This is called *data type definition* in ML. For example, similar to Pascal enumeration types, we can define the new type color as

```
datatype color = red | white | blue;
```

This definition defines a new type color and three *value constructors* for it. These value constructors are simple and do not take any parameters. In general, we may have more complex value constructors. In any case, the name color has now been defined as a new type. We may use the new constructors to build new values. For example, [red, blue] is of type color list.

Value constructors may take parameters. We might define a new type to help us keep track of a person's publications in journals and conferences,

```
datatype pubs = nopubs | journal of int | conference of int;
```

based on three value constructors: nopubs, journal, and conference. The first constructor takes no arguments, while the latter two are monadic constructors. Examples of constant values of this new type are nopubs, journal(5), conference(7).

We can also provide recursive data type definitions. For example, we might define a binary tree as

```
datatype 't Btree = empty | Node of 't * 't Btree * 't Btree;
```

We have defined a Btree of a particular type 't as being either empty or consisting of a node that has three components. One component is simply a value of type 't. The other two components are each a 't Btree themselves. An example of int Btree is Node(3, empty, empty), which represents a tree consisting of a single node.

To show the power of value constructors in defining new types, we define a stack in terms of the operation push that can be used to construct it:

```
datatype 't stack = empty | push of 't * 't stack;
```

This definition says that the following are example values of the stack data type:

```
empty
push(2, empty)
push(2,(push(3,push(4,empty))))
```

Here we have used push as a value constructor rather than an operation defined on stacks. Indeed, the list data type of ML is defined in a similar way as

```
datatype 'a list = nil | :: of 'a * 'a list;
```

For this definition of list to really work, we also need to say that :: is used as an infix operator. We can do that by using

```
infixr ::;       (*this says that the operation :: is infix and right-associative*)
```

Going back to our definition of 't stack, we can define functions such as pop and top on the new data type stack. For example, we might define pop and top as shown here:

```
exception error;
fun pop(empty) = raise error
|   pop(push(x,xs)) = xs;
fun top(empty) = raise error
|   top(push(x, xs)) = x;
```

This stack does not hide its representation from its clients. If we want to do that, we must use an *abstract data type definition*, which is the third way to define a new type in ML. An abstype defines a new type and hides its concrete representation. For example, Figure 7.2 shows a lifo abstract data type. This

```
abstype 'a lifo = Stack of 'a list
with    exception error;
        val create = Stack nil;
        fun push(x, Stack xs) = Stack(x::xs);
        fun pop(Stack nil) = raise error
        |   pop(Stack [e]) = nil
        |   pop(Stack(x::xs)) = Stack xs;
        fun top(Stack nil) = raise error
        |   top(Stack(x::xs)) = x;
        fun lenght(Stack nil) = 0
        |   length(Stack(x::xs)) = length(Stack xs) + 1;
end;
```

FIGURE 7.2   An abstract data type stack in ML

type defines the operations create, push, pop, top, and length and one exception called error for the abstract type lifo. The definition of the type gives the representation of the type (after the =), followed by the supported operations (after the with). Internal to the type, we represent a stack as a Stack type made of lists. From the outside, the representation of lifo, which is a list, is not accessible. A lifo object may only be manipulated through its exported operations.

Given this definition, we may use the following operation:

```
val z = create;       (* create an empty 't lifo and assign it to z *)
```

The type of variable z is still polymorphic because its value is nil. After pushing a value, the resulting object will get a concrete type:

```
val w = push(2, z); (* w is a singleton int lifo *)
val x = push(1, push(2, push(3, create))); (* create a new int lifo with 1,2,3 *)
```

Notice that even though x is represented as a list, we may not manipulate it as a list. It is truly an abstract data type.

We can see that ML has a rich type system. Every value has a type, but the type may be polymorphic (*polytype*). The use of type variables supports the creation of polymorphic types. These types may then be used to write polymorphic functions. Because of ML's strong type system, type errors are caught as soon as the system encounters an expression that violates the type requirements.

7.4.3.6 Type inference

Earlier functional languages used dynamic typing, in which a variable simply takes on the type of the value that is assigned to it. Both LISP and APL are based on such dynamic type systems. ML tries to achieve the advantages of a strongly typed language without burdening the user with the requirement for type declarations. A name always has to be declared before it is used, but its type is not required in the declaration. The ML system infers the types of variables based on their use. Because the language is strongly typed, each value produced by the program has to be assigned a particular type expression. These type expressions are used to perform type checking on operations. If the system cannot use the inferred types to guarantee the type safety of a program, an error message is produced at compile time identifying the offending definitions. The programmer must specify the type in such situations. For example, an expression x>y does not contain enough information to infer whether x and y are integers or reals. If a function of x and y contains such an expression and no other indication of the types of x and y, then the program must declare the type of either x or y. Only one type declaration is necessary because the other one is constrained to have the same type. This was the reason that in the definition of the function square in Section 7.3.1, we had to declare the type of the argument as being int, while in the definition of the factorial function we did not have to declare the type of the argument. The ML system uses the expression "if x = 0" in the definition of factorial to infer the type of x to be int. Rather than requiring the programmer to declare the types of variables, the ML system uses such information to do its static type checking.

ML combines type inference with extensive support for (parametric) polymorphism. Consider a simple polymorphic identity function that returns its argument as its result. This function does not care what the type of its argument is. If we were to write such a function in C or Pascal, we would have to write a function for each type that we expect to use. In ML, we only need one function:

```
fun id(x) = x;
```

We could write a similar function in C++ using templates, where the type of the parameter is a template parameter (Exercise 15). This function may be applied to a value of any type and it will return the same value. Of course, we may apply id to a function also, for example, to itself: id (id) returns id.

The signature of this function is id: 'a -> 'a; that is, it maps from a domain of some type to a range of the *same* type. From its signature, we can see clearly that the function is polymorphic. Such a function can be type-checked statically even though we do not know what type will be passed at the time the function is applied. Each application of a function uses the type of the argument to produce a value of the appropriate type as result. For example, id(3) returns an integer and id(id) returns a value of type 'a->'a.

Some built-in functions such as list handling functions are naturally polymorphic. For example, hd has signature hd: 't list->'t. Some operators, on the other hand, limit the polymorphism in programs and also constrain the ability of the system to do type inferencing. For example, the function max, defined as

```
fun max(x:int, y) = if x > y then x else y;
```

requires declaration of the type of x because the system cannot tell whether, for example, the signature of max should be (int*int)->bool or (real*real)->bool. The signature ('t*'t)->bool is not correct either because not all types are acceptable. Only types that support the > operator are acceptable. We can also use the signature facility of ML to specify the requirements of operations. The use of such signatures is discussed in the next section.

One particularly important class of types is the *equality* types, denoted by "a. These are types that support the equality and inequality operators = and <>. If we define a function eq,

```
fun eq(x, y) = x=y;
```

the type of the function is eq: "a*"a-> bool. That is, eq is a polymorphic function that requires two values of an equality type and returns a boolean. Of course, a type expression including a type variable "t has stricter requirements than one having only 't variables.

7.4.3.7 Modules

We have already seen an example of an ML module in Chapter 5. ML modules are separately compilable units. There are three major building blocks:

1 A *structure* is the encapsulation unit. A structure contains a collection of definitions of types, data types, functions, and exceptions.
2 A *signature* is a type for a structure. A signature is a collection of type information about some of the elements of a structure: those we wish to export. We may associate more than one signature with a structure.
3 A *functor* is an operation that combines one or more structures to form a new structure. We will not discuss functors here.

As an example of a module, Figure 7.3 shows a stack definition encapsulated in a structure. A structure is like a package in Ada: it packages a number of related entities. In this figure, we are defining a structure named S. The structure contains definitions of an exception called error, a type Stack, and a number of operations. These operations are packaged together using the

```
structure S = struct
    exception error;
    datatype 't Stack = 't list;
    val create = Stack nil;
    fun push(x, Stack xs) = Stack(x::xs);
    fun pop(Stack nil) = raise error;
    |   pop(Stack [e]) = nil
    |   pop(Stack(x::xs)) = Stack xs;
    fun top(Stack nil) = raise error;
    |   top(Stack(x::xs)) = x;
    fun lenght(Stack nil) = 0
    |   length(Stack (x::xs)) = length(Stack xs) + 1;
end;
```

FIGURE 7.3 A stack module in ML

struct...end construct after the =. In this figure we have defined a simple polymorphic stack implemented as a list, similar to the one in Figure 7.2. Our new
definition of Stack is polymorphic in the type of elements stored in the stack.
It may also be compiled separately. A structure exports all the entities that it
defines. We use the dot notation to access to the entities defined in the structure. For example, we may create a Stack by S.create. And we may push a
value on a Stack by S.push(2, S.create).

A structure exports all of its defined entities. But signatures allow us to
define interfaces for modules. For example, we may define a simple interface
to a lifo module as

```
signature lifo = sig
    type q;
    val push : 't * q -> q;
    val pop: q -> q
end;
```

This signature defines an interface to a module that provides a type q and
operations push and pop. We may use this signature with the module that we
defined in Figure 7.3 to build a new module with fewer operations visible to
clients. We may do this by using the signature like a type declaration:

```
structure lifo1 :lifo = S;
```

This statement defines a new structure (i.e., module) that has the interface lifo
and the implementation S. Since the implementation defined in the module
does meet the requirements stated in the interface lifo, this is a valid construction. As long as the implementation provides at least what the signature promises, it is possible to use the interface with that implementation.

```
signature stringStack = sig
    exception error;
    type string Stack;
    val create: string Stack;
    val push: string * string Stack-> string Stack;
    val pop:  string Stack-> string Stack;
    val top:  string Stack-> string;
end;
```

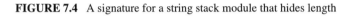

FIGURE 7.4 A signature for a string stack module that hides length

We can also use signatures to specialize a structure. For example, we can specialize the polymorphic stack of Figure 7.3 to a stack of strings. In Figure 7.4 we define a signature for a stack of strings that supports the operations create, push, pop, and top, but not length. A signature may be viewed as a specification for a module. It contains no implementation and is similar to a Java interface. Several signatures may be associated with the same module, and the same signature may be used with different modules. For example, we can use the signature of Figure 7.4 with the structure of Figure 7.3 to create a new structure:

```
structure SS:stringStack = S;
```

In this statement, we create a new structure called SS, with the implementation provided by the structure S and the interface provided by the signature stringStack.

Structure elements may be accessed selectively by using dot notation (e.g., SS.push("now",SS.create)) or by "opening" the structure and gaining access to all the elements:

```
open SS;
push("now", create);
```

ML also provides functors for combining structures to build a new structure by combining other structures.

7.5 Functional programming in C++

In this chapter, we have studied the style of functional programming as supported by languages designed to support this style of programming. It is interesting to ask to what degree traditional programming languages can support functional programming techniques. It turns out that the combination of classes, operator overloading, and templates in C++ supports some degree of programming with functions. In this section, we explore these issues.

7.5.1 Functions as objects

A C++ class encapsulates an object with a set of operations. We may even overload existing operators to support the newly defined object. One of the operators we can overload is the *application* operator, i.e., parentheses. This can be done by a function definition of the form: operator()(parameters...){...}. We can use this facility to define an object that may be applied, that is, an object that behaves like a function. Figure 7.5 shows the outline of such a class called Translate. We call such objects *function objects* or *functional objects*. Such objects are defined as objects but they behave as functions.

```
// definitions of types word and dictionary
...
class Translate {
private: ...;
public:
    word operator()(dictionary& dict, word& w)
    {
        //  look up word w in dictionary dict
        //  and return result
    }
};
```

FIGURE 7.5 Outline of a function object in C++

We may declare and use the object Translate in this way:

```
Translate Translator(); //construct a Translate object using default constructor
cout << Translator(EnglishGermanDict, "dog");
```

which would presumably print "Hund" if the dictionary is correct.

The ability to define such objects means that we have already achieved an element of functional programming: we can construct values of type function, assign them to variables, pass them as arguments, and return them as result.

7.5.2 Functional forms

Another element of functional programming is the ability to define functions by composing other functions. The use of such high-order functions is severely limited in conventional languages.

With the use of templates in C++, however, we can somewhat simulate high-order functions. First, we notice that the Translate constructor builds a function that takes two parameters: a dictionary and a word to translate according to that dictionary. Is it possible to construct a specialized Translate function that uses a predefined dictionary? Because the Translate function is being constructed inside the Translate object, we can use a private variable of the Translate object to hold the value of the desired dictionary. Then all we have to do is to provide a new constructor for Translate that takes on a single parameter denoting the dictionary to be used. By constructing a translator object this way, we bind the dictionary and produce a function object that works only with that dictionary.

The new class definition and its use are shown in Figure 7.6. In this figure, we construct two different translator objects, each with its own dictionary. The general concept we have used here that of a closure. A *closure* is a function with some of its free variables bound. It is like a lambda expression with an environment that contains bindings for some of the function's free variables. It is a common functional programming technique. In this example, the function application operator () uses d as a free variable. We use the constructor to bind this free variable. We can bind it to different values in different instantiations of the object.

```
// definitions of types word and dictionary
...
class Translate {
private:
    dictionary D; //local dictionary
public:
    Translate(dictionary& d): D(d) {} // constructor
    word operator()(word& w)
    {
        //   look up word w in dictionary D
        //   and return result
    }
};
...
//construct a German to English translator
Translate GermanToEnglish (GermanEnglishDictionary);
//construct an  English to Italian translator
Translate EnglishToItalian (EnglishItalianDictionary);

...
cout << EnglishToItalian (GermanToEnglish("Hund"));
...
```

FIGURE 7.6 Outline of a partially instantiated function object in C++

The 1995 standard for the C++ library contains a number of function objects and associated templates to support a functional style of programming. For example, it includes a predicate function object greater that takes two arguments and returns a boolean value indicating whether the first argument is greater than the second. In other words, it encapsulates the > operator as a function object. We can use such a function object, for example, as a parameter to a sort routine to control the sorting order. We construct the function object in this way: greater<int>().

The library also includes a higher-order function find_if, which searches a sequence for the first element that satisfies a given predicate. This find_if takes three arguments: the first two indicate the beginning and end of the sequence, and the third is the predicate to be used. Find_if uses the iterators that we discussed in Chapter 5. Therefore, it is generic and can search arrays, lists, and any other linear sequence that provides a pointer-like iterator object. Here, we will use arrays for simplicity. To search the first 10 elements of array x for an element that is greater than 0, we may use something like the following statement:

```
int* p= find_if (x, x+10, "...positive..." ); //predicate positive needs to be detailed
```

What function can we use to check for positiveness? We need to check that something is greater than 0. Given template function objects such as greater, we can build new functions by binding some of their parameters. The library provides *binder* templates for this purpose. There is a binder for binding the first argument of a template function object and a binder for binding the second argument. For example, we might construct a predicate function positive from the function object greater by binding its second argument to 0 in the following way:

```
bind2nd (greater<int>(), 0)
```

The library also provides the usual high-order functions such as reduce, accumulate, and so on for sequences. The combination of the high level of genericity for sequences and the template function objects enable the use of a functional style of programming in C++, although the syntax of the language does not make it as natural for this purpose as a functional programming language. For example, contrast the convenience of ML's approach to constructing a function object from a built-in operator (as we saw in Section 7.4.3.4) such as (op+), with the greater template function here. Further, the approach in C++ is limited. Here, we only have two binders defined, rather than a general binderN function to be able to bind any parameter position.

7.5.3 Type inference

The definition of the template facility in C++ requires that the compiler perform a fair amount of type inference. For example, consider the polymorphic max function given in Figure 7.7. The type of the arguments is simply stated to be of some class T. The C++ compiler accepts such a definition as a polymorphic function parameterized by type T. We have seen that the ML type-inferencing scheme rejects such a function because it cannot infer the type of the operator > used in the function definition. It forces the programmer to state whether T is int or float. C++, on the other hand, postpones the type inferencing to template *instantiation* time. Only when max is applied—for example, in an expression ...max(a, b)—does C++ do the required type checking. This scheme allows C++ to accept such generic functions and still do static type checking. At function definition time, C++ notes the fact that the function is parametric based on type T, which requires an operation > and a copy constructor (so that it can be passed and returned as an argument). At instantiation time, it checks that the actual parameters satisfy the type requirements.

```
template <class T>
T max (T x, T y)
    {if (x>y) return x;
        else return y;
}
```

FIGURE 7.7 A C++ generic max function

We have already contrasted the C++ polymorphic functions with those of ML in terms of type inference. It is also instructive to compare them with those of Ada. In the definition of a polymorphic function based on a type parameter T, neither C++ nor ML require the programmer to state the requirements on type T explicitly: they infer them from the text of the function definition. For example, both discover that the type must support the > operation. ML rejects the function definition because of this requirement and C++ accepts it. In Ada, in contrast, the specification of the function must state explicitly that the type T must support the operation >. This is intended both as documentation and to allow the function specification to be compiled separately from the body of the function. Both ML and Ada accord special treatment to the assignment and equality operators: Ada refers to types that support these two operations as **private**, and ML infers a type that uses the equality operator as an *equality* type. Each language tries with its decisions to balance the inter-related requirements of strong typing, ability to describe highly generic functions, separate compilation, writability, and readability.

7.6 Final remarks

In this chapter, we have examined the concepts and style of functional programming and some of the programming languages that support them. The key idea in functional programming is to treat functions as values. Functional programming has some of the elegance of mathematical functions and, therefore, it is easier to prove properties about functional programs than about iterative programs. On the other hand, because of its reliance on mathematics rather than computer architecture, it is more difficult to achieve efficient execution in functional programs.

Modern functional languages have adopted a number of features, such as strong typing and modularity, that have been found useful in conventional languages. In turn, conventional languages such as C++ and Ada have adopted some functional programming ideas that make it easier to treat functions as objects.

7.7 Bibliographic notes

Lambda calculus was invented by Alonso Church [Church41]. [Landin64] describes the SECD virtual machine for interpreting lambda calculus. The foundations of LISP are developed in the classic paper by John McCarthy [McCarthy60]. In it, McCarthy introduces LISP and its interpreter eval. A fascinating history of the development of LISP is given by McCarthy in [Wexelblat81]. Common LISP, an attempt to unify the different LISP dialects, is described in [Steele84]. Scheme is a popular variant of LISP that is used heavily in teaching. The textbook [Abelson85] is based on Scheme.

APL was defined in the book *A Programming Language* [Iverson62]. ML was developed by Milner in the 1970s. The formal definition of Standard ML is available in [Milner90]. Books on ML are [Ullman94] and [Paulson96]. The document by Bob Harper, available on the Net, is a handy introduction to ML and is the source of several examples in this chapter.

Even though work on functional programming dates back to the 1930s, interest in functional programming was sparked by the Turing award lecture of John Backus [Backus78]. In this paper, the inventor of FORTRAN argued that imperative programming simply could not support programming in the large and that mathematically based functional programming had a much better chance. He introduced a family of functional programming languages called FP as a candidate language.

Many functional languages have been developed over the years. Hope [Burstall80], is an early functional language with static typing. Haskell [Thompson96] is a proposed standard for a functional programming language. It is an attempt to standardize the functional programming syntax. Both Haskell and Miranda [Turner85] feature lazy evaluation. [Hudak89] is a treatise on functional programming languages.

7.8 Exercises

1. Reduce the lambda expression [y/x]((λy.x)(λx.x)x).
2. Reduce the lambda expression (λx.(x x))(λx.(x x)). What is peculiar about this expression?
3. Write a LISP program to evaluate arithmetic expressions containing parentheses and operations +,–, *, and /. Run the program on your local implementation.
4. Write a LISP program to compute the first 100 prime numbers.
5. Write a factorial program in APL.
6. What is the type of this ML function?

```
fun f(x, y) = if hd(x) = hd(y)
              then f(tl(x), tl(y))
              else false;
```

7. Write an ML function to merge two sorted lists.
8. Write an ML function to sort a list using the sort-merge method. Use your merge function from the previous exercise.
9. Explain why the following ML function bigger gives a type error:
   fun bigger(x, y) = if x> y then x else y;
10. Write a function in ML to compute the distance between two points, represented by (x, y) coordinates. Next, based on this function, define a new function to compute the distance of its single argument from the origin.
11. Define an ML module (structure and signature) that implements an abstract data type for sets, with the usual algebraic operations on sets.
12. Define the two functions of Exercise 10 in C++.
13. In C++, we can use a function template to write a function bigger similar to the one in Exercise 9:

```
template<class N>
bool bigger(N x, N y)
   {if (x>y) return x; return y;}
```

Why does this program not cause a type error at compile time?
14. Use Exercise 9 and Exercise 13 to compare the type inference support in C++ and ML in terms of flexibility, generality, safety, and power.
15. Write the identity function of Section 7.4.3.6 in C++ (using templates).
16. Define a signature for the Stack of Figure 7.3, which exports only create and push. Is it useful to have a signature that does not export create?

17. In this chapter, we have seen the use of partially instantiated functions in both C++ and functional programming languages. In Chapter 4, we saw the use of default values for function parameters. In what sense is the use of such default values similar to constructing a closure, and in what ways is it different?

18. Consider the following generic signature in ML:

```
signature DictLookupSig = sig
    exception NotFound;
    val lookup : 't * ("t * "t) list -> int
end
```

Does the signature match the structure of Figure 5.16? Does it match the signature of Figure 5.18?

Logic and rule-based languages

Facts belong to the problem domain, not to the solution.
(Wittgenstein)

C H A P T E R **8**

This chapter presents two unconventional classes of languages: logic and rule-based languages. Such languages are different from procedural and functional languages not only in their conceptual foundations, but also in the programming style (or paradigm) they support. Programmers are involved more in describing the problem in a declarative fashion than in defining details of algorithms to provide a solution. Thus, programs are similar to specifications, rather than implementations in conventional programming languages. Such languages are, therefore, more demanding of computational resources than are conventional languages.

8.1 "What" versus "how": Specification versus implementation

A software development process can be viewed abstractly as a sequence of phases through which system descriptions become progressively more detailed. As we discussed in Section 1.1, starting from a software requirements specification, which emphasizes *what* the system is supposed to do, the description is progressively refined into a procedural and executable description, which describes *how* the problem actually is solved mechanically. Intermediate steps are often standardized in software development organizations, and suitable notations are used to describe their outcomes (referred to as "software artifacts"). Typically, a *design* phase is specified to occur after *requirements specification* and before *implementation*, and suitable software design notations are provided to document the resulting *software architecture*. Thus the "what" stated in the requirements is transformed into the "how" stated in the design document; i.e., the design specification can be viewed as an abstract implementation of the requirements specification. In turn, this can be viewed as the specification for the subsequent implementation step, which takes the design specification and turns it into a running program.

In their evolution, programming languages have become increasingly higher-level. For example, as we saw in Chapter 5, a language such as Ada, Eiffel, or C++ can be used in the design stage as a design specification language to describe the modular structure of the software and module interfaces in a precise and unambiguous way, even though the internals of the module (i.e., private data structures and algorithms) are yet to be defined. Such languages, in fact, allow the module specification (its interface) to be given and even compiled separately from the module implementation. The specification describes "what" the module does by describing the resources that it makes visible externally to other modules; the implementation describes "how" the internally declared data structures and algorithms accomplish the specified tasks.

All of the stated steps of the process that lead from the initial requirements specification to a code implementation can be guided by suitable systematic methods. They cannot be done automatically, however: they require engineering skills and creativity by the programmer, whose responsibility is to map—that is, translate—requirements into executable (usually, procedural) descriptions. This mapping process is time-consuming, expensive, and error-prone.

An obvious way to avoid these problems is to make specifications directly executable, thus avoiding the translation step from the specification into the implementation altogether. Logic programming tries to do exactly that. In its simplest (and ideal) terms, we can describe logic programming in the following way: A programmer simply declares the logical properties that describe the problem to be solved. The problem description is used by the system to find a solution to the problem (*infer a solution*). To denote its distinctive capabilities, the run-time machine that can execute a logic language is often called an *inference engine*.

In logic programming, problem descriptions are given in a logical formalism based on first-order predicate calculus. The theories that can be used to describe and analyze logic languages formally are thus naturally rooted in mathematical logic. Our presentation, however, will not delve into deep mathematical concepts and will mostly remain at the same level in which we studied more conventional languages.

The above informal introduction and motivations point out why logic programming is often said to support a *declarative* programming paradigm. As we will show, however, existing logic languages, such as PROLOG, match this description only partially. To make the efficiency of the program execution acceptable, a number of compromises are made that dilute the purity of the declarative approach. Efficiency issues affect the way programs are written; that is, the programmer is concerned with more than just the specification of what the program is supposed to do. In addition, nondeclarative language features are also provided, which may be viewed as directions given by the programmer to the inference engine. These features in general reduce the clarity of program descriptions, because they intermix the problem description with implementation concerns.

8.1.1 A first example

To clarify the distinction between specification and implementation and to introduce logic programming, let us specify the effect of searching for an element x in a list L of elements. We introduce a predicate is_in(x, L) that is true whenever element x is in the list L. The predicate is described using a self-explaining hypothetical logic language, where operator "•" denotes the concatenation of two lists, operator [] transforms an element into a list containing it, and "iff" is the conventional abbreviation for "if and only if."

```
for all elements x and lists L: is_in(x, L) iff
    L = [x]
    or
    L = L1 • L2 and
        (is_in(x, L1) or is_in(x, L2))
```

This specification describes a search procedure in a declarative fashion. The element is in the list if the list consists exactly of that element. Otherwise, we can consider the list as composed of a left sublist and a right sublist whose concatenation yields the original list. The element is in the list if it is in either sublist.

Let us now proceed to an implementation of the above specification. Besides other details, an implementation must decide

- How to split a list into a right and a left sublists. An obvious choice is to split it into two sublists of either the same length (if the list contains an even number of elements) or such that their lengths differ by at most one.
- How to order the elements stored in the list. An obvious choice is to keep the list sorted, so that one can decide whether to search the left or the right sublist or avoid searching both.

• How to speed up the search. Instead of waiting until a singleton list is obtained via repeated splitting, the algorithm can check the element that separates the two sublists. If the separator equals the desired element, the search can stop. Otherwise, depending on the value of the separator, it proceeds to check either in the right or in the left sublist generated by the splitting.

These are the kinds of decisions we have to make during the design of a system in order to achieve an efficient implementation of an abstract specification. Such design decisions often restrict the domain of applicability of the chosen solution. For example, by choosing to keep the list sorted as new elements are added or deleted, the resulting search procedure is more efficient, but less general—it works only for lists that are sorted.

A possible C++ implementation of the specification is shown in Figure 8.1. By comparing the logic specification and the C++ implementation, one can appreciate the differences between the two approaches in terms of ease of writing, understandability, and confidence in the correctness of the description with respect to the initial problem.

```
int binary_search(const int val, const int size, const int array[]) {
// return the index of the desired value val, if it is there, otherwise return -1
    if size ≤ 0 {
        return (-1);
    }
    int high = size; // the portion of array to search is
    int low = 0;     // low .. high-1
    for ( ; ; ) {
        int mid = (high + low) / 2;
        if (mid = low) {
            // search is finished
            return (val != array[low]) ? -1 : mid;
        }
        if (val < array[mid]) {
            high = mid;
        }
        else if (val > array[mid]) {
            low = mid;
        }
        else {
            return mid;
        }
    }
}
```

FIGURE 8.1   A C++ implementation of binary search

Instead of transforming the specification into an implementation, one might wonder whether the specification can be executed directly or used as a starting point for a straightforward derivation process yielding an implementation. To illustrate how this might be done, we can read the above declarative specification procedurally, as follows:

Given an element x and a list L, to prove that x is in L, proceed as follows:
(1) prove that L is [x];
(2) otherwise, split L into L1 · L2 and prove one of the following:
    (2.1) x is in L1, or
    (2.2) x is in L2

A blind mechanical executor that follows the procedure can be quite inefficient, especially if compared to the C++ program. Although direct execution is understandably less efficient than execution of an implementation in a procedural language, a declarative description requires less effort to write and to prove correct.

8.1.2 Another example

Suppose we wish to provide a logical specification of sorting a list of integers in ascending order. Our goal is thus to describe a predicate sort(X, Y) that is true if the nonempty list Y is the sorted image of list X. The description of such a predicate can be provided in a top-down fashion by introducing two auxiliary predicates: permutation(X, Y), which is true if list Y is a permutation of list X, and is_sorted(Y), which is true if list Y is sorted. We can in fact write

for all integer lists X, Y: sort(X, Y) iff
    permutation(X, Y) and sorted(Y)

To describe the predicate sorted, let us assume that our logic notation provides the notion of an indexable sequence of integers (we use subscripts in the range 1..length(X) for this purpose):

sorted(Y) iff forall j such that $1 \leq j <$ length(Y), $Y_j \leq Y_{j+1}$

To describe the predicate permutation(X, Y), we assume that the following built-in predicates are available for lists (of integers). All such predicates, except for the first, are defined only for nonempty lists.

- is_empty(X), true iff list X is empty;
- has_head(X, Y), true iff the integer Y is the first element in the (nonempty) list X;
- has_tail(X, Y), true iff Y is the list obtained by deleting the first element of the (nonempty) list X;

- delete(X, Y, Z), true iff list Z is the result of deleting an occurrence of element X from list Y.

Predicate permutation(X, Y) can now be specified as follows:

```
permutation(X, Y) iff
    is_empty(X) and is_empty(Y)
    or else
    has_head(Y, Y1) and has_tail(Y, Y2) and delete(Y1, X, X2) and permuta-
    tion(X2, Y2)
```

(The logical connective "or else" has the following meaning: A or else B means A or ((not A) and B).)

The declarative specification can be read procedurally as follows, assuming that the two lists X and Y are given:

Given two integer lists X and Y, to prove that the sort operation applied to X yields Y, prove that Y is a permutation of X and prove that Y is sorted.

To prove that Y is a permutation of X, proceed as follows:
(1) prove that both are empty;
(2) otherwise, if they are not both empty, select the first element of Y and delete it from both X and Y, thus producing X2 and Y2, and prove (recursively) that Y2 is a permutation of X2.
To prove that Y is sorted, prove that each element is less than or equal to the one that follows it.

The declarative specification can also be read as a constructive recursive procedure. Assume that X is a given list and we are interested in producing its sorted image Y:

Given an integer list X, construct its permutations and select one such permutation Y that is sorted.

To construct Y, a permutation of X, proceed as follows:
(1) if X is an empty list, then Y is the empty list;
(2) otherwise, construct Y as a list whose head is an element X1 from X and whose tail Y2 is constructed as follows:
(2.1) delete X1 from X, thus obtaining the list X2;
(2.2) construct Y2 as a permutation of X2.
To check if a permutation Y is sorted, check if each element is less than or equal to the one that follows it.

This example confirms that a direct implementation of the specification, according to its procedural interpretation, can be quite inefficient. In fact, one might need to generate all permutations of a given list before generating one that is sorted. All different permutations can be generated because, in step 2 above, there are many ways of choosing an element X1 from X. Any such way provides a different permutation, and all such different permutations might need to be generated until a sorted one is finally found.

In general, a declarative specification contains many sources of nondeterminism, such as "select an element of Y." Direct execution of such a description has to resolve the nondeterminism by making a specific choice. In procedural programming, the programmer resolves the nondeterminism by choosing an efficient alternative, e.g., by selecting the smallest element of Y. The nondeterminism of the declarative description contributes to its high-level nature but hampers its efficient execution.

8.2 Principles of logic programming

To understand exactly how logic programs can be formulated and how they can be executed, we need to define a reference syntax and its semantics. This would allow some of the concepts we used informally in Section 8.1 (such as "procedural interpretation") to be stated rigorously. This is the purpose of this section. Specifically, Section 8.2.1 provides the background definitions and properties that are needed to understand how an interpreter of logic programs works. Based on these preliminaries, Section 8.2.2 presents an interpretation algorithm for logic programs. The interpreter provides a rigorous definition of the program's "procedural interpretation." The interpreter is thus analogous to SIMPLESEM for imperative programs.

8.2.1 Preliminaries: Facts, rules, queries, and deductions

Although there are many syntactic ways of using logic for problem descriptions, the field of logic programming has converged on PROLOG, whose core is a simple subset of first-order logic. Hereafter we will gradually introduce the notation used by PROLOG.

The basic syntactic constituent of a PROLOG program is a *term*. A term is a constant, a variable, or a compound term. A *compound term* is written as a *functor symbol* followed by one or more arguments, enclosed by parentheses, which are themselves terms. A *ground term* is a term that does not contain variables. Conventionally, constants are written as lowercase letter strings (representing atomic objects) or strings of digits (representing numbers). Variables are written as strings starting with an uppercase letter. Functor symbols are written as lowercase letter strings.

```
alpha        --this is a constant
125          --this is a constant
X            --this is a variable
```

```
abs(-10, 10)          --this is a ground compound term; abs is a functor
abs(suc(X), 5)        --this is a (nonground) compound term
```

The constant [] stands for the empty list. Functor "." constructs a list out of an element and a list; the element becomes the head of the constructed list. For example, .(alpha, []) is a list containing only one atomic object, alpha. An equivalent syntactic variation, [alpha, []], is also provided. Another example is

```
.(15, .( toot, .(duck, .(donald, [])))) 
```

which can also be represented as

```
[15, [toot, [duck, [donald, []]]]] 
```

The notation is further simplified by allowing the above list to be written as

```
[15, toot, duck, donald]
```

and also as

```
[15 | [toot, duck, donald]]
```

In general, the notation

```
[X | Y]
```

stands for the list whose *head element* is X and whose *tail list* is Y. This is similar to the ML notation X::Y.

A predicate is represented by a constant or by a compound term. For example,

```
it_rains
```

is a constant predicate;

```
less_than(5, 99)
```

states the "less than" relationship between objects 5 and 99.

A PROLOG program is written as a sequence of *clauses*. A clause is either a single predicate, called *fact*, or as a *rule* (called *Horn clause*) of the form

```
conclusion :- condition.
```

where :- stands for "if," conclusion is a single predicate, and condition is a conjunction of predicates, that is, a sequence of predicates separated by a comma, which stands for the logical and. The rule can be read as "conclusion is true if condition is true." Facts can be viewed as rules without a condition part (i.e., the condition is always true). Thus we will use the term "rule" to indicate both facts and rules, unless an explicit distinction is necessary. A rule's conclusion is also called the rule's *head*. Clauses are implicitly quantified universally. That is, a PROLOG rule

```
conclusion :- condition.
```

containing variable X1, X2, ..., Xn would be represented in the standard notation of mathematical logic as

$$\forall X1, X2, ..., Xn \ (\text{condition} \supset \text{conclusion})$$

where $\supset$ is the logical implication operator. In a procedural program, it would be represented as

if condition **then** conclusion;

For example, the program

```
length([], 0).      --this is a fact
length([X | Y], N) :- length(Y, M), N = M + 1.      --this is a rule
```

says that

- The length of the null string is zero.
- For all X, Y, N, M, if M is the length of list Y and N is M + 1, then the length of a nonnull string with head X and tail Y is N.

As another example, the sort problem of Section 8.1.2 can be written in PROLOG as shown in Figure 8.2.

```
sort(X, Y) :- permutation(X, Y), sorted(Y).
sorted([]).              --the empty list is sorted
sorted([X | []]).        --the singleton list is sorted
sorted([X | [Y | Ys]]) :- X ≤ Y and sorted([Y | Ys]).
permutation([], []).
permutation(X, [Y | Ys]) :- delete(Y, X, Z), permutation(Z, Ys ).
delete(A, [A | As], As).
delete(A, [B | Bs], [B | Cs]) :- delete(A, Bs, Cs).
```

FIGURE 8.2 A PROLOG sort program

The examples we have given so far show implicitly that PROLOG is a dynamically typed language. No type declarations are provided for variables. The value that is bound dynamically to a variable determines the nature of the object and thus the legality of the operations applied to it. For example, in the case of sort, operators "less than or equal to" must be applicable to the elements of the list: it might be a list of numbers or a list of characters.

Facts and rules are used to express the available knowledge for a particular domain: they provide a declarative specification of that knowledge. Given a set of facts and rules, we may solve a problem by posing the problem as a *query* against them. A query can also be viewed as a *goal* that must be proved.

From a logical viewpoint, the answer to a query is YES if the query can be derived by applying *deductions* from the set of facts and rules. For example,

?-sort([3, 2, 7, 1], [1, 2, 3, 7]).

is a query that can be read as "can we deduce from the rules given above that sort([3, 2, 7], [2, 3, 7]) is true?" Intuitively, we expect the answer to this query to be YES.

To understand how deductions are made from a logic program, we need to provide some mathematical preliminaries. A *substitution* is a function, defined as a (possibly empty) finite set of pairs of the form $<X_i, t_i>$, where X_i is a variable and t_i is a term, $X_i \neq X_j$ for all i, j with $i \neq j$, and X_i does not occur in t_j for all i, j. The definition of a substitution μ may be extended to apply to terms; i.e., it is applied to the variables appearing in a term. The result of applying a substitution μ to term t_1, $\mu(t_1)$, yields a term t_2, which is said to be an *instance* of t_1. A substitution may also be applied to a rule; i.e., it is applied to all its component terms to produce an instance rule.

For example, the substitution

{<A, 3>, <B, beta(X, xyz>}

applied to term

func(A, B, C)

yields

func(3, beta(X, xyz), C)

The fundamental rule used for making deductions in logic is called *modus ponens*. This rule can be stated as follows, using the syntax of logic programming:

From the rule R:

P :- Q1, Q2, ..., Qn

and the facts

F1, F2, ..., Fn
if D :- F1, F2, ..., Fn is an instance of R

then we can deduce D as a logical consequence
For example, from the rule

grandfather(X, Y) :- father(X, Z), father(Z, Y).

and the facts

father(john, charles).
father(charles, james).

we can deduce

grandfather(john, james).

since

grandfather(john, james) :- father(john, charles), father(charles, james).

is an instance of the rule via substitution

<X, john>
<Y, james>
<Z, charles>

If we submit a ground query to a logic program, the answer to the query is YES if the repeated application of modus ponens proves that the query is a logical consequence of the program. Otherwise, if such a deduction is not possible, the answer is false. For example, the answer to the query

?-sorted([2, 3, 7])

is YES because the following deduction steps can be performed using modus ponens:

1 sorted([7| []])
2 From the previous step, our knowledge that $3 \leq 7$, and from the rule sorted([X | [Y | Ys]]) :- $X \leq Y$ and sorted([Y | Ys]) we can deduce sorted([3 | [7 | []]]).

3 From the previous step, our knowledge that $2 \leq 3$, and from sorted([X | [Y | Ys]]) :- X ≤ Y and sorted([Y | Ys]) we can deduce sorted([2 | [3 | [7 | []]]]), i.e., sorted([2, 3, 7]).

PROLOG allows existential queries to be submitted. An *existential query* is a query that contains a variable. For example,

    ?-sort([3, 2, 7], X)

means "is there an X such that sort([5, 1, 33]) gives X?" To accommodate existential queries in the deduction process, another rule, called the *existential rule*, is provided. The rule states that an existential query Q is a consequence of an instance of it, μ(Q), for any μ. In the above sort example, the answer would be YES since

    1 sorted([2, 3, 7]) can be proved by repeated application of modus ponens, as shown above.
    2 permutation([3, 2, 7], [2, 3, 7]) can be proved in a similar way.
    3 From 1 and 2 we can deduce sort([3, 2, 7], [2, 3, 7]).
    4 From the existential rule, we can conclude that the answer to the query is YES (i.e., there is an X such that sort([3, 2, 7], X), and [2, 3, 7] can be such an X).

Modus ponens and the existential rule are the conceptual tools inherited from mathematical logic that can be used to support deductive reasoning. But to make logic specifications executable, we need to devise a practical approach that is amenable to mechanical execution: we need to interpret logic programs procedurally.

Intuitively, the *procedural interpretation* of a logic program consists of viewing a query as a procedure call. A set of clauses for the same predicate can, in turn, be viewed as a procedure definition, where each clause represents a branch of a case selection. The basic computational step in logic programming consists of selecting a call, identifying a procedure corresponding to the call, selecting the case that matches the call, and generating new queries, if the matched case is a rule. This is in accordance with the concepts of case analysis and pattern matching that were introduced in Section 4.5, and it resembles the definition of functions in ML. For example, the above query

    ?-sort([3, 2, 7], [2, 3, 7])

which is matched by the sort rule, generates the following queries:

    ?-permutation([3, 2, 7], [2, 3, 7]).

and

?-sorted([2, 3, 7]).

The procedure corresponding to the call described by the first of the above two queries has two cases:

```
permutation([], []).
permutation(X, [Y | Ys]) :- delete(Y, X, Z), permutation(Z, Ys ).
```

To select the appropriate case, a special kind of pattern matching is performed between the query and the head of the rule describing each case. Intuitively, in our example, the query does not match the first case, which is the rule for empty lists. The match against the other rule's head binds X to [3, 2, 7], Y to 2, Ys to [3, 7], and generates two further queries:

```
delete(2, [3, 2, 7], Z)
```

and

```
permutation(Z, [3, 7])
```

Interpretation proceeds in the same manner for each generated query until all queries are processed by the interpreter. The intuitive, yet informal, treatment of the interpretation procedure described so far will be formally described in the next section.

8.2.2 An abstract interpretation algorithm

In this section we discuss in detail how an abstract processor may interpret logic programs in a procedural way. As we mentioned earlier, the abstract processor must be able to take a query as a goal to be proven and match it against facts and rule heads. The matching process, which is a generalization of the concept of the procedure call, is a rather elaborate operation, called *unification*, which combines pattern matching and binding of variables. Unification is a generalization of pattern matching, as supported by languages such as ML. In ML, actual parameters of a function invocation are bound to values in the function's domain when the function is called. In a logic language, such as PROLOG, the query that is matched against a fact or a rule's head can contain unbound variables that become bound as a consequence of unification.

Unification applies to a pair of terms t1 (representing the goal to prove) and t2 (representing the fact or rule's head with which a match is tried). To define it, we need a few other background definitions. Term t1 is said to be *more general* than t2 if there is a substitution μ such that $t2 = \mu(t1)$, but there is no substitution π such that $t1 = \pi(t2)$. If there are both a substitution μ such that t2 = μ(t1) and a substitution π such that t1 = π(t2), t1 and t2 are said to be *variants*; i.e., they are equal up to a renaming of variables. For example, term f(X, Y) is more general than f(a, Y); terms f(X, Y) and f(Z, W) are variants.

Two terms are said to *unify* if a substitution can be found that makes the two terms equal. Such a substitution is called a *unifier*. For example, the substitution

s1 = {<X, a>, <Y, c>, <Z, b>, <W, c>}

is a unifier for the terms f(X, b, Y) and f(a, Z, W). A *most general unifier* is a unifier μ such that μ(t1) = μ(t2) is the most general instance of both t1 and t2. A *most general instance* of terms t1 and t2 is a term t that is an instance of both and such that there is no other such instance that is more general than t. It is easy to prove that all most general instances are variants. We will therefore speak of "the" most general instance and "the" most general unifier (MGU), since they are unique up to a renaming of variables. In the previous example, s1 is not the MGU. In fact, the substitution

s2 = {<X, a>, <Y, T>, <Z, b>, <W, T>}

is more general than s1, and it is easy to realize that no unifier can be found that is more general than s2. The term f(a, b, T) is the most general instance of f(X, b, T) and f(a, Z, W).

MGUs may be computed by the unification algorithm shown in Figure 8.3. The algorithm is written in a self-explanatory notation. If the two terms given to the algorithm do not unify, the exception unification_fail is raised. The second and third cases in the repeat loop in Figure 8.3 show that the unification algorithm does not attempt to unify such pairs as <f(...X...), X>, since the two terms do not have any finite common instance. The identification of such pairs is achieved by the so-called *occurs check*.

We are finally in a position to provide a precise meaning for "procedural interpretation" by showing how logic programs can be interpreted The interpretation algorithm is given in Figure 8.4. The unification step of the algorithm either succeeds or fails. If it fails, none of the actions defined by this step occurs (in particular, SG does not change). If it succeeds, all variables appearing in the rule are automatically renamed with brand new variable names, and SG is updated. The renaming ensures that variables with the same name appearing in different clauses of the logic program are treated as different. This is necessary since clauses are implicitly quantified universally.

The algorithm shown in Figure 8.4 is *nondeterministic*; i.e., it describes several possible computations for a given input goal. The goal is solved successfully if there is at least a computation that stops with the answer YES. In

The algorithm operates on two terms t1 and t2 and returns their MGU.
It raises an exception if the unification fails.
It keeps a working set WS of pairs of terms to unify, initialized to contain the
pair <t1, t2>.

```
MGU = { };          --initialize MGU to the empty substitution
WS = {<t1, t2>};    --initialize working set
repeat
    remove a pair <x1, x2> from WS;
    case
        • x1 and x2 are two identical constants or variables:
            do nothing
        • x1 is a variable that does not occur in x2:
            substitute x2 for x1 in any pair in WS and in MGU;
            insert <x1, x2> in MGU;
        • x2 is a variable that does not occur in x1:
            substitute x1 for x2 in any pair in WS and in MGU;
            insert <x2, x1> in MGU;
        • x1 is f(y1, y2, ..., yn), x2 is f(z1, z2, ..., zn), f is a functor, and n ≥ 1:
            insert <y1, z1>, <y2, z2>, ..., <yn, zn> into WS;
        otherwise
            raise unification_fail;
    end case;
until WS = { } --working set is empty
```

FIGURE 8.3 Unification algorithm

Given a goal G submitted as a query to a logic program P, the algorithm
    answers
    YES, and provides bindings for the variables appearing in G, or it answers
    NO
```
SG = {G}; --initialize the working set of goals to G, the submitted query
repeat
    begin unification step:
        remove an element E from SG and
            select a (renamed) clause X :- X1, X2, ..., Xn from P (n = 0 for a fact)
            such that <E, X> unifies with MGU μ;
        insert X1, X2, ..., Xn into SG;
        apply μ to all elements of SG and to G;
    exception
        when unification step fails => exit;
    end;
until SG = empty;
if SG = empty then
    the answer is YES and G describes a solution
else
    raise fail
```

FIGURE 8.4 A nondeterministic interpretation algorithm

such a case, if the goal contains variables, when the interpreter stops, all variables are bound to a ground term. A computation may raise the exception fail if the attempt to solve a goal fails during the process. It is also possible that a computation does not terminate; i.e., the set of goals to be proven never becomes empty.

To illustrate how the nondeterministic interpretation algorithm operates, consider the logic program shown in Figure 8.5, which describes a binary relation (rel) and its closure (clos). Predicate rel lists all object pairs that constitute the relation. Pairs belonging to the closure are specified by the recursive predicate clos.

```
(1)    rel(a, b).
(2)    rel(a, c).
(3)    rel(b, f).
(4)    rel(f, g).
(5)    clos(X, Y) :- rel(X, Y).
(6)    clos(X, Y) :- rel(X, Z), clos(Z, Y)
```

FIGURE 8.5   A sample logic program

Suppose the query

?-clos(a, f)

is submitted to the nondeterministic interpreter of Figure 8.4. Some of the many possible computation paths for the query are shown in Figure 8.6. Computation paths are described by showing how goals are matched successively against facts or rule heads, and new subgoals are generated after the match. The goal chosen at each step for the match is shown in bold in the computation path. Since clauses are numbered in the logic program, clause numbers are shown in the computation paths to indicate the clause selected by the unification algorithm.

Figure 8.6 shows that in case (b) the computation terminates and solves the goal; cases (a) and (c) describe computations that fail because of the wrong selections made at nondeterministic decision points; case (d) describes a nonterminating computation where clause 6 is chosen repeatedly by the unification procedure.

To provide a deterministic implementation of the nondeterministic interpretation algorithm, one needs to understand exactly what happens when a decision point is reached and, in particular, what the effect of a particular choice made during execution is. First, when a goal is being solved, it may be necessary to choose one out of several clauses to attempt unification. It may

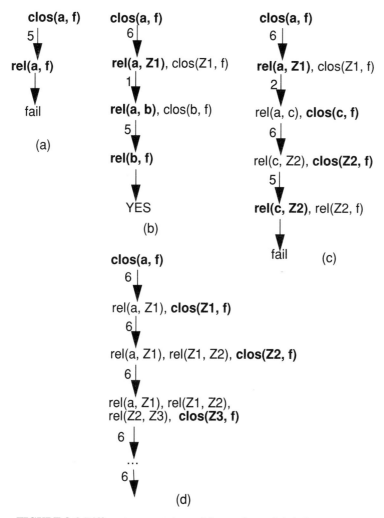

FIGURE 8.6 Different computations of the nondeterministic interpreter

happen that the choice we make eventually results in a failure, whereas another choice would have led to success. For example, the goal clos(a, f) matches both clause 5 and clause 6 of the algorithm in Figure 8.4. In the case of computation (a) in Figure 8.6, the choice of clause 5 instead of clause 6 for the first match leads to a failure. Second, when several goals can be selected from SG, there is a choice of which is to be solved first. For example, when the goals to be solved are rel(a, Z1), clos(Z1, f), computations (c) and (d) in Figure 8.6 make their selection in a different order. In general, when we have to choose which of two goals G1 and G2 is to be solved first, it can be shown that, if there is a successful computation choosing G1 first, there is also a successful computation choosing G2 first (in fact, both goals must be eventually satisfied). The choice can only affect the efficiency of searching for a solution. From now on, we will assume that whenever a goal unifies with a rule's head, the (sub)goals corresponding to the right-hand side of the rule will be solved according to a predefined deterministic policy, from left to right.

Another way of capturing the behaviors of the nondeterministic interpreter shown in Figure 8.6 is to view them as a tree of computations (called the *search tree*). The arcs exiting a node represent all possible clauses with which unification can be performed. Figure 8.7 shows the search tree for the query clos(a,f).

To implement the nondeterministic interpreter on a conventional processor, it is necessary to define a traversal of the search tree according to some policy. One possibility is to search all branches in parallel (*breadth-first* policy). Another possibility is a *depth-first* search, for example, always choosing the first clause in the list for unification. In such a case, when the computation fails along one path, it is necessary to *backtrack* to a previously unexplored choice to find an alternative path. A breadth-first searching algorithm is said to provide a *complete proof procedure* for logic programs: it guarantees that if there is a finite proof of the goal, it will be found. In addition, the breadth-

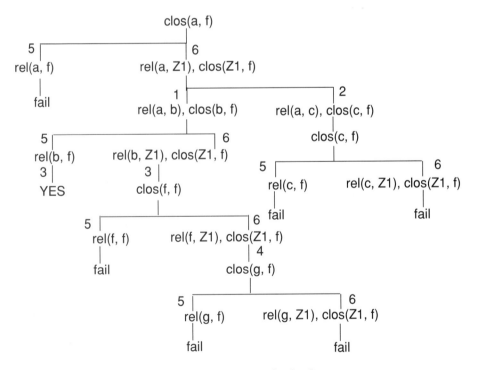

FIGURE 8.7 Search tree for the query clos(a, f)

first algorithm is said to provide a *sound proof procedure*, since any answer derived by the interpreter is a correct answer to the query (i.e., it is a logical consequence that can be derived from the program via modus ponens and the existential rule). Completeness and soundness are indeed the most desired properties of a proof procedure. Depth-first search is also a sound procedure, but it is not complete, since the searching engine might enter a nonterminating computation, preventing backtracking to another path that might lead to the solution.

Conventional logic programming languages, such as PROLOG, follow a depth-first search policy, as we will see in the next section. Several experimental languages have tried to improve the search method by supporting breadth-first search via parallel execution of the different branches of the search tree.

As a final point, let us discuss when the answer to a query submitted to a logic program can be NO. This can only occur if all computations for that query terminate with a failure; i.e., the search tree is finite, and no leaf of the tree is labeled YES. Similarly, a goal submitted as a query ?-not Q yields YES if Q cannot be proven from the given facts and rules. This happens if the search tree is finite, and all computations corresponding to the different branches fail. In other terms, logic programs are based on the concept of *negation as failure*. A common way to describe negation as failure is to say that logic language interpreters work under the "closed world assumption." That is, all the knowledge possessed by the interpreter is explicitly listed in terms of facts and rules of the program. For example, the answer to the query

    ?- rel(g, h)

would be NO, which means that "according to the current knowledge expressed by the program, it cannot be proved that rel(g, h) holds."

8.3 PROLOG

PROLOG is the most popular example of a logic language. Its basic syntactic features were introduced informally in Section 8.2. PROLOG solves problems by performing a depth-first traversal of the search tree. Whenever a goal is to be solved, the list of clauses that constitutes the program is searched from top to bottom. If unification succeeds, the subgoals corresponding to the terms in the right-hand side of the selected rule (if any) are solved next, in left-to-right order. This particular way of operating makes the behavior of the interpreter quite sensitive to the way programs are written. In particular, the ordering of clauses and subgoals influences the way the interpreter works. Although from a conceptual viewpoint clauses are connected by the logical operator "or" and subgoals are connected by "and," these connectives do not exhibit the commutativity property associated with logical operators.

As an example, Figure 8.8 shows all possible permutations of terms for the closure relation described by the program of Figure 8.5. It is easy to verify that any query involving predicate clos would generate a nonterminating computation in case 4. Similarly, a query such as ?-clos(g, c) causes a nonterminating interpretation process in cases 2 and 4, whereas in cases 1 and 3 the interpreter would produce NO.

(1) clos(X, Y) :- rel(X, Y).
     clos(X, Y) :- rel(X, Z), clos(Z, Y).

(2) clos(X, Y) :- rel(X, Y).
     clos(X, Y) :- clos(Z, Y), rel(X, Z).

(3) clos(X, Y) :- rel(X, Z), clos(Z, Y).
     clos(X, Y) :- rel(X, Y).

(4) clos(X, Y) :- clos(Z, Y), rel(X, Z).
     clos(X, Y) :- rel(X, Y).

FIGURE 8.8 Variations of a PROLOG program

PROLOG provides several *extralogical* features, which cause its departure from a pure logical language. The first fundamental departure is represented by the *cut* primitive, written as "!," which can appear as a predicate in the condition part of rules. The effect of the cut is to prune the search space by forbidding certain backtracking actions. Its motivation, of course, is to improve efficiency of the search by reducing the search space. It is the programmer's responsibility to ensure that such a reduction does not affect the result of the search. The cut can be viewed as a goal that never fails and cannot be resatisfied. That is, if during backtracking one tries to resatisfy it, the goal that was unified with the left-hand side of the rule in which the cut appears fails.

To illustrate how the cut works, consider the following rule:

A :- B, C, !, D, E

Suppose that, after a match between the rule's head and a goal A', subgoals B, C, and D (with suitably applied substitutions) have been solved successfully. If subgoal E fails, the PROLOG interpreter backtracks and tries to solve D by matching it to the next available rule's head, if any, found in scanning the program clauses from top down. If no successful match can be found and no cut is present in the rule, the PROLOG interpreter backtracks further, trying to find a new solution for C and then B. Eventually, if all these fail, the match of A' with the rule would fail and another rule or fact would be tried. The presence of the cut, however, forbids the backtracking procedure from retrying C, then B, and then a further alternative for the match with A': the current goal A' would fail right away. In other terms, the cut, viewed as a predicate, always succeeds and commits the PROLOG interpreter to all the choices made since the goal A' was unified with the head of the rule in which the cut occurs.

Let us consider as example the simple program shown in Figure 8.9(a). The program contains the relational predicate $\leq$. *Relational predicates* (i.e., $<, \leq, =, \neq, >, \geq$) are also treated in a special way. They are such that when a goal, like $A \leq B$, is to be solved, both operands A and B must be bound to arithmetic expressions that can be evaluated (i.e., if they contain variables, they must be bound to a value). The goal $A \leq B$ succeeds if the value of A is less than or equal to the value of B. If not, or if A and B cannot be evaluated as arithmetic expressions, the goal fails. The presence of the cut implies that if the first alternative is chosen (i.e., $X \leq Y$), the backtracking that may occur due to the failure in the proof of some later goal will not try to find another solution for max, because there is no possibility for the second alternative to be chosen.

Relational predicates represent another departure of PROLOG from the ideal behavior of a logic language. As an example, the evaluation of the goal

?- 0 < X

which should be read as

does a positive value for X exist?

does not succeed by binding X to a positive number, as the logical reading of the clause might suggest. It simply fails, since X in the query is unbound, and the arithmetic expression cannot be evaluated. To guard against such a situation, the programmer must ensure that only bound variables participate in expression evaluations.

The fragment of Figure 8.9(b) defines an if_then_else predicate. If clause

max(X, Y, Y) :- X ≤Y, !.   if_then_else(A, B, C) :- A, !, B.
max(X, Y, X) :- X > Y, !.   if_then_else(A, B, C) :- C.

(a)   (b)

FIGURE 8.9 Sample PROLOG fragments using cut

A describes a goal whose proof succeeds, then goal B is to be proved. If the execution fails to prove that A holds, then C is to be proved. A possible use is shown by the following query, where rel was introduced by the program in Figure 8.5, and, we assume that some clause exists in the program for goal g:

?- if_then_else(rel(a, X), retract(rel(a, X)), g(X)).

The example shows another extralogical feature of PROLOG: retract. This feature removes from the program the first clause that unifies with its argument. Thus the effect of the query is to remove from the relation rel a pair whose first element is a, if there is one. If the choice of executing retract is made, it cannot be undone through backtracking. Instead, if a pair whose first element is a does not exist, goal g is solved.

The reciprocal effect of retract is provided by the extralogical primitives assert and asserta, which allow their argument to be added as a clause at the end of the program or at the beginning, respectively. Thus retract and assert allow logic programs to be modified as the program is executed. They can be used, for example, to add new ground facts to the program in order to represent new knowledge that is acquired as the program runs.

Another departure from logic is represented by the assignment operator is, illustrated by the PROLOG program of Figure 8.10, which defines the factorial of a natural number. When the operator is encountered during the evaluation, it must be possible to evaluate the expression on its right-hand side (i.e., if the expression contains variables, they must be bound to a value); otherwise the evaluation fails. If the left-hand-side variable is also bound to a value, then the goal succeeds if the variable's value is equal to the value of the expression. Otherwise, if the left-hand side variable is unbound, the evaluation succeeds and the variable becomes bound to the value of the expression. In the example, when the subgoal

F is N * F1

is encountered in the evaluation, N and F1 must be bound to some values. For example, suppose that N and F1 are bound to 4 and 6, respectively. If F is also

```
fact(0, 1).
fac(N, F) :- N > 0, N1 is N - 1, fact( N1, F1), F is N * F1.
```

FIGURE 8.10 Factorial in PROLOG

bound, the value bound to it must be equal to the value evaluated by the expression (24, in the example). If F is not bound, it becomes bound to the value of the expression.

As the above discussion illustrates, PROLOG variables behave differently than variables of a conventional procedural programming language. As in functional languages, logic language variables can be bound to values, but once the binding is established, it cannot be changed.

The extralogical features of PROLOG have a profound effect on the semantics of the language. All represent a departure from pure declarativeness and add concepts inherited from von Neumann languages. In fact, most such features can be understood only by considering the order of execution of individual steps of computation. In addition, features like assert and retract can be used to modify the state of the computation by adding and deleting information represented as PROLOG facts. Furthermore, such features allow the program to be changed, even as the computation is in progress, by adding both facts and rules. This powerful—but potentially unsafe—feature is similar to what can be achieved in LISP and in Smalltalk by allowing a program to be viewed as data that can be modified during execution. Programming languages that support this feature are called *reflective languages*.

8.4 Functional programming versus logic programming

The most striking difference between functional and logic programming is that programs in a pure functional programming language define *functions*, whereas in pure logic programming they define *relations*. In a sense, logic programming generalizes the approach taken by relational databases and their languages, such as the Standard Query Language (SQL) (see sidebar on page 397). For example, consider the simple PROLOG program shown in Figure 8.11, consisting of a sequence of facts. Indeed, a program of this kind can be viewed as defining a relational table—in the example, a mini-database of classical music composers, which lists the composer's name, year of birth, and year of death.

In a function there is a clear distinction between the domain and the range. Executing a program consists of providing a value in the domain, whose corresponding value in the range is then evaluated. The domain constitutes the *input*; the range constitutes the *output*. In a relation, there is no predefined notion of which is the input and which is the output. In fact, all of these possible queries can be submitted for the program of Figure 8.11:

```
?- composer(mozart, 1756, 2001).
?- composer(mozart, X, Y).
```

```
composer(monteverdi, 1567, 1643).
composer(bach, 1685, 1750).
composer(vivaldi, 1678, 1741).
composer(mozart, 1756, 1791).
composer(haydn, 1732, 1809).
composer(beethoven, 1770, 1827).
composer(schubert, 1797, 1828).
composer(schumann, 1810, 1856).
composer(brahms, 1833, 1897).
composer(verdi, 1813, 1901).
composer(debussy, 1862, 1918).
```

FIGURE 8.11 A PROLOG database

```
?- composer(X, Y, 1901).
?- composer(X, Y, Z).
```

In the first case, a complete tuple is provided as input, and a check is performed to see if the tuple exists in the database. In the second case, the name of the composer is provided as input, and the birth and death years are evaluated by the program as output. In the third case, we only provide the year of death and ask the program to yield the name and year of birth of a composer whose year of death is given as input value. In the fourth case, we ask the system to provide the name, year of birth, and year of death of any composer listed in the database.

Most functional languages are not purely functional, and **PROLOG** is not a pure logic language either. Consequently, it is not fully relational in the above sense. In particular, the choice of the input domains of a query is not always free. This may happen if the program contains relational predicates, assignment predicates, or other extralogical features. For example, the factorial program of Figure 8.10 cannot be invoked as follows,

```
?- fact(X, 6).
```

to find the integer whose factorial is 6. The query would in fact fail because the extralogical predicate is fails. Similarly, the query

```
?- max(X,99, 99).
```

for the program fragment of Figure 8.9 does not yield a value less than or equal to 99, as the logical reading might suggest. It fails, since one of the arguments in the invocation of $\leq$ is not bound to a value.

8.5 Rule-based languages

Rule-based systems (also called *production systems*) are tools for developing expert systems. Intuitively, an *expert system* is a program that behaves like an expert in some specific application domain. A rule-based system consists of a *knowledge base (KB)* and an *inference engine (IE)*. The knowledge base provides an explicit description of the knowledge that is specific to an application domain. It might, for example, describe the relationships between the symptoms of patients and a possible diagnosis in a medical consultation system. The language provided to describe such knowledge (called the *rule-based language*) provides two simple kinds of constructs: facts and rules. These constructs are similar to their PROLOG counterparts. Rules, also called *production rules*, express knowledge in the conditional form

```
if X then Y
```

where X and Y are the *antecedent* and the *consequent* parts of the rule, respectively. The interpretation of the rule performed by the inference engine is that if the antecedent can be satisfied, the consequent can too. When the consequent is an action (e.g., printing or sending a message), the effect of satisfying the antecedent is to schedule the consequent for execution. When the consequent is a conclusion, the effect is to infer the conclusion as a new fact.

Some rule-based languages allow conclusions to be stated with a "degree of certainty." For example, the MYCIN system for medical consultation allows rules of this kind to be written:

```
if
    description of symptom 1, and
    description of symptom 2, and
    ...
    description of symptom n
then
    there is suggestive evidence (0.7) that the identity of the bacterium is ...
```

With knowledge represented using production rules, the inference engine draws conclusions from an initial set of facts that represent the *current situation (CS)*. For production rules, there are two basic ways of reasoning: *forward chaining* and *backward chaining*. Different rule-based languages provide one or both of these methods.

To understand forward and backward chaining, let us introduce a simple example described via production rules. The knowledge base provides a model of a supervisory system that can be in two different danger states, characterized by levels 0 and 1 and indicated by the state of several switches and lights:

```
if switch_1_on and switch_2_on
    then notify danger_level_0.
if switch_1_on and switch_3_on
    then assert problem_1.
if light_red or alarm_on
    then assert problem_2.
if problem_1 and problem_2
    then notify danger_level_1.
```

An equivalent representation for the set of production rules is described by the and/or tree representation of Figure 8.12, which uses the convention introduced in Section 4.6.

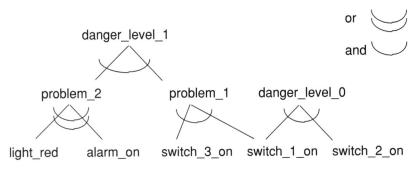

FIGURE 8.12 An and/or tree representation of production rules

Consider the following initial CS: the alarm is on and switches 1 and 3 are on. The inference engine should help the supervisory system determine the danger level. Forward chaining proceeds by matching the CS against the antecedents of the rules stored in the KB (i.e., from the leaf nodes of the and/or tree). If the condition is matched, the "then" part is "concluded"; that is, it is asserted as a new fact or it is executed, depending on the nature of the consequent. In this specific example, the asserted new facts are added to CS. In particular, alarm_on leads to the assertion of problem_2; switch_1_on and switch_3_on lead to the assertion of problem_1. Subsequently, danger_level_1 is asserted, since both problem_1 and problem_2 have been discovered.

Suppose now that the purpose of the reasoning procedure is to understand if we are in level 1 of danger. Forward chaining worked fine in the example, since the deduction succeeded. But, in general, for a large KB, the same facts might be used to make many deductions that have nothing to do with the goal

Relational database languages

A relational database can be viewed as a table of records called *tuples*. This form is quite similar to a logic program written as a sequence of ground terms. For example, the logic program of Figure 8.11 can be represented in a relational database as a table (relation) COMPOSER with fields NAME, BIRTH_YEAR, and DEATH_YEAR. The best known and standard language for relational databases is SQL. In SQL, retrieval of data from the relational database is accomplished by the SELECT statement. Here are two sample SQL queries:

```
SELECT BIRTH_YEAR
FROM COMPOSER
WHERE NAME = 'BEETHOVEN'
```

This query says to first search the database called COMPOSER for any records that have the NAME field equal to 'BEETHOVEN'; then from the selected records, return the value of the field BIRTH_YEAR.

The following query selects all tuples representing composers who were born in the 19th century:

```
SELECT *
FROM COMPOSER
WHERE BIRTH_YEAR ≥ 1800 and BIRTH_YEAR ≤ 1899
```

We can see that the query language specifies the selection of information stored in the database declaratively, by stating the logical (relational) properties that characterize such information. Nothing is said about how to access the information through suitable scanning of the database. Earlier generations of database systems, however, were imperative, requiring the user to state how to find the desired tuples through pointers and other such mechanisms. The current declarative approach is more oriented to the end-user who is not necessarily a computer programmer.

Logic and relational databases fit together quite nicely. In fact, extensions have been proposed to relational databases that add PROLOG-like rules to relational tables.

---

we wish to check. Thus, if we are interested in a specific possible conclusion, forward chaining can waste processing time. In such a case, backward chaining can be more convenient because it starts from the hypothesized conclusion we would like to prove (i.e., a root node of the and/or tree) and executes only the rules that are relevant to establishing it. In the example, the inference engine would try to identify if problem_1 and problem_2 occur, since these would cause danger_level_1. On the other hand, there is no need to check if danger_level_0 is true, since it does not affect danger_level_1. To signal problem_1, switches 1 and 3 must be on. To signal problem_2, either the alarm is on or the light is red. Since these conditions are stated as facts in the CS, we can infer both problem_1 and problem_2, and therefore the truth of danger_level_1.

Expert system languages based on production rules are commercially available. An example is KEE. It is also possible to implement production rules and different reasoning methods in other languages. The implementation is rather straightforward in PROLOG, but it is also possible with more programming effort in a procedural language like C++ or in a functional language like LISP. CLIPS is a C-based expert systems tool based on production rules (see sidebar on page 399).

The main difference between logic and rule-based languages is that logic languages are based on the formal foundations of mathematical logic, whereas rule-based languages are not. Although they have a similar external appearance, being based on rules of the form "if *condition* then *action*," rule-based languages allow any kind of state-changing actions to be specified in the *action* part.

8.6 Bibliographic notes

The reader interested in the theory of logic, upon which logic programming is founded, can refer to [Mendelson64]. [Kowalski79] pioneered the use of logic in computer programming. [Lloyd84] provides the foundations for logic programming languages. PROLOG and the art and style of writing logic programs are discussed at length in [Sterling86].

[Bratko90] discusses the use of PROLOG in artificial intelligence applications. For example, it shows how PROLOG can be used to write a rule-based expert system along with different searching schemes (forward and backward chaining). OPS5 [Brownston85] and CLIPS [NASA95] are examples of commercially available rule-based systems. For more information on rule-based expert systems, the reader may refer to [Buchanan84]. This book also contains a description of MYCIN, which was mentioned in Section 8.5. The Turing Award lecture of Feigenbaum [Feigenbaum96] concentrates on the relationship between the "what" and the "how" in programming and the contributions of artificial intelligence in bridging the gap.

Relational databases and the SQL query language are presented in most textbooks on databases, such as [Ullman88] and [Ullman89].

CLIPS

CLIPS is a multiparadigm expert system tool developed by the Software Technology branch of NASA/Lyndon B. Johnson Space Center. It was originally written in C to support the goals of high portability, low cost, and ease of integration with other languages. For example, CLIPS can be embedded in procedural code, called as a routine, and integrated with languages such as C, FORTRAN, and Ada. A version of CLIPS developed entirely in Ada is also available.

Knowledge representation is supported in CLIPS by integrating rule-based, functional, and object-oriented programming. In particular, rules and objects form an integrated system since rules can pattern match on both facts and objects. Rules are expressed in the CLIPS LISP-like syntax as follows:

```
(defrule rule_name
     (pattern_1);
     (pattern_2);
     ...
     (pattern_n)
=>
     (action_1)
     (action_2)
     ...
     (action_m))
```

The CLIPS inference engine follows a forward chaining strategy. The left-hand side of rules have an implicit AND among conditions, described by patterns. If all patterns are matched by known facts, the rule is said to be *activated*, and its instance is put on the so-called *agenda*. CLIPS selects from the agenda the rule with the highest priority to fire. Priorities can be associated with rules as integers in the range $-10,000 \ .. \ +10,000$, with a default value of 0. Instances with the same priority are handled according to a last-in/first-out policy. Firing a rule instance consists of performing the actions specified in the right-hand side. Actions may imply deriving new facts, executing certain functions, or sending messages to objects.

8.7 Exercises

1. Comment on the following statement: "In logic programming, a program used to generate a result based on a certain input value can also be used to check that a certain input value generates a particular result." Discuss how existing programming languages approximate this general statement.

2. Find the most general unifier for

$$f(X, g(a, Z, W), a, h(X, b, W))$$

and

$$f(h(a, Z), g(a, h(Z, b), X), Z, h(d, b, a))$$

3. Given the PROLOG sort program of Section 8.1.2, show the search tree for the query

   ?-sort([3, 5, 1], [1, 3, 5]).

4. Show the different computations of the PROLOG interpreter for the program of Figure
   8.5 for the following queries:

   ?-rel(a, b).
   ?-rel(a, c).
   ?-rel(b, f).
   ?-rel(f, g).

5. Predicate even(n) is true for all even numbers. Write a PROLOG program to implement
   predicate even.

6. Write a PROLOG program that checks whether a list contains another as a sublist. The
   program returns YES for queries of the following kind:

   ?-sublist([1, 5, 2, 7, 3, 10], [5, 2, 7]).

   What is the intended meaning of the following queries?

   ?-sublist([1, 5, 2, 7, 3, 10], X).
   ?-sublist(X, [5, 2, 7]).
   ?-sublist(X, Y).

   Does the behavior of the PROLOG interpreter correspond to the expected meaning if
   these queries are submitted for evaluation?

7. Consider the program of Figure 8.10. Discuss what happens if the query ?-fact(-5, X) is
   submitted. If the program does not behave as expected, provide a new version that
   eliminates the problem.

8. Consider the following PROLOG program.

   belongs_to(A, [A | B]) :- !.
   belongs_to(A, [C | B]) :- belongs_to(A, B).

   – What does this program do?
   – Can the cut be eliminated from the first clause without affecting the set of solutions
     computed by the program?

9. Consider the fragment of the previous exercise. Suppose you eliminate the cut from the
   first clause and, in addition, you interchange the two clauses. Describe the behavior of the
   PROLOG interpreter when the following goal is submitted:

   ?-belongs_to(a, [a, b, c])

10. The special goal fail is yet another extralogical feature provided by PROLOG. Study it in
    a PROLOG manual and discuss its use.

11. It has been argued that the cut can be viewed as the logical counterpart of the goto
    statement of imperative programming languages. Provide a concise argument to support
    the statement.

12. Write a PROLOG program that defines the predicate fib(I, X), where I is a positive integer
    and X is the I-th Fibonacci number. Remember that the first two Fibonacci numbers are 0

and 1, and any other Fibonacci number is the sum of the two Fibonacci numbers that precede it.

13. Take the list of courses offered by the computer science department and the recommended prerequisites. Write a PROLOG application that can answer questions on the curricula; in particular, it should be able to check whether a certain course sequence conforms to the recommendations.

14. Write a PROLOG program that recognizes whether an input string is a correct expression with respect to the EBNF grammar illustrated in Section 2.2.1. You may assume, for simplicity, that expressions only contain identifiers (i.e., numbers cannot appear), and identifiers can only be single-letter names.

15. Suppose you are given a description of a map in terms of the relation from_to. The term from_to(a, b) means that one can reach point b from point a directly. Assume that from any point X one cannot return to the same point by applying the closure of relation from_to (i.e., the map contains no cycles). A special point, called exit, represents the exit from the map. Write a PROLOG program to check if, given a starting point, one can reach exit.

16. Referring to the previous exercise, write a PROLOG predicate to check if the assumption that the map contains no cycles holds—i.e., from any point X one cannot return to the same point by applying the closure of relation from_to.

17. Consider the fragment of Figure 8.9. Suppose that the second rule is changed in the following way: max(X, Y, Y).

    Is the new fragment equivalent to the previous one? Consider, as an example, the following queries:

    ```
    ?- max(2, 5, A).
    ?- max(5, 2, B).
    ?- max(2, 5, 3).
    ?- max(2, 5, 5).
    ?- max(2, 5, 2).
    ```

18. Consider the PROLOG sort program discussed in Section 8.1.2. Discuss if (and how) the goal specified by the following query can be solved:

    ```
    sort(X, [1, 3, 5, 99]).
    ```

19. Consider a problem of the kind shown in Figure 8.12. Write a PROLOG implementation that does both forward and backward chaining, as illustrated in Section 8.5. (You might consult [Bratko90] for a discussion of the implementation of forward/backward chaining in PROLOG.)

Languages in context

C H A P T E R   9

This chapter serves as an epilogue to our whirlwind tour of the world of programming languages. During the tour, we stressed the fundamental concepts of languages, rather than specific details of each individual language encountered. Rather than a feature-by-feature presentation of a long list of languages, we have examined the concepts that provide a framework in which languages can be studied, analyzed, and compared. Thus, if we are told that a certain language is, say, statically scoped, strongly typed, and polymorphic, we immediately grasp some important semantic properties that characterize the language. Although we miss the syntactic aspects and other details of the language, the concepts provide deep insights into the language. These concepts enable us to examine not only the languages we have already seen, but also those that are yet to be developed.

The concepts we have studied provide an *inside* view: what are the pieces that make up a language? In this chapter, we will take an *outside* view: what are the environments in which languages are used? These environments impose requirements on programming languages and influence the future development of languages. The outside view helps us understand *why* certain features may be needed in a language; the inside view answers the question of how and *whether* the feature can be smoothly integrated in combination with other features of the language.

We studied the concept of binding time in Chapter 2 and used it extensively to analyze language features. In particular, we stressed the notion of compile time versus run time. The same distinction may also be used to study the context in which languages are used: the context during execution of a program and the context during the development of a program.

- *Execution context*: What is the environment in which programs are executed, and how do programs interact with that environment? One particularly important component of this context is the interaction with the user of the program.
- *Development context*: What is the environment in which programs are developed and how do programmers interact with it?

In the next two sections, we examine each of these contexts. The study of the outside view helps us understand why languages have evolved the way they have and helps us anticipate future developments.

9.1 Execution context

The execution environment of programs has gone through a tremendous amount of change since the early days of computing. The simple "calculating machines" of yesterday have been replaced by "multimedia" computers with sophisticated user interfaces. We can see several general trends in the development of the execution context:

1 *User interfaces.* User interface technology has replaced simple input/output devices with point-and-click windowing devices. The simple text input/output model of early programming languages has had to evolve to deal with window-based input/output. This is generally done through graphic user interface (GUI) libraries, and it certainly changes the way programming languages can look at the I/O question. An early debate among language designers was whether I/O should be part of the language or supported by a supporting library. Pascal and FORTRAN made it part of the language, whereas the Algol family and C rely on a library. It is clear that the simple character I/O model is inadequate for today's sophisticated environments. The key point is the development of an appropriate model of I/O with an appropriate interface in the programming language. The object-oriented model has been the most common approach used for building GUI libraries.

2 *Computation model.* Simple CPUs are being replaced with multiprocessor machines communicating over a network. The standard von Neumann model of computation that is the foundation of conventional languages has had to be extended to deal with this new environment. As we have seen, several models of concurrency exist, and different ones have been introduced in various languages. In contrast to the von Neumann model of computation, which is shared by all sequential languages, there is no consensus on the appropriate model of concurrency for languages. Threads, events, monitors, data parallelism, and others are competing models of concurrent computation that are finding their way into languages. All programming paradigms have been extended for parallelism. Because of the lack of side effects, functional programming languages support concurrency most naturally.

Generally, the concurrent model of computation assumes that data are shared among the concurrent tasks. The Ada tasking model and the Java threads are based on this model. The distributed model of computation is characterized not only by the presence of concurrency, but also by the notion of the distribution of data. That is, the data are not shared by the concurrent tasks. As a result, explicit messages have to be passed between tasks to communicate the needed data. This model is based on sending the data to where the code is. Another possibility is to send the code to where the data are located.

Some networked models of computation are based on the concept of *mobile* programs that can travel through the network and execute on different computers. The Java language and others are trying to address this issue.

Middleware is a collection of software intended as a layer between the language run time and the networked environment. Middleware frees the programmer from dealing specifically with network programming issues. Remote procedure calls, atomic actions, and distributed transactions are examples of ways of dealing with distributed environments and represent the kinds of functionalities one finds in middleware. Some of these middleware libraries are being standardized and provide interfaces to programming languages. For example, CORBA (Common Object Request Broker Architecture) is a standard for the naming and locating of resources in a network environment. CORBA interfaces with all of the popular languages have been defined. Conventional languages may be modified to accommodate this new distribution model. For example, Distributed Smalltalk extends Smalltalk with CORBA facilities. ORB, the *Object Request Broker* part of CORBA, makes it possible for programs written in different languages to communicate and *interoperate*. A program may ask an ORB where a certain resource is located and what interfaces it supports. In this way, for example, a program written in C++ may contact an ORB, which will direct it to an object written in Distributed Smalltalk.

3 *Dealing with time.* Another interesting requirement of some of the new execution environments is the ability to deal with the passage of time. The traditional model in most programming languages assumes that a program starts execution, reads the data it needs, processes the data, produces its output, and terminates. In many environments, such as so-called *embedded systems*, this model is inadequate. The program is expected to respond to events, such as the pressing of a button or the reception of a sensor signal, within a predefined time limit. Such real-time systems are gaining importance as software is applied to control devices such as in automobiles and airplanes. Writing software that meets such time limits is challenging and requires specialized design techniques. Some languages have features to deal specifically with these environments. For example, Ada has facilities for specifying *timeouts*. A timeout indicates that the operation should be abandoned if it cannot be completed within the specified time period. There is no consensus on a model of computation to handle time. As a result, we are likely to see different languages with experimental approaches in this area.

4 *Database integration.* Another change in the execution environment has been the emergence of databases and the availability of vast amounts of data on-line. Again, the simple model of a program that does input, processing, and output is inadequate. Instead, the program may interact with the user, manipulate some data in a database, and even store data in a database for processing in a later execution of the program. The concept of such *persistent data* is being explored in various language design efforts as one way of interfacing programming languages with databases. Current approaches simply provide database manipulation through libraries. A coherent persistency model will enable a more integrated view of programs and databases.

The common property among the solutions to these trends seems to be that appropriate models are being developed and progressively standardized. Such standard models make it easier for a language to interact with its execution environment. The impact of future standardizations will be felt by both the language and its implementation.

9.2 Development context

The program development environment has also undergone a tremendous evolution. We can identify two related trends. One is the way programs are entered in the computer, debugged, etc. Another is the way that programs are assembled from existing parts rather than being written from scratch. Visual languages combine the two trends in providing a visual programming interface in which existing parts are assembled together using point-and-click rather than textual input.

1 *Visual interfaces.* The sophisticated GUI technology that we discussed in the last section has enabled a new generation of programming environments that gives the programmer a *visual* interface. Such interfaces allow GUI interfaces to be constructed visually, rather than by entering the program as a sequence of characters: the constituents of the user interface are represented as icons (e.g., buttons, windows), and actions associated with those icons are entered textually. For example, we can design an interface to our program by selecting from a predefined set of icons, such as dialog boxes, menus, and buttons, and then clicking on each icon to specify the procedures to be invoked based on the user's actions. The program development environment is then responsible for assembling the complete program based on the programmer's interaction with the system. The concept of the programmer typing in a program and then compiling it is being replaced by this kind of incremental development and assembly of programs from text and icons.

2 *Programming by assembling software parts.* Another important trend in the software development context is the building of software not from scratch but from existing *parts* or *standard components*. This is indeed a significant fundamental challenge facing the software industry. A successful example is, as we have just discussed, in the area of user interface development, where such high-level concepts as dialog boxes and

menus are routinely reused by programmers. The visual interface referred to above make this easy to do.

But building from parts is important for software as a whole—not just for the user interface component. This problem is addressed in several phases of the software development process, including architecture and design. Programming languages can support the development of highly reusable parts with certain desired features. For example, inheritance and genericity are two fundamental concepts for building components that may be reused for building or instantiating new components. Language concepts such as polymorphism underlie such features.

3 *Visual languages.* Taking advantage of both visual interfaces and software parts is a particularly interesting prospect. Some environments represent software parts as icons and support programming entirely through a direct-manipulation visual interface. That is, the programmer selects appropriate icons that represent program components and draws lines between icons to reflect communication among those parts. The concept of a textual program is completely replaced by a visual program. In these so-called visual languages, the ideas of syntax and programming are replaced by selection and configuration or assembly.

9.3 Final remarks

As we develop concepts and models to facilitate the understanding of existing programming languages, developments in technology force programming languages to evolve and incorporate new features that require newer concepts and models or refinements of the older ones. For example, the FORTRAN language, originally developed in 1957, has evolved through Fortran 66 and Fortran 77 to the current standard of FORTRAN 90, which incorporates many of the newer language concepts. Also, several current versions of FORTRAN support various models of parallel computation. In this chapter, we have identified two kinds of forces that impose requirements for evolution on existing languages and give impetus to the development of new languages. The pace of change and the constant interplay among technology, models, and the implementation of models make the study of programming languages a truly exciting activity.

9.4 Bibliographic notes

This chapter concerns mostly other areas of computer science and their impact on languages. Further references can be found in the literature of other specialties. Probably the best source of up-to-date information on recent developments is the Internet. The home page for this book is located at http://www.infosys.tuwien.ac.at/pl-book. CORBA was developed by the Object

Management Group; you can find the latest copy of the standard at http://www.omg.org. At least two commercial versions of Distributed Smalltalk exist. Visual Basic is the most successful example of both the visual approach to programming and the reuse of standard parts in software development. [Kopetz97] is a textbook on real-time systems, their requirements, and their design. The design of user interfaces, particularly GUI interfaces, is covered in [Schneiderman87].

Appendix
Language references

Ada

[ISO95a]
[Barnes96]

ALGOL 60

[Dijkstra62]
[Naur63]

Algol 68

[vanWijngaarden76]
[Lindsey77]

APL

[Iverson62]
[Gilman84]

BASIC

[Kemeny85]
[ISO91b]

C

[Kernighan88]
[ISO90a]

C++

[Stroustrup92]

CLIPS

[NASA95]

CLOS

[Bobrow88]
[Keene89]

CLU

[Liskov81]
[Liskov86]

COBOL

[ISO85]

Concurrent Pascal

[BrinchHansen75]
[BrinchHansen77]

Eiffel

[Meyer88]
[Meyer92]

Euclid

[Lampson77]

FORTRAN

[ISO91a]
[Brainerd95]

Icon

[Griswold90]

Java

[Arnold96]
[Gosling96]
[Lindholm96]

LISP

[Steele84]
[Winston89]

Mesa

[Geschke77]

ML

[Ullman94]
[Paulson96]

Modula-2

[Wirth82]

Modula-3

[Nelson91]

Oberon-2

[Reiser92]
[Mössenböck93]

OPS5

[Brownston85]

Pascal

[Jensen85]
[ISO90b]

Perl

[Wall96]

PL/I

[ISO79]

PROLOG

[Sterling86]
[Clocksin87]

Python

[Lutz96]

Scheme

[Abelson85]

SETL

[Schwartz86]

SIMULA 67

[Birtwistle73]

Smalltalk

[Goldberg83]

SNOBOL4

[Griswold73]

Tcl/Tk

[Ousterhout94]

Bibliography

[Abadi96] M. Abadi and L. Cardelli. *A Theory of Objects*, Monographs in Computer Science. Springer-Verlag, Berlin, 1996.

[Abelson85] H. Abelson, G. J. Sussman, and J. Sussman. *Structure and Interpretation of Computer Programs*. MIT Press, Cambridge, MA, 1985.

[ACM87] *ACM Turing Award Lectures—The First Twenty Years*. Addison-Wesley, Reading, MA, 1987.

[Aho86] A. Aho, R. Sethi, and J. Ullman. *Compilers—Principles, Techniques, Tools*. Addison-Wesley, Reading, MA, 1986.

[Andrews91] G. R. Andrews. *Concurrent Programming—Principles and Practice*. Benjamin-Cummings, Redwood City, CA, 1991.

[Apple92] Apple Computer. *Dylan, an Object-Oriented Dynamic Language*. Apple, Cupertino, CA, 1992.

[Arnold96] K. Arnold and J. Gosling. *The Java Programming Language*. Addison-Wesley, Reading, MA, 1996.

[Backus78] J. Backus. Can programming be liberated from the Von Neumann style? A functional style and its algebra of programs. *Communications of the ACM,* **21**(8):613–641, August 1978.

[Barnes96] J. Barnes. *Programming in Ada 95*. Addison-Wesley, Reading, MA, 1996.

[Ben-Ari90] M. Ben-Ari. *Principles of Concurrent and Distributed Programming*. Prentice-Hall, Englewood Cliffs, NJ, 1990.

[Bergin96] T. J. Bergin and R. G. Gibson. *History of Programming Languages II*. Addison-Wesley, Reading, MA, 1996.

[Birtwistle73] M. G. Birtwistle, O. J. Dahl, B. Myhrhaug, and K. Nygaard. *Simula Begin*. Petrocelli/Charter, New York, NY, 1973.

[Bobrow86] D. Bobrow, K. Kahn, G. Kiczales, L. Masinter, M. Stefik, and F. Zdybel. Common-Loops: Merging Lisp and object-oriented programming. *ACM Conference on Object-Oriented Programming Systems, Languages and Applications (OOPSLA '86)*, p. 17–29, 1986.

[Bobrow88] D. G. Bobrow, L. G. De Michiel, R. P. Gabriel, S. E. Keene, G. Kiczales, and D. A. Moon. Common Lisp object system specification. *ACM SIGPLAN Notices*, **23**, September 1988.

[Booch94] G. Booch. *Object-Oriented Analysis and Design with Applications*, 2nd edition. Benjamin-Cummings, Redwood City, CA, 1994.

[Brainerd95] W. Brainerd, C. Goldberg, and J. Adams. *Programmer's Guide to Fortran 90*. Springer-Verlag, Berlin, 1995.

[Bratko90] I. Bratko. *PROLOG Programming for Artificial Intelligence*, 2nd edition. Addison-Wesley, Reading, MA, 1990.

[BrinchHansen75] P. Brinch Hansen. The programming language Concurrent Pascal. *IEEE Transactions on Software Engineering*, **1**(2):199–207, June 1975.

[BrinchHansen77] P. Brinch Hansen. *The Architecture of Concurrent Programs*. Prentice-Hall, Englewood Cliffs, NJ, 1977.

[Brooks95] F. P. Brooks Jr. *The Mythical Man-Month: Essays on Software Engineering*. Addison-Wesley, Reading, MA, 1995.

[Brownston85] L. Brownston, R. Farrell, E. Kant, and N. Martin. *Programming Expert Systems in OPS5*. Addison-Wesley, Reading, MA, 1985.

[Bruce96] K. Bruce, L. Cardelli, G. Castagna, G. T. Leavens, B. Pierce, and T. H. O. Group. On binary methods. *Theory and Practice of Object Systems*, **1**(3):221–242, 1996.

[Buchanan84] B. G. Buchanan and E. H. Shortliffe, editors. *Rule-Based Expert Systems*. Addison-Wesley, Reading, MA, 1984.

[Burstall80] R. M. Burstall, D. B. MacQueen, and D. T. Sannella. Hope: An experimental applicative language. Conf. Record of the 1980 LISP Conference, pp. 136–143, August 1980.

[Cardelli85] L. Cardelli and P. Wegner. On understanding types, data abstraction, and polymorphism. *ACM Computing Surveys*, **17**(4):471–522, December 1985.

[Castagna95] G. Castagna. Covariance and contravariance: Conflict without a cause. *ACM Transactions on Programming Languages and Systems*, **17**(3):431–447, May 1995.

[Church41] A. Church. The calculi of lambda conversion. *Annals of Mathematics Studies*, 6, Princeton University Press, Princeton NJ, 1941.

[Clocksin87] W. F. Clocksin and C. S. Mellish. *Programming in Prolog*, 3rd edition. Springer-Verlag, Berlin, 1987.

[Cohen81] J. Cohen. Garbage collection of linked data structures. *ACM Computing Surveys*, **13**(3):341–68, 1981.

[Cox86] B. Cox. *Object-Oriented Programming: An Evolutionary Approach*. Addison-Wesley, Reading, MA, 1986.

[Cristian95] F. Cristian. Exception handling and tolerance of software faults. In M. Lyu, editor, *Software Fault Tolerance*, pp. 81–107. John Wiley & Sons, New York, 1995.

[Dahl72] O. J. Dahl, E. W. Dijkstra, and C. A. R. Hoare. *Structured Programming*. Academic Press, New York, 1972.

[DeRemer76] F. DeRemer and H. Kron. Programming-in-the-large versus programming-in-the-small. *IEEE Transactions on Software Engineering*, **2**(2):80–86, June 1976.

[Dijkstra62] E. W. Dijkstra. *A Primer of ALGOL60 Programming*. Academic Press, New York, 1962.

[Dijkstra68a] E. W. Dijkstra. Goto statement considered harmful. *Communications of the ACM*, **11**(3):147–149, March 1968.

[Dijkstra68b] E. W. Dijkstra. Cooperating sequential processes. In F. Genuys, editor, *Programming Languages*, pp. 42–112. Academic Press, New York, 1968.

[Feigenbaum96] E. A. Feigenbaum. How the "what" becomes the "how." *Communications of the ACM*, **39**(5):97–104, May 1996.

[Fischer91] C. N. Fischer and R. J. LeBlanc. *Crafting a Compiler with C*. Benjamin-Cummings, Redwood City, CA, 1991.

[Fowler97] M. Fowler. *Analysis Patterns: Reusable Object Models*. Addison-Wesley, Reading, MA, 1997.

[Fraternali95] P. Fraternali and L. Tanca. A structured approach for the definition of the semantics of active database systems. *ACM Transactions on Database Systems*, **20**(4):414–471, December 1995.

[Geschke77] C. M. Geschke, J. H. Morris, Jr, and E. H. Satterthwaite. Early experience with Mesa. *Communications of the ACM*, **20**(8):540–553, August 1977.

[Ghezzi91] C. Ghezzi, M. Jazayeri, and D. Mandrioli. *Fundamentals of Software Engineering*. Prentice-Hall, Englewood Cliffs, NJ, 1991.

[Gilman84] L. Gilman and A. J. Rose. *APL: An Interactive Approach*. John Wiley & Sons, New York, 1984.

[Goldberg83] A. Goldberg and D. Robson. *Smalltalk-80: The Language and Its Implementation*. Addison-Wesley, Reading, MA, 1983.

[Goodenough75] J. B. Goodenough. Exception handling: Issues and a proposed notation. *Communications of the ACM*, **16**(12):683–696, December 1975.

[Gosling96] J. Gosling, B. Joy, and G. Steele. *The Java Language Specification*. Addison-Wesley, Reading, MA, 1996.

[Griswold73] R. E. Griswold and M. T. Griswold. *A SNOBOL4 Primer*. Prentice-Hall, Engle-wood Cliffs, NJ, 1973.

[Griswold90] R. E. Griswold and M. T. Griswold. *The Icon Programming Language*, 2nd edition. Prentice-Hall, Englewood Cliffs, NJ, 1990.

[Hoare74] C. A. R. Hoare. Monitors: An operating system structuring concept. *Communications of the ACM*, **17**(10):549–557, October 1974.

[Hoare78] C. A. R. Hoare. Communicating sequential processes. *Communications of the ACM*, **21**(8):666–677, August 1978.

[Hoare81] C. A. R. Hoare. The emperor's old clothes. *Communications of the ACM*, **24**(2):75–83, February 1981.

[Horowitz78] E. Horowitz and S. Sahni. *Fundamentals of Data Structures*. Computer Science Press, Potomac, MD, 1978.

[Hudak89] P. Hudak. Conception, evolution, and application of functional programming languages. *ACM Computing Surveys*, **21**(3):359–411, September 1989.

[ISO79] International Organization for Standardization. PL/I. Technical report ISO 6160. ISO, Geneva, 1979.

[ISO85] International Organization for Standardization. COBOL. Technical report ISO 1989. ISO, Geneva, 1985.

[ISO90a] International Organization for Standardization. C. Technical report ISO/IEC 9899. ISO, Geneva, 1990.

[ISO90b] International Organization for Standardization. Pascal. Technical report ISO 7185. ISO, Geneva, 1990.

[ISO91a] International Organization for Standardization. FORTRAN. Technical report ISO 1539. ISO, Geneva, 1991.

[ISO91b] International Organization for Standardization. Full BASIC. Technical report ISO/IEC 10279. ISO, Geneva, 1991.

[ISO95a] International Organization for Standardization. Ada. Technical report ISO/IEC 8652. ISO, Geneva, 1995.

[ISO95b] International Organization for Standardization. Programming Language C++. Draft X3J16/94-0095,WG21/N0482. ISO, Geneva, 1995.

[Iverson62] K. E. Iverson. *A Programming Language*. John Wiley & Sons, New York, 1962.

[Jazayeri95] M. Jazayeri. Component programming: A fresh look at software components. *Fifth European Software Engineering Conference (ESEC'95)* (Sitges/Barcelona, September 25–28), pp. 457–478, 1995.

[Jensen85] K. Jensen and N. Wirth. *Pascal User Manual and Report*, 3rd edition. Springer-Verlag, Berlin, 1985.

[Johnston71] J. Johnston. The contour model of block-structured processed. *SIGPLAN Notices*, **6**(2):55–82, February 1971.

[Keene89] S. E. Keene. *Object-Oriented Programming in Common LISP: A Programmer's Guide to CLOS.* Addison-Wesley, Reading, MA, 1989.

[Kemeny85] J. G. Kemeny. *True BASIC.* Addison-Wesley, Reading, MA, 1985.

[Kernighan88] B. W. Kernighan and D. M. Ritchie. *The C Programming Language*, 2nd edition. Prentice-Hall, Englewood Cliffs, NJ, 1988.

[Knuth69] D. E. Knuth. *The Art of Computer Programming.* Addison-Wesley, Reading, MA, 1969.

[Knuth74] D. E. Knuth. Structured programming with goto statements. *ACM Computing Surveys*, **6**(4):261–301, December 1974.

[Koenig96] A. Koenig and B. Moo. *Ruminations on C++.* Addison-Wesley, Reading, MA, 1996.

[Kopetz97] H. Kopetz. *Real-Time Systems.* Kluwer Academic, Norwell, MA, 1997.

[Kowalski79] R. A. Kowalski. *Logic for Problem Solving.* North-Holland, Amsterdam, 1979.

[Lampson77] B. Lampson, J. Mitchell, and E. Satterthwaite. Report on the programming language Euclid. *SIGPLAN Notices*, **12**(2), February 1977.

[Landin64] P. J. Landin. The mechanical evaluation of expressions. *Computer Journal*, **6**(4):308–320, 1964.

[Lindholm96] T. Lindholm and F. Yellin. *The Java Virtual Machine Specification.* Addison-Wesley, Reading, MA, 1996.

[Lindsey77] C. H. Lindsey and S. G. van der Meulen. *Informal Introduction to ALGOL68.* North-Holland, Amsterdam, 1977.

[Liskov81] B. Liskov, R. Atkinson, T. Bloom, E. Moss, J. C. Schaffert, R. Scheifler, and A. Snyder. *CLU Reference Manual.* Springer-Verlag, Berlin, 1981.

[Liskov86] B. Liskov and J. Guttag. *Abstraction and Specification in Program Development.* MIT Press and McGraw-Hill, New York, 1986.

[Liskov94] B. H. Liskov and J. M. Wing. A behavioral notion of subtyping. *ACM Transactions on Programming Languages and Systems*, **16**(6):1811–1841, November 1994.

[Lloyd84] J. W. Lloyd. *Foundations of Logic Programming.* Springer-Verlag, Berlin, 1984.

[Lutz96] M. Lutz. *Programming Python.* O'Reilly, Sebastopol, CA, 1996.

[Madsen93] O. L. Madsen, B. Moller-Pedersen, and K. Nygaard. *Object Oriented Programming in the Beta Programming Language.* Addison-Wesley, Reading, MA, 1993.

[Marlin80] C. D. Marlin. *Coroutines.* Lecture Notes in Computer Science 95. Springer-Verlag, Berlin, 1980.

[McCarthy60] J. McCarthy. Recursive functions of symbolic expressions and their computation by machine. *Communications of the ACM*, **3**(4):184–195, 1960.

[Mendelson64] E. Mendelson. *Introduction to Mathematical Logic.* Van Nostrand Reinhold, New York, 1964.

[Meyer88] B. Meyer. *Object-Oriented Software Construction.* Prentice Hall International, Hemel Hempstead, 1988.

[Meyer92] B. Meyer. *Eiffel: The Language.* Prentice-Hall, Englewood Cliffs, NJ, 1992.

[Milner90] R. Milner, M. Tofte, and R.M. Harper. *The Definition of Standard ML.* MIT Press, Cambridge, MA, 1990.

[Mössenböck93] H. Mössenböck. *Object-Oriented Programming in Oberon-2.* Springer-Verlag, Berlin, 1993.

[Moon86] D. A. Moon. Object-oriented programming with Flavors. *ACM Conference on Object-Oriented Systems, Languages and Applications* (Portland, Oregon), pp. 1–8, 1986.

[Musser96] D. R. Musser and A. Saini. *STL Tutorial and Reference Guide.* Addison-Wesley, Reading, MA, 1996.

[NASA95] NASA/Johnson Space Center. *CLIPS Version 6.0 Reference Manual.* NASA, 1995.

[Naur63] P. Naur, editor. Revised report on the algorithmic language ALGOL60. *Communications of the ACM,* **6**(1):1–17, 1963.

[Nelson91] G. Nelson. *Systems Programming with Modula-3.* Prentice-Hall, Englewood Cliffs, NJ, 1991.

[Nelson95] M. Nelson. *C++ Programmer's Guide to the Standard Template Library.* IDG Books, Foster City, CA, 1995.

[Ousterhout94] J. K. Ousterhout. *Tcl and the TK Toolkit.* Addison-Wesley, Reading, MA, 1994.

[Parnas72a] D. L. Parnas. A technique for software module specification with examples. *Communications of the ACM,* **15**(5):330–336, May 1972.

[Parnas72b] D. L. Parnas. On the criteria to be used in decomposing systems into modules. *Communications of the ACM,* **15**(12):1053–1058, December 1972.

[Paulson96] L. C. Paulson. *ML for the Working Programmer.* Cambridge University Press, New York, 1996.

[Raj91] R. K. Raj, E. Tempero, H. M. Levy, A. P. Black, N. C. Hutchinson, and E. Jul. Emerald: A general-purpose programming language. *Software—Practice and Experience,* **21**(1), January 1991.

[Reiser92] M. Reiser and N. Wirth. *Programming in Oberon—Steps Beyond Pascal and Modula-2.* Addison-Wesley, Reading, MA, 1992.

[Schneiderman87] B. Schneiderman. *Designing the User-Interface.* Addison-Wesley, Reading, MA, 1987.

[Schwartz86] J. T. Schwartz, R. B. K. Dewar, E. Dubinsky, and E. Schonberg. *Programming with Sets: An Introduction to SETL.* Springer-Verlag, Berlin, 1986.

[Snyder86] A. Snyder. Encapsulation and inheritance in object-oriented programming languages. *SIGPLAN Notices,* **21**(11):38–45, November 1986.

[Steele84] G. J. Steele, Jr. *Common LISP.* Digital Press, Burlington, MA, 1984.

[Sterling86] L. Sterling and E. Shapiro. *The Art of PROLOG*. MIT Press, Cambridge, MA, 1986.

[Stroustrup92] B. Stroustrup. *The C++ Programming Language*, 2nd edition. Addison-Wesley, Reading, MA, 1992.

[Stroustrup94] B. Stroustrup. *The Design and Evolution of C++*. Addison-Wesley, Reading, MA, 1994.

[Taivalsaari96] A. Taivalsaari. On the notion of inheritance. *ACM Computing Surveys*, **28**(3):438–479, September 1996.

[Tanenbaum87] A. S. Tanenbaum. *Operating Systems: Design and Implementation*. Prentice-Hall, Englewood Cliffs, NJ, 1987.

[Tennent78] R. D. Tennent. Another look at type compatibility in Pascal. *Software—Practice and Experience*, **8**:429–437, 1978.

[Tennent81] R. D. Tennent. *Principles of Programming Languages*. Prentice-Hall, Englewood Cliffs, NJ, 1981.

[Thompson96] S. Thompson. *Haskell: The Craft of Functional Programming*. Addison-Wesley, Reading, MA, 1996.

[Turner85] D. A. Turner. Miranda: A non-strict functional language with polymorphic types. *Functional Programming Languages and Computer Architecture*, Lecture Notes in Computer Science 201, pp. 1–16. Springer-Verlag, Berlin, 1985.

[Ullman88] J. D. Ullman. *Principles of Database and Knowledge-Base Systems*, Vol. I. Computer Science Press, Rockville, MD, 1988.

[Ullman89] J. D. Ullman. *Principles of Database and Knowledge-Base Systems*, Vol. II. Computer Science Press, Rockville, MD, 1989.

[Ullman94] J. D. Ullman. *Elements of ML Programming*. Prentice-Hall, Englewood Cliffs, NJ, 1994.

[Ungar87] D. Ungar and R. B. Smith. Self: The power of simplicity. *SIGPLAN Notices*, **22**(12), 1987.

[vanWijngaarden76] A. van Wijngaarden, B. J. Mailloux, J. E. L. Peck, C. H. A. Koster, M. Sintzoff, C. H. Lindsey, L. G. L. T. Meertens, and R. G. Fisker. *Revised Report on the Algorithmic Language ALGOL68*. Springer-Verlag, Berlin, 1976.

[Wall96] L. Wall, T. Christiansen, and R. L. Schwartz. *Programming Perl*, 2nd edition. O'Reilly, Sebastopol, CA, 1996.

[Wegner87] P. Wegner. Dimensions of object-based language design. *Proceedings of OOPSLA '87*, pp. 168–182, 1987; *ACM SIGPLAN Notices*, **22**(12), 1987.

[Welsh77] J. Welsh, M. J. Sneeringer, and C. A. R. Hoare. Ambiguities and insecurities in Pascal. *Software—Practice and Experience*, **7**:685–696, 1977.

[Wexelblat81] R. L. Wexelblat, editor. *History of Programming Languages*. ACM Monograph Series. Academic Press, New York, 1981.

[Wilson96] P. R. Wilson. Uniprocessor garbage collection techniques. *ACM Computing Surveys*, 1996.

[Winskel93] G. Winskel. *The Formal Semantics of Programming Languages.* MIT Press, Cambridge, MA, 1993.

[Winston89] P. H. Winston and B. K. P. Horn. *Lisp*, 3rd edition. Addison-Wesley, Reading, MA, 1989.

[Wirth82] N. Wirth. *Programming in Modula-2*, 2nd edition. Springer-Verlag, Berlin, 1982.

[Wirth88] N. Wirth. Type extensions. *ACM Transactions on Programming Languages and Systems*, **10**(2):204–214, February 1988.

[Wittgenstein63] L. Wittgenstein. *Tractatus logico-philosophicus.* Frankfurt am Main, Berlin, 1963.

[Wood93] D. Wood. *Data Structures, Algorithms, and Performance.* Addison-Wesley, Reading, MA, 1993.

Index